communication
personal & public

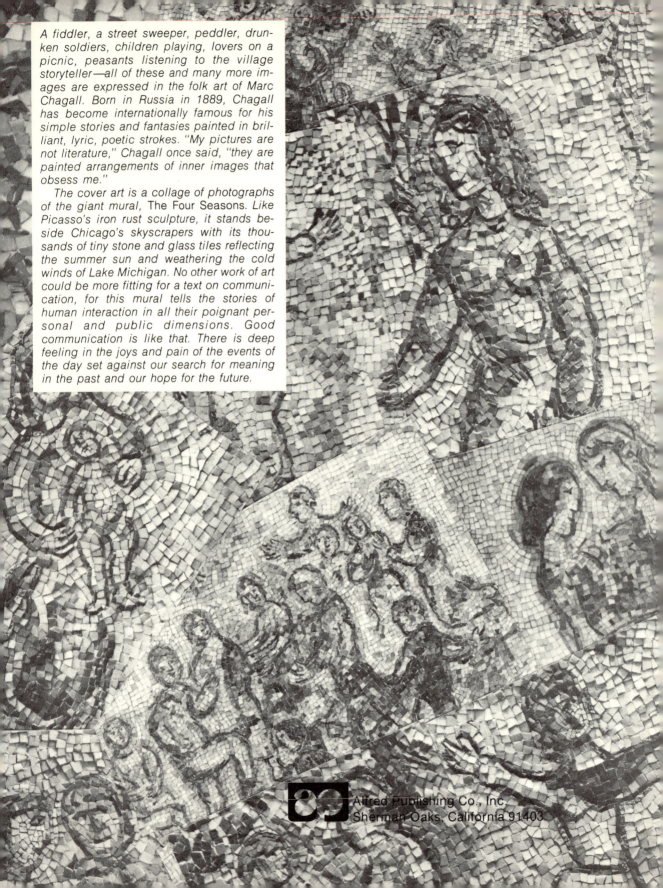

A fiddler, a street sweeper, peddler, drunken soldiers, children playing, lovers on a picnic, peasants listening to the village storyteller—all of these and many more images are expressed in the folk art of Marc Chagall. Born in Russia in 1889, Chagall has become internationally famous for his simple stories and fantasies painted in brilliant, lyric, poetic strokes. "My pictures are not literature," Chagall once said, "they are painted arrangements of inner images that obsess me."

The cover art is a collage of photographs of the giant mural, The Four Seasons. Like Picasso's iron rust sculpture, it stands beside Chicago's skyscrapers with its thousands of tiny stone and glass tiles reflecting the summer sun and weathering the cold winds of Lake Michigan. No other work of art could be more fitting for a text on communication, for this mural tells the stories of human interaction in all their poignant personal and public dimensions. Good communication is like that. There is deep feeling in the joys and pain of the events of the day set against our search for meaning in the past and our hope for the future.

Alfred Publishing Co., Inc.
Sherman Oaks, California 91403

communication
personal & public

william i. gorden

KENT STATE UNIVERSITY

Credits and Permissions

p. 3 Culver Pictures, **p. 5** Copyright © 1977, G. B. Trudeau/Distributed by Universal Press Syndicate, **p. 11** UPI, **p. 14** Copyright © 1974 by Sol Gordon. Reprinted by permission of Quadrangle/The New York Times Book Co. From *You: The Teenage Survival Book by Sol Gordon,* **p. 27** UPI, **p. 29** Magnum, **p. 31** all UPI, **p. 35** Steven Manus, **p. 49** UPI, **p. 53** UPI, **p. 56** 2 photographs UPI, Brown Brothers, **pp. 66–67** 4 photographs UPI, A. Marshall Licht, **p. 71** UPI, **p. 79** American Telephone & Telegraph Company, **p. 85** Culver Pictures, **p. 89** Graphics Two, **p. 94** UPI, **p. 103** A. Marshall Licht, **p. 107** UPI, **p. 111** © 1973 Daily Mirror Newspapers Ltd. ANDY CAPP ® Dist. Field Newspaper Syndicate, **p. 115** UPI, **p. 135** Douglas Moore, **p. 137** UPI, **p. 144** 2 photographs A. Marshall Licht, 2 photographs UPI, **p. 163** UPI, **p. 167** Drawing by Mahood; © 1977 The New Yorker Magazine, Inc., **p. 191** 2 photographs Mimi Forsyth from Monkmeyer Press Photo, Hugh Rogers from Monkmeyer Press Photo, **p. 195** UPI, **p. 204** UPI, **p. 213** Bill Anderson from Monkmeyer Press Photo, Hugh Rogers from Monkmeyer Press Photo, UPI, Brown Brothers, **p. 219** Drawing by Lorenz; © 1977 The New Yorker Magazine, Inc., **p. 227** UPI, **p. 237** Copyright © 1977, G. B. Trudeau/Distributed by Universal Press Syndicate, **p. 242** UPI, **p. 253** Douglas Moore, **p. 273** all UPI, **p. 287** Culver Pictures, **p. 303** ® Joy is a registered trademark of Jean Patou, Inc., **p. 319** National Archives, **p. 325** UPI, **p. 330** Drawing by H. Martin; © 1977 The New Yorker Magazine, Inc., **p. 339** Robert Pachero, **p. 341** UPI, **p. 349** THE WIZARD OF ID by permission of Johnny Hart and Field Enterprises, Inc., **p. 351** The New York Historical Society

Production Credits

Design: Steven Manus and Karen McBride
Photo Research: Gene Vlazny, Graphics Two
Composition: Lienett Company, Inc.
Printing: Kingsport Press

Cover Art: This cover is a montage of photographs of *The Four Seasons* by Marc Chagall, a 128 panel mosaic of hand-chipped stone and glass fragments located in the First National Bank Plaza, Chicago.
Cover Design: Marylynn Conte
Cover Photography: Steven Manus

Published by Alfred Publishing Co., Inc.
15335 Morrison St., Sherman Oaks, CA 91403

Library of Congress Cataloging in Publication Data

Gorden, William I 1929–
   Communication: personal and public

   Bibliography: p.
   Includes index.
   1. Communication. I. Title
P90.G55   001.5   76-30803
ISBN 0-88284-041-X

contents

preface

This is personal—from me to you—as personal as I know how to communicate in print. I have tried not to hide my values and biases. But I hope you will find what I say unpretentious, direct and generally free from jargon.

We all have certain expectations out of life and in our everyday activities we expect (indeed we often take for granted) communication. You, as a student taking a course in communication, have certain expectations. And as I wrote this book, I had certain expectations in mind. On a general note, I want the book to provide a special experience for those who read it. I want to brighten your eyes from time to time with a new idea and a well-put phrase. I want to touch readers who may be anxious about their interpersonal relationships and communication abilities. I want the substance and spirit of this book to assist young adults in developing communication behaviors needed in their careers and community life—to discover effective alternative ways of coping, cooperating and competing to achieve what is good for them and others. I want to help students increase their sense of personal and public identity—to become more articulate, accurate and humane in expressing their own wants and ideas.

More specifically, I want this text to present a credible resource. The book progresses from concepts to applications in interpersonal and public transactions. The first part, *General Expectations*, is designed to draw attention to phenomena common to all manner of communication. Early focus on these ideas is in harmony with that pedagogical principle which suggests theory should precede and accompany prescription. In this section a framework is structured to help the student and his instructor better talk about the complex and multidimensional communication process. The second part, *Interpersonal Expectations*, attends to interpersonal skills important in one-to-one and small group communications. The last part, *Public Expectations*, examines speech preparation and delivery, the speaker/audience relationship, ethics, influence and mass media communications. The explicit statement of the text rests in the communicator's dual concern for understanding his own motivations and for addressing his listeners' expectations.

In addition to the illustrations and frequent use of everyday examples, the book has two special features to help achieve my goals for it. The work acknowledges the relationship, if not the wedding, of the science and art of communication. Therefore, space is given throughout the book to abstracts of the growing body of research intended to accurately describe the communication process. My hope is that special attention to the growing body of research will help readers to understand why some "common sense" ideas about human interaction are reliable, but others are not. And through this understanding we can temper our expectations of others.

The second feature is the use of what I choose to call, "Initiatives." Each chapter concludes with a number of experiential activities, the purpose of which is to open opportunities to test the theoretical material presented in the chapters. Involvement in these "Initiatives" will also help readers to refine their expectations of communication experiences.

No book is ever totally the product of one person's efforts. In early drafts of the manuscript I received help from Ray Heisey, Hugh C. Munro, and Gene R. Stebbins. I wish to thank the publisher for assistance in the writing of Chapter Eleven, and I especially thank Charles G. Waugh of the University of Maine for writing the chapter on mass media. It is a fine contribution to the work and except for small sections which I wrote, all credit for it is his. I also wish to thank James Waickman, Ed Swingle and Ed Pappas for critically reading the manuscript. Nancy Schmitz typed two drafts of the book and successfully persisted in obtaining the permissions. Linda Beikirch worked with the final draft and Phyllis Thomas assisted with endless typing of bits and pieces. Special credit goes to Linda Moore, who is co-author of the *Instructor's Manual*. And finally, I am grateful to the many students who have helped me to understand communication and forgiven me when I didn't.

This text might never have been written had not John Stout, College Editor at Alfred Publishing Company, convinced me that his firm genuinely wanted such a book as I envisioned and would publish a beautiful volume. For that stimulus I thank John. For making good that promise, I thank Morton Manus, President of Alfred Publishing.

A Note on Language

In connection with my goals for this book, I want to say a few words about my choice of language. Careful readers may notice obvious efforts to avoid stereotyped or traditional roles for women in both the text and the selection of photographs. At one point in the writing, for a certain chapter I had changed all generic, "he" pronouns to "she"; but then I decided that such changes were unacceptable and distracting tokens. Since no word has yet come to be accepted to mean either "he" or "she" (such as "chee"), I have reluctantly stayed with "he." But whenever either pronoun would suffice, I tried to find an alternative way to make the statement, keeping in mind that "one" often seems cold and impersonal and not very consistent with the book's tone and style.

To my parents and other young people.

communication
personal & public

part one

general expectations

1 identity & communication

TO NAME IS TO INFLUENCE

None of us can wholly escape the influence of our names. At the same time babies learn words to label everything outside themselves, they learn their names as labels for themselves, and subsequently their identity—which will further develop. Whether the label they learn for themselves is more or less common to their culture will influence how well accepted they feel they are by their society. Some Puritans tried to influence their children by giving them virtuous names such as Fearnot and Flie-Fornication. One Pilgrim in 18th Century Rhode Island bore the name Through-much-tribulation-we-enter-the-Kingdom-of-Heaven Clapp. Even today some parents assign their children names like Joy, Grace, Faith, and Chastity.

Some parents appear insensitive to the consequences of extremely unusual or humorous combinations such as Ima and Ura Hogg, or Pansy and Leafy Plant.

John and Mary and William and Elizabeth, in our culture, are more traditional and respected than most other names. Some studies have shown that popularity and better grades are related to respected names such as David and Michael, as compared to less respected names such as Hubert and Elmer. Conversely, "functional psychosis" was found in four times as many men who carried odd names such as Oder and Lethal.

Paraphrased from "The Name of the Game," *Akron Beacon Journal,* November 11, 1973, pp. 23–28. Also see Mary G. Marcus, "The Power of a Name," *Psychology Today,* Vol. 10, October, 1976, pp. 75–76, 106.

We live in a communication-dependent society. That is, we are in constant interaction with people around us and, in turn, are constantly affected by their actions. Often, communication comes in the form of media bombardment. Television, radio, movies, and newspapers flood us with information, and their advertisements attempt to persuade us in almost every aspect of our daily behavior. Some of this environment is beyond our control: we are born in a certain country, of particular parents, with varying abilities, liabilities, and potentials. Society passes laws which we are told to obey and develops customs to which we are encouraged to conform. Much of the time we are not even aware of the many ways our lives are influenced by these outside forces.

As you begin this chapter, repeat your name—if not aloud, then in a whisper. Listen to its sound. Do you like it? A large percent of college students, when asked whether they would have chosen their own names, say no. Some, because their names are too common, others, because they are not common enough. At one stage of adolescence, as we struggled to establish some degree of individuality, most of us hated our name merely because it was imposed by our parents.

A name, like any communicative act, cannot be taken back. It is irreversible. Even those who change their names cannot erase it from their memory. The sound of a name: Marilyn, Janice, Lenny, Malcolm, Bobby, Abraham, Martin and John—they stir images of charismatic lives and tragic deaths. On stage and on record, in concert, film, or politics, their voices and images captured our attention and imagination. Only a few, in any society, achieve popular recognition during their lives, and fewer still after their deaths. Yet each of us wants to have a good sounding name for our friends, our loved ones, our professors, and our employers.

Not only do the names we are given at birth subtly influence our lives, but also the labels we are given influence how others think about us and, perhaps more important, how we perceive ourselves. For example, to be labeled *"easy"* affects how one is treated by the opposite sex. To be labeled a good or poor listener, or outgoing or introverted, most certainly will affect one's social well-being and, possibly, one's career.

DOONESBURY

by GB Trudeau.

The goals we set for our lives, in a very real sense, create new labels for ourselves. To set a goal, say to become knowledgeable and articulate in a chosen field, sets a positive attitude about oneself. Such an attitude identifies what one can become. As individuals, we strive to assert control over our lives and destinies. The capacity to learn frees us from repeating set patterns and allows us to become a new person daily. What we learn changes not only what we can do, but how we think and feel about ourselves and others.

In order for change to occur, we must understand the factors that influence our lives and develop the skills necessary to control them. In this chapter, we will examine the learning relationship important to developing communication skills. In addition, we will examine the universal concern for self-confidence and how communication skills may contribute to one's self-image. Finally, we will examine the relationship between these skills and achievement in our careers and life goals.

THE LEARNING RELATIONSHIP

It is very difficult, if not impossible, to learn to dance by self-instruction. And just as it takes two to tango, it takes you plus someone else to develop your communication skills. This text, therefore, can be only an invitation to join with others in the study and observation of the dynamic and complex social process we call *communication.* A book cannot *speak* to share the insights gained across the centuries by the scholars of the communication process. I, as an author, am restricted to print, to the words, sketches and photographs on these pages. I cannot make you want to learn. It is the working human relationships between you and your instructor, and you and your social environment that will motivate you to improve or not improve your communication skills.

Learning at its best is a love relationship. We may, of course, learn avoidance behaviors, such as not touching a hot stove or jumping in front of a car, by the negative stimuli of a slap on the wrist or a shout from a parent. But developing positive social competencies is generally the product of a loving relationship *between* teachers and learners.

Facts, figures and formulas become meaningful when there is someone explaining them who I believe has my welfare at heart. Without goodwill, there is little credibility; without love, there is isolation, frustration, alienation and failure. Without the assurance that my instructor cares for me, I find it difficult to take criticism. In short, no teacher can teach me if I do not want to learn.

So it is with communication skills. Only you can determine if you need to know more about the process and if you need to improve certain interaction skills. Not everyone does. Even though we live in a communication-oriented society, many people do survive socially and do satisfy the demands of their careers with little formal training in communication skills. You may have brothers or sisters who are mechanics, druggists or microbiologists, who have taken no course, yet are successful in their chosen careers and are reasonably articulate in exchanging opinions with friends about the news of the day and matters of concern.

It is also a fact that even speech defectives, such as Leonardo da Vinci, Thomas Jefferson, Lewis Carroll, Clara Barton, Theodore Roosevelt, and George Washington Carver (most of them stutterers), have achieved fame.[1] Moreover, in spite of the sloppy pronunciation practiced by millions of Americans, the business of living has not come to a screeching halt.

In short, you can exist and our society will go on even if you never study interpersonal communication and if you never learn to deliver a speech. If you choose, you can avoid most formal speaking by electing a career that is not communication-oriented. But many need communication skills and one of that many may be you.

In my job I must be able to communicate with all types of people with a good attitude while telling them about the product. I must be able to speak to customers, but also to listen to their thoughts.
—Beer Truck Driver, Male, 1 year's experience

COMMUNICATION COMPETENCE AND CAREERS

The reasons for studying the communication process and developing skills are many. But first we should ask, "Who needs it?"

SELF-CONFIDENCE   A primary consideration important to answering that question is knowing the components of self-confidence. People who suffer communication apprehension tend to avoid encounters that involve talk. They seldom participate in class discussions and prefer to work alone. Extremely quiet individuals generally are considered by others as less credible, less attractive as social companions and less likely to be opinion leaders.[2]

Self-confidence or the lack of it varies from situation to situation. One may, for example, be confident of one's ability to drive a car and at the same time lack confidence to dive into a pool. The question before you is: In what areas do you want to and in what areas can you attain a level of competence which merits a reasonable measure of self-confidence? To put it another way, are your present communication skills sufficient for the needs of your career, your social interaction, and your public and private life?

Think for a moment about several varied situations and then make a judgment about how able you are within them. If you feel highly uncomfortable in a situation, you are likely not very competent in that area. What we do well, we feel comfortable doing.

Most students increase confidence in their ability to communicate during a course in basic communications. This confidence seems to spring from two sources: increased knowledge about theory and increased ability to think on one's feet. It makes sense, doesn't it? Once I know more about what makes a message understood and impressive, I feel more confident. And after I have had the practical experience of making several presentations and answering questions about what I've said without falling on my face, and having seen signs that my audience liked my presentations, I gain confidence. There is considerable evidence that speech training has resulted in a dramatic gain in confidence in the speaking situation for some students.[3] Speech anxiety goes down for most students and they say they have learned how to utilize the tension natural to facing an audience.[4]

Admittedly, hard evidence that instruction in speech communication skills increases confidence is not easy to come by. Some studies that report increased self-confidence may simply result from a comfortableness with one's classmates toward the conclusion of the course. Moreover, to get data on the long-range effects of taking a course in communication would require follow-up studies years afterwards. The many intervening variables and the expense of such studies has left us with little data.

Nevertheless, there is sufficient evidence to believe that your attitudes toward yourself as a communicator will improve after you take a course in speech.

Some students may suffer severe speech anxiety at the thought of making a speech. Not many colleges and universities are equipped with special programs to map out a strategy for dealing with extreme reticence. The essential question is this: Do you avoid speaking encounters? As unscientific as this question may sound, if your answer is "yes" you ought to consult privately with your instructor. Together you may be able to structure a program to deal with your speech avoidance.

Yet another word should be said concerning general self-confidence. Some studies have revealed the college years to be a time when many students suffer a decrease in self-concept. Their high expectations of childhood and adolescence frequently are shattered by the harsh realities of a competitive society in which social and financial success are more limited than expected. Brooks and Platz found that 75% of a freshman class that was enrolled in a speech course had a significant improvement in their view of themselves as communicators while the other 25% shifted downward toward a lower self-concept.[5]

To expect a course in communication skills to counteract such psychological and political awakenings is unrealistic and unfair. A communication course may increase one's general knowledge; it may enhance one's career effectiveness; it may assist one to be a more able student in other classes; it may improve one's conversational and public speaking skills; and such a course may stimulate one to be a more sensitive, humane person.

CAREERS

Let us now consider those in communication-oriented careers: lawyers, clergymen, politicians, teachers, salesmen, advertising managers, actors, counselors, public relations workers, newsmen and entertainers. The list is staggering. Reading, writing, listening and, most of all, oral communication are the channels for input and output of millions of messages which are a daily part of these careers.

In addition, surveys of course requirements of professional schools of agriculture, business, education, engineering, home economics, law, journalism, music, nursing and pharmacy reveal that training in written and oral communication is required of all their students.

In the legal profession, the ability to communicate by either the oral or written medium is of paramount importance. Without either of those skills, the attorney will just not be able to ply his trade.

—Attorney, Female,
2 years' experience

HOW MUCH DOES THE COP TALK?

Basic Question: What kinds of communication activities are used by urban police officers and what are their attitudes to these activities?

Method: Fifty police officers in Lubbock, Texas, a medium-sized city, were asked to keep a careful on-duty record of the kind of communication used over ten weeks. Each fifteen minutes of their eight hour day they were to log the form and extent of communication activities: for example, did they write a report, read, listen or talk and to whom. The researchers, in addition, rode in a lot of patrol cars observing firsthand the officers' activities. The fifty officers were enrolled in an oral communication course during the time of the survey. At the outset and at the end of the term their attitudes toward their several communication activities were measured on a seven-point scale.

Results: Consistent with reports on white collar workers and business executives, 72% of the on-duty time of the 50 officers surveyed is spent in communicative behavior. The major portion of their communication time was spent listening (36%) and talking (30%). Reading (18%) and writing (16%) were also important in police officers' workdays. Within the department most communication was directed to others of the same rank.

Communication Contacts Within The Department

Percent of Communication Time Within Dept.	Communication With Officers of Like Rank	Communication With Superiors	Communication With Subordinates
40%	75%	15%	10%

Communication Contacts Outside

Percent of Communication Time Outside Dept.	General Public	Witnesses	Suspects	Lawyers	Informers
60%	55%	20%	15%	5%	5%

At the beginning of the course, the officers' attitudes generally were more negative than positive. After the course was completed, the officers' confidence in their effectiveness both within and outside their departments shifted to the positive.

Implication: Police work involves much communication. This survey tends to support and extend previous studies which revealed that only a small percentage of police work focuses upon crime control and that most police encounters with the public require interpersonal communication skills. Police officers, like many in service careers, do need communication skills. Moreover, such training increases their confidence in their communicative effectiveness.

T. Richard Cheatham and Keith Erickson, "Auditing Police Communication," a paper presented at Speech Communication Association Convention, Chicago, December 29, 1974.

To fail in communication is to fail as an educated person. The most essential characteristics of such a person are that he or she be literate and articulate.[6] Robert Oliver, Professor of Speech Communication, Emeritus, Pennsylvania State University, offers the following:

> At the highest levels of government, business, and community life, the most capable people are well aware that their ability to communicate orally and directly, in face-to-face situations, is the last great capacity they must master.
>
> At the lowest levels, the under-employed and the unemployable suffer special disabilities because they do not properly interpret what is said to them and because they lack skill in presenting themselves in acceptable form.[7]

There is a general agreement of those in business that their work involves communication skills, human relations, effective speech, conference leadership and participation. Many corporation presidents have stated their belief that a definite relationship exists between employee productivity and communication with management.[8] This is the dollars and sense reason American big business has spent millions to improve communication in past years.

These sentiments led Lynn A. Townsend, at that time president of Chrysler, to suggest:

> *Internal communication must be recognized as an essential tool of good management.* There is a particular need for every manager to understand that good communication is a way to achieve corporate objectives; it's a way to build better teamwork, it's a way to *make money* . . .
> . . . effective communication as an important motivating force. It can help managers become better leaders. It can develop constructive attitudes. It can make employees feel they are working with a company—not just for it. It can build employee confidence in management. Good communication can achieve better quality and safety records, increased production, and reduction of waste and spoilage.[9]

Top executives of corporations speak for business. They testify at government hearings. They carry their views to city clubs and to college campuses. But it is not only the person at the top who must tell his company's story. Thousands of companies such as General Motors, General Electric, Standard Oil and the 3-M Company field speakers' bureaus. Their representatives speak on topics of plant safety, minority hiring, ecology and free enterprise.[10]

You be the judge. Did Lowell Thomas, the world-famous traveler and news commentator, overstate the importance of communication skills when he said: "The ability to speak is a shortcut to distinction. It puts a man in the limelight, raises him head and shoulders above the crowd"?[11]

But formal speaking and writing messages likely is not in your future if your choice is largely aimed toward doing things, such as working on an assembly line, being a professional athlete, handling a large diesel, or playing a musical instrument. You may avoid formal speaking and writing in many careers that are essential to our society.

This one striking fact, however, is unavoidable: Almost no career, even those listed above, is isolated from conveying and receiving messages. Messages are either *internal* to your business

DO REAL PEOPLE EVER GIVE SPEECHES?

Blue collar workers in surprising numbers do speak to audiences of ten or more fairly frequently. A carefully drawn sample of working class people in Albany, New York, in an interview were asked, "In the past two years, how many times have you spoken to a group of ten or more people at once?"

Forty-three percent stated they had presented one or more speeches. "Speaking at church" was the most frequently mentioned occasion. Bowling banquets, speeches to day-care parents, driver safety lectures, kitchen staff and union were other speaking experiences listed.

Kathleen Edgerton Kendall, "Do Real People Ever Give Speeches?" *Central States Speech Journal* (Fall 1974), pp. 233–235.

organization, from supervision above, between and among workers, between management and unions, or *external*, between the organization and the public. The quality of communication in business is what makes the difference.

So far in this chapter, we have explored the relationship between communication and self-confidence and considered the importance of communication to career choices and life goals. Now we are ready to set some personal goals and map out a program for achieving them.

Oral and communication skills are among the most important management criteria.
—Division Plant Manager, Telephone Co., Male, 19 years' experience

PERSONAL GOAL SETTING

Let us first consider short-term goals, those related to your success and well-being during the next several weeks. What are some of your immediate objectives? Might you want to make a favorable impression in other classes—to be able to ask and answer questions and to comment intelligently? Will you be active in a social or professional organization? Will you be assigned to present a report of a committee of which you are a member? Will you want to join in a conversation with new acquaintances? Would you stumble hesitantly when discussing current events with some friends? Are you as articulate as you would like to be at this stage of your life? Do you want to be able to talk knowledgeably about the favorite topic of a boy or girl friend? Do you want to persuade your parents to let you go on a trip over the next vacation? Or might you simply want to develop a closer friendship

I was one of five candidates for one job opening. The interview was decisive.
—Pricing Manager, Oil Co., Male, 23 years' experience

Written by someone who <u>really</u> understands the problems, the feelings and the thoughts of young people today. Dr. Gordon's approach and way of communicating to young people is outstanding. — Dr. Lee Salk

YOU

THE PSYCHOLOGY OF SURVIVING AND
☆ ☆ ☆ ☆ **ENHANCING YOUR** ☆ ☆ ☆ ☆

$6.95

Social Life
Love Life
Sex Life
School Life
Work Life
Home Life
Emotional Life
Creative Life
Spiritual Life
Style of Life
Life

by SOL GORDON with Roger Conant ★★

with them? Might you soon be interviewed for a job, a loan, or admission to a professional school?

All of the above are potential goals for you and your classmates—goals that are related to your communication skills in addition to your special talents and personality. It is unrealistic to aim too high and to try to do too much. No one can be brilliantly conversant on all subjects. Life is too short and the mountains of knowledge too steep. But each of us can begin this term to achieve in a particular area.

A fellow, for instance, may want to be able to talk intelligently with a girl friend about the movement for equal opportunities for women. A coed, on the other hand, may want to increase her ability to speak on behalf of her chosen career. One student, majoring in recreation for the physically handicapped, for example, set as one short-term goal the ability to design and present a speech to persuade more physically handicapped students to participate in recreational activities on campus. *Short-Term Goals*

Achieving short-term goals are the stepping stones to long-range goals. A student who some day wants to host a television talk show must begin by becoming an articulate, informed student. To achieve this involves many intermediate experiences. He may want to learn how to interview local sports stars. He may want to attend a cocktail party reception for a local artist and ask questions about his work. He may want to record a conversation with a member of the local clergy about the state of the church. At a political rally, he might sample and compare on-the-spot opinions of participants and onlookers. An important step in his program might be monitoring popular talk show hosts and making a list of questions they asked. In so doing, he could perhaps discover what order the interview took . . . which questions stirred the most dialogue . . . which fell flat. These are just a few ideas for setting one's goals and developing a step-by-step program designed to achieve them.

What can a course in basic communication skills do for you? Let's brainstorm, and from the list of potentials, you may decide on a plan for achieving one or more of these potential benefits. *General Goals*

Self-improvement books, though always popular, have in recent years become particularly hot sellers. Whether concerned with interpersonal skills, management techniques, or lovemaking, these books stress the importance of self-confidence.

1 Acquaint you with the complex dynamic components in the communication process. Consequently, you may be able to adjust to, if not always prevent, misunderstandings.

2 Arm you against salesmen who would sell you products or policies not in your best interests.

3 Provide an understanding of and experiences in building your credibility with an audience.

Be concise and to the point, be objective and say what you feel. Be aware of feedback and practice active listening.
—Teacher, Female, Six months' experience

4 Help you become a more interesting conversationalist.

5 Increase your question asking and answering skills.

6 Increase your confidence to express your ideas and feelings with friends and acquaintances. Give you an appropriate sense of self-confidence socially and professionally.

7 Enhance your leadership abilities—to give you theory and practice as a task leader in a small group or panel.

8 Develop your organizational abilities—to help you divide your ideas to make them clearer to you and your audience.

9 Give you a theoretical and practical understanding of informative and persuasive message construction and delivery.

10 Alert you to think first of adapting your ideas to your listeners and of seeking their feedback, both verbal and nonverbal.

These are only potential benefits. Only you can say whether any or all of them are important to your life goals and career choices. But everyone—students, professors, businessmen, artists, musicians—needs both long-range and intermediate personalized goals, a program and a schedule.

Many teen-agers and young adults have a need not to need their parents. It is a natural and healthy impulse toward independence. Developing our knowledge and skills is yet another step toward independence. For some, communication skills may become a shortcut to success. For most of us, developing our communication skills is one giant step beyond independence. It is the step toward being heard and treated as someone whose voice counts and matters to others. It is the step toward interdependence—adult to adult. It is gaining both a sense of self-identity and an identity with others.

SUMMARY

This first chapter has focused upon the individual's needs and goals in a communication-oriented society. One's ability to function in both social and career relationships hinges upon one's communication competencies. To be educated, in the best sense of the word, is to be literate and articulate.

Self-confidence in different social situations is intimately related to one's ability to communicate ideas and feelings. Our individual identity and independence depend upon the way we communicate. The quality of citizenship, the salvation of the environment, and the management of organizations, likewise, depend upon the quality of communication. Civilization itself is not possible without communication.

People who gain understanding of the complex dynamic process of human communication and who translate that understanding into communication competencies have reason to gain in self-confidence. Testimony to that fact can be found in the universities of ancient Greece and Rome as well as the universities of today.

Business and industry are also increasingly dependent upon translating theoretical knowledge into new products and applications. To do so requires accurate and efficient exchange of information and coordination of human resources. To be sure, some individuals may find careers that are less concerned with formal communication skills, but no one can escape the necessity for some measure of receiving and conveying information.

But little if any learning about communication can take place in isolation. It takes feedback and interaction to develop and perfect one's abilities to listen and to speak well.

INITIATIVES

Each chapter includes several student-initiated actions designed to illustrate, clarify and reinforce learning. If the text might be thought of as a window through which the student looks at concepts, the initiatives are then doors that open to learning by doing. When the student takes the initiative to open the door, the experience can be theirs. Usually there will be more initiatives than time will permit. The student may elect those that appear most interesting and/or those the instructor suggests will complement his instruction. I like my students to begin immediately all three of the initiatives at the close of this chapter. Action 1 can be completed in ten minutes, but Action 2 may take several weeks to achieve, and Action 3 about three weeks.

INITIATING ACTION 1   This inventory is designed to help the student define where it is that he or she cannot function with ease. Do not assume that all discomfort is bad. It is a fact that often we can do things that we fear or feel uncomfortable doing. It is also true that a certain amount of anxiety may motivate us to train and prepare well for something, such as a job interview. I recommend that you complete this inventory of your feelings, ranging from Highly Uncomfortable to Comfortable, as you begin this course. Note where it is that you find a communication event uncomfortable. Analyze why and consult with your instructor. Perhaps together you can outline several concrete steps you may take to function more adequately and with greater ease. At the end of the term, again complete this Comfort Index,* but use a different colored pen. Examine those items in which you have circled different numbers. Why? Reflect upon why, if you have changed.

---

*Also see James C. McCroskey, "Measure of Communication-Bound Anxiety," *Speech Monographs* 37, (November 1970), pp. 269–277. McCroskey's Scale may be used by the instructor who wishes to do a pre-post test of speech anxiety. The instrument, titled PRCA-College, has twenty items such as "I have no fear of facing an audience" and "I always avoid speaking in public if I can avoid it." The Comfort Index is not designed for testing, i.e., the items have not been worded in opposite fashion, nor has it been validated. Its purpose rather is to alert the student to a range of communicative situations and to his own feelings of discomfort or comfort about them, and consequently, to better enable him to set his own individual goals.

COMFORT INDEX

WHEN	I GENERALLY FEEL				
Circle the number representing your feelings	Highly Uncomfortable				Highly Comfortable
1. Eating alone in a cafeteria	1	2	3	4	5
2. Observing a sports event with a companion	1	2	3	4	5
3. Talking with a *friend* of same sex on the phone	1	2	3	4	5
4. Talking with a *friend* of opposite sex in person	1	2	3	4	5
5. Talking with a *new acquaintance* of *same* sex	1	2	3	4	5
6. Talking with a *new acquaintance* of *opposite* sex	1	2	3	4	5
7. Social conversation with several acquaintances, same age, both sexes	1	2	3	4	5
8. Social conversation with several older persons	1	2	3	4	5
9. Thinking in my room about having to recite in class	1	2	3	4	5
10. Participating in classroom discussion	1	2	3	4	5
11. Participating in a panel discussion before a class	1	2	3	4	5
12. Answering questions asked by a teacher	1	2	3	4	5
13. Thinking in my room about having to present a speech two weeks away	1	2	3	4	5
14. Thinking about a speech the night before I am to present it	1	2	3	4	5
15. *Getting to my feet* to speak in a business meeting	1	2	3	4	5
16. *Getting to my feet* to present a speech in which I am the main speaker of the occasion	1	2	3	4	5
17. Actually presenting a speech	1	2	3	4	5
18. Going for a job interview	1	2	3	4	5
19. Chairing a committee	1	2	3	4	5

20. Talking with acquaintances about sports	1	2	3	4	5
21. Talking with acquaintances about music, dance or theater	1	2	3	4	5
22. Talking with acquaintances about current events	1	2	3	4	5
23. Talking with acquaintances about philosophy and ethics	1	2	3	4	5
24. Talking with a friend about things I dislike about his or her behavior	1	2	3	4	5
25. Talking to a disliked person	1	2	3	4	5

INITIATING ACTION 2.

NAME _____

MY GOALS
A PERSONAL PLAN FOR DEVELOPING COMMUNICATION SKILLS

Check those goals that are important to you.
Double check those goals that are especially important to you.

_____ To understand how to develop my credibility.

_____ To be more able to ask and answer questions clearly and effectively.

_____ To be more able to express my feelings which may hinder communication if I keep them bottled up.

_____ To be more able to present an organized persuasive message which I've prepared.

_____ To be more able to think on my feet and to debate an issue with my peers.

_____ To be more able to make others laugh.

_____ To be a more interesting conversationalist.

_____ To be more able to know when someone is manipulating me and to respond in my best interests.

_____ To be more able to lead a panel, to make introductions, and conduct a discussion.

SPECIFY:

Long-range Communication Skills that will be important to my career are:

_____

_____

My Intermediate Communication Skills Goals are: _____

_____

Some Concrete Steps I will undertake during these coming weeks to achieve one or more of my Intermediate Goals:

1. _____

_____

2. _____

_____

3. _____

_____

INITIATING ACTION 3.

Who Needs It? People with experience in a career can provide sound suggestions for the kinds of communication skills needed in their jobs. Doing your own survey is one way to discover more about communication skills that may someday be important to earning your own bread. Out of my experience with this project, I make the following recommendations.

1 Each student should select three people working in careers which hold some interest for him or her. These people may be relatives, parents of friends, or new contacts. (Relatives are usually very cooperative.)

2 Prepare a business-like letter explaining your genuine interest in learning how important various communications are in their careers. The ability to write such a letter is an act of persuasion in itself which your instructor may wish to discuss. For example, the letter may reveal your intentions clearly or ambiguously. It may express goodwill or reveal little goodwill. It may demonstrate how well you adapt or fail to adapt your language to that of your reader. Prepare letters for two of the three persons you have selected. Be sure to specify a date when you need the material and stress that these answers should be printed clearly.

3 Interview the third person. Think through how you will arrange to get the interview. What you will say when making the first contact, probably by phone. What questions you will ask to get the person talking? What you will do to make sure you have written down exactly what the interviewee has expressed. (It may be good to read back what you have written down.) Also take notice of the place of the interview. What have you learned about the communication aspects of the job by observing the working conditions.

4 Write your report. From the forms upon which you have gathered data, see if there are any commonalities and/or major differences. Summarize your findings in not more than three paragraphs. Be cautious about generalizing.

5 Compare your data with your classmates'. Likely the instructor will set aside part of one period to report and compare findings.

A sample form that could be used as the data instrument for the interviews follows. (This particular form was used effectively by the author and his colleague in a mailed survey.)

Please type or print your answers clearly.

1. Occupation _____

   Years of experience _____

2. How did you get your job? (a) phone call _____ (b) letter _____ (c) interview _____ (d) other _____

3. Do you think your ability to communicate (a) helped _____ or (b) had little influence in your hiring _____ ? Why? _____

   _____

4. Is there any part of your occupation that involves communication?

   ____ (a) giving instructions or orders

_____ (b) following instructions or orders

_____ (c) written reports or briefings

_____ (d) oral reports or briefings

_____ (e) staff meetings

_____ (f) buying or selling face-to-face or by phone

_____ (g) working with committees or small groups

_____ (h) speaking to larger audiences within your plant

_____ (i) speaking to community audiences or to conferences

_____ (j) Please describe more fully the kinds of communication skills you are expected to

possess: _____

_____

_____

5. Are there any specific recommendations you would make to young people about develop-

ing their abilities to read, write, listen and speak? _____

_____

_____

_____

Signature   Date

I give permission for my above comments to be used in educational materials. Check here if you do not want your name used _____ . Thank you for your cooperation. Your answers may help students to seek an education that is a practical benefit to them and their community.

Please write any additional comments on the back and return to us immediately.

NOTES

1. Carol Schwalberg, "The Secrets of Better Speech," *Pageant,* October, 1961, p. 9.

2. James C. McCroskey and Virginia P. Richmond, "The Effects of Communication Apprehension on the Perception of Peers," *Western Speech Communication,* Vol. XI, Winter 1976, pp. 14–31.

3. Larry Judd, "Research in Improving Self-Concept in the Basic Course: Review and Recommendations," *Today's Speech,* **21,** Summer, 1973, p. 51.

4. James C. McCroskey, "The Effects of the Basic Course on Student Attitudes," *The Speech Teacher,* 16 (March, 1967), pp. 115–117; and Wayne N. Thompson, *Quantitative Research in Public Address and Communication* (New York: Random House, 1967), pp. 149–203.

5. William D. Brooks and Sara M. Platz, "The Effects of Speech Training Upon Self-Concept As a Communicator," *The Speech Teacher,* Vol. 17, January 1968, pp. 44–49.

6. J. Jeffrey Auer, "Speech as a Social Force," *National Educational Journal,* November, 1960. This statement is a paraphrase of the words of Lawrence M. Gould, President of Carleton College, from a speech he delivered to a University of Michigan graduating class. In addition, J. Jeffrey Auer, Chairman of the Department of Speech and Theatre, Indiana University, reported: "A recent study published by the Institute of Higher Education surveyed 182 professional schools of agriculture, business, education, engineering, home economics, journalism, music, nursing, and pharmacy. A majority of the 3400 teachers and administrators surveyed designated speech training as important enough to be required of every student. This same endorsement was given for only four other subjects in the liberal arts curriculum: English composition, mathematics, history, and chemistry [p. 22]."

7. Robert T. Oliver, "A View Ahead: The Speech Profession in 1984," *Today's Speech,* **20,** Summer, 1972, p. 11. For a more cynical view consider the opinion of H. F. Harding, University of Texas at El Paso, Professor of Speech, "Speech Communication in 1984," *Today's Speech,* **20,** Summer, 1970, p. 6. "Will good writing and good speaking be considered essential for the well educated man? No. This is a screwy old idea that does not *relate* now. The best writers will be those least understood. The best speakers will be teleprompter readers."

8. R. E. Lull, F. E. Funk, and D. T. Piersol, "Business and Industrial Communication of the Corporation President," Purdue University, 1954 (mimeographed), pp. 2, 5, 11. Returns from 51 corporation presidents from the 100 largest U.S. corporations: "Do you believe there is a relationship between communication and employee productivity? [p. 2]"

Definite Relationship	48
Slight Relationship	2
No Relationship	0

"98% thought oral communication was at least as important and 40% thought it was even more important than written in their company [p. 5]." "The vast majority of the respondents indicated that effectiveness of management personnel is greatly dependent upon ability in oral communication [p. 11]."

Also see Harold P. Zelko, "Adult Speech Training: Challenge to the Speech Profession," *Quarterly Journal of Speech,* XXXVII, February, 1951, p. 57. Data from 206 industries and businesses involving 2,809,500 employees and

221,900 supervisors; representatives in the firms were asked to check their communication needs:

    1. Human Relations   92%
    2. Effective Speech   76%
    3. Conference Leadership   82%
    4. Conference Participation   60%
    5. Parliamentary Law   10%

9. Lynn A. Townsend, "A Corporate President's View of the Internal Communication Function," *Journal of Communication,* XV, December, 1965, pp. 208–215.

10. John R. Miller and William I. Gorden, "Survey of the Fortune 500 Speaker's Bureau," Kent State University, 1974, Unpublished. Subsequent data was gathered in this survey.

11. Dale Carnegie, *How to Win Friends and Influence People.* New York: Pocket Books, 1935, 1970, 82nd printing, p. 6.

SUGGESTED READINGS

Brown, Charles T., and Charles Van Riper, *Speech and Man.* Englewood Cliffs, N.J.: Prentice-Hall, 1966.

——— , *Communication in Human Relationships.* Skokie, Ill.: National Textbook Co., 1973.

Civikly, Jean M., *Messages: A Reader in Human Communication.* New York: Random House, 1974.

Eble, Kenneth E., *A Perfect Education.* London: Collier-Macmillian, 1966.

Nadeau, Ray E., *Speech-Communication: A Career Approach.* Reading, Mass.: Addison-Wesley, 1974.

Postman, Neil, and Charles Weingartner, *The Soft Revolution.* New York: Dell Publishing Co., 1971.

Ratcliffe, Sharon A., and Deldee M. Herman, *Adventures in the Looking Glass.* Skokie, Ill.: National Textbook Co., 1973.

Stewart, John., *Bridges Not Walls.* Reading, Mass.: Addison-Wesley, 1973.

Wilmot, William W., and John R. Wenburg, *Communication Involvement: Personal Perspectives.* New York: John Wiley and Sons, 1974.

2 communication functions

The word *communication* comes from the Latin word *communis,* meaning *common.* In a very real sense, that is what communication is all about, establishing commonness with yourself or with one or more members of a group. When we send a message, we are requesting that the listener pay attention to us and find something with which he might identify. Communication involves three elements: expressing, receiving and interpreting. *Communication may be briefly defined as a dynamic human transaction involving ideas and feelings.*

Communication may be better understood if it is described according to its various functions in society. This is to say that talking to oneself, prayer, cocktail party conversation, and a public speech involve different characteristics and purposes. The categories of communication which will be considered in this chapter are: (1) Social, (2) Expressive, (3) Ritual and (4) Instrumental. Every kind of communication serves one or more of these four functions; often a communication includes all of them. In later chapters we will examine the processes by which these different types of communication occur.

SOCIAL COMMUNICATION

People are gregarious. We come together for a number of reasons. First, because we, even before our initial cries, were dependent upon a mother and then a family. The family is dependent upon other families in the community and, obviously, in this whirling globe with several billion people, states and nations are dependent upon each other for trade, services, ideas and security.

Few people can survive alone, or choose to. The baby or young child who is isolated and deprived of human interaction is delayed in the development of his sensual acuity, his intellectual and emotional well-being, and may be emotionally wounded for a lifetime. An individual who is deprived of human contact is soon disoriented. People, as a popular song says, need people. As babies we need to be held, cuddled and assured that we are

physically well and emotionally alive. We need each other throughout our lives to assure us that we are not alone in the struggle for survival. We need each other to provide models and alternative lifestyles against which to measure our own.

We need human contact to learn who we are. Man is constantly developing his self-image. History and tradition provide a meaningful structure for the present. In short, man thrives best when he has roots. But each of us seeks an individual distinctiveness so that not only are we recognized as one of the group, but also as one with an individual identity.

Social communication is the social interaction that helps each person keep in contact. "Hello" and "How are you?" are examples. Expressions of coming and going, hugs, handshakes and general inquiries about family, health and weather also may be so classified. Sometimes, though, the greetings and farewells become so automatic that we may go to a doctor's office and greet him with "How are you?" and leave him with "Let's do this again sometime."

At a party, much of our conversation is *relational:* that is, we are primarily concerned with telling others who we are, what we think of them, and how we wish to be viewed. In such a situation, the relational component of a long conversation on politics, for example, might simply be, "I'm smart. Please like me."

We are each other's mirror. My reflection in the bathroom mirror tells me whether or not I am well shaved. It cannot, however, tell me whether my behavior seems pushy, wishy-washy or withdrawn. I must see in you who I am. Gaining accurate feedback for development of self will be discussed more in later chapters. For now, it is sufficient to say that you tell me that I *am.* Communication confirms our human existence and that is vital to each of us.

EXPRESSIVE COMMUNICATION

A man stops his car just past a horseshoe bend and yells out so he can hear his voice echo back from the canyon walls. He is enjoying expressing and then hearing himself. We are all emotional beings with stories being told within our bodies, so we transform these emotions into forms of art, dance, music, poetry and speech. A dance on the seashore does not have to be performed before an audience of even one to have profound meaning for the expressor. Expressive communication may occur in the presence of others, but its main function is to provide a form for the feelings of the expressor. The expressor does not intend for his communication to influence anyone.

Some philosophers argue that such expression is a part of the "thinking-out-loud" process. There are also psychologists who suggest that expressive communication is the more authentic "You" because it is closer to involuntary behaviors which are free from intellectual weighing and consequent self-censoring.

Incongruity may sometimes be observed between the nonverbal "expressive" message and the verbal message. For example, we frequently observe a person standing in a slouch as if to say, "It just doesn't matter," while at the same time he is saying, "You really should try it. It's fantastic!" Something about that double message, indeed, is incongruous. Today, scholars of nonverbal communication suggest that we all tend to believe the nonverbal, probably because we have learned, unconsciously, that it provides a truer message.

There are two important reasons why being aware of expressive communication is of value. First, the communicator is now more conscious of emotional reactions. Learning another's feelings associated with a communication event should be sought out

These four examples of expressive communication exhibit distinctly different emotional states. However, as viewers we often have difficulty interpreting these expressions when seen out of context.

rather than ignored. The way a man feels about where he works influences how he goes about a job assignment. The alert supervisor, therefore, is concerned about the story going on inside the employee as well as the employee's productivity. Perhaps the example is clearer if we suggest that the teacher must take note of the expressive communication of the pupil if he is to understand those things that frustrate learning. We are not therapists when we recognize the expressive messages, but simply communicators in touch with the nature of man.

Second, it may free the individual in the sense that she now understands a bit more about herself by listening to and observing her own feelings, rather than bottling up and suppressing the story going on within. There is, in this sense, real cathartic and therapeutic value.

Once we realize that we all have feelings, we then feel free to make expressive communication a part of all our communication. The speaker who can talk about as well as show his anxiety caused by an event will help his listeners perceive a more accurate message than he would if he suppressed and did not verbalize these feelings.

The speaker who is able to put into verbal and nonverbal expression his joy or grief in relationship to his subject helps his listener understand more accurately his involvement with the message. Expressive speech, then, is linked to a thoughtful message.

RITUAL COMMUNICATION

Reciting a pledge, singing an anthem, and repeating a prayer are examples of communication that may be called ritualistic. The experience is an emotional one. Those participating reaffirm a commitment to a particular belief or way of life. In the case of a flag salute, the senses join the verbal affirmation. The eyes see both the red stripes stitched onto the muslin and the white stars set against the blue, while the flag is raised towards the heavens. The music accompanying the ceremony is heard by the ear while the drum cadences are felt by the body. The contagion of standing, saluting and singing, all combine to complete a moving communicative experience.

In addition to ritual, the flag ceremony may serve social and

RITUAL MUST BE RIGHT

A ritual is a bit of drama that must be carried off flawlessly, lest illusion and reality will become confused. The front stage and back stage can be no more clearly separated than in the rituals surrounding death. The undertaker of the past who played a minor role in the funeral drama, now is the funeral director who choreographs the drama. Since it is a one shot affair, it must be beautifully executed to the satisfaction of the bereaved and community in order to preserve the all-important reputation of the mortician and his business.

Backstage the body is washed, shaved, sprayed, powdered, waxed, stitched, painted, enbalmed, and finally the naked body is dressed and positioned in the casket. Bodies are referred to as "floaters" (one who has drowned), "warm" (recently received) or cold (one frozen) by the backstage crew, and there is laughter, joking, singing, discussion of politics, sexual remarks or reference to the size of the body, and the like. Whereas, out front the backstage work if mentioned at all is referred to as restorative art. Signs in the front stage may encourage the participant in the ritual to remember that "the preparation room becomes sacred when a family entrusts us with one of its most precious possessions." Out front the mortician keeps a respectful two or three feet distance and does not touch the body. He must not strut or appear mousy, but rather should speak in a demeanor of dignity and confidence, of one in control. He orchestrates drivers and pallbearers (who may be honorary so that a paid staff can insure that the casket is not dropped). Sometimes he coaches the mourners how to act, and the minister (so that he, too, will carry off the denial and reality of death). He may be seen subtly checking the flowers, braided ropes and general flawless decor inside the often proud and wealthy buildings of the mortuary. Anything incongruous such as electric guitar rather than traditional organ music is skillfully kept out of the ritual.

The language, as well as the many non-verbal symbols, deny death. Metaphors in the American funeral are of sleep, transition to other worlds and eternal life. Mr. Jones reposes in a slumber room and poetry and music use words such as "death is a dream" and "the beloved is still with us." The funeral is a morality play, emphasizing the good deeds of the deceased. Whatever that was less than sterling done by the dead is overlooked or obscured in juggling the facts or in retreats to euphemism. The funeral director may justify his role in all this by thinking of himself as grief therapist and a mood manager.

Based in large part upon an analysis by Ronny E. Turner and Charles Edgely, who studied 15 funeral homes and analyzed the content of the literature of the profession, "Death As Theater: A Dramaturgical Analysis of The American Funeral," *Sociology and Social Research*, Vol. 60, July 1976, pp. 377–392.

expressive functions as well: social because assembling for a ceremony provides an occasion in which humans affirm their interdependence, and expressive because the ritual provides an opportunity for an emotional outlet.

Ritualistic communication may sometimes be of a mystical character. An act of faith unites the communicants to a metaphysical phenomenon and to each other. Beliefs codified into ritual and then into an institution have been great motivating forces with most, if not all, civilizations. The Aztecs, for example, were ruled by strong despotic rulers who gained part of their power from religious rites, which even included human sacrifice.

Speech becomes magical when people believe in a special effect inherent in the words themselves. Reverential tones often accompany the words. For example, "In Jesus' name, Amen," is used in the typical closing words of blessing of food in a Christian home. The religious customs, such as eating bread, drinking wine and laying on of hands, involve the total body and a commitment. Such ritualistic experiences command a continuing affirmation by the individual to previously agreed-upon goals and behavior.

At times of change from one role to the next, most cultures perform certain ceremonies, termed by anthropologists as the rites of passage. Major examples are christenings, bar mitzvahs, graduations, weddings, and funerals. By these ceremonies, the community grants its official approval to pass on to another role. Sometimes a new name or title is conferred in recognition of the new role.

In practical terms, rituals mean that people who participate in the ceremonies belong to a select company and this company must speak with a united voice. For the individual, it means he must support the group (i.e., family, business, club, church, government) with time, money, energy and, perhaps, his life.

Another common example of ritual is the annual birthday party. The giving of gifts, the birthday cake and the singing of "Happy Birthday" come to be expected. They carry a loud message to the individual who has completed another year of life. The type of gift received may tell the individual whether he is looked upon as continuing in a role, or ready for a new one, such as a teenager.

Gifts can be instrumental in that they carry messages of identity and control. Identity: The little girl who receives a make-up mirror has been told by the giver that it is expected that females be concerned about appearance. Gifts, as you can see, convey very

The wedding, in almost all societies, is a highly ritualized event. Even after the formal ceremony, there are many ritualized behaviors associated with the day of marriage. Throwing rice has traditionally communicated a wish for fertility and happiness.

loud messages about sexual and vocational roles. Control: We give, we say, because we love and not because we want something in return. But gifts are a means to influence another in being receptive to the giver as well as conveying a message of how I want you to behave.

THE MESSAGES COMMUNICATED BY GIFTS ILLUSTRATE CERTAIN MEANS OF SOCIAL CONTROL IN INTERPERSONAL RELATIONSHIPS

1. How do gifts impose an identity on the receiver? If a man receives a box of dominoes from one woman and a *Playboy* subscription from the other what does this tell him about the sender's control of the receiver? How do the gifts of parents reinforce certain desired roles upon their children?

2. How do gifts impose an identity on the giver? Think of such examples as a new father giving out cigars.

3. How may gifts be degrading?

4. What gifts dramatize group boundaries? Family loyalties? Joint gifts? Ranking and priority?

5. How do gifts send messages of apology and atonement?

6. What is the message of the Christmas card, the gift exchange and Santa Claus?

7. What gifts have you recently given and received? What was the intended message?

Based upon Barry Swartz's "The Social Psychology of the Gift," *The American Journal of Sociology*, Vol. 72, No. 1, July, 1967, pp. 1–11.

INSTRUMENTAL COMMUNICATION

By instrumental communication (sometimes called persuasive communication) we mean messages designed to convey information or to influence towards a particular end. This kind of communication is affirmed in the mechanical analogy: The written and spoken word are social tools. Communication, when conceived to influence, then, is an instrument for social change or reinforcement of existing social behavior. When I look at my students and say, "It's hot in here," I am expressing a feeling. But since I say it in the presence of others, I also may be checking their feelings about the temperature against my own. If there appears to be general agreement, then someone in the room has the group's "ok" to open the door or window, or turn on the air conditioner. This is an example of very subtle instrumental communication.

Classical scholars described three kinds of formal instrumental communication (although it was not called that but rather known as *rhetoric*): (A) speeches of praise and blame (epidictic), (B) speeches of arguing points of law (forensic) and (C) speeches of policy (political).

The study of formal persuasive speech, indeed, has a classical heritage. Rhetoric was one of the first, if not *the* first, courses of instruction in the schools of ancient Greece; and man, the speaker, was studied as man the influencer. Aristotle defined rhetoric as "the faculty of discovering in the particular case what are the available means of persuasion."[1] Instrumental communication, therefore, ranges from making policy and extending power, to practical words that are used to get the plumbing repaired.

Instrumental communication has several possible general purposes: (1) to amuse and entertain, (2) to inform and teach, (3) to impress and stimulate, (4) to change belief and convince, and (5) to move to action. An interpersonal exchange between two people, a group discussion or a public speech may include any or all of these general purposes. Requesting a loan from a bank officer may involve a reference to an amusing incident, a personal history, an account of future plans, a rationale for the needed money, a signing of a note, and finally the counting out of the cash.

Often, the several functions of communication can be found to occur in one event, as in the occasion described below. In the antiphonal sermon, the assembling of the congregation is a *social* event, the emotional shouts and singing are *expressive,* participation in a litany is *ritualistic,* and seeking to influence behavior is *persuasive.*

To be effective, talk that is designed to persuade, as is this sermon, should be in a form acceptable to the listener. The antiphonal [responsive alternation] sermon housed in the black church provided the proper form in the right place. The rituals of prayer, scripture and song emotionally linked the desired behavior (continuation of the boycott) to the symbols and values treasured by those people. The give and take of the sermon with its vigorous audience response symbolized a joint endeavor in which leader and followers supported one another. The antiphonal rhythmic redundancy stamped in the message and provided an ego-involving public commitment to belief and action. The message, indeed, was instrumental, an effective social communicative tool.

AN ANTIPHONAL SERMON

Comments upon a sermon by the Reverend James Wilburn, a black minister. This sermon was preached at the Providence mass meeting in Atlanta, Georgia, on March 12, 1961, at the peak of the struggle to desegregate lunch counters in that city.

The total length of the sermon was 3,050 words and totaled 26 minutes, 3.7 seconds or about 117 words per minute (the usual conversational rate is approximately 125 words per minute). But also during this time there were some 382 interrupting responses by the audience! These varied from many encouraging individual interruptions such as the intoned "hum" (19 counted), "preach doctor" (11), "yeah" (89), "yes" (144), "yes sir" (148) to more unusual "dirt" (1), "watch out" (2), "rich" (2), "right" (3), "pretty" (4), "go to hell," "help yourself" (7), etc. There were some 81 times when the audience responded as a group. Of these 81 times, crowd applause was noted 19 times. Many of the responses thunderously echoed the pastor with such phrases as "what a moment" (1), "nobody" (2), "stay there" (8).

SERMON
(DIVIDED INTO THIRDS)

Words	Time	Responses	Sentences	Average words per sentence
1,000	9 min. 8.2 sec.	76	63	16.2
1,000	8 min. 2.9 sec.	130	67	15.0
1,050	8 min. 2.6 sec.	176	130	10.0
3,050	25 min. 13.7 sec.	382	260	11.36

The chart points up the accelerated rate of speaking, congregational responses and shortening of sentence length. During the last 1050 words of the sermon, the preacher averaged about six words between responses. These crowd responses followed in tone and intensity Pastor Wilburn's series of short, shouted, frenzied ejaculations:

You who've got backbone, *(Yes)*
You who've got character, *(Yes)*
You know the way that God is moving, *(Yes)*
Keep on moving. *(Yes, keep on moving.)*
You've got a song to sing, *(Yes)*
Don't let nobody *(Yes)*
Turn you around. *(Yes, applause.)*

I want'a tell you tonight, *(applause, cheers)*
Nobody, *(Nobody)*
Nobody, *(Nobody)*
Knows you're right. *(Stay there)*
Stay there. *(Stay there)*
Stay there. *(Stay there)*
Stay there. *(Stay there)*
If mamma doesn't like it, *(Like it)*
Well, I'm sorry, *(Shout it)*
———— * *(Shout it)*
———— * *(Applause)*
Stay there, *(Stay there)*
Stay there, *(Stay there)*
Til heaven gets happy *(Yes)*
And hell gets mad. *(Yes)*

*Unintelligible

Toward the end of the sermon the link and relationship was spelled out in uncompromising language, and definite, precise, terse style:

For this is God's world *(Yes God's world)*
And you are God's kind. *(That's enough, Doctor, Amen*

That's enough, Doctor
That's enough, Doctor, heh, heh)
God forbid *(Yes sir, yes sir)*
That I would ever go downtown again *(All right, well say it then)*
And buy a suit of clothes for a hundred dollars at one time *(Yes, go ahead now)*
And walk over to another counter and say, "May I have a ten-cent cup of coffee?" *(Um)*

You'd take my Easter money with one hand *(Yes)*
And then you tell me to get the hell out of there with the other. *(Applause, cheers, yes sir, yes sir, yes sir, yes sir, yes sir)*
I tell you never, *(applause continuing)*
Long as I live. *(Yes)*
I'm going to have a little more sense than that. *(Yes)*
I tell you never, *(Never)*
I don't care what you want'a do on your own, *(Yes sir)*
But never, *(Never)*
As long as my head stays warm and black *(Yes)*
Never will I do this thing again. *(Yes sir, never, yes sir.)*

William I. Gorden, "Antiphonal Preaching Success in Georgia," *Preaching Today,* Vol. 6, No. 3, March, 1972, pp. 17–20.

SUMMARY

The nature of communication may be better understood when categorized into four broad functions: social, expressive, ritual and instrumental. These functions should not be thought of as distinct but as overlapping.

Social communication utilizes the expected greetings and salutations common to everyday interaction, such as "Hello." "How are you?" "How are the children?" "Brrr, it's cold." The words expressed tend to center on one's health, the weather, and the family. To be able to chat on such things in some cultures is a necessary prerequisite to doing business. Getting a feel for the mood of the other person as well as having the time to get your own thoughts in order appears to be a very important human communication act.

Expressive communication makes audible and visible one's inner feelings. Anger, boredom, sorrow and love, for example, are common emotions we express in swearing, poetry, song, dance and gesture.

Rituals are communicative procedures, often of a participatory character, which focus upon tangible symbols. These symbols, over a period of time, become expected in certain institutions and occasions. To participate in such rituals identifies one with that institution. It becomes a vote of approval, an affirmation of allegiance to the institution sponsoring the ritual. Not to participate, or not to conform to the ritualistic act, may identify one as an outsider, possibly opposed to that institution.

Instrumental communication defines attempts to exchange information and to influence. It is this dimension of communication which, perhaps, most distinguishes humans from other animals. Symbols in speech, gesture and written language enable man to store knowledge, and to coordinate and plan human enterprise.

INITIATIVES

Observing Ritual. Attend a religious service and participate in the ritual when permitted. Secure copies of the ritual. Analyze the message:

- What is the basic proposition of the ceremony?
- Upon what myths is it based?
- Upon what facts, if any?
- What metaphors are used? Do these metaphors carry certain messages, e.g. convey a message of pretending and role playing. It may also imply back stage behavior which is closer to reality, but which also might imply acting for a smaller audience.
- What words are used most frequently?
- To get an idea of the personal quality of the message, count the personal pronouns "I, me, my, we, our, you, etc."
- Study the length of the sentences, pause and stress. Is the impact one of quieting the mind and body; is it one of creating awareness of others present; does it call forth feelings of commitment and determination?
- Particularly, note whether there is an honest challenge to the proposition. Ritual may attack other beliefs but only rarely does it present convincing counterargument. To do so is to move from ritual to deliberation.
- How did the ritual affect the emotions?
- Now that you have experienced and reflected upon an experience of ritual, discuss with your classmates and friends other rituals in the society. How important are rituals to an organization and to institutions? Are any of these rituals demeaning to an educated person? Why? Should a thinking person shun ritual in his or her life?

INITIATING ACTION 1

Antiphonal Affirmation. Try your hand at composing an affirmative statement similar to that in the sermon at the end of the chapter. Design it to involve the class. The instructor may arrange for the class to open with some of these. Leading them provides an interesting communication experience. I see the following benefits:

INITIATING ACTION 2

- Reading one's own writing promotes involvement.
- Seeking an oral response from an audience demonstrates experientially the focus of communication.
- Reading antiphonally calls forth important attributes of delivery: enunciating, appropriate stress and rate to convey meaning, and variety of volume.
- Reading antiphonally provides a communication event that carries only minimal threat. First, it is short; second, it is written by the leader; third, it involves others in addition to oneself. My classes have found them creative and entertaining.
- Student written affirmations may serve as springboards for a discussion of the place of ritual and the importance of being able to make an affirmation.

Here is an example of an antiphonal affirmation which one student wrote and performed with her class.

Sunshine

Leader: Sunshine!
Response: Sunshine!

Leader: Bold and Bright,
Response: Sunshine!
Leader: Warm and light,
Response: Sunshine!
Leader: Flowers Grow,
Response: Sunshine!

Leader: Raindrops—
Response: Raindrops—
Leader: Crystal clear
Response: Raindrops—
Leader: Soft to hear
Response: Raindrops—
Leader: Speckle leaves
Response: Raindrops—
Leader: Dance on trees

Leader: Sunshine!
Response: Sunshine!
Leader: Beaming down
Response: Sunshine!
Leader: Soaks the ground
Response: Sunshine!

Leader: All the way
Response: Sunshine!
Leader: Every day.

by Kathy Finneran
1977

Gifts. Bring to class some tangible object that has some meaning **INITIATING ACTION 3**
because someone gave it to you. The class may sit in a circle or in
small groups if the instructor prefers. Each class member then
takes turns showing his or her gift and asks the class to guess
who gave it and what form of control or influence that gift
represents.

You think–I think. Divide into small groups. Predict each other's **INITIATING ACTION 4**
reactions to the following statements. Circle your reaction to each
statement and underline what you predict will be the position of
your group. Do not reveal your reaction until after the group has
predicted your reaction. Then after you have revealed your reaction, disclose whether the group's predictions were as you expected.

Statements

1 Our military deserves less criticism and more support.
   Strongly Agree, Agree, Disagree, or Strongly Disagree.
2 The greatest experience in my life will be to be a parent.
   Strongly Agree, Agree, Disagree, or Strongly Disagree.
3 Every person ought to have a religion.
   Strongly Agree, Agree, Disagree, or Strongly Disagree.
4 If asked to pose nude by a famous artist would you politely
   decline, ask what will I be paid, or do it for free?

Word Magic. List and describe several words used by your family **INITIATING ACTION 5**
and/or community which possess a measure of magic. Consider
words which arouse anger (such as four-letter words considered
to be obscene), reverence (such as religious approbations) and
patriotic (such as references to past heroes).

Alone–Together. List the things you do alone on one half of a **INITIATING ACTION 6**
sheet of paper. On the other half list those you do with others.
Compare and classify the type of communication involved: social,
expressive, ritual or instrumental, or a combination of these.

INITIATING ACTION 7   *To Praise to Action.* Listen to the evening news. Record the times someone or thing was praised. Compare what was praised with what was blamed. Now what course of action might accrue from the praise or blame? Was a course of action directly connected to the praise or blame or was it assumed?

NOTE

1. Aristotle, *Rhetoric,* 1355b 27.

SUGGESTED READINGS

Burgoon, Michael, *Approaching Speech/Communication.* New York: Holt, Rinehart and Winston, 1974.

Condon, John C., Jr., *Semantics and Communication.* New York: The Macmillan Co., 1966.

De Vito, Joseph A., *Communication Concepts and Processes.* Englewood Cliffs, N.J.: Prentice-Hall, 1971.

Giglioli, Pier Paolo, *Language and Social Context.* Baltimore: Penguin Books, 1972.

Goffman, Erving, *The Presentation of Self in Everyday Life.* Garden City, New York: Doubleday and Co., 1959.

Harms, L. S., *Human Communication.* New York: Harper and Row, 1974.

Pace, R. Wayne, and Robert R. Boren, *The Human Transaction.* Glenview, Illinois: Scott, Foresman and Co., 1973.

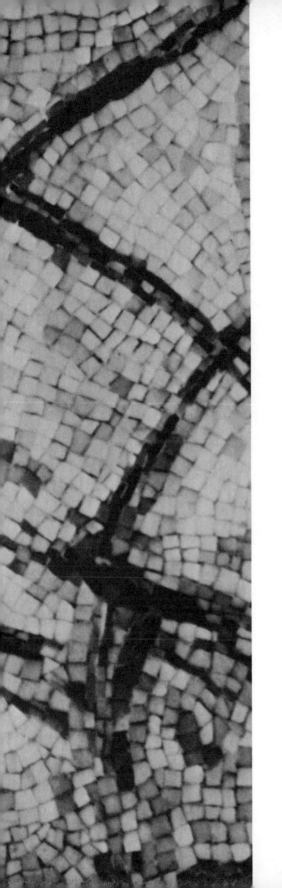

part two

interpersonal expectations

3 nonverbal cues

January 22, 1852. When a man asks me a question, I look him in the face. If I do not see any inquiry there, I cannot answer it. A man asked me about the coldness of this winter compared with others last night. I looked at him. His face expressed no more curiosity or relationship to me than a custard pudding. I made him a random answer. I put him off till he was in earnest. He wanted to make conversation.

— *Thoreau's Journal*

We live in such a verbal world, with tens of millions of words spoken and written each day, that it is difficult to realize that much of what we really think and feel is expressed nonverbally. The purpose of this chapter is to alert us to the nonverbal messages given off all about us and to raise our level of sensitivity to what the world about us is trying to say in more than words. More accurately, when I speak of messages given off, I mean meanings assigned in the brain to nonverbal phenomena. For example, in 1956 when Adlai Stevenson was running for the presidency, he was photographed wearing a shoe with a hole in its sole. Such a photo was assigned several meanings: thriftiness, unconcern about nonessential items and identification with the common man. However, if the sole of the foot is exposed in Moslem countries, it is likely to be interpreted as an insult. You can see how a similar event in another context can be interpreted quite differently.

Obviously, not all things and actions are meant to convey specific messages. However, there are few man-created objects or actions to which meanings have not been attached. Communication, indeed, largely involves assigning meanings to nonverbal codes. These codes involve everything about us: paintings, photos and film, space and time, artifacts and objects that convey status, and certain human performances such as rituals and gestures. Some researchers suggest that only a small percentage of communication is verbal — one gives the figure at no more than 35%, another says 7%.[1]

This chapter moves from the general to the specific, from the universe to the human senses. The first section describes messages from space (distance, structure and size, boundaries, and focus). The next sections discuss messages of time (tradition, appointments, timing) and those of the body (the five senses). Finally, we examine how the body itself and even silence are used in rhetorical ways.

MESSAGES OF SPACE

"Incredible" is the only word possible to explain how you and I ended up on a tiny planet somewhere in space. In comparison to the rest of the cosmos, our earth is like a speck of sand in the ocean. The messages given off by the stars, for both the religiously inclined and the scientific minded, silently tell us of the finite nature of this creature we call man, who seeks meaning in infinite space. The mystery of why we were born and exist on a thin crust of a spheroid planet racing about a blazing sun has provided endless speculation for the guru and the sage. There will always be attempts to derive meaning out of the vastness of space and the uncertainty of life. There is one common feeling shared by all people, and that is the wish to understand and to explain.

To become aware of the many cycles in our bodies is to be more tolerant of the subtle influences on our own and others' moods. The sun affects the physical well-being and maturation of all of us. Those born in polar climates far from the sun have found survival difficult. Those who must bear the heat of the equatorial sun have been forced to adapt the activities of their days to the cooler hours. The famous Norwegian playwright Henrik Ibsen illustrates in some of his plays the depression created by long gray winters. Jet pilots who criss-cross time zones are more susceptible to accident. Criminologists have charted an increase of aggressive crimes and riots during the dog days of summer. It is clear that the emotional and physical states of people are definitely influenced by the physical environment.

DISTANCE

Americans are a mobile people, so much so that we have been labeled a nation of strangers. The vast riches of this land stimulated the pioneer spirit of individualism and materialism of our industrial expansion. A certain measure of prestige is associated with the ability to go places and cover large distances with great speed. The high status of a Marco Polo is relived again and again by those of us who describe the long journeys of our summer vacations.

Electronic communication and high speed travel have reduced our world to a fraction of its former size. We are instantly in communication with other voices thousands of miles away, and with little inconvenience, visit friends and relatives across town or country. Nevertheless, we still are deeply affected by the distances we are from others. We prefer to keep family and friends physically close. Members of similar ethnic groups or income levels tend to cluster together, obviously separated from differing groups. For many, the dense urban center is a place of comfort and excitement. For others, the distances of suburban homes, close but not too close, are most pleasing. For a few, the large separation in rural areas is the desired distance. Social distance, the degree of closeness in our interactions with others, is very much reflected and controlled by physical distance.

STRUCTURE AND SIZE

Just as man stands in awe of the size and order of his universe, so is he impressed by architectural triumphs. Massiveness, since the days of the pyramids, has spoken loudly of power and served as graphic evidence of permanence and position. Hitler, who thought of himself as the master builder, designed massive structures, and in so doing, told the world, "We are the super race." The site of the Nuremburg rally, for example, was 15 times the size of the standard football field. Hitler's stone viewing stand was backed by a colonnade of 170 stone pillars, 60 feet tall and illuminated by 1,200 spotlights. The nonverbal message of the physical setting added to the verbal and the roars of nearly a million voices reinforced their feelings of superiority.[2]

ARCHITECTURE MAY COMMUNICATE POLITICAL MESSAGES

Living forms, especially human beings, add a distinctive frame of reference to the characteristic effect physical energies and particles have on one another.

The novelty lies in the symbolic use that man makes of his surroundings and the symbolic complexity of the way he interprets an altered environment. A transformed habitat changes the experience and the behavior of man. In common with all living forms man seeks to maximize his preferred events, such as power and wealth, when he utilizes the environment. Physical resources are modified to give expression to the perspectives of individuals and groups who are influential in the body politic.

. . . The physical changes introduced for political purposes by architects, planners, and engineers are guided by the subjectivities—the perspectives—of designers. A completed structure influences both the symbolic outlook and the behavioral activities of the people who adapt to its existence.

Harold D. Lasswell "The Signature of Power," *Society: Transaction Social Science and Modern Society*, Vol. 14, November/December, 1976 p. 82.

This photo, taken during a massive Nazi rally, gives solemn testimony to Hitler's use of size and structure as a propagandistic tool. This awesome spectacle surely ignited strong patriotic feelings in most Germans and proclaimed to the world Germany's power and unity of will.

There are other examples of governing bodies conveying messages through architecture. We have our presidential libraries and memorials in stone, and some of our airports and bridges are named for political leaders. Heavy Romanesque columns and domes have come to represent Western concepts of law and order. Gothic cathedrals with their towering spires, assert the "higher loyalties" of the believers. Moreover, the ringing of the bells from many a church steeple are daily reminders of spiritual obligations.

Community planners have recently learned that some buildings may appear impressive but are not emotionally satisfying. Monolithic prison structures isolating criminals have been miserable failures in rehabilitation. Destructive riots may not be blamed on architecture, but the traditional prison building does signal our failure to discover an effective program for the antisocial individual. Large brick buildings to house the poor and aged are gradually being abandoned in favor of smaller, more homey structures. And on many campuses, high-rise dormitories are giving way to smaller living clusters.

The sterility of smooth white walls, long halls and uniform boxlike rooms, at one time typical of our sanitariums, hospitals,

Architects, in general, appear to have difficulty in communicating ideas. I believe there are two basic reasons for this. First, the architect's training relies heavily on graphics as the chief means of communication. Some practicing architects expect that the graphics they produce will make everything perfectly clear. This is rarely the case. Most persons do not easily interpret graphic communications because they have had little or no training or experience in the visual arts. The architect must be able to articulate verbally the intent of his graphics. He may even have to clarify the intentions of architecture. Thus, part of the architect's task is to educate the layman.

Second, the architect possesses a vocabulary that is completely foreign to others. (Not unlike the other professions.) The architect must learn to communicate ideas so that they are comprehensible and meaningful to the person or group receiving the message. For example, it is insufficient for an architect to say to a financier, "I think your building will become more beautiful if we use a two story lobby." It would be better to suggest that "A two story lobby will assure that the offices on the second floor will be visible from the main entry. Therefore, these offices will be more marketable and should generate additional income."

Finally, I would like to suggest that effective communication cannot be fully accomplished either by the choice of the most precise words or by well articulated graphics. Nonverbal and nongraphic communication can be quite profound. I became particularly aware of this when traveling in foreign countries where I did not know the language. To my amazement I discovered that I could tell what people were talking about without knowing the meanings of any of the words they were saying.

— Architect, Male, 10 years' experience

WHAT EFFECT DOES A ROOM HAVE ON MOOD?

Question: Does the beauty or ugliness of a room influence our mood?

Experiment: Three rooms were designed for the experiment. One, a Beautiful Room, with beige walls, soft armchair, mahogany desk, bookcase, Navajo rug, drapes, paintings and sculptures. Two, an Ugly Room with battleship-gray walls, an overhead bulb with a dirty torn shade, furnishings to give the impression of a janitor's storeroom. The room was dusty and had unemptied ashtrays. Three, an Average Room appeared to be a clean office of the professor with a mahogany desk, couch and straight chairs and battleship-gray walls. The subjects, 16 college students in the Beautiful Room, 16 in the Ugly Room and 10 in the Average Room, were asked by a "naive" experimentor to describe negatives of faces. The naive experimentor thought he was discovering if certain types of faces elicited stereotyped reactions. That is, does Shakespeare's Cassius provoke a "lean and hungry look." After ten minutes, experimentors in each case were instructed to excuse themselves from the room and then to return after two minutes. The unannounced intention being to cause the student to focus upon the room rather than the ratings of the pictures which were in the possession of the experimentor.

Results: The table below summarizes the ratings. An average score below 35 indicates that the subjects in the rooms generally rated the faces as "fatigued" and "displeased" while above 35 indicates the subjects rated the faces as having "energy" and "well being."

	Number of Subjects	Average Rating
Ugly Room	16	31.81
Average Room	10	34.00
Beautiful Room	16	37.99

The average ratings in the Beautiful Room were well within the "more energy" and "well being" range while the ratings in the Average and Ugly Rooms were within the "fatigued" and "displeased" range.

Implications: Our environments do influence our moods. Every communication takes place some place. Efforts to make that place pleasant may pay off.

A. H. Maslow and N. L. Mintz, "Effects of Esthetic Surroundings: 1. Initial Effects of Three Esthetic Conditions upon Perceiving 'Energy' and 'Well-Being' in Faces," *Journal of Psychology,* Vol. 41, April 1956, pp. 247–254.

and to some extent our schools, is being replaced by textured walls of varied colors, by rooms carpeted and varied in size with nooks and corners. Not only do certain types of structures tend to be signs of specific institutions, but we come to associate certain types of communication with each structure—"Amen" in a church, "Dee-fense" at a stadium. The message of size and structure, whether consciously or unconsciously perceived, is always present.

Top. We feel closer to people and things we like. I will work, play, drink or bathe with anyone regardless of race, creed or color—but do I? Often where we live isolates and separates us from persons with different lifestyles.

Left. Like it or not, most living creatures stake out their land. Man is skilled at building fences and armies to protect and, too often, expand his territory. Battleships cruising in a sea carry a very loud message.

Right. The population explosion and the crowding complexity of civilization make it even more imperative that a man's home should provide private space.

It is a law of physics that no two bodies may occupy the same space at the same time. Survival thus dictates that animals defend the territory which they inhabit. So it is that we come to set up territorial boundaries and to use personal symbols to mark our own space. Man's first bubble extends about as far as he can reach. To have this bubble invaded without permission causes discomfort, if not hostility. In close quarters, such as an elevator, we reluctantly reduce the size of our bubble, but we do not like to be crowded or pushed.

BOUNDARIES

Since space and territory are in limited supply, the larger the territory under one's command, the greater one's status. Not only do prominent people often own large estates or office buildings, but they frequently travel with an entourage who protect their bigger bubble. The desk of the company president is usually larger, constructed of more expensive materials, and placed in a more spacious room than the desk of a clerk. Corner offices, which tend to be larger and contain more windows, therefore, are assigned to managers with higher status. The physical space in which one lives and works is frequently a rather telling message of one's income level and job ranking.

The focal structure of a place provides clues as to what the people consider important. Was it not a round table that helped King Arthur change a motley, swarthy hoard of gluttons into responsible knights? Even today, the shape of a table will cause us to focus our eyes and attention on the leader. Such is the message of a long rectangular table with the chairman of the board at the end position. Or the authority may be more equally dispersed, as in a circular or horseshoe arrangement.

FOCUS

Priests in primitive cultures knew well the impact of elevation. Sunlight and position focused all eyes toward the symbol of sacred authority. The rules of dominance grew out of the focus derived by structure, position, height, lighting and facial direction. No words have to be uttered to indicate who is the king. Throne, height and focal structure tell all.

In our society, we know the effect of a conversation pit as contrasted to a TV lounge. In one instance, the structure brings us together; in the other, it isolates by facing us all toward the tube. Observe the mood created by a classroom's arrangement. Is there a difference between a room where all chairs are in neat rows facing a desk as compared to one where chairs are clustered in small circles with no desk for the instructor?

We usually know before we go to hear a message much about it from the structure in which it is housed, or for that matter, whether it is housed at all. We learn from our physical world to seek balance between contending forces. That which appears in conflict or contrast gains our attention. We attend to that which appears more powerful and dominant by its being comparatively higher, larger, louder, brighter, separated by distance and having the visual focus of more people.

MESSAGES OF TIME

Time silently speaks. We live on a planet that has had perhaps 40,000 years of human history, is some four and one-half billion years old, in a universe scientists now estimate to be about 18 billion years old. The Age of the Universe Clock (AUC) is a digital voltmeter clock that registers the year, month, day, hour and second since it all began.[3] On January 1, 1980, it will read:

18,807,631,980	1	1	1	1	01.1
Years	Month	Day	Hour	Minute	Second

This knowledge, in addition to striking the same kind of awe as does the physical size and structure of the universe, speaks a message of infinite patience. The wheels of history turn slowly. Man appears impatient for change when compared to the seemingly endless movement of time.

TRADITION   Because time is so much a part of man's being, it is celebrated in many ways. The change of seasons is marked by rites and festivals. Each person's life is annually marked by a birthday celebration, as are important events of local communities and countries. Consequently, we have our centennials and Independence Day celebrations.

In the musical *Fiddler on the Roof,* Tevya opens with the rousing song "Tradition," and he philosophizes that "Tradition tells us who we are." Tradition assures us that there is order, that there are ideals which are changeless, and ways of life to cling to and believe in. This is probably why we celebrate symbolic reenactments of significant events. To sing the old songs and to take journeys to historic sites reinforce a sense of identity. We know, then who we are.

APPOINTMENTS

We live by the clock. The hunger for structure, so apparent in architecture and tradition, also shows up in our ability to fill days with dates, meetings and activities. So it is that we have watches, clocks and appointment books which order our day.

The time a communication takes place speaks loudly. Moreover, how early, late or on time we are conveys a message about how important we feel an appointment is. In some instances, to arrive early will seem crude, when the expectation is to come fashionably late. In some cultures, punctuality is not so rigidly prized. Mañana may not be tomorrow, but some indefinite time in the future—nor should one be offended to wait for several hours to see a high official. But even in this country, how long we wait is directly related to status. The higher the status of the other person, the longer one will wait.

TIMING

A persuasive message may fall on deaf ears because the timing was off. As persuasion is the gradual process of securing cooperation, knowing "when" and "how long" is an essential part of the

TIME SPEAKS

A Sense of Timing: He said to his wife, "Well, I guess we'll have to go to bed so that these folks can go home."

Lateness: Whatever my excuses, my absence or tardiness tells you that some other occasion took priority over being with you. When I keep you waiting, I cause you to wonder about how important you are to me.

Earliness: For you to arrive a few minutes early tells me you are considerate of my time. If you usually arrive very early, I may think you have nothing very important to do.

Fashionable Lateness: I expect you to be late when I invite you to a party at my place. To come a little late tells me that you realize that I have a lot to do before I am ready to be your host.

Overly Punctual. Social relationships are strained when I insist that you must live by my clock.

Pace: If you walk beside me, I can tell how content you are with my pace. When we talk there are times when our speech will be as slow as death, and other times as rippling as a brook. I do not like to be rushed or pressed for an answer, but I am pleased you asked, "What do you think?"

Departures: Don't rush. Tell me you must go, if you must. But say goodbye as though you hate to leave. Too much of my life is made up of saying goodbye and never again hello.

THE INCREDIBLE HUMAN BEING!

What are we made of? Of flesh and blood and a bit of hair? The body contains 60,000 miles of blood vessels. In less than a minute, the heart pumps the blood one complete tour of the body. In a day it pumps the equivalent of 2,000 gallons and 55 million gallons in a lifetime. We each possess 6,000 muscles, and 206 bones, more than half of which are in the hands and feet. 5,000 pounds per square inch of pressure are normally exerted on the bones and up to 20,000 pounds are exerted during athletic events.

Where do we come from? The ovum is the largest cell produced by the body and the sperm is one of the smallest of which approximately 200 million are produced each day. The body increases 10,000 times in size the first month of life and when mature consists of 60 trillion cells.

A biophysicist today has put to rest the low estimate of past chemists who asserted that the chemical components of the body were worth only 98 cents. If we were crass enough to estimate the current value of a person in cash terms, a pound of flesh would be worth over $11,000 and the whole body around six million dollars. In addition to these raw materials of the flesh, we have yet to estimate the brain with its chemical-electric consciousness and intelligence in its billions of cells. Add six thousand trillion dollars. This astronomical figure is based upon such prices for rare body producing ingredients as $17 million a gram for prolactin, or the $5 million a gram for follicle-stimulting hormone, or DNA at $768 a gram, acetate kinase at $8,860 a gram, and alkaline phosphatase at $225 a gram. To simulate the human mind, a computer would have to be almost the size of the Earth.

Based in part upon Sidney J. Harris "Strictly Speaking: 98¢ We're Worth A Fortune!" *Chicago Daily News*, February 25, 1977.

process. The speaker who is conscious that time is money adjusts his message to the time of the customer. He not only does his best to find a suitable time, but he clearly estimates the time he needs, and then he scrupulously honors the time allotted. Whether it be a public address or a visit with a friend, it is wise to check out and honor the time expected for the communication event. The "how-often" and the "when" of a communication may sometimes influence opinion as much or more than the "what" of a message.

BODY MESSAGES

It is impossible not to communicate because of the many channels sensed by our bodies. That is to say, you cannot *not* communicate. Any communication event consists in a large part of reading nonverbal body messages. Indeed, how our nonverbal messages are interpreted has a great impact on what others think of our verbal messages. We may contradict a confident verbal statement with a nervous movement of hands and eyes. On other occasions, nonverbal clues amplify verbal messages as, for example, when an expression of affection is accompanied by a hug or a squeeze of the hand. In all of our communicative acts, nonverbal messages give listeners important clues to our true inner feelings and thoughts.

Let us examine some of the variables that determine how our nonverbal messages are interpreted. The research in these areas is now rapidly expanding but the findings are still quite tentative. After a brief look at the senses, we will examine the nonverbal cues associated with physical appearance and dress, body movement and gesture, eye contact, and even silence.

THE SENSES

Touch

Handshakes, cuddling and hugging are interpersonal messages perceived through the sense of touch. Gentle strokes, whether they be physical or psychological, are sought by us all. Tactile communication is much more important than verbal to the infant and for adults, touching can often be as important for feelings of love and assurance. On the other hand, pushing, bumping, striking and other forms of violent physical contact, transmit messages of punishment and coercion.

Taste

Knowledge of the world around us would indeed be limited if taste and smell were our only perceptors. But they can tell us a lot about our social interaction. Breaking bread together has long symbolized strong social binding. The cocktail party and the banquet are important social indicators of belonging. To be invited or not to cocktails may tell whether one is "in" or "out" in many places.

Smell

Perception of odors communicates such messages as breakfast, fire and sex. The smell of toast and coffee may announce breakfast even more clearly than a call from the cook, and certain perfumes may announce the sex of a house guest, even to one with a cold.

Hearing

The auditory sense extends man into his environment even farther than the senses mentioned (touch, taste, smell), particularly when we consider the telephone and radio. Nonverbal messages can also include rhythm and tone. Hearing someone humming, whistling, or patting their leg, will indicate emotions even more than words themselves. We will talk more about sound in Chapter Four.

Seeing

The visual sense enables man to reach miles beyond in an

instant. Yet it also delivers the bulk of body signals from those right next to him. These include spatial relationships, body posture and eye contact. Compared to touch, taste and smell, the communication channels of sight and hearing are less intimate but more important.

APPEARANCE   Like it or not, we tend to judge each other by appearance. There is general agreement within a culture, for example, about who is and who is not good looking. And in some cultures the greater a person's status, the taller he is perceived to be. Make-up, grooming and dress can influence the attitudes of an audience. And even though they are frequently wrong, people tend to judge others with a different physical appearance to have certain character traits.

The pretty as compared to the ugly do have an easier time of it. There are many instances of job discrimination toward people who veer too far from the norms set for acceptable height and weight. Some studies indicate what we all know, that people attractive to the opposite sex receive greater attention and exert more influence than those who are less appealing.

SENSES COMMUNICATE

Taste: Sweet-sour, hot-cold, and spicy are words that find their messages in the nerve endings in our taste buds and skin. Much of our language is in direct touch with our taste.

Smell: She smelled like Lilies of the Valley, he like English Leather. The child, whose hands they held, smelled like peanut butter.

Touch, the Most Primitive Sense: Before birth the world is no larger than that which the unborn can feel. After birth, if we had no other senses than touch, we would flail about with arms and legs to become acquainted with our environment.

Touching Another Human: From the birth spank on we are hugged, stroked and rubbed by those who tell us with Tender Loving Care that the world can be a secure and comforting place. It is good to be in hands that care. It is unpleasant to have people "rub us" the wrong way.

Sight: It is through sight that we know our world is so much bigger than this spot of land upon which we stand and so much older than this moment in time. The light from stars, some of which have burned out, just now reaches our eyes. Buckminster Fuller said, "Vision is an unlimited universal language; speech is local and limited. We can see 70 sextrillion miles, seven followed by 22 zeroes, in any direction in the universe and do so at 700 million miles mph."[4]

Sensory Deprivation: One of the meanest punishments known to prison is the hole—a small cell removed from human contact, without light or sound. The prisoner in such confinement may soon become disoriented.

CAN A PRETTY FACE PERSUADE ME?

Question: Will frankly stating our desire to influence enhance or hinder our effectiveness? And will it help if we are attractive? What if we are not attractive to the audience?

Experiment: Opinions of college students on a number of items were gathered some two months in advance of the experiment. The day of the experiment the professor asked the students to take another similar questionnaire upon such topics as "Every college student should receive a broad education" and "Students should not be forced to take courses to make them well rounded." But before doing the questionnaire he requested that they briefly think about their answers. He suggested to aid this thinking that someone in the class might read his or her answer aloud. A girl (a confederate in the experiment) volunteered in one case and, in another, feigning reluctance to read her answer was chosen by the professor. She was attractively groomed upon these two occasions. Then upon two other occasions she was unattractively groomed. Her clothing was ill-fitting, her hair was messy, her skin was oily and a trace of mustache was etched upon her upper lip.

Under each of the four conditions the confederate responded to the question: "How much would you like to influence the views of others on this issue?" In the persuade condition (that is, when she had more effect on others' opinions) her response was "Very much." In the nonpersuade, her response was "Not at all."

Results: The results are summarized in the table:

Measures of Favorability to General Education

Four Experimental Conditions	N	Pretest	Posttest
1. Attractive "I want to influence."	24	24.3	41.8
2. Attractive "I do not want to influence at all."	18	23.8	37.0
3. Unattractive "I want to influence."	26	23.8	31.8
4. Unattractive "I do not want to influence at all."	29	23.8	37.8

The data demonstrates that an openly stated desire to influence made by the attractive girl did affect the male audience. But that when the girl was "unattractive" and stated her desire to influence it had no apparent effect. A second experiment's results were similar.

Implications: We must always be cautious in generalizing from test tube experiments. But it is safe to conclude that we are sometimes influenced by appearances, that we may consciously or unconsciously try to please some attractive person of the opposite sex who admits a desire to influence. Such an experiment should alert us to do our own thinking regardless of appearance, providing we do not want to be puppets of a pretty face or handsome body. It also suggests that we do not need to hesitate to frankly state our desire to influence, provided of course that we do not act dogmatically and conceited.

J. Mills and E. Aronson, "Opinion Change as a Function of the Communicator's Attractiveness and Desire to Influence," *Journal of Personality and Social Psychology,* Vol. I, No. 2, 1965, pp. 173–177.

The way one dresses gives various clues about the individual. Conformity in dress, for example, has been found to correlate with conformity in other areas. One of the most effective signs of role is the uniform. It is widely used to provide readily visible signs of job classifications. In one trip to a hospital, I noted uniform and color differentiating practical nurses from registered nurses. There were ladies in gray, candy stripers, blue orderlies, green maintenance personnel, technicians in white pants suits, nurses in white gowns, surgeons in unironed green, and doctors in suits.

Dress conveys many meanings: decorative functions (fashionability or lack of style), sexual role (degree of concern for femininity or masculinity), formality (suitability for formal or informal occasions), conformity (uniforms or similarity of dress to others with whom one associates), and finally, but of less importance to many people, comfort and economy.

One's dress, like one's physical appearance, has much to do with self-image. A positive self-image of one's body appears to be directly related to feelings of security, and a negative image to insecurity. A prosperous cosmetics industry and plastic surgery practice thrive on the belief that looks influence how favorably one fares socially and vocationally. Make-up, clothing, hair style and glasses, if extreme, may detract from an individual's social and professional acceptability.

BODY PLACEMENT

The placement of one's body tells us such things as who is in charge, who is the Chief and who are the Indians. Elected officials tend to sit in head chairs, such as at end positions at rectangular tables. People who are more influential tend to sit where they are able to see more people. Those with little influence tend to sit on the fringes and do not take head positions. People turn toward those with whom they wish to interact and turn away from those to whom they do not wish to speak or listen. Generally, we approach and come close to those things and people we like and keep our distance from those we dislike. Our body tends to be more open toward those with whom we feel comfortable and closed toward those with whom we feel discomfort.

People of higher status, as compared to subordinates, tend to take larger strides, to command larger territory, use larger, more definite gestures, to be less rigid, stand taller, be more open in posture and talk more loudly.[5] Do not infer that talking loudly means crudity and ill manner. People of higher status are not generally unsophisticated loudmouths.

Three crucial clues that appear to make nonverbal signs readable are (1) the degree to which positions permit much or little
visibility, (2) the degree to which positional distance facilitates
involvement or frustrates interaction, and (3) the size and strength
of movement.

**MOVEMENT AND
GESTURES**

We have a number of conventional gestures that signal such
messages as come, stop, and approval (thumb and first finger
touching). The vigor of descriptive gestures may convey messages of enthusiasm; the size of gestures correlates with power
and status. Man has an inclination for symbolic gestures such as
the forked fingers in a Victory or Peace sign, the raised, clenched
fist signaling black power, or the upraised middle finger, indicat-
ing an angry, obscene response.

Gestures, just as body movement which precedes or accom-
panies words, may focus attention and emphasis on the verbal
message. Gestures are extensions of thought and feeling into
visual spatial symbols. When they appear to spring spontaneously
from the message, they confirm. When they appear stilted and put
on, they contradict the message. Gestures, therefore, at their best
(1) express the mood of the speaker and listener, (2) assist
communicators in depicting spatial relationships, (3) aid in the

CUES OF TOGETHERNESS AND CONFLICT

Two psychologists interviewed fifty
newlywed couples. They asked them to
complete a questionnaire designed to measure conflicts they were having in the first
few weeks of marriage. Many of them, it
turned out were experiencing serious
conflicts. Then each couple was videotaped
as he or she talked about their marriage.
Afterwhich the type and amount of nonverbal communication was analyzed. They discovered:

"The happy couples would sit closer together, look more frequently into each

other's eyes, would touch each other more
often than themselves and would talk more
to their spouses. The happier couples in
short, were able to create for each other a
more comfortable, supportive, bodily environment."

"The couples who were experiencing the
most conflict sent out more distant vibrations. They tended to cross their arms
and legs, had less eye contact, and touched
themselves more frequently than they
touched each other."

Ernst G. Beir, "Nonverbal Communication: How We
Send Emotional Messages," *Psychology Today*, Vol. 18,
October, 1974, p. 53–56.

Lover's Distance. The space I stand upon belongs to me. But you may come so close to me that I feel you breathing and can easily hear you whisper. You may make love to me.

Private Distance. Within arm's length, even if you are a stranger, you may stand quietly to my side in a crowded elevator. However, I feel uncomfortable with your face close to mine. Face close to face is reserved for intimate affection and sometimes for anger.

Personal Distance. Within two to three arm's lengths, we can talk business or chat about old times. At this close distance, you control my attention. If you would invade my bubble, please leave off the garlic.

Social Distance. From four to twenty feet you are not so important to me. I can look at others. Yet we can talk to each other without raising our voices. If I want our relationship to become more personal, I will approach you and await your gaze and smile. But, if you are much more important than I, I will keep a proper distance.
Public Distance. Twelve feet or more. From this distance I must speak more carefully and enlarge my signals to you. If I do not motion you to come closer, it is a clue to you that our relationship is more formal than social.

dramatic account of human interaction and (4) signal cultural taboos.

The act of touching is a "sign of power," a "subtle physical threat used to remind people of their status," that in the opinion of Nancy Henley, is used particularly by men against women.[6] In some 50 hours of observation (incidentally by a male research assistant) it was discovered that those who did the most touching were of a higher socioeconomic status and older than the persons touched. There were 41 cases observed of men touching women, but only 21 where women touched men. "Cues of Togetherness and Conflict" reports an interesting study of the use of touch among married couples.

TEACHER FINDS LIES IN FACIAL EXPRESSION

ATHENS, Ohio, Sept. 24—A 43-year-old journalism professor is at work on a doctoral thesis that could assist observers in recognizing truth.

Roger E. Bennett, a former newspaper reporter and editor who is now teaching at Ohio University, has tentatively proved that split-second facial expressions known as "micromomentaries" occur at the precise moment a person is telling a lie.

"We know that a psychopath, a psychopathic liar, can beat a polygraph test," Mr. Bennett says. "But to the best of my knowledge, he can't beat this."

What Mr. Bennett has discovered and photographed on videotape is that the human subsconscience produces bizarre expressions around the face, characterized by rapid eye movements, when a falsehood is uttered.

Must Be Significant Lies

The operative idea here is that the deeper the emotional attachment to the lie, the more exaggerated the eye movements," he says. "I found that they have to be lies of significance."

He says that these micromomentaries take place at one-sixtieth of a second, distinguishing them from the normal blinking process, which occurs at a relatively slower one-fifth of a second.

Although Mr. Bennett's early research proved that micromomentaries appeared in clinical settings between mental patients and their psychiatrists, he wanted to know if they would show up in a news setting, his preferred application for the new technique.

He put his theories to the test while teaching and working on his master's degree at the University of Texas in Austin. In 1973, he set up a bogus "speakers bureau" consisting of some of the students in his magazine journalism class. He told the speakers in addressing the class to use the details of their own background but to fabricate some aspect.

For example, one student, a former legislative aide to a member of the Texas House of Representatives, announced that he was running against the very man he had worked for, a man whom he greatly respected and admired. Mr. Bennett says. "The fabrication was that he was running because he hated this man, had a drastic split with this man he had worked for," Mr. Bennett says.

Mr. Bennett says that when the speaker told his lie, the micromomentaries startlingly showed up.

The New York Times, September 25, 1977

EYE CONTACT   People seeking interaction tend to look at each other, and conversely, people look away and avoid eye contact when they do not wish to interact, or when they are in a competitive situation. Looking is usually an invitation to talk. In addition, it is a clue to wanting affiliation, inclusion and involvement. One researcher observed, for example, that women in bars situate themselves so they may view approaching men peripherally and then look longer at those who appear interesting. He found that the second look serves as a signal that they want to be approached.[7] Conversely, looking away may signal a desire not to be included, dislike or just plain boredom. Eye contact provides a psychological bond

when separation by distance makes the channel of touching unavailable.

In our culture it is commonly believed that a person who avoids
eye contact is insecure and afraid of being rejected or else they
are feeling guilty about something. Research on feelings of security is still quite tentative, but psychologist R. V. Exline and his
colleagues have tested the belief about guilt. First they gave their
subjects a personality index to determine whether they were
"manipulators" or not. Some students got low scores while
others turned out to be real "people pushers." Then they had the
subjects participate in an experiment. During the experiment they
deliberately but subtly encouraged the subjects to cheat. Some
did, and some didn't. Finally Exline and his colleagues interviewed the students to see if they would look them in the eye
while discussing the experiment.

The students who had not cheated engaged in normal eye
contact during their discussion with the experimenters. Students
who had cheated showed two kinds of reactions. Those who had
scored low as "manipulators" on the personality index avoided
direct eye contact with the experimenters. But those subjects who
had tested high as "people pushers" stared calmly into the eyes
of the interviewers. The findings indicate that people who are
"manipulators" or enjoy using others do not have the same guilt
reactions as those who are less manipulative.

The eyes are particularly important in face-to-face communication. People who want to communicate try to make eye contact.
However, when about to begin a long talk, a person looks away,
likely because getting one's thoughts together and planning what
to say takes concentration. Perhaps it is because the brain can
process only so much information that we look at the person to
whom we are speaking in short glances that vary from three to ten
seconds and make eye contact only about one-third as often
when talking as when listening. Eye contact is greater with those
whom we have reason to expect approval and support. Eye contact is also related to the degree of intimacy. There tends to be
more eye contact when less personal topics are discussed. There
is less eye contact during hesitancies. We tend to look up when
completing a message, as though to say, "Now it's your turn."
Both looking at another beyond the usual length and failure to
make eye contact may be disruptive and tension-producing in
interpersonal communication. When a person's eyes are looking
straight at you and they are wide and bright, you know they are
open to what you have to say.

MY, WHAT BIG EYES YOU HAVE!

The size of the pupil of the eyes serves as a signal between individuals, usually at an unconscious level. The size of the pupil is measured by photographs taken during an experiment or by an electronic pupilometer. Hungry subjects (those who had not eaten at all for the past five to eight hours) were found to have larger pupils when shown a picture of food than those who had eaten within the past two hours.

Larger pupil size appears to be a consistent cue to assigning more positive traits. Men attributed to a woman's picture retouched to make the pupils either larger or smaller, correspondingly "more feminine" or "pretty" to that with the larger pupils and "hard," "selfish" or "cold" to that same photograph with the pupils made smaller.

Additional experiments have revealed that bigger pupils elicit a more positive response from the individual looking at the person or picture with big pupils. Babies were found to smile more when a woman stranger had had her pupils chemically dialated than when they were chemically constricted.

In one experiment two individuals (secretly one with dilated and the other with constricted pupils) of the opposite sex were introduced to an individual. The task was for this individual to chose between the two as a partner for an experiment. Both men and women tended to choose the individual with the larger pupils.

Persons of all age groups were found to have their own pupils widen when they were shown pictures of eyes with large as compared to small pupils. An additional finding, which has no clear explanation is that blue-eyed people were found to have greater increase in pupil size than brown-eyed.

These experiments and others on the eyes are reported in Eckhard H. Hess, "The Role of Pupil Size in Communication," *The Social Animal*, Second Edition, edited by Elliot Aronson (San Francisco: W. H. Freeman and Co., 1977) pp. 350–362.

The eyes help us gather information, signal we want to communicate, establish affiliation, demonstrate power and dominance, and indicate our desire to be seen or concealed (averted eyes may indicate a desire not to be involved). When a relationship changes, eye contact changes, as do physical proximity and the amount of smiling.[8]

BODY RHETORIC "Put your body on the line" and "Vote with your bodies" became important battle cries during the civil rights movement. Parades, marches, picketing, sit-ins, kneel-ins and wade-ins were some of the tactics used to rally support and focus national attention on entrenched discrimination. Rhetoric was characterized as empty; commitment was gauged by willingness to be physically present at a demonstration.

In the early years of television, those who desired to make the evening news were compelled to find visual symbols. Body rhetoric took on greater importance, perhaps, than it had since the days of the Crusades. What got attention one day would not make the news the next unless the tactic could somehow be visually different. Consequently, we witnessed an escalation of confrontations, sometimes taking on destructive behaviors, during the prolonged protests against the U.S. involvement in Vietnam. The strategy escalated and became one of coercion—seeking to bring business-as-usual to a grinding halt.

The results of body rhetoric were both effective and counterproductive. They rallied support and focused attention, but when escalation progressed to ridicule and mockery and then exploded into violence, the opportunities for meaningful dialogue diminished.

The rhetoric of the streets, as it has been called, seems to be the only method some groups can use to attract attention to their unhappy conditions. When landlords will not repair the broken plumbing and the city will not exterminate rats, assembling angry bodies may embarrass officials and get action. But dramatic demonstrations may deteriorate into a prolonged struggle if creative dialogue and negotiations do not accompany them.

Individuals and groups who elect body rhetoric must be prepared for sacrifice and a long battle, counterdemonstration and failure. They must guard against bitterness which turns to violence and closes the channels to dialogue.

MAINTAINING APPROPRIATE CONTACT

The best researched general finding about personal space is that positive feelings, friendship, and attraction are associated with closeness. Subjects in a number of experiments indicated a preference for sitting closer to friends than to strangers or casual acquaintances. Outside the laboratory close friends were observed approaching more closely than friends or acquaintances, but mainly this appears to be more true of women than men. We also assign "liking" to those whom we observe seated at closer distances, say at 4 ft. as compared to 12 ft. Moreover, we know that how directly people face each other corresponds to liking. Those who dislike one another adopt less direct body orientation, tending to turn away. Of course, under stress and hostility, two persons may approach each other very directly and close, in nose to nose combat.

There is evidence that we prefer and expect persons with less pleasant facial expression and unfavorable personal attributes (such as low intelligence, low prestige, low personal adjustment) to stay more distant than persons with the opposite positive traits. We tend to expect closer proximity between persons with like values. It is sad but true that studies also reveal that when a person is physically handicapped or otherwise stigmatized, that many non-handicapped people maintain a relatively large distance from them.

Several studies found that psychological comfort depended upon distance. When individuals were seated less than 5 feet apart they would prefer to be seated side by side rather than face to face. And when persons were seated at a distance of 4 feet, facing each other, they felt more pressured, unfriendly and irritated than when at 8 feet. At close interacting distances in experiments, subjects nervously touched their own bodies more often than at larger distances. At distances of 1, 3, and 9 feet, looking into another person's eyes, there was less anxiety and as registered by a GSR (Galvanic Skin Response measures perspiration) at 9 feet less anxiety than at closer distance. Persons seated 2 or 3 inches side by side in a discussion group found persons who were closer with more palmar sweat. There is abundant evidence that when personal space is invaded that anxiety increases and often efforts are made to preserve that space with barriers or flight results. We also avoid or hesitate to invade another's territory, for example, taking a drink from a water fountain when someone is standing close to it.

The behavioral scientists have discovered that we tend to seek a balance of eye contact, distance, directness and topical intimacy *appropriate* to an interpersonal relationship. That is to suggest that we may adjust downward the amount of eye contact or we may turn slightly away if another person comes too close for the stage of the relationship.

There appears to be an optimal (neither too close nor too far apart) distance that becomes smaller with friends and larger if individuals do not intend or expect to interact. Comfortable distance varies according to function: seated vs. standing, intimacy of the topic, sex of those interacting, directness of the body and crowding as well as other factors such as the size of the space.

Based on the summary of the research literature and theorizing of Eric Sundstrom and Irwin Altman, "Interpersonal Relationships and Personal Space: Research Reviews and Theoretical Model," *Human Ecology*, Vol. 4, No. 1, 1976; pp. 47–67.

The silent body carries a very loud message. It speaks in count- **SILENCE**
less ways. It is in silence that we prepare to speak and it is in
silence that we contemplate what we have said. Not to speak may
be thought of as disagreement, boredom or contempt. Not to
speak, oddly enough, sometimes signifies agreement. Not to
speak may also be caused by lack of information, doubt, indeci-
siveness or fear. Slowness to speak, however, may be interpreted
as respect for the spoken word.

Quietness has been adopted by most religions as a sign of
reverence and holiness. Quietness may be considered as aloof-
ness, sophistication, rudeness or shyness. Silence may be used to
punish and like distance, may isolate. In silence, we may gently
enter into another's sorrow. In silence, we may join another's
daydreams and in silence, we may unite in passion. Silence, indeed, carries a very loud message.[9]

SUMMARY

To be alert to nonverbal messages enhances our interpersonal sensitivity. In this chapter, we have examined the messages people assign to nature, space, time, the body and silence.

Space speaks a silent language. Man's poetic and scientific interpretations of the earth and cosmos provide a perspective and purpose for his existence. The cycles of nature appear also in body rhythms. Awareness of these internal tides may help us understand more about human nature.

Man has a sense of territoriality. He marks and defends his space against violation and crowding. He has developed certain norms of distance to correspond to social interaction. Generally, the more formal the occasion, the greater the distance among the parties involved. Size, structure, texture, color, height, lighting and focus are yet other ways in which messages are conveyed. Massive stone structures, for example, tend to be assigned meanings of strength and permanence. It is also true that the warmth and beauty of one's surroundings, as compared to ugliness, appear to affect emotional well-being.

In addition to space, we infer much from how time is used. Tradition is a universal way for all cultures to preserve a sense of identity. Artifacts may take on sacredness and thus serve as a form of social control. Time also has come to signify importance and status. Students, for example, will wait longer for a late professor than a late instructor, and longer still for a popular musical group. Repetition, pace and timing of a message are other ways time may be used to influence.

The five senses of the body are the means by which an individual perceives and assigns meaning to the outside world. Each sense serves special communicative ends. Touching, for example, may be more important at times than words. The closeness of one body to another, obviously, influences which senses are more important. When people are very close, touch and smell are important. At a greater distance, eye and ear take precedence. Generally, we approach those things and people we like and avoid those we do not. The physical openness and closeness of body and gestures provide additional clues to the degree of comfort in interpersonal communication.

Dress and appearance carry great importance. To wear a uniform, for instance, symbolizes one's commitment to an institution or a group. People carry certain ideal images for body and appearance. One's own self-concept is related to how closely one compares to that ideal. Attractiveness is frequently related to one's choice in marriage and vocational success.

The eyes are particularly important to nonverbal communication. Eye contact provides a signal that communication is desired and looking away tells that it is not. Eye contact may provide a psychological bond between persons separated in a crowd. The brain, apparently, is able to process only so much information at one time and when planning what to say and while talking, a person tends to look away more than while listening. Leaders tend to take positions that enable them to see many people. Those who are minimally involved sit behind others or on the fringes of a group where eye contact is restricted.

We tend to believe nonverbal messages because they seem to spring more from involuntary, natural behavior as compared to words which may be planned for effect. Let us be cautious, however, when assigning meaning to nonverbal behavior. A gesture or movement should not be interpreted in isolation but in combination with other cues and in the situational context. Look for clusters of gestures. To read too much into nonverbal behaviors may be as unwise as being insensitive to the very loud messages of silence all about us.

INITIATIVES

INITIATING ACTION 1   *Factory Visit.* Visit the work areas of a local industrial firm. What are the sizes of the working spaces? Is space a sign of status? In what ways?

INITIATING ACTION 2   *Space and Wealth.* Drive through the residential areas of a city. Note the number of police in various sections of the city. In addition, note what comments are valid about trash collection in districts where population is high, is low.

INITIATING ACTION 3   *Attend a Play.* What could you tell about relationships from the height, distance and focus?

INITIATING ACTION 4   *Time-Bound.* Write a description of *you* and *time.* Consider your sense of identity based upon your knowledge and contacts with your past. Note those events to which you have arrived early and late. Does anyone turn you off by his punctuality or lack of it? Whom do you consider old? Middle aged? Young? How does age affect your relationships?

INITIATING ACTION 5   *Delete Verbal to Observe Nonverbal.* Have a group of students roleplay a situation such as the meeting of people from different lands. Let each person take the role of a different culture or subculture. From an adjoining room, those not performing should observe this action through a one-way glass, but should not hear the skit. After it is over, rejoin the performers and describe what you observed nonverbally.

INITIATING ACTION 6   *Invasion of Space.* Ride a commuter train. By trial and error discover how people react when others stand close to them, side-by-side, face-to-face, and back-to-back. If you want to live dangerously, chew a string which you let dangle from your mouth. Observe the behavior of persons standing or seated near you.

INITIATING ACTION 7   *Room Size–Conversation Distance.* Measure distance between chairs in a home living room. Compare this distance with the distance between people conversing in a large lounge. In both places the people talking likely are good friends. How does the room size affect the distance?

Blindfold. Carry on a five-minute conversation while both parties have their eyes covered with a blindfold. Did the other senses become more important? How important is eye contact?

INITIATING ACTION 8

Beautiful Room. Replicate the beautiful-ugly room experiment.

INITIATING ACTION 9

Body Rhetoric. Prepare a slide show of nonverbal symbols used to promote a movement. Include such symbols as flags, uniforms, marches, picketing, religious ceremony, cross, Star of David, medals, trophies, salutes, gestures.

INITIATING ACTION 10

NOTES

1. R. L. Birdwhistle, *Kinesics and Context* (Philadelphia: University of Pennsylvania Press, 1970), p. 158. Albert Mehrabien, "Communication Without Words," *Psychology Today*, Vol. 2, 1968, pp. 51–52.

2. See Charlotte L. Stuart, "Architecture in Nazi Germany: A Rhetorical Perspective," *Western Speech*, Vol. 37, Fall 1973, pp. 253–263.

3. Hendrik Hertzberg and David C. K. McClelland, "Marching On," *Harper's*, Vol. 248 (January 1974), p. 10.

4. R. Buckminster Fuller, "Outlook: Cutting the Metabilical Cord," *Saturday Review World*, September 9, 1974, p. 56.

5. Proxemics and Kinesics, Slide-cassettes, Columbus, Ohio, Center for Advanced Study of Human Communication, 1974.

6. Kenneth Goodall, "Bi Line," *Psychology Today*, Vol. V, January 1972, p. 26.

7. Mark Cary, Paper presented at the Eastern Psychological Association, 1974; Abstract "That Second Glance: Invitation to Conversation," *Psychology Today*, Vol. 8, (July 1974), p. 91.

8. Michael Argyle and Janet Dean, "Eye-Contact, Distance and Affiliation," *Sociometry*, Vol. 28, 1965, pp. 289–304.

9. These musings on silence were due in part to several thoughtful articles and books, principally, Edward T. Hall, *The Silent Language,* and Richard L. Johannesen, "The Functions of Silence: A Plea for Communication Research," *Western Speech*, XXXVIII, Winter 1974, pp. 25–35.

SUGGESTED READINGS

Barnlund, Dean C., *Interpersonal Communication: Survey and Studies*. Boston: Houghton Mifflin Co., 1968.

Beebe, Steven A. "Eye Contact: A Nonverbal Determinant of Speaker Credibility," *The Speech Teacher*, Vol. XXIII (January 1974), pp. 21–25, abstract presented with permission by The Speech Communication Association, New York, N.Y.

Birdwhistle, R. L. *Kinesics and Context*. Philadelphia: University of Pennsylvania Press, 1970.

Hall, Edward T., *The Hidden Dimension*. Garden City, New York: Doubleday, 1966.

————., *The Silent Language*. Greenwich, Conn.: Fawcett Publications, 1967.

Knapp, Mark L., *Nonverbal Communication in Human Interaction*. New York: Holt, Rinehart and Winston, 1972.

Leathers, Dale, *Nonverbal Communication Systems*. Boston: Allyn and Bacon, 1976.

Mehrabian, Albert, *Silent Messages*. Belmont, Calif.: Wadsworth Publishing Co., 1971.

Nierenberg, Gerald I., and Henry H. Calero, *How to Read A Person Like a Book*. New York: Hawthorn Books, 1971.

Rockefeller, David, "The Generation Gap and Its Meaning for Business," *The University of Chicago Magazine* (July/August 1968), pp. 2–8, quoted with permission from the *University of Chicago Magazine,* Copyright © 1968, The University of Chicago.

Slides and cassettes (audiovisual resources) on "Proxemics" and "Kinesics". Columbus, Ohio: Center for Advanced Study of Human Communication, 1974.

4 verbal cues

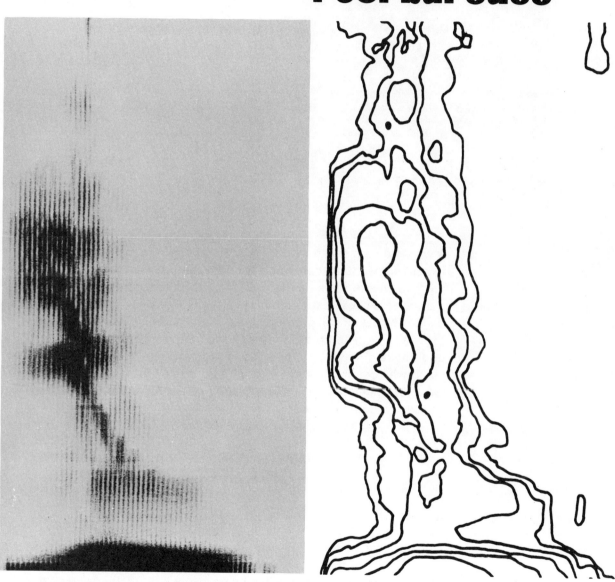

Two forms of the voiceprint are the "bar" form, left, and the "contour" form, at right. Both voiceprints represent the word "you" spoken by the same person.

In each of the two forms, time is plotted from left to right. That is, the beginning of the word "you" is at the left, and the end of the word is at the right. The lower pitch of sound appears at bottom and the higher pitch toward the top. Greater intensity of sound at each frequency for a particular time is represented by darker lines in the form at left, and by peaks in the "contour-map" form at right. People detect patterns more readily in the form at left. But the contour form at right is more easily analyzed by computer and is also more easily reproduced in print.

Think about how often you speak. Right now you are reading, true, but think about how often you speak from the time you awaken to the time you go to sleep. The answer psychologists give is approximately *seven hundred* discrete utterings, that is, those which aren't parts of a "conversation" but actually different occasions to say something. Investigators say some people utter 12,000 sentences every day, which averages out to almost 100,000 words! Put differently, an average American can *speak* the equivalent of two novels per day, although he *reads* less than three books per year.

From *Egospeak: Why No One Listens to You* by Edmond G. Addeo and Robert E. Burger, (Radnor, Pennsylvania: Chilton Book Company, 1973), p. 258.

A wise man once said that the biggest mistake we mortals make is to *assume* we have communication. In the last chapter we examined nonverbal cues — now we will consider verbal symbols. In particular, we will explore why the words we speak and listen to cannot be taken for granted. After a brief look at the vocal process, we will take up the message process, the language system, and finally, the psychological set and feedback. To better understand why communication is such a complex process, we should have an understanding of the basic components and processes needed to communicate verbally.

THE VOCAL PROCESS

Our ability to express widely variable symbolic sounds such as a whisper or a scream depends upon adequately functioning muscles, organs and nervous system. The synchronization of these body processes is no small miracle. How do the lungs, which become a vacuum chamber for in-rushing elements that provide oxygen for the red corpuscles, become a source for puffs of air which flutter through the taut folds of the larynx? And how do these inaudible vibrations which get amplified in the larynx, nose and mouth, then to be modified by the tongue, teeth and lips, become a noise or symbol?

VOCAL ELEMENTS

There are four generally agreed upon elements necessary for the vocal process to operate fully. There first must be an *energy source*, something to supply air that powers the whole system. Second, a *vibrator* must create sound so the *resonators* (the third element) can amplify it. And finally, the sound must be *modified* into precise and conventional symbols usually recognized by others.

Energy Source

The *energy source* is our breathing equipment, mainly consisting of our lungs. Because our breathing is affected by our physical state (have we just awakened or finished jogging), we need be aware of the various ways the vocal mechanism will perform when the energy source is varied. Emotional stress can also affect our breathing pattern and such everyday matters as ventilation, comfortable clothing and good posture are crucial in determining the energy available for effective speech.

Vibrator

The *vibrator* is the set of vocal cords located in the larynx. Air is forced up the trachea (windpipe), mainly by the use of the diaphragm, through the vocal cords. When the cords vibrate sound is produced and this occurrence is called *phonation.* Most of us have had the experience, at one time or another, of food going down the wrong pipe. This occurs when we have tried to swallow and speak at the same time. At the top of the larynx is a flap of skin called the epiglottis. When we are breathing, it remains open so air can get into and out of the trachea. When we are swallowing, it closes so food will go down through the esophagus to the stomach. When food does get into the trachea, a situation that can sometimes be fatal, a cough usually clears the particles.

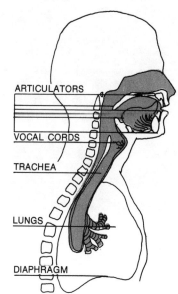

ARTICULATORS

VOCAL CORDS

TRACHEA

LUNGS

DIAPHRAGM

Although the vocal cords are hearty, they can be abused. Repeated straining, such as cheering or shouting commands, can cause temporary loss of sound and over a long period of abuse, the cords can be permanently affected. Smoking and excessive drinking are, among other things, also damaging to the vocal cords.

Resonator

While the entire head is used as a *resonator,* the mouth and nose cavities are the primary resonators. The effect, for example, of swelling on the nasal passages and the sinuses caused by a cold are noticed immediately by others. And while everyone's aural cavity differs, when you shape your mouth or shift your tongue, the quality of sound is also affected.

Modifiers   The lips, teeth, tongue, jaw and soft palate all function as *modifiers.* Their importance is most noticeable in consonant sounds such as the *b* in *bang* or the *p* in *punt,* and they work in combination with vowels and other consonants to mold the sounds into meaningful symbols of communication.

VOLUME   Since sound is the final product of the vocal process and one of the main ingredients needed for the verbal message, a few important observations are necessary before discussing voice quality. It is amazing, first, that muscles and organs, whose primary function is the supplying of oxygen and the processing of food, can also make sounds upon command. But it is even more amazing to know that approximately 100 muscles must be coordinated to express a word. Yet, for all this complexity, the sounds are produced with a very small expenditure of energy; for example, "2 million people talking at once would use no more energy than that required to light a 25 watt bulb."[1]

The college student in a speech communication course does not have to learn to produce words and sentences. He is far beyond the basic steps of learning a language. However, the student must learn to produce a message with a volume appropriate for the occasion. While audibility is both a physical and psychological matter, there exists an aesthetic sophistication related to volume. A child from four to six years old may often speak at a level suited to the playground. He has little sense of the distance his voice will carry. His models are older children who get their way by shouting, and so must he. We can see how far a ball will go when it is kicked but it is more difficult to estimate the level of our voice at various distances and situations.

Sound levels are measured by the voice scientist in decibels. The threshold of hearing is 0 decibels and the level where sounds become painful is in the 140 decibel range. A whisper is 20-30 decibels and conversational speech at three feet is 60-70 decibels.[2] Students speaking to their classmates could be heard with comfort in the rear of the room some 30 feet away when their decibel level was in the 60-70 decibel conversational range. When a person speaks slowly and with precise enunciation, he can be heard with less volume than that. However, listeners in the front of my classroom did not report their classmates spoke too loudly

THE DECIBEL SCALE

dB	
0	THRESHOLD OF HEARING
10	NORMAL BREATHING
20	LEAVES RUSTLING IN A BREEZE
30	EMPTY MOVIE HOUSE
40	RESIDENTIAL NEIGHBORHOOD AT NIGHT
50	QUIET RESTAURANT
60	TWO-PERSON CONVERSATION
70	BUSY TRAFFIC
80	VACUUM CLEANER
90	WATER AT FOOT OF NIAGARA FALLS
100	SUBWAY TRAIN
120	PROPELLER PLANE AT TAKEOFF
130	MACHINE-GUN FIRE, CLOSE RANGE
140	MILITARY JET AT TAKEOFF
160	WIND TUNNEL
175	FUTURE SPACE ROCKET

THE SOUNDS WE HEAR

Sound: A sound that is just barely audible has an approximate intensity of 1/10,000,000,000,000,000 watts per square centimeter. The necessary sound pressure for an audible sound seems almost nil. Speech in conversation averages about 60 decibels in intensity relative to the above. This corresponds to an actual intensity which is 1,000,000 times greater (10–16 watts per centimeter squared).*

Decibel: A decibel represents the amount of sound that can be picked up at a given distance, and it is scaled logarithmically; that is, each measure of 10 decibels represents a tenfold increase. Hence the volume of 120 decibels is 10 times the volume of 110 decibels. Some 16 million Americans work where on-the-job noise level is severe enough to endanger hearing. A climbing jet, for example, even 2,000 feet above the ground is 130 decibels. A typical disco puts out 115 decibels and there are instances of permanent deafness of rock musicians who played approximately 11 hours per week. Even home noise at 80 decibels can produce fatigue.†

Noise: The Environmental Protection Agency estimates that 10 million Americans of all ages live in areas where the sound outside their dwellings averages 60 to 70 decibels, a level equal to a loud conversation heard four feet away. Five million have decibel levels of 70 to 80 outside their homes, noise equal to traffic heard from 50 feet.

A study of noise levels outside and inside a high-rise apartment building near a busy highway found that noise levels at the top of the building were less than at the bottom. In addition, it revealed that children who had lived there for four or more years on the lower floors scored lower in reading skills and in their ability to understand speech than those living on upper floors.‡

*Frederick Williams, *Language and Speech Introductory Perspectives* (Englewood Cliffs, N.J.: Prentice Hall, 1972), pp. 10–11.

†Edwin Kiester, Jr., "Noise, Noise, Noise," *Family Health,* Vol. VI, January, 1974, pp. 20–21, 48–52.

‡Patrick Young, "Noise Can Hinder Kids," *The National Observer,* February 8, 1975, p. 4.

even when the voices occasionally peaked in the 80-90 decibel range.

The conversation range, 60-70 decibels, conveys a person-to-person message. Lower or higher ranges may, because of their contrast, gain attention and emphasize certain ideas. My recommendation to a public speaker is to stay within the conversational range, but not to hesitate to increase or decrease volume when excited about or when underlining special points. And in face-to-face communication your listener will usually signal you if you are too loud or too soft.

For every communicative transaction to be received accurately, one must send a signal that is more noticeable than competing signals and *nonsymbolic* sound (general noise). If a message is overwhelmed by noise, a listener may give a signal that tells the speaker he is not getting through and, therefore, to increase his signal. For example, he might lean forward and turn his head slightly so his ear is closer to the speaker, or the speaker might put his message into another channel. Children do this frequently. When they do not get attention by calling, they may grab hold of their mother's arm.

Beginning students of speech communication are often uninformed about their own appropriate volume for intelligible speech in different situations. Moreover, they are usually less aware of how pleasing or not their own voice volume and quality are when speaking at varying distances. The responses given have usually been indirect and unsystematic. Initiative 1 at the end of the chapter provides an opportunity to get information about your speaking volume and intelligibility.

VOICE QUALITY   Besides volume, there are other qualities connected with sound production that impair communication. Hoarseness, harshness, nasality, breathiness and pitch are all problems that must be dealt with. While voice quality is a product of cultural models, physical structure and emotional well-being, the student can make improvements with these problems by taking a voice/diction or acting course that provides vocal training. A tape recorder can also aid in voice quality refinement by allowing the student to hear himself. By listening attentively, the student may, as an example, be able to mellow his voice quality by merely lowering his pitch. While student attention to voice quality is important, very serious problems should be referred to a speech therapist. Be cautious about striving for pear-shaped vowels and distinctly enunciated consonants—you may appear as affected as a student in a tuxedo at the local pizza hut. Minimum essentials of voice quality are best judged by attention to reactions from your instructor and your peers under various circumstances.

Many speakers with unpleasant voice qualities are able to minimize the audience's attention to them by good humor, sincerity and eloquence. Speech should not draw attention to itself. The voice, like the gesture, should not get in the way of the message. When the vocal system is in good health, the quality of the voice, except in rare cases, will be unobtrusive and not noticed by the listeners. If the ideas are exciting, your listener will adjust to a slightly unpleasant voice.

The attributes of voice, in addition to volume and quality, in-

clude pitch, rate, duration (length of a vowel), regularity and rhythm, articulation and pronunciation, stress and silence. Certain expectations are developed for these attributes and influence the communication. An excessively high rate of speech, for example, may be associated with loss of control and defensiveness. An excessively slow rate (many hesitancies), may be associated with uncertainty. Both excesses disrupt communication and may be caused by emotional stress or physiological deficiencies.

The voice carries an information component in verbal symbols and an emotional component in quality. Emotional tension is noticeable through one or more of the voice attributes, particularly volume, pitch, rate, rhythm and silence. To understand a speaker's emotional state, we need not hear his words or see his face and body movements—quality alone provides ample cues. Emotions of contempt, grief, anger, fear, determination, doubt and joy may be conveyed with a high degree of accuracy, for example, by simply repeating the letters of the alphabet.

In the enormously popular Broadway musical and movie "My Fair Lady," cockney, lower-class Eliza Doolittle (Audrey Hepburn) is turned into an English gentlewoman by her teacher, Henry Higgins (Rex Harrison). Many speech qualities are learned during language acquisition and are therefore culturally determined. These learned qualities can be altered through imitation of preferable speech models.

THE MESSAGE PROCESS

There are minimum essentials for survival both in the wilderness and in the center of highly congested cities. What some of these minimum essentials are becomes eloquently evident on a trip to a new environment where the culture and language are different from our own. For example, I walked into a hotel in Oaxaca, Mexico, to wait for my family, who was shopping in a nearby market. As I entered the small lobby, a young boy confronted me. In rapid fashion he told me something. I heard sounds but I could not understand. Shaking my head, I sat down, a bit uneasy about my presence there but anxious to rest my tired feet. No sooner had I eased into a chair when a man I assumed to be the hotel manager, a woman, and the teenage boy approached me. This time the boy spoke some English. He asked, "What do you mean?" The message was clearer now. I must justify my presence or get out. Fortunately, I had been told that this place was the headquarters of a group from the states with whom we would be associated while in the area. My password to acceptance had to be used, so I clearly said, "Claudia." The three who surrounded me smiled and the manager nodded understanding, "Si, Claudia." They knew Claudia was the leader of the Gringo.

DIAGRAM OF A SIMPLE COMMUNICATION TRANSACTION

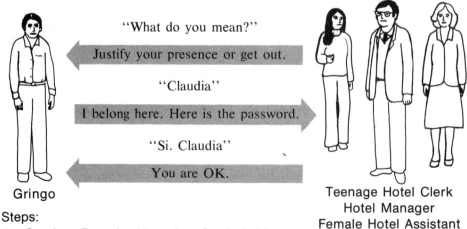

"What do you mean?"

Justify your presence or get out.

"Claudia"

I belong here. Here is the password.

"Si. Claudia"

You are OK.

Gringo

Teenage Hotel Clerk
Hotel Manager
Female Hotel Assistant

Steps:
1. Sender ← Encodes Idea → Into Symbols Message
2. Message sent in a channel (speech in air waves and gestures in visual light waves)
3. Heard, seen and decoded by Receivers
4. Who Respond With Feedback (words, smiles and nods)

What fundamental conditions were needed for this transaction? First, I had to express a message that was heard, next I had to use a sign or symbol that would be interpreted as "I'm okay," and finally, to discover the effect of my message, I had to receive some signals of response (feedback).

If we consider my experience in the hotel more carefully, we can see that several processes were actually occurring at the same or almost the same time. I had first to think of a message that would be meaningful to my listener. I then had to dig into my memory containing information about the visit and sort out a symbol I hoped would be recognized. Once I had filtered through all the details of hotel names, cities visited and people associated with on my trip, I selected, "Claudia."

After making a selection of a message symbol, I had to put it into a form I knew would be recognized. This process is called *encoding.* I then *transmitted* (sent) the symbol to the receiver using a channel (speech and gestures) I knew the manager would hear and see. In this case, I was fortunate to have a symbol my listener could recognize. Now he was able to think through the people associated with tourists and especially those permitted to use the hotel as a meeting place. This process is called *decoding.* Once my listener decoded the message and signaled (*feedback*) me he understood, the message circle or loop was complete. And remembering that his feedback was also a message similar to mine, we can say communication has occurred.

Looking at the Diagram of a Simple Communication Transaction and the Diagram of Communication Components carefully, we can conclude that the message process is continual. We can also conclude that the basic component of the message process is the *signal* or *symbol.* In verbal communication, the symbol is usually a word or group of words, and that now brings us to the language system.

THE LANGUAGE SYSTEM

The basic element in language, the *symbol,* is some object, image or sound that represents something other than itself. For example, the written symbol "dog" represents the idea of a dog. The letters themselves are not the dog. Without symbols to exchange meanings, it would be an almost impossible task to ex- **SYMBOLS**

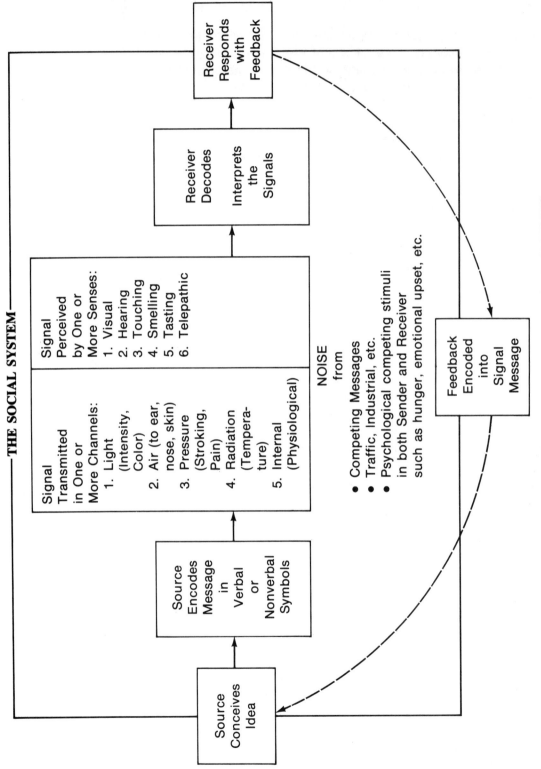

DIAGRAM OF COMMUNICATION COMPONENTS

change information. We would need all objects and places present in order to act out our message. It is the symbol, codified into language, that enables us to store knowledge, coordinate human activity and to plan for the future. And most importantly, symbols are the keys that make thought and problem-solving possible.

There are certain characteristics that all symbols (verbal and nonverbal) share and in order to better understand our language system, we need to recognize what they are and their limitations. The symbol is *arbitrary*—it is a sound or sign that does not mean exactly the same thing to everyone as we all have a different perception of the world. The symbol is also *ambiguous* because it represents different people's perceptions and interpretations and, therefore, has a variety of potential meanings. Moreover, it may result in diversified effects. Some who hear the symbol will be its intended listeners, others will not. Finally, a symbol competes with *noise* (sounds other than the signal) in the channel and may be heard incorrectly (see Diagram of Communication Components).

A symbol is not only arbitrary and ambiguous, but it is also *situationally dependent*—the meaning of a symbol changes and is colored by the context in which it occurs or is uttered. The receiver of a communication transaction, and sometimes those not intended, may not only be influenced by a symbol but they may, in turn, also influence the user of the symbol. In a face-to-face encounter, source and receiver are mutually subject to each other's influence. The source of a message and a receiver may be separated by distance, as in the case of a radio broadcaster and listener, or they may be separated by time, as in the case of an

SYMBOLIC REPRESENTATION OF "DOG" IN CHINESE

Pictograph (1400 B.C.)   Chou Era (500 B.C.)   Modern

In the historical development of language, symbols have become progressively more abstract in their representation of meaning. For example, the Chinese pictograph for dog closely resembed the animal itself in 1400 B.C. Over the millenia, the symbol for dog has become progressively more and more abstract.

author and reader. In such cases, feedback and the circular nature of communication are not so apparent.

To illustrate the situationally dependent character of symbols, let us consider a red light. When someone sees the light, the visual nerve endings differentiate that color from surrounding colors. Cultural conditioning helps the person identify the nerve impulse and by learning the word that describes "red," gives it meaning. If the red light is at a street corner, a driver may automatically press down on the brake. If the light is shining in a house window during the Advent season, someone who respects the Christian faith will respond with reverence. And at a hockey game, a red light over the net signals a goal scored, igniting a wild burst of enthusiasm from the fans. Just as symbols are situationally dependent, so also are words and messages that function as symbols.

WORDS   A more complete idea of how dependent words are on situations for their meaning can be gained by looking through a dictionary. The entries following the word "hand" fill nearly half a page in one dictionary. Definitions range from "that part of the human arm that extends below the wrist" to "the cards one may hold in a card game" and "an increment of measure for large animals."

There are many examples of situation-bound messages, and most of them are closely linked with ethnic, subcultural or occupational differences. To a student, the word "book" may mean the verb "to study" or it may mean a collection of printed pages required to be read to gain information. To a street-wise urbanite, "book" may mean "to bet on horse races." And to a minister, the good "book" will mean "the Bible."

Oral symbols are frequently likened to maps by semanticists. These scholars of meanings are fond of the well-known metaphor, "The map is not the territory. The word is not the thing." Maps only represent a certain place. They cannot tell everything about an area. Moreover, maps cannot tell anything about the reader of the map; they only provide clues to what the cartographer knows about the territory. Communication between the map maker and map reader depends, then, on a set of symbols common to both. The more similar the language and travel experience, the greater likelihood the messages intended will overlap with the messages interpreted.

THE VOCABULARY OF MEANING IN THE STUDY OF COMMUNICATION

This list contains definitions and concepts usually used by communications scholars.

Communication sometimes is intentional—those acts in which a person deliberately puts his ideas or feelings into a symbol to elicit a response.

Communication sometimes is unintentional—those times when a meaning is assigned to a symbol, object or action which was not deliberately planned.

Communication sometimes creates meanings—symbols grow from those things and interactions we experience and share.

Symbols are words or nonverbal acts which stand for some thing, person, place, act, thought or feeling—that reality which may be referred to as a referent.

Symbols have a denotative meaning—that association connecting an object or event in environment to thought and symbol. A name of something is denotative.

Symbols have a connotative meaning—those emotional and personal feelings generated by a symbol. Pleasure or anger, for example, may be feelings associated with certain symbols because of one's past experiences.

Beliefs are what we think or feel to be true or false, good or bad, desirable or undesirable about the world around us.

Attitudes consist of an organization of beliefs around an object or situation. An attitude predisposes us to a certain way of responding.

Values are deep enduring beliefs about how we should or should not behave or values may be beliefs in end-states of existence which are or are not held to be worth attaining.

Relationships at times may involve interactions that are symmetrical—that is the participants are similar and tend to mirror each other and tend to be competitive.

Relationships on the other times may be complementary—that is the participants are different or opposite, what one does tends to produce contrasting behavior in others. Members in an orchestra bringing music from their differing contributions is complementary or symbiotic.

Artifacts are objects and things which tell us about the society—buildings, tools, clothing, literature, forms of exchange that reflect the culture.

Even when people possess a common language, there still exists a concern for finding symbols that carry like-meaning between sender and receiver. The basic awareness which the beginning student of communication should gain is stated simply in one sentence, "Meanings are in people and not in symbols themselves." Symbols mean only what meaning people give to them. The communicator must always be aware that his meaning may not be conveyed by the symbols he uses. A talk about shared experiences will assure both the sender and the receiver that the symbols they are using mean the same thing to each of them, that certain words have a common meaning. Only by understanding the listener's background and point of view and by obtaining

**CONVEYING
MEANINGS**

I DON'T UNDERSTAND

I know that you believe you understand what you think I said, but I'm not sure you realize that what you heard is not what I meant.

Don't you know that we still can't believe what we think we heard you say, but you must realize that we know that you know that what we heard you say is what you meant.

I'm not sure I understand why you still can't believe what I want you to think I said and I'm not sure I know what you meant by what I think I heard you say about what I said but I'm not sure you realize that what you heard is not what I meant.

We're sure we understand what we think we heard you say and we're sure we understand that what we heard you say is what you meant, but we don't understand how you can't be sure about what you heard us say about what you said and we don't understand why you want us to believe what we didn't hear you say when you said something that you didn't realize you meant to say when we heard you say it and you must realize that we're sure we understand you meant what we heard you say.

I'm not sure I understand why you're sure you understand what I said previously because if you understand what you think you heard me say, you would realize that what I meant then explained what you thought you had heard me say originally and I don't understand how you can't believe what I want you to think you heard me say when you must realize that what I said was meant for you to understand and believe the way you heard it and you must realize I believe that I think I don't understand . . . ?

L. & D. Janke, "I Don't Understand," *The Daily Kent Stater,*
February 13, 1975, p. 2.

The English language, as recorded by *The Oxford English Dictionary*, consists of approximately half a million words. The average person has a vocabulary amounting to 60,000 to 80,000 words (*Encyclopedia Americana*, 1969 ed., p. 202). The English language, however, may be communicated adequately through the use of only 800 words.

Martin P. Anderson, E. Ray Nichols, Jr., and Herbert W. Booth, *The Speaker and His Audience* (New York: Harper and Row, Second Ed., 1974), p. 199.

feedback on whether the message was properly interpreted can we be confident that we have communicated effectively. We will discuss experience and feedback later in this chapter but for now we can say that because of the inexact nature of words and language, we must constantly be aware of the possibilities for misunderstanding. Knowing this, then, what general rules can we offer to increase the frequency of effective communication:

1 We should use symbols with care. We should learn to use words that have specific meanings to our listeners.

2 We should move down the ladder of abstractions to the most precise meanings we can find. Such words as "freedom" and "success" must be described in more tangible terms. Ambiguity is more likely with only a few abstract words than with many more concrete, descriptive words.

3 We should be willing to say it again. To overexplain may be to bore, but to be willing to repeat and say it in another way is to be aware of the need to find symbols that have your meaning to others.

4 We should be aware that in spite of all efforts to be clear, listeners will still, at times, find our directions confusing and incomplete, may still find us unpersuasive, and may still take things the wrong way. We should be more tolerant of our own misunderstandings and of inaccurate directions from others. Misunderstandings are expected and are not exceptions.

To summarize, we communicate differently when we are conscious of the fragile nature of our codes and if we are alert to the intimate, personal relationship between man and his symbols.

THE PSYCHOLOGICAL SET AND FEEDBACK

PSYCHOLOGICAL SET

Two closely linked communication ideas are *psychological set* and *feedback.* Psychological set refers to a person's readiness to receive a communication. Feedback refers to the manner in which a person responds to a communication, and is usually determined by the person's psychological set. We all have a certain readiness to believe some things and not others. How often have we heard someone say, "I just can't believe she would say such a thing." We believe what we want to believe. This has been referred to as *autistic* thinking. Jean Piaget, the Swiss biologist, defines autism as "truth confused with desire."[3] Many psychologists have broadened the meaning of autism to include a "hostile reaction to favorable inputs about popular things we don't like."[4] This definition would explain the statement, "My mind's made up, don't confuse me with facts."

Probably the most important part of a person's psychological set is *self-esteem.* Hundreds of studies have been done showing

The clearly opposing psychological sets of these two antagonists will probably prevent them from breaking out of the simple feedback chain, "I'm right! You're wrong!" They probably perceive the other as pig-headed, yet, blind to the existence of their own psychological set, they see themselves as being rational and open-minded. While a third person may be able to point out the dilemma, antagonism over fundamental perceptions of reality may never be resolvable.

people reacting to various kinds of communications. Some of these communications were to persuade the subjects to action (such as to quit smoking) and others were to change attitudes. Among the kinds of variables determining reactions, self-esteem was most consistently related to readiness to accept new information or change attitudes.[5] Those people with low self-esteem were more susceptible to persuasion than those with high self-esteem. This is not surprising when you consider that a person with a high opinion of himself is likely to value his own ideas highly and may be reluctant to accept others' ideas.

In addition to self-esteem as an element of the psychological set, *prior experience* is extremely important. Prior experience was essential when I had my conversation with the hotel staff in Mexico. And in our discussion of symbols, prior experience was necessary for some words to become meaningful. But similar to self-esteem, prior experience is especially important in communications that are persuasive or instrumental (Chapter 2). Studies, in which subjects were told that someone was going to try to change their minds about something have shown that when fore-warned about such attempts, people have a tendency to resist the message. Further, people who have successfully resisted mild attacks against some belief are even more resistent to subsequent attacks.[6] The explanation offered for this finding is that people whose opinions are only mildly attacked become motivated to defend them, and as they acquire more practice by defending a position, they become more skilled and even more reluctant to change. An important lesson to be gained from this is that when certain beliefs we hold are never challenged, we can lose sight of why we hold them. By challenging our own ideas from time to time, we can see their valuable and vulnerable points. We then will reinforce our original position or, perhaps, reevaluate and change it.

These descriptions of the importance of prior experience do not adequately describe the full range of influence that it has on psychological set. In terms of our goals for achieving a better understanding of the communication transaction, it is important to remember that everyone we contact is carrying a psychological set made up of their own kind of autistic thinking, self-esteem, and prior experience. The way our message is received will be colored by these factors.

FEEDBACK

Earlier in this chapter we said that feedback is a *response* by a listener to a message and is closely linked with the listener's psychological set. It is, however, often difficult to tell where feed-back begins and ends. Even before we speak, we react to verbal and nonverbal cues from our listener. In turn, our message may be viewed by the listener as feedback to his visual appearance. Most communication, in fact, consists of chains of messages and feedback which each member of the transaction perceives differently. When we interpret feedback incorrectly, there is confusion; but it is more often a very useful tool in achieving effective communication.

The quality of a communication event is determined, to a great degree, by the ability of people to predict and interpret each other's feedback. Feedback helps us to refine and correct our message so we may be more accurate and complete. In teaching situations, this notion becomes essential and is clearly illustrated in studies that examined the value of feedback. And in a world where discussion, negotiation, and collective bargaining grow increasingly important, feedback can be crucial to peace, trade and social progress.

DO ASK

Basic Question: Will a message be more accurately understood if the listeners have an opportunity to ask questions and make comments?

Subjects and Treatment: Eighty students in four groups were given instructions by two instructors about how to reproduce simple geometric designs. The designs consisted of various arrangements of six rectangles (domino shapes).

The instructors presented the designs in four different ways: 1. Zero Feedback in which the instructor spoke from behind a blackboard. The audience was asked to remain completely silent. 2. Visible Feedback in which the instructor was permitted to see his silent audience. 3. Yes-No Feedback in which the instructor answered questions from his audience with a yes or no. 4. Free Feedback in which the instructor, while presenting his instructions, responded to any questions or comments by the audience. The instructors were allowed to use all the time they wanted.

Results: The greater the feedback permitted, the more rectangles were correctly drawn by the 80 students and more time was taken by the instructors in giving their instructions.

	Zero Feedback	Visual Feedback	Yes-No Feedback	Free Feedback
Average Number of the correctly reproduced six figures	4.7	5.3	5.5	5.6
Average Time used given in seconds	229	249	316	363

A follow-up experiment using triangles, lines and circles with ten additional classes met with the same general results. The instructors noted that students' feedback was more hostile when Free Feedback followed a Zero Feedback situation.

Implications: Encourage feedback when giving directions, but expect it to take more time. When we want to have a message accurately understood, we should permit questions and comments during our presentations.

Harold J. Leavitt and Ronald A. H. Mueller, "Some Effects of Feedback on Communication," *Human Relations*, 4, 1951, 401–411.

The journey from source-idea to symbol to receiver-response is a complex, human phenomenon. Because of noise in the channel and other distractions competing with a signal, it is sometimes miraculous that communication is ever accurate. But opportunity for ample feedback increases our chances for good communication significantly by adding six important elements to the transaction. Feedback (1) helps us discover common symbols in the language code, (2) increases redundancy to ensure a signal is received, (3) prevents misinterpretations from going unchecked, (4) helps us to accomodate different attention spans, (5) provides opportunity for expression and the discovery of new ideas, and most importantly, (6) forces us to share the responsibility for getting the message clear.

MY INTRODUCTION TO FEEDBACK

It was Dr. Martin Luther King, Jr. who first introduced me to the importance of communicating in dialogue rather than monologue.

The occasion was a cool March night in Atlanta in 1961. My family and I listened to a blaring loudspeaker from outside the Warren Street Methodist Church in the heart of the black community. We couldn't get into the church because some 2,000 persons filled the building and jammed the entrances.

The crowd appeared displeased at the very time a Black Liaison Committee had signed a contract with the Chamber of Commerce to desegregate the lunch counters of over seventy eating places in the city. Black Muslims circulated handbills accusing the Liaison Committee of "selling out."

The rumored part of the contract which so displeased many in the black community was a promise to call off the boycott of downtown stores in exchange for an opening of lunch counters on a desegregated basis upon an undetermined, unspecified future date. The Negro attorney who helped the Liaison Committee complete the agreement, when trying to explain the necessity for maintaining confidentiality was laughed and jeered off the platform after he said, "There's no doubt about if it's going to take place; we have it in black and white. You'll have to take my word for it."

For two and three-quarter hours the activists spoke against the Liaison Committee, urging the community to continue the boycott and to overthrow the negotiations of their own Liaison Committee.

In the eye of this turbulent storm, Dr. King addressed the crowd. Calm, deliberate and forceful, he acknowledged that he had heard the feedback to the Liaison Committee of which he was an advisor. He did not argue with the students' militant determination to continue the boycott until the lunch counters were in fact desegregated as he made these points: (1) We have a right to be angry and discontented; (2) But our own differences must be solved with mutual respect; and (3) Only then will our goals of first class citizenship be achieved within the nonviolent way. At one point, he said:

> If I had been on that committee that met Monday afternoon, I wouldn't mind anybody saying, "Martin Luther King, Jr., you made a mistake." I wouldn't mind anybody saying, "Martin Luther King, Jr., you should have thought it over a little longer." I wouldn't have minded anybody saying to me, "Martin Luther King, Jr., maybe we made a tactical blunder." But I would have been terribly hurt if anybody said to me, "Martin Luther King, Jr., you sold us out!" (Applause) I would have been hurt by that.[7]

He argued that a misunderstanding is never solved "trying to live in monologue; you solve it in the realm of dialogue." And at the conclusion of his sermon predicted victory. "We have now brought the football of civil rights to about the 50-yard line, . . . and with the proper leaders in the backfield and a great team of linemen, within the next ten years we will go all the way across the goal line to human dignity."

I tell this story, so moving to me, because it represents one of the most basic principles of grassroots democracy, and that is that: *Trust depends upon keeping the channels open for feedback.*

—William I. Gorden
(see footnote 7)

SUMMARY

In this chapter, we have examined the basic components of verbal communication: the vocal process, the message process, the language system, and the psychological set and feedback. The ability to make sound is a secondary function for the body's muscles and organs that are used for breathing and eating. The four elements necessary in the vocal process are: energy source, vibrator, resonator and modifiers. Vocal sound is a product of the vocal process, and it contains certain measurable qualities of its own that work together to form our voice.

The voice also has many attributes that aid the communication of ideas, feelings, and beliefs. Volume, pitch, rate, duration, regularity and rhythm, articulation and pronunciation, and stress are all factors of voice quality; and they all affect the manner in which we communicate verbally.

The message process consists of deciding on a signal (encoding), sending the signal (transmitting), having the signal received (perceiving—hearing and seeing), having the signal assigned meaning (decoding), and having the meaning acknowledged (feedback). Diagrams may show these activities happening in sequence but in actuality, much of the process is simultaneous and continual.

The language system is essential to the verbal message process. The basic element in the language system is the symbol or word. They carry most of our verbal cues. As with many other symbols, words are arbitrary (they do not mean the same thing to all people), they are ambiguous (their meanings are not always clear), and they are situationally dependent (their meanings may change from one context or user to another).

Psychological set and feedback help us to eliminate much of the ambiguity of words in the verbal message process. Psychological set refers to people's readiness to perceive a communication. Autistic thinking, self-esteem, and prior experience are the main ingredients of the psychological set.

Feedback is the manner in which we respond to a message and is often determined by a person's psychological set. It is particularly useful in determining how effective our verbal message has been, and is essential for effective teaching and instructional messages.

INITIATIVES

How Loud Am I? In teams of three and four, check out your **INITIATING ACTION 1**
volume levels within the following situations and distances:
- around a table in a quiet restaurant,
- in a group on a noisy street,
- in a living room at distances of 4 feet, 6 feet and 8 feet,
- at various distances in a classroom,
- from the pulpit of a church or synagogue or stage of a theater
  at distances of 20, 30, 50, 100 feet.
- speaking with the aid of microphone in a gymnasium.

Each person should deliver a short written paragraph for these
tests and should also answer a question or two asked from the
listeners. The listeners should confer before feeding back their
perceptions of what the speaker said. Signals of "louder," "softer,"
"about right" and additional suggestions concerning articulation
should be given. If there are real difficulties of intelligibility, the
instructor may suggest drills such as speaking in a whisper. Your
instructor may recommend a light-activated microphone to aid in
such drills. The level of sound required to "light" the lamp may be
adjusted. In addition, in such cases the aid of an instructor who
specializes in voice and diction may be solicited.

A Partial Failure. Now let's try several exercises designed both to **INITIATING ACTION 2**
help the sender deal with feedback and to help the listener ask
the kind of questions which will bring out the essential message.
Each class member should bring a three-minute presentation on a
general topic such as "The State of the Church," "The State of
Professional Sports," "The State of Marriage." These presentations should be made to clusters of 4–6 other students. During
and after the presentation it is the special duty of each listener to
ask one of the following or similar questions:

(1) Do you mean _____ ?

(2) How do you know _____ ?

(3) What difference will it make if _____ ?

These questions should be asked whenever they seem honestly
appropriate. After the exercise is completed for all members of

the cluster, the class as a whole may share their reactions to the proposition that most communication is a partial failure. The class might also discuss how feedback revealed and helped alleviate the misunderstanding, but perhaps sometimes only led to more misunderstanding.

INITIATING ACTION 3 *Blind to Feedback*. In order to gain some feeling for the importance of visual feedback, try the following:

Blindfold a person and have him instruct the class to reproduce a geometric design he has seen (no questions permitted).

Have a class member wear very dark sunglasses and, if possible, with shiny reflective exteriors. Have the class bombard this individual with questions about his beliefs. After a few minutes, talk about the feeling generated by this exercise.

INITIATING ACTION 4 *Zero Feedback*. Reread the abstract of the now classic experiment by Harold Leavitt and Ronald Mueller, "Do Ask." Reproduce the zero to free feedback activities in your classroom.

INITIATING ACTION 5 *Interpersonal Feedforward*. Pair with another classmember. Take turns talking for a minute or two about each of the following topics. After each one speaks, paraphrase what you have heard into a short phrase or sentence. Then proceed to the next topic if the paraphrase captures the essence. If it does not, restate what you said.

Topics:
a. My home town is. . .
b. This past week, I felt. . .
c. An event which changed the direction of my life. . .
d. The things that motivate me or demotivate me are. . .

INITIATING ACTION 6 *Identity Symbols*. Secretly bring to class something that has personal meaning for you. Place it in a box or pile and shuffle it with others' objects. Then, have someone take turns drawing out one object and guessing whose it is. The owner may compare his reason for bringing the object with those meanings assigned by the class.

INITIATING ACTION 7 *Discovering Meanings*. This week jot down examples from your own experience of the following.

Intentional communication. . .
Unintentional communication. . .

Created meanings. . .
Denotative meaning of a new symbol. . .
Connotative meaning of a symbol you encounter. . .
A belief you refer to as true or false. . .
A belief you refer to as good or bad. . .
A belief you refer to as desirable or undesirable. . .
An attitude you become aware of. . .
A value you live by to attain something. . .
A value you hold as an end-state. . .
A relationship which is symmetrical. . .
A relationship which is complementary. . .
An artifact which tells about your values. . .

Value Clarification. Rank the following list of values from most to **INITIATING ACTION 8** least important to you:

A comfortable life	National security
An exciting life	Pleasure
A world of peace	Salvation
A world of beauty	Self-respect
Equality	Social recognition
Family security	True friendship
Happiness	Wisdom
Inner harmony	

Now compare your list to a classmate's. Try to understand the reasons and feelings behind his or her list. Do not try to change each others' ordering. Next cluster with another pair and discuss which values seem to be the driving force within our current government's domestic and foreign policies. The purpose of the discussion is not to change but to see the reasoning and feeling which generates one another's opinions.

An extension of this exercise is to rank the following instrumental values (means to achieve an end):

Ambitious	Imaginative
Broadminded	Independent
Capable	Intellectual
Cheerful	Logical
Clean	Loving
Courageous	Obedient
Forgiving	Polite
Helpful	Responsible
Honest	Self-controlled

In your cluster of four, take turns providing an illustration which shows your feelings about one of these instrumental values.

This exercise should increase your awareness of the root experiences which motivate ourselves and others.

(Based on Milton Rokeach, *The Nature of Human Values* (Boston: The Free Press, Macmillan Publishing Co., 1973)

NOTES

1. Carol Schwalberg, "The Secrets of Better Speech," *Pageant,* October 1961, pp. 9–10.

2. Edwin Kiester, Jr., "Noise, Noise, Noise," *Family Health,* Vol. VI, January 1974, pp. 20–21, 48–52.

3. Jean Piaget, *The Child's Conception of Physical Causality.* London: Routledge and Kegan Paul Ltd., 1930. p. 302.

4. James V. McConnell, *Understanding Human Behavior.* New York: Holt, Rinehart, and Winston, Inc., 1974. p. 755.

5. Eliot Aronson, *The Social Animal.* San Francisco: W. H. Freeman and Company, 1972, p. 80.

6. Ibid. p. 81.

7. Martin Luther King, Jr., Personal Tape Recording, March 6, 1961. See William I. Gorden and Lionel Newsom, "A Stormy Rally in Atlanta," *Today's Speech,* Vol. 11, April 1963, pp. 18–21.

SUGGESTED READINGS

Berlo, David C., *The Process of Communication.* New York: Holt, Rinehart and Winston, 1960.

Brooks, William D., *Speech Communication,* 2nd ed. Dubuque, Iowa: W. C. Brown, 1974.

Clevenger, Theodore, Jr., and Jack Matthews, *The Speech Communication Process.* Glenview, Illinois: Scott, Foresman and Co., 1971.

Peterson, Brent D., Gerald M. Goldhaber, and R. Wayne Pace, *Communication Probes.* Chicago: Science Research Associates, Inc., 1974.

Ross, Raymond S., *Speech Communication: Fundamentals and Practice,* 3rd ed. Englewood Cliffs, N.J.: Prentice-Hall, 1974.

Scheidel, Thomas M., *Speech Communication and Human Interaction.* Glenview, Illinois: Scott, Foresman and Co., 1972.

Swanson, David L., and Jessie G. Delia. *The Nature of Human Communication,* MODCOM. Chicago: Science Research Associates, 1976.

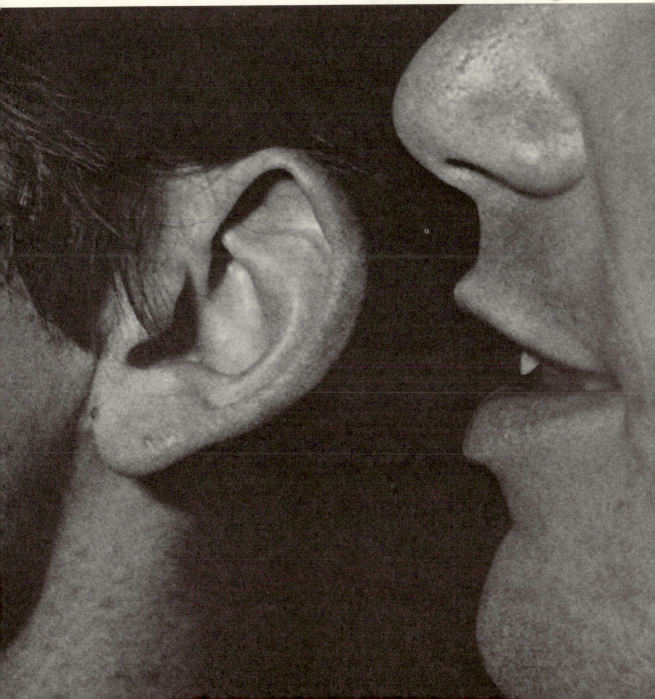

5 listening

FRIENDSHIP

In Bangwa, a country in West Africa, friends are known as twins. Friendship is fervent and visible. Verbalizing affection, giving gifts and going on trips together are important parts of friendship. In other countries friendship is shown in more unusual ways. In one part of Western Africa, men throw excrement at each other and comment loudly about the size of the genitals of their respective parents. In Tanzania, when a man meets a woman who is his special friend, yet not his sexual partner, he may insult her and playfully treat her like a punching bag. Special friendships are celebrated in many cultures.

Yet in America, perhaps because of some of our Judeo-Christian teachings which encourage that we love God first and everyone else equally, special friendship is not so important. Instead, friendship for adults is supposed to be found in the marriage bond or in expedient social-business relationships.

Perhaps the emotional poverty and loneliness of adult life would be lessened if friendship were taken more seriously. When one's identity is a badge number in a large complex organization, belonging might replace alienation if friendships were institutionally encouraged. The Japanese do this by expecting that each employee has a godfather who will intercede for and counsel him throughout his career. Let us find enduring relationships.

Based in large part on Robert Brian, "Somebody Else Should Be Your Own Best Friend," *Psychology Today*, Vol. II, October, 1977, pp. 83–84, 120–121.

In the previous chapter we were concerned with the components of the message process and those things necessary to understand the communication system. And, although we discussed feedback as an integral part of the message process, we did not go into the details of the main prerequisite of feedback, *listening*. In this chapter, we will consider the listening process, the purposes of listening, the need for empathy and definitions, the problems of listening, and ways to improve listening habits. Finally, we will look at the important role interaction and listening play in the development of our self-concept and the maintenance of a healthy approach to dealing with conflict and stress.

Like many of our human experiences, we take listening for granted. Much of the time we think we are listening, we really are not. And when we are listening, we often do not make a conscious effort to select the important things to remember, nor do we decide why we are listening to a particular message or person. As we spend so much of our time listening, it is not surprising that we do take it for granted. Studies have shown that among the verbal activities, we spend 16% of our time reading, 9% writing, 30% talking, and 45% or more in listening.[1] The amount of time we spend engaged in listening may vary somewhat depending on occupation, personality, and other socio-economic factors. It is, however, a crucial factor in human verbal interactions and its absence can usually be the single, most important ingredient in misunderstandings and communication breakdowns.

THE LISTENING PROCESS

Listening is a process of several activities occurring partly in sequence and partly at the same time. Though it may seem to be, listening is not a simple process at all. It is actually a combination of three phases: *reception* (hearing), *perception* (using all the senses as described in Chapter 3), and *interpretation*.

Reception refers to the occurrence of the tympanic membrane (eardrum) being struck by sound waves. The membrane then vibrates and transfers its message to the cranial nerves which lead to the cortex of the brain. There the decoding process and perception and interpretation begin. Volumes have been written about *perception,* but for purposes of understanding listening, we can say it is the process in which all the stimuli being sensed by the body are identified and recognized, to be used in combination with sound in an interpretation process. *Interpretation* is the process of cataloging and arranging all the stimuli (including sound) in a sequence that will permit assigning meaning to the sound and to refine, amplify, or correct this meaning by using all the other senses. This is the phase where all you have learned before, your psychological set, and your experiences from the past begin to influence how you interpret the sound. This is where you begin preparations for delivering feedback.

FACTORS THAT AFFECT LISTENING   It is important to keep in mind that the process just described is ongoing and fleeting. Just as the sequence of events is difficult to arrange into a reliable pattern, so also are the factors that influence listening difficult to categorize. But there are some we know of, and we can try to be aware of them when we are listening.

Loudness and *noise* both have a direct impact on the first phase of listening and they are also influential on the thinking process that goes on in the perception and interpretation phases. We do not need a measuring device to know when someone is speaking too loudly for comfort. This may result in our listening more to how loudly a person is speaking than to what he is saying. A person who finds it necessary to have sounds amplified 15 to 20 percent over the normal hearing range is said to be suffering from a hearing loss.

We experience a large number of unspecified sounds that are too loud to be comfortable. Heavy traffic (both on land and in the air) and industrial activity create a noise backdrop for most city dwellers that is unrelenting competition for normal communication. In conversation in rooms where most outside noise has been eliminated, there are always at least two other kinds of noises. The *extrinsic* noise is made up of background sounds, movements, and other sensations we are perceiving while someone is speaking to us. The *intrinsic* noise (distracting thoughts) is going on in our minds while we are listening.

Prolonged exposure to loud sounds can result in *hearing fatigue,* and studies of people in urban communities who are

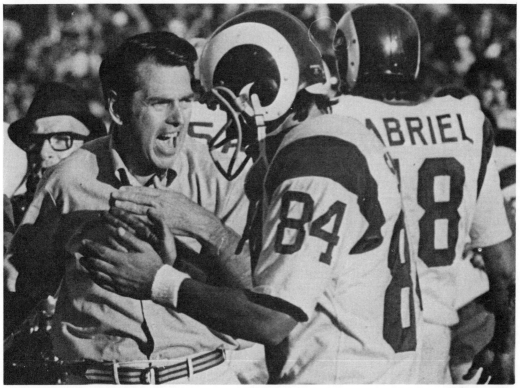

In a football game, the roar of the crowd can often interfere with effective communication among the participants. Since it is impossible to silence the huge crowd, players must learn to attend to only those sounds relevant to their job. Of course, for the home team, the crowd's roar can communicate the excitement which aids victory.

exposed to prolonged loud noise and those exposed to loud rock music indicate that their experiences can result in some long term hearing loss. We will discuss other factors that influence listening later in the chapter when we talk about problems of listening.

PURPOSES OF LISTENING

How we go about listening and how much listening we take for granted will be largely determined by our reasons for listening. There are three generally agreed upon purposes for listening. In the interpersonal setting, we usually are (1) listening to gain information or (2) to evaluate or arrive at some decision. Lastly, (3) we listen just for the fun of it, for the pleasure and enjoyment it brings. But just as the process of listening cannot be easily separated, the reasons for listening can be combined into infinite combinations and do not fall into neatly defined categories. Just the same, we know that the most effective listening and remembering occurs when we listen for a specific purpose and not just for some general or undefinable reason.

LISTENING FOR INFORMATION

A popular radio comedian once said that with the popularity of television, the human body will one day evolve eyes the size of sliced pineapples and ears the size of peas. Perhaps he belittled the ears because he observed such great interest in visual, slapstick comedy and much less interest in verbal humor. When we listen for information, we usually either want to be helped with a problem, receive directions on how to go someplace or do something, or we just want to be informed about the opinions of others, the news of the day, or details of an upcoming examination. But in all listening for information, we usually appear to be more involved than the comedian indicated.

Listening for information requires us to listen accurately and with some organization in mind. Messages come to us in various states, and we usually can remember better what we can put into patterns: sequential, spatial, temporal, or functional (equipment needed, cost and uses). We also remember better that for which we can find a purpose. Motivation to listen is based on use to us.

Listening accurately requires us to be particularly careful to note what the speaker actually said. When we can recall what the speaker claimed to be factual and not just what we think is factual, we know we have listened accurately.

LISTENING TO EVALUATE

This kind of listening is also referred to as *listening critically.* Before we can listen critically we must be able to think critically. The two essential components of critical thinking are analysis (the skill of asking probing questions) and synthesis (the skill of finding meaningful relationships and arriving at solutions or general thoughts about specific data). We usually take pride in our critical thinking ability and it is not too difficult a task to apply it to listening techniques.

In listening critically, there are a few cautionary notes to be observed. When listening to a message intended only to inform, we may miss much of the information if we are busy making judgments about each point. By so doing, we are prone to making snap judgments and misinterpreting the speaker's message. It is usually best to wait until the informative message is completed before judging the validity and usefulness of the newly gained information. Conversely, if we are listening to gather information on which to base a decision or on which to form or change an opinion, we may prefer to evaluate each point as it is presented. For messages that are lengthy and complex, we need to select the data we feel is relevant and discard the rest. Making these distinctions as the information is presented allows us to handle large amounts of important data more easily.

LISTENING FOR ENJOYMENT

This kind of listening is also referred to as *listening for appreciation.* Attending a movie, a play, a poetry reading, listening to the radio or television, and swapping stories of travel or work all fall under this category. Listening is often hard work, particularly listening for information. We need to be able to relax occasionally and just enjoy the company of others. To be listening for enjoyment does not mean we do not learn anything, but it does mean we can select the levels of energy we want to expend on an experience.

EMPATHY AND DEFINITIONS

Earlier in this chapter we discussed the factors that affect listening (loudness, noise, hearing fatigue). There are also two more general problem areas in listening that we must consider in order to more fully understand the listening process. Listening *empathically* and developing common *definitions* can contribute much to our listening ability.

LISTENING EMPATHICALLY

Listening empathically is sometimes called listening *actively.* The empathic or active listener is one who not only listens to verbal cues but also observes all the behavior of the message sender (movements, gestures, facial expressions, posture, etc.). But to listen empathically means much more than just perceiving everything around you and the speaker.

A dear old woman I once knew will always symbolize an empathic, active listener to me. Sarah was a widow with a heart of gold. Her legs were not strong and she had many aches and pains, but she would forget her troubles if she could help others, no matter how many hours it took. And when she was being told anything, she was always ready with some signal of genuine interest and understanding. We cannot all be Sarahs, even a part of the time, but we can be interested in others and genuinely try to understand them. Empathy means sharing feelings and emotions. In order to share those feelings, however, we must try to understand them in others.

The empathic listener is also open-minded. Will Rogers typified the empathic listener when he said, "I never met a man I didn't like." The empathic listener assumes good intentions on the part of the speaker until he is proven wrong. By remaining open to all ideas, the empathic listener avoids biases that could prevent him from sharing the feelings of the speaker.

While it is important to be an understanding listener, it is not always easy. In some, the need for understanding is greater than for others. They may crave sympathy and demand attention beyond that which we are willing to give. We cannot be all things to all people. We must decide how much time we can give others. Sometimes, to meet our goals and responsibilities, we must candidly tell others there is a limit to the time we can spend with them. Openness about such relationships may not be free from some emotional hurt but it will make for a much more genuine and rewarding relationship.

One final word about empathy is important to remember. Just as some peoples' needs for understanding may be greater than others', so are abilities to give sympathy apparently quite varied. Most research on the topic indicates that the ability to predict or judge another's behavior (the sign that is typically used to identify empathic ability) varies widely from person to person but most findings are still incomplete. All that has definitely been established is that people who seem to have good ability to understand others and to predict or describe others' feelings accurately also seem to be most effective in interpersonal relations. And the abilities of these individuals all reflect a readiness to accept new ideas, tolerate imperfections in others, and wait for all available data to be gathered before making judgments about certain matters.

THE NEED FOR DEFINITIONS

In Chapter 4, we discussed the elusive nature of words and symbols. You may recall that we said words alone do not carry much meaning. Careful listening is the method to use to ensure we are in agreement with the speaker and it is the responsibility of everyone in the message process to arrive at common definitions for certain words and ideas. When we are listening for information to arrive at decisions, definitions become especially important.

Straight thinking and straight talk begin with a definition of terms. The unknown in a formula cannot be found until the other symbols are defined. A surveyor cannot find the boundaries of a property you wish to buy until he knows the section markers; nor can a lawyer defend his client until the charges are defined. And we, in our everyday business of living, cannot even get our food prepared to suit our taste unless we agree upon the meaning of such terms as "well done," "medium" and "rare."

"Living together," "open marriage" and "liberated" are rather important terms to define before getting involved with another who may have very different definitions from yours. Such definitions are not found in *Webster's* or *Funk and Wagnall's,* but are worked out by much discussion and consultation. Nor are they definitions which, once defined, are unchangeable. Rather, they become working definitions upon which some very crucial life decisions are based until modified by new experiences.

What, then, are the ways terms might be defined? Any one of these ways may be sufficient to help two parties talk with clarity. Terms may be defined by: (1) opinions from authority, (2) descriptions of function, (3) example, (4) description of what it is not (negation), (5) analogy, and (6) operationally specified behaviors.

Ways of Defining

In any exchange, definitions are either assumed or explicit. In a public hearing before a city council over the inclusion of certain periodicals in the city library, a number of ways of defining occurred.[2] The first speaker, a Pentecostal woman minister, held up a photograph from a magazine she found in the library as an example of what should not be there. It was a tangible definition of obscenity to her (defining by *example*). The second speaker, a dignified woman who was Chairperson of the Library Commission, stated that it was the Commission's responsibility to determine what was "lewd and indecent." Although she did not define what was obscene, she made it clear that the Commission had determined that the magazines were not obscene. (She defined by *negation* and by the *authority* of the Commission.) Yet someone else, a Committee member of "Ban the *Barb*," said that a subscription to the *Barb* read "Not for Sale to Minors," defining that magazine as obscene. (This definition was, for that person, *operational;* anything which was so labeled was obscene.) She added, "When I see dirt, I clean it up. When there is garbage around, it is thrown in the garbage can. Help us, please, to keep the dirt from cluttering the library shelves." (She was now defining by *analogy*.)

An Episcopal priest and a member of a Commission on Public Morals argued that there is no responsible scientific survey which has ever shown that pornography has influenced or stimulated sex crimes. (He did not define pornography but stated what function it will not perform.) Later he read from the *Song of Solomon* references to urine, sexual organs and erotic behavior, and stated that these materials did not hurt anybody. And he added that if the definition of obscenity advocated by those asking the library not to carry magazines which include explicit sexual matter could be applied, then the *Holy Bible* would also have to be banned. (In so doing, he was defining a *functional* result of holding such a definition.) Another speaker stated that Section 311 of the Penal Code specified what, in fact, was punishable by law. (He used this statute as an authority to define.)

DEFINING "OBSCENE FOR CHILDREN"

General	Pictorial or printed matter pertaining to sexual arousal.	USA Children under 16
	Pictorial or printed matter pertaining to sexual arousal such as exposure of the genitals.	USA Children under 16 in the city of Puritanville, Massachusetts
	Printed matter pertaining to exposure of the genitals with the exception of materials specified for health education in a state-approved program.	Our children in this school district
Specific	For example, this picture I found in a magazine in our corner newsstand is what I call obscene for children.	My Johnny and Sally

In this extended debate, there was no consensus possible about what was obscene. Defining in cases such as this is obviously not an objective matter, but it is an important first step in the reflective thinking process. It is part of the orientation period in which people who wish to communicate begin to familiarize themselves with each other's values. When a definition of almost any word is taken from outside the communicator's experience (such as from a dictionary), it is only a beginning for people who are to work together, for they must then agree on what the definition means to *them.*

Once a word has been defined, however, it is not defined absolutely and for all time. Words are like chameleons: they take on different colorings in new surroundings. Moreover, as they age they take on other meanings and personalities. Consider the changing character of a word like "hit" in the various settings of a baseball game, an automobile accident, a date, a crime movie, and a popular song.

Both listening empathically and establishing common definitions are important regardless of the purpose for which we are listening. Yet, there are times when they are more important than others. For example, you may not feel the need to empathize with a political candidate who is trying to convince you to vote for him; or you may not need to concern yourself with definitions when you are listening to a play for the pure enjoyment of the experience; and we do not go about our daily chores with these two listening components in the front of our minds. But in the general scheme of becoming a better communicator and improving our personal relationships, we should be sensitive to the need for empathy and the way we define our world; and we should be constantly improving our methods for employing them.

LISTENING PROBLEMS

Although empathy and language are general problems for all listening, there are more specific problems of listening that we can look for in ourselves and others. These more narrowly defined listening problems are identifiable and we can usually eliminate them by careful observation and good practice habits.

CAPACITY

One problem that is not always detected, but becomes more apparent once you have looked for it, is that of *capacity.* Our brain can only process a certain amount of information at any given time, and it is possible to overload the processing center by trying to listen to too many messages at once. Think of the frustration of listening to a very important announcement while someone is talking to you. Have you ever "shushed" someone during the evening news?

In some, there may be neurological impairments that prevent listening to verbal messages. Stroke victims commonly suffer some temporary or permanent damage to the cranial nerves that carry verbal messages to the brain. Loss of some hearing is common to the aged as nerves within the ear lose their sensitivity. Such loss is not limited to senior citizens, however. Hearing loss is one of the most chronic health problems in the United States with over 13.4 million Americans afflicted with a significant degree of impairment. For hundreds of thousands of people, deafness begins in childhood. But there are warning signs that may help detect difficulties in preschool children. Delayed speech or language development is one of the most important symptoms. Another clue is poor speech or strange sounds from a child.[3] Most public school programs have regularly scheduled hearing examinations for children, and many hard of hearing victims are identified and helped. We can help ourselves communicate better by watching for any sign that a normally spoken message is not being received. And finally, when we know or suspect that someone has a hearing deficiency, we can make a conscious effort to speak loudly and slowly, enunciate clearly, and if there is one, in the direction of their favored ear.

ATTITUDE   Remembering our discussion of psychological set in Chapter 4, our attitude can greatly affect how we receive a message. The problem of attitude is not just apparent in instrumental (persuasive) communication situations; we may be unwilling to listen to certain kinds of messages at all. We may think the topic is dull, unimportant, or we know all there is to know about it. These are reactions everyone is guilty of, but they are to be guarded against. Keeping an open mind can often reward us with surprising, unexpected, and important information; and by forcing ourselves to listen to seemingly unwanted news we may find solutions to problems that have troubled us.

EXPERIENCE AND BACKGROUND   Thinking of psychological set once again, we know that our experience shapes the way we respond to certain messages. But in terms of listening we must be alert to the possibility that we do not know enough about the subject for the speaker's message to be meaningful. Another possibility is the language being used is too technical for us (such as an audiophile discussing the components of a sophisticated stereo system). Although we may be interested in learning something about stereos, we may find listening in this situation very frustrating and we may tune out the speaker altogether.

MAINTAINING ATTENTION

Earlier in the chapter we discussed the problem of noise and its impact on our ability to hear. Closely related to intrinsic noise is the problem of maintaining attention. Our thought processes work so rapidly that most of us are able to comprehend messages much faster than others can send them. As a result, we often find our attention wandering while we wait for the speaker to formulate his ideas and send another message. In addition, in interpersonal relations, a common cause of communication breakdown is our not listening to another because we are too busy thinking of what we are going to say as soon as the speaker takes a breath.

DEFINING PURPOSE

When we do not know why we are listening to a message, we have difficulty organizing the speaker's main points and concentrating on them. We may focus on unimportant data or derive an

This special education teacher is emphasizing the word "apple" as she attempts to teach autistic children how to talk. The severely autistic is virtually incapable of communication with others, apparently "lost" in what may be a highly creative and complex inner world. Though the cause of the disease is not known, teachers of the autistic have stressed language skills as being the fundamental step toward normalcy.

THE MESSAGE BEHIND THE QUESTION

In everyday conversation, questions may veil our real purposes to manipulate. Being questioned, therefore, often makes one feel uneasy, resistent and even hostile. At school, most questions, for example, seem designed to point up what we don't know rather than what we do know. When we question, the focus shifts from us'to the person who must answer. We thus often avoid what's going on inside ourselves. Our feelings become less important than external facts. To avoid discounting our feelings and escaping from expressing them when we feel a question coming on, we could start *listening* to ourselves. Then identify those feelings and express them in statements rather than hiding behind a question.

Here are some everyday questions that work better as honest statements:

What time is it?
I'm tired. I'd like to go home now.

Is it far?
I don't feel up to a long trip this weekend.

Do you love me?
I wish you'd spend more time with me. You work every day and read in the evenings.

How much did you pay?
I hope we have some money left for the rest of the week.

Is it good?
I need to know if you like my soup, if I made it the way you prefer.

Jacques Lalanne, "Attack by Question", *Psychology Today*, Vol. 9, No. 6 November, 1975, p. 134.

altogether different meaning than the one the speaker intended. Have you ever listened to a friend and asked yourself, "Why is she telling me this?" Deciding on what the speaker's purpose is helps considerably in determining what our purpose is for listening.

In public speaking situations, it is often easier to decipher the speaker's purpose than in interpersonal ones. In such instances we may have to ask probing questions, agree on definitions, and empathize as much as possible before we are able to fully appreciate the speaker's intent.

MEMORY   Closely related to defining your purpose for listening is the problem of remembering all that is included in a message. This may not be quite apparent in interpersonal settings, but in more formal situations, such as classroom lectures or public speeches, it can become a problem. Earlier in the chapter we observed that motivation can influence how well you recall. When you know why you are listening to a message, it is easier to separate the important ideas from the less important, and to remember them.

When we describe the tendencies of disturbed people to talk too much or too little, we are describing much which passes for normal social conversation. Let us analyze one aspect of the cause of this problem. I call it "blurred listening." The blurred listener is in a sense anonymous. He loses his identity in the conversational circle and feeds on the drama of others. His characteristics seem innocuous: he is agreeable, attentive, understanding and seemingly empathic. But by being the seemingly ideal listener, he fails in exploring the topics more deeply. All is too well and issues never develop.

SOCIAL CONVERSATION

The blurred listener knows the importance of posture. He assumes a reflective stance, makes appropriate gestures, even maintains eye contact that signals he is involved, but actually he is not. He contributes such forgettable responses as "um," "uh huh," "of course," "naturally," and "that's to be expected." He never disagrees, offers a controversial opinion, or becomes argumentative.

We all may blur in certain stages of fitting into a social situation. But when we have a sense of our own worth, we no longer hide our own opinions. Rather, we exchange and test them with others. Characteristics of healthy and disturbed listeners in conversation have been effectively contrasted by Dommick A. Barbara, psychoanalyst and speech consultant:

> Listening is most effective when one is closest to being his real self. The effective listener is one who feels himself able to express his opinions openly and to meet justifiable criticism, anger, or hostility. On the other hand, a person who feels divided and disorganized is unable to make use of all his resources. His entire organism, especially his hearing, becomes defective in function. The communication system breaks down as messages are poorly received and erroneously transmitted to others. As a result, both speaker and listener become tense and anxious, feedback systems become jammed, misunderstanding occurs, and the ultimate situation is one of confusion and misunderstanding, anger, and hostility.[4]

The end result of how a rumor gets changed as it passes from one person to another points up some interesting characteristics of people and what they remember. Generally, a story that moves from one telling to another loses many details. Those details that remain are sharpened by stressing the numbers of people, the things involved, and what was said or done. The time in which the event took place tends to be the immediate present.

RUMORS

Details concerned with movement and action are remembered well. The setting is often recalled accurately, particularly when it is described at the beginning. Retellers of a story, however, tend to extend, explain and interpret to help make the story complete.

Rumors tend to be shortened and sharpened in accordance with the attitudes and life–styles of the tellers. Many items become reported as one would *expect* them to happen, rather than as they *actually* occurred. The tellers change the wording of the story to fit their own vocabulary. In addition, they often change the stories to fit their interests and prejudices. A rumor is carried most accurately, obviously, when it involves the life of the teller.[5]

What might this knowledge about the transmission of rumors mean to us now that we know it? First, it should influence the way we listen. We should expect that more or less happened than was told. We should expect that repeaters of a story sharpen those details that capture their attention and fit their attitudes. Second, we should realize the need to probe for more information to ascertain the truth of a situation. Third, as transmitters we can be aware of these tendencies to bring our own values into a message, and consequently, improve our reporting of an event or secondhand message we are passing on.

DIALOGUE   Dialogue is much more than simple social conversation. It is a term which has come to mean that time when persons truly come in mental contact with one another. The theologian Martin Buber proposed that dialogue occurs when the divine in one man addresses and responds to the divine in another.[6]

Parallel concerns for meaningful human exchange are evident in dissimilar movements: disciples of charismatic religious leaders, the political cell, the Round Table of the Air, The Great Books Study Groups, and more recently, the various consciousness-raising groups. Robert Hutchins, while President of the University of Chicago, popularized the idea that the quality of a people could be no greater than the exposure of that people to the ideas of the great minds of the world's civilizations.[7] Upon his retirement he established the Center for Democratic Institutions around the concept that bringing great minds together to talk is an essential step in creating a world free from starvation, fear and war.

Dialogue is not to be construed as avoidance of disagreement, but as contact of one mind and spirit with another. Dialogue is openness. Facade is torn away. Masks crack and personal statements and questions are all that matter. Dialogue has been aptly characterized by Richard Johannesen as:

1   genuineness,
2   accurate empathic understanding,
3   unconditional positive regard,
4   presentness, i.e., full concentration, a participant willing to reveal himself,
5   spirit of mutual equality, and
6   a supportive psychological climate, i.e., one that allows free expression and avoids judgments that stifle.[8]

Monologue is talking *at.* It is manipulative and linear. Dialogue consists, rather, of an interaction between and among people who prize each other's essential dignity and mutual welfare. People engaged in dialogue do not avoid trying to influence. Genuineness implies saying, "Here I stand, here are my feelings and thoughts. Test them. But remain free to dispute and reject them."

Dialogue is more than tuning into another's mind. It is a reaching out to another's feelings and aspirations. How often do we ask, "How do you *feel?*" and then genuinely listen to the answer? Dialogue is an evolution of trust and disclosure—a sharing of dreams; and it is the setting for extensive use of *empathic listening.*

SELF CONCEPT AND INTERACTION

The basis of good mental health is a good self concept. Our self concept begins very early. Every baby comes equipped for a conversation with its mother. The dialogue of the first 18 months is critical. If the infant is deprived of formation of close human bonds a chain of emotional misfortune will follow through adulthood. Emotionally deprived children develop a powerful appetite for strong sensations such as those found in drugs and brutality. Human contact is both a biological and psychological need.[9]

Emotional deprivation in youth and adult life also is costly. Loneliness and social isolation too often chain into unhappiness, depression, physical illness, suicide, bizarre homicide and dying of a broken heart. The medical researchers who have studied the leading causes of death in America, heart disease and cancer, to fire and auto accidents, find mortality of the divorced, widowed and unmarried are two to five times higher than for people who are not alone. Of course smoking, poor diet, excess weight and failure to exercise take their toll, but it is the broken and lonely heart that is the number one killer.[10]

INEFFECTIVE COPING WITH STRESS ON SELF

The self concept continues to be shaped by the dynamics of the work setting. In that interpersonal field, both positive and negative feedback interact with one's self image. Feedback which is consistent with one's good image of self tends to increase one's feeling of self-worth. When one receives feedback which is inconsistent with a good self image, feelings of self-worth are decreased. The individual who receives negative feedback must find ways of dealing with this stress upon his psyche. Under stress people may elect defensive and ineffective ways of coping. Virginia Satir suggests that four major ineffective methods of coping are: placating, blaming, distracting and computer-like responding.[11]

Placating. The placater tends to agree even when he does not agree. He wants so much to avoid disagreement and fighting, that whatever another says is OK. He or she is forever blaming himself and apologizing so much that others feel sorry for him or feel guilty. He is passive, dependent, withdrawing, faceless, a people pleaser and a yes-man. He hides his own feelings by praising, agreeing, humoring and consoling. He counts himself out. "You count, I don't count." He plays underdog.

Blaming. The blamer is as disagreeable, bossy, and cantankerous as the placater is agreeable and phony. He finds fault, is aggressive and rebellious. He says, "I count, you don't count." He is judging, advising, dominating and puts others down. Almost every aggressive roadblock to communication is his: ordering, directing, commanding, threatening, moralizing, preaching, judging, criticizing, name-calling, ridiculing and shaming. He attends neither to the content or the feelings of other's messages, but rather discredits and devalues. He must be top dog.

Distracting. The distracter is always changing the subject. He is busy, busy, busy. In his hyperactivity he escapes discomforting feedback. He may take on a "live it up" or "who cares" posture. He ignores cues from others regarding their own needs. His roadblocks to communication are interrupting, diverting, and withdrawal. His frenetic flight behavior may be a plea for attention. He is not underdog or top dog but rather is a barking dog.

Analyzing. In a cool computer-like fashion the analyzer says, "Let's be reasonable." By analyzing he protects himself from his own hurt feelings. He has the right words and can find an intellectual explanation for everything. His head trip is so pronounced that he is boring, bland and devoid of emotion. His roadblocks to good communication are interpreting, diagnosing, lecturing, and logical arguments. He is the family psychologist, the little professor, the disqualifier. Gestures are absent or neutral. He is a cool poodle.

EFFECTIVE COPING WITH STRESS ON SELF

Positive coping requires a riskier posture. The mask is cracked. He is real and he levels with others about his feelings, values and opinions. He can express either positive or negative feelings without trying to make points or put another down. He can criticize without blaming. He can shift subjects without trying to get off the hook. His messages are straight rather than circuitous, and yet not without tact. He can analyze without turning off his feelings. What he says is truth for him, without contriving ways to cover up feelings of weakness or helplessness. His body is expressive and congruent with his words. He is open, alive, trustworthy and you know where he stands. He says, "I'm OK, you're OK," but he does not see the world through rose-colored glasses.

Effective coping begins with experiencing rather than covering up one's own feelings. Others do have their bad parts. A person who practices leveling communication may find the following steps helpful:

1 Describe specifically the behavior you dislike.
2 Express the feelings you have about that disliked behavior.
3 Suggest a better alternative, and
4 Involve the other person by coming up with alternative solutions.

Levelers are essential to creating healthy environments. Feedback, to be really reinforcing of behaviors we like, must respond to other's good parts. Here are three simple steps to make that positive feedback more effective.

1 Describe the behaviors you like specifically.
2 Express the way the liked behavior makes you feel, and
3 Encourage the other person to keep doing those good things.[12]

REFLECTIONS ON LISTENING ATTENTIVELY

1. To effectively communicate with others when there are numerous distractions that usually take my attention away, I will:
   A. Concentrate on every word and ask to have a sentence repeated if it is blocked out by some loud noise.
   B. Keep my eyes on the person during our talk.
   C. Listen critically to everything that is said.
   D. Continue the conversation even if there is a distraction.
   E. Ignore all inside distractions, like other thoughts or tensions.
2. What I can do towards improving my communication:
   A. Talk to people in less distracting surroundings.
   B. Keep up with the person's rate of speech and not feel embarrassed to ask him to slow down if I can't keep up.
   C. Not look away at the slightest noise.
   D. Ask people I know well if they've noticed any difference in my attention span.
3. Signs that the goal has been successfully achieved:
   A. A person who told me I was obnoxious three months ago, solely because I was easily distracted, noticed a change.
      1. I looked at him the whole time we talked.
      2. I found that he was more interested in my conversation when it was directed to him.
   B. My grades are averaging out better.
      1. They have become better since I took the time to really listen to the professors and block out distractions.
      2. My complete attention is on the speaker during a lecture now and I find I can recall facts better during an exam.
      3. I've found that my exams are easier to take because I have learned to ignore all distractions.
   C. I feel people are responding much better to me.
      1. I hear people out instead of trying to get in the last word.
      2. Patience was gained through experience.
   D. My mother noticed I would let her finish talking before I would leave the room.
      1. At supper, I sit at the table until we are all finished.
      2. We no longer fight because I would not hear her out.
      3. Before, I would jump to the wrong conclusions.
      4. She told me I had changed my attitude towards her because we are getting along much better.
      5. She also said I was not as stubborn in my views.
   E. A girl friend of mine told me I didn't play the deaf role anymore.
      1. I would keep all my attention on her, because before I would have to ask her to repeat herself after I had been distracted by something.
      2. Even as we walked someplace, I would keep my eyes on her so I wouldn't lose the conversation.
      3. She really appreciated it.

—This outline is a report on a listening project by Linda M. Schultz

WAYS TO IMPROVE LISTENING

The listening problems we have just surveyed are not always present in every communicative experience. And as we noted earlier, we cannot be constantly thinking about how we are listening or we will miss a good many of the messages being sent. But we can take stock of our listening habits and try to improve on them. Here is a list of suggestions that can help you improve your listening effectiveness in interpersonal settings as well as in more formal situations such as classroom lectures or public speeches.

Consider the advantages of knowing many things about many topics. In conversation, a broad knowledge of several topics can help you feel more comfortable and make you a more interesting person to be with. One method of keeping an open mind is to ask honest questions, ones that reflect your own true interest about a subject and not ones that you think will appear intelligent, sophisticated or what others are interested in.

DEVELOP AN OPEN MIND

Try to choose a place for your conversations as free from physical and psychological distractions as possible. Close out noise from surrounding areas and in interpersonal settings, choose a place to have serious discussions that will allow for full concentration by you, your partner, and friends.

PROPER SETTING

Be aware of your biases and guard against letting them prejudice the message. Although you may have held a certain opinion for a long time, each new speaker deserves the chance to tell you what they know about a topic. The advantages of listening without bias are similar to those of having an open mind. New insights may be available to you, and you may discover someone whose company and support you appreciate.

BIAS

In public and formal settings, do not be afraid to take notes. Taking notes can help you focus on the main points of the message. Later, when referring to your notes, it will help you organize the message so you can remember it more accurately and

TAKE NOTES

evaluate it more objectively. As you list points in your notes, ask yourself about them. Consider how well the ideas fit together and how well the evidence supports the points as compared to what you already know.

RESERVE JUDGMENT   Do not make up your mind until you have heard the entire message. Although you may think you know the direction in which the speaker is headed, he may introduce new information at the end of the message that will require you to reconsider. By reserving judgment, you also give yourself a chance to reflect on all the data of your own concerning the message.

DISCOVER COMMON GROUND   Ask yourself what things you know about the speaker that you share with him or her. While you are searching for things in common with a public speaker, consider the way he presents himself. Be careful to look beyond dress, to language usage, posture, gestures and movements; and any other mannerisms that may give you more insight into background, personality, and character. Certainly we all know the danger of forming opinions based on first impressions, but the empathic listener keeps that in mind while searching for any signs that will help him get closer to the speaker's feelings. One good suggestion is to put yourself in the speaker's shoes. And when you have begun to develop empathic listening, balance it with discriminative (critical) listening.[13]

REMAIN SILENT   Do not be afraid to remain silent. If you find yourself in the middle of a conversation that you do not feel genuinely a part of, or when you really are not motivated to join, do not try to fake interest by offering thoughtless comments. You are an interesting person in your own right, and defensive or inadequate feelings about not taking part in certain conversations will not help you in your efforts to develop empathy, understanding, and clarity.

SUMMARY

Listening is a process just as message sending is. It is made up of three general phases. *Reception:* hearing the message; *perception:* using all the other senses to help refine the message; *interpretation:* decoding all the signals by indexing, cataloging and arranging them in a sequence that will allow us to assign meanings. Some of the immediate factors that affect listening are loudness and noise, and hearing fatigue.

The three general purposes of listening are: *listening for information; listening to evaluate;* and *listening for enjoyment.* All three of the reasons for listening may overlap and be operative at one time, but we know that we listen more effectively and accurately when we have a goal or purpose in listening. Purpose is also important to remembering the message.

Two closely related concepts of listening that are influential in all kinds of listening are empathy and the need for definitions. To *listen empathically* means to become psychologically involved with the speaker. It means that you try to understand and share his feelings and appreciate the point of view he is expressing. The need for definitions is apparent when you consider all the different possible meanings a single word can have. And in order to share someone's feelings, the first step is to be sure you both have the same meaning of crucial words in mind.

The problems of listening are probably as many and varied as there are people in the world, but for our purposes we identified six general problems: (1) capacity, (2) attitude, (3) experience and background, (4) maintaining attention, (5) defining purpose, and (6) memory. Social conversation, dialogue and rumor were introduced as three common settings in which listening problems are easily observed. Good mental health is based on a good self-concept. When the self-concept is under stress, one tends to turn toward ineffective coping communication: placating, blaming, distracting and analyzing. Positive coping requires openness in communication.

Finally, we suggested six things to do that can help improve our listening effectiveness: (1) developing an open mind, (2) freeing the setting from distractions, (3) being aware of our own biases, (4) taking notes, (5) reserving judgment, (5) searching for common ground, and (6) remaining silent on occasion.

Now that we have covered verbal and nonverbal messages, and looked closely at the listening process, we are ready to begin a closer examination of the communication process in such interpersonal settings as dyads, small groups, and larger working groups.

INITIATIVES

INITIATING ACTION 1   *Checking*. Divide into groups of four. Each member should complete this statement: This place is like a _____ because . . . (In a short paragraph describe this place.)

To increase our skills in listening accurately, practice summarizing what the speaker expressed as factual and then ask him if your feedback summary was what he said. Do not be surprised if the speaker says, "No, I did not say that." The feedback was an abstraction, and/or the speaker may have meant to say something different from what he said. The exercise, therefore, may be valuable in helping both the speaker and listener to be more accurate. After each statement, another member takes his turn at feedback.

INITIATING ACTION 2   *Defining*. In clusters of four or five, define "obscenity." Remember there are many ways to define a term: by (*a*) authority, (*b*) function—what it does, (*c*) example, (*d*) negation—what it is not, (*e*) analogy, and (*f*) operationally specified behaviors. Now write your definition on the board. Take turns having a member of another group read the definition and then, based on what he reads, take a position in support of or contrary to what he sees implied in the definition. The group that prepared the definition should then react to the position taken: Did the member of the outside group understand your definition? The important lesson in such an exercise is the realization that (*a*) a word must be narrowly defined if it is to be correctly used and, (*b*) a defining word is not simply a pronouncement of meaning, but an exchange and agreement upon symbols.

INITIATING ACTION 3   *Exercise in Description of Feelings*.
Step 1. Break into clusters of four students. One member of the cluster should go first. He should complete this statement in two minutes.

One thing I did this last week was _____

_____

Because _____

_____

Step 2. After he has completed the above statement in a paragraph or two, a second member in the cluster briefly describes the *feelings* he felt as the person talked. Remember, empathic feelings come from getting into another person's feelings, words, tone of voice, rate of speaking, posture, facial expression, and muscle tension.

Step 3. After step 2, the first person confirms, modifies or adds to the feedback to help the listener know if his feedback came close. Sometimes the feedback helps the sender to better understand his own feelings. The exercise proceeds to the next person in turn, in the same format.

Broadening Your Interests. Jot down a list of things you don't like. Follow it with a list of things you do like. Compare your list with that made by one other member of the class. Place a plus beside those items you both like and a minus beside those you both dislike. How many such items are there? Now draw a picture of your relationship.

INITIATING ACTION 4

From Conversation to Dialogue. Keep a log of your own attempts to improve your conversation skills. Particularly, reflect upon and describe those times when you experienced dialogue. A sample of a student's log is included here to use as a guide and to see what someone else experienced.

INITIATING ACTION 5

A STUDENT'S LOG

Goal: To be more at ease, be myself, and say what I want to say when I meet people for the first time.

Reason: When I first meet people I have a very hard time being myself. The person that I am when I am around strangers is definitely not at all like me. When I am around strangers I am very quiet and sober, when actually I border on being loud and sometimes overly comical. When I am around strangers, I can't express how I really feel, when actually I am a very opinionated person.

How To Achieve This Goal

Most of what I have to do is psychological training, since that is the root of my problem.

1. I must put myself in a situation where I am meeting new people all the time. (I am now doing that as vice-chairman of the Commuters and Off-Campus Students Organization.)

2. I must learn not to worry about my physical appearance. This is the hardest thing for me, since I have no idea how to get over it other than lose the undesired weight (which for me would be harder than any speech correction!).

3. I have got to learn to pretend that the people around me are all long known friends, whether they are or not. If I do this, then I am able to communicate with others on a normal level, which I think is pleasing. I can do this when there are people around that I know, but it is really hard—impossible in fact—when I am surrounded by unknowns.

4. When meeting strangers, I must train myself to the idea that I am what I am, I say what I feel, and if a stranger doesn't like it, we'll not be friends anyway. (Being fake is letting the person like someone that you really aren't. A front can't be kept up forever and the friendship will eventually end.)

5. I must overcome the fear of rejection. I must understand that I have friends that like me for what I am, and that there are other people in the world that would like me for the same reasons another person rejected me. Nobody has, or could have, every person in the world as a friend.

Tuesday, Oct. 16

The Commuter Student Services has a room off the cafeteria reserved every Tuesday and Wednesday so commuters can have lunch together.

I took a friend with me and I met Jack Smith. I felt a lot of anxiety but I was able to be myself although it took a great deal of concentration. It wasn't at all natural. I included him a lot in the conversation.

Friday, Oct. 19

I was invited to a party hosted by one of my friends who does not share many friends of mine. I wasn't going to go because I didn't want to be around a bunch of people I didn't know.

Well, I went to the party and it was full of strangers. I felt very uneasy at the start of the party. It seemed like everyone knew each other except me, which made me feel like everyone was sitting around saying, "Who's the fat dude?"

Knowing that I was trying to improve a problem made me feel even more anxious, even at the point of shaking hands. Well, as the night went on, I opened up to people.

I think I was myself. But I didn't want to be different from the others! I had a good time so I guess I was successful in being myself.

Tuesday, Oct. 23

Went to the Commuter lunch again, because it seemed like a good place to meet strangers. The anxiety was great again.

I noted something I did; I introduced myself as vice-chairman of the Commuters and Off-Campus Students Organization. The whole conversation was around COSO. I just wonder what we would have talked about if I introduced myself as just myself and not the vice-chairman.

I think that the person didn't really get to know me but he got to know a little about COSO. I really do think I used my title as a crutch.

I failed miserably at being myself, because I put on an air of intelligence that I don't normally exhibit.

Wednesday, Oct. 24

A new girl started work today at the library. I had to train her. After we finished the training session and she completed her test, we just talked about each other. I really got to know a lot about her, even though it probably was stuff she'd tell anyone. I also wasn't intimate with her, but she got to know a lot about me. I think we will get to be friends if she gets to keep her job. (She nearly flunked the test!)

I thought maybe my training her may have affected her openness with me, but not really. I think it was my initial openness that got us started. I think I was successful today but the anxiety was still there.

Friday, Oct. 26

Got into a terrible argument today with the chairperson of COSO. I never said what I wanted to say; I guess my anger interfered with my ability to speak to the core of the problem.

We ended the argument not mad at each other, but both of us probably felt bad about the argument. At least I did. Nothing was resolved. The point or the core of the argument was never discussed.

Saturday, Oct. 27

I worked from 9:00 AM until noon today, then I went to the lobby of the Student Center to wait for a friend. While I was sitting by the fountain, I started a conversation with a guy next to me about how I hated to wait for people who were late.

This was really good for me, because I initiated the conversation. Didn't get to know the person at all but enjoyed meeting him. My friend came a half hour late but no conflict resulted, as he had a good excuse. He had a flat tire.

Monday, Oct. 29

Met a girl in chemistry class today. We talked about how much we hated chemistry. We had one other point in common: we were both food and nutrition majors.

She initiated the conversation, so I had no anxiety about her not wanting to talk to me.

Thursday, Nov. 1

A student came into the COSO office today with a housing complaint. After we got the complaint, and took care of it, I decided to initiate a discussion over the cost of going to college. Somehow the conversation evolved to the philosophy of education.

I learned a lot about the girl through her opinions, and she learned a lot about me. The conversation led to her promising to come up and help out at COSO. I think I was successful, as I really was "myself."

Wednesday, Nov. 21

I went home today to find my family's living room full of very attractive coeds from my sister's college. Today is my sister's birthday and she came home to celebrate the event with her friends. Well, normally I would have avoided the room completely, but I went right in and sat down.

Found out they were all Alpha Xi's, their majors, *etc.* We talked about all sorts of things. They wanted me to go downtown with them, but I didn't go! (My sister can't cut loose with me around.)

Campus Talk. Conversation needs active listening and responding. One study found that supportive responses tend to increase the number of opinions ("I think" type statements).[14] The supportive responses used included verbal and nonverbal agreement such as, "Yes, you're right," "That's so," smiles, and nods. The study, in addition, demonstrates that withdrawal of such supportive behavior and/or disagreeing with opinions expressed tended to extinguish opinions given. Some people in the study became disturbed or angry. When a conversation partner elicits silence, he frequently expresses some reason to leave—"to study," "to go to dinner." As a class, experiment with making conversation with a friend or new acquaintance on a campus bus, in the student union, etc. Half of the students should try to increase the rate of

INITIATING ACTION 6

opinion triggered by supportive responses such as: "Yes, you're right," "That's for sure," smiles, and nods. The other half should paraphrase (briefly repeat and rephrase opinions expressed). In the first five minutes do not use supportive responses and keep track of the number of opinions expressed ("I think" type phrases) by seeming to idly doodle on a note pad or margin in a book. In the second five minutes use the supportive responses and see if the rate of opinion statements rises. Probably it is unnecessary and unwise to disclose to the friend or new acquaintance what you are doing. Class members who wish to carry the experiment a bit further may, after the reinforcement with supportive responses has been working, then try the extinguishing behavior: e.g., withdraw the supportive responses and/or disagree with the opinions given. Of course, all of this, including the recording of the rate of opinions given, will have to be subtly and unobtrusively executed.

INITIATING ACTION 7   *Rumors.* Some member of the class or the instructor should clip an article from the newspaper and count the details within it. Five or six members of the class should be asked to volunteer for an exercise in rumor transmission. They are asked to wait in the hall. A first person is then invited in from the hall to hear the article. Upon hearing it, he tells it to a second person invited in, and so forth, until all have heard it. Meanwhile, the class members record those details which suffer from shortening and sharpening. If possible, video or audio tape the original and subsequent telling. Afterwards dicuss the characteristics of rumors, and how these principles apply to both interpersonal and public communication.

INITIATING ACTION 8   *Saying Goodbye.* Ending a relationship, even temporarily, may be uncomfortable. People take leave of each other for a number of reasons: one or both tire of conversation, may have vocational obligations, or may desire social interaction with others. Terminating interpersonal interaction usually balances making oneself unavailable and assuring the other that the interpersonal relationship is a good one. In order to learn more about saying goodbye let's do some field work. Observe a number of conversations in which you and your friend engage. Note the cues signaling:

(a) *Inaccessibility,* such as: quick movements like a slap on the side of the arm; an embrace; handshake; looking away; glancing at one's watch; shift of position preliminary to rising to one's feet, etc.

(b) *Supportiveness*, such as: expressions with superlatives (fantastic, swell); inquiries about the other person's professional or personal life in contrast to the subject of the conversation; expressions of appreciation and of goodwill—nodding, smiling, winking, touching, etc.[15]

"I-Talk." Pick out a controversial subject and carry on a two-minute conversation about it. Deliberately avoid the use of "I," "me," or "my." Discuss the problems of leaving oneself out of the conversation. Were you able to do so? Was the conversation interesting?

INITIATING ACTION 9

You might be interested to learn that an analysis of normal American usage of "I" is approximately 4,000 "I"s per million words; and that an anlysis of the taped discussions between President Nixon and those who spoke with him in his oval office revealed that Mr. Nixon used the word "I" some 4,390 times in 100,000 words.

Again, discuss a controversial topic. Use the "I" personal pronoun. Notice when you do and don't use it. Have an observer tally the times you use such terms as "People think," "One would think," "We feel," as compared to "I" statements.

Blind Walk. Pair off. Touch fingertips. One member of the pair serves as a guide; the other member with eyes closed follows in a short walk. Change roles, only this time the person with eyes closed holds the guide's arm. Take a walk around the surroundings. Get a drink of water. Play the roles seriously. Discuss your *earning* and *giving* of trust.

INITIATING ACTION 10

Fall. Approximately fifteen people stand in a close circle. One member of the class stands with arms folded, eyes closed, in the center. He or she, with feet in one position, permits his body to fall. The group catches and transfers the body to another. Note the feelings of hesitancy and trust which grow with the earned successful care of that person. Several persons may wish to try this experience.

INITIATING ACTION 11

Rocked. Six to eight persons form a hand stretcher. One person is then gently rocked by those composing the stretcher. Discuss the feelings you have about taking part in this childhood game. Is there a good feeling that comes over one from being cared for gently, and from giving that care?

INITIATING ACTION 12

NOTES

1. C. H. Weaver, *Human Understanding: Processes and Behavior*, Indianapolis, Ind.: Bobbs-Merrill Co., 1972, p. 72.

2. "What Shall They Read," Pacifica Radio Station, San Francisco, 1971 (Record).

3. Vernon McCay and Judith Athey cited in "Deafness in Children Often Overlooked," *The Los Angeles Times*, December 5, 1976, Part IV, p. 4.

4. Dommick Barbara, "Listening With a Modest Ear," *Today's Speech,* Vol. IX, February, 1961, p. 3.

5. T. M. Higham, "The Experimental Study of the Transmission of Rumour," *British Journal of Psychology*, Vol. 42, (March-May, 1951), pp. 42–55; also reprinted in *Interpersonal Communication Survey and Studies*, edited by Dean C. Barnlund (Boston: Houghton Mifflin Co., 1968), pp. 273–291.

6. Martin Buber, *I and Thou*, translated by Ronald George Clark Smith (Edinburg: T. and T. Clark, 1937). Also see Reuell Howe, *The Miracle of Dialogue* (New York: The Seabury Press, 1963). Howe defines dialogue as "the serious address and response between two or more persons, in which the being and truth of each is confronted by the being and truth of the other (p. 4)."

7. Robert H. Hutchins, "The Great Conversation," in *The Great Books of the Western World*, Vol. I, Morton Adler, Associate Editor, p. 1.

8. Richard L. Johannesen, "The Emerging Concept of Communication as Dialogue," *The Quarterly Journal of Speech*, Vol. LVII, December, 1971, pp. 373–382.

9. Selma Fraiberg, *Every Child's Birthright:* In *Defense of Mothering*. New York: Basic Books, 1977.

10. James J. Lynch, *The Broken Heart: The Medical Consequences of Loneliness*. New York: Basic Books, 1977.

11. Virginia Satir, *People-Making*. Palo Alto, California: Science and Behavior Books, Inc., 1972.

12. C. U. Shantz and K. E. Wilson, "Training Communication Skills in Young Children," *Child Development,* 1972, Vol. 43, pp. 693–698.

13. Larry Barker, *Listening Behavior*, Chapter 5, Englewood Cliffs, N.J.: Prentice-Hall, 1971.

14. William I. Verplanck, "The Control of the Content of Conversation," *Journal of Abnormal and Social Psychology,* Vol. 51, No. 3, 1955, pp. 668–676.

15. Mark L. Knapp, Roderick P. Hart, Gustav W. Frederick and Gary Shulman, "The Rhetoric of Goodbye: Verbal and Nonverbal Correlates of Human Leave-Taking," *Speech Monographs,* Vol. 40, August, 1973, pp. 182–198.

SUGGESTED READINGS

Adler, Ron, and Neil Towne, *Looking Out/Looking In.* San Francisco, Calif.: Rinehart Press, 1975.

Barker, Larry L., *Listening Behavior.* Englewood Cliffs, N.J.: Prentice-Hall, 1971.

Brown, Charles T., and Paul W. Keller, *Monologue to Dialogue.* Englewood Cliffs, N.J.: Prentice-Hall, 1973.

Johnson, David W., *Reaching Out.* Englewood Cliffs, N.J.: Prentice-Hall, 1972.

Keltner, John W., *Elements of Interpersonal Communication,* 2nd ed. Belmont, Calif.: Wadsworth Publishing Co., 1973.

Matson, Floyd W., and Ashley Montagu, eds., *The Human Dialogue: Perspectives on Communication.* New York: The Free Press, 1967.

Mortensen, C. David., *Communication: The Study of Human Interaction.* New York: McGraw-Hill, 1972.

Oliver, Robert T., *Conversation: The Development and Expression of Personality.* Springfield, Illinois: Charles C. Thomas, 1961.

Samples, Bob, and Bob Wohlford, *Opening.* Reading, Mass.: Addison-Wesley, 1973.

Sathre, Freda S., Ray W. Olson, and Clarissa I. Whitney, *Let's Talk: An Introduction to Interpersonal Communication.* Glenview, Illinois: Scott, Foresman and Co., 1973.

Wilmot, William C., *Dyadic Communication: A Transactional Perspective.* Reading, Massachusetts: Addison-Wesley, 1975.

6 communication in groups

Understanding the world and our relationship to it is obviously influenced by much more than just our perception and recall of stimuli. What role we play in life's drama is dependent on our human relationships; and as we grow to understand the world more accurately, we often alter or modify this role. How we evaluate our behavior and find our identity is, to a large degree, determined by how we compare ourselves and interact with others. For these reasons, and for many others, we seek out people and spend large amounts of time in their company.

The Reference Group   Most of the time we choose (although not in the case of our families) those with whom we wish to associate. These associations can be categorized into various kinds of groups. The smallest group would be, naturally, that with just one other person. The next larger group is that of three people, followed by small groups of even more people. We will look at the interactions within each of the group categories and their reasons for being in this chapter, but one that is most important to us is called the *reference group.* Even though we may not know all the members of our own reference group, it is the group we use to evaluate our status. Social psychologists have determined that we all tend to compare ourselves with certain people or groups rather than the entire population, and we use that group as a standard to gain our own status and guide our own behavior. The categories of comparison may include social standing, prestige, popularity, intellectual or economic ability, and even occupational status.

A college student may, for example, be in the 90th percentile on all standard test scores and be aware that she is academically more successful than 90% of all other college students who have taken the same tests. Yet, she may be unhappy because her friends have done even better. These people are her reference group and they, not the total population of college students, function as her criterion in judging academic ability.[1]

Of course, we do not only compare ourselves with others for status. Our attitudes, values and beliefs are shaped and refined by the people with whom we associate, and by those not known personally whose opinions of certain matters we respect. So although we may not always be evaluating our status, we usually are performing some kind of self-appraisal when involved with a

From our reference group, which usually consists of peers, we develop many of the values and goals which help make up our self-definition. Furthermore, we rate ourselves (looks, intelligence, personality, etc.) not in comparison to society in general, but to other members of our reference group.

reference group and, in addition, there may be several groups who operate for us in this manner.

The reference group is especially important to the study of group communication because so much of our behavior is influenced by it. The most important idea for us to remember is that reference groups are essential to what sociologists call *socialization*. Socialization is usually described as the process of developing who we are in our preparation for life. The process does not end at some age or point because we continue self-appraisal and changing throughout a lifetime. Getting along and working effectively in groups is an integral part of the socialization process.

Whether or not a group functions as a reference group for us, our effectiveness as communicators and our ability to work successfully within groups can be enhanced by our understanding of the influence groups have on us. It helps to know, for instance, that there are various types of groups with qualities that are different than others and that the task or purpose for which a group is formed determines its size and behavior. In the rest of this chapter, we will consider various types of groups, their structural and behavioral features, the different kinds of group behavior we may experience, and how we interact within certain group settings. In Chapter 7, we will look at these group characteristics in regard to problem-solving and decision-making.

FORMING GROUPS

Primary Groups   Almost all of us were born into families and spent our early years as members of this *primary* group. We were taken to community gatherings, to school, and to church or temple. We aspired to belong to and be like people who belonged to certain groups. When we belong to teams, clubs, gangs, fraternities, sororities, we are the *in-group.* Occasionally, we say that others are not one of us—they are the *out-group.* In our lifetimes, we are members of many groups. One sociologist estimates that the average person belongs to five or six groups at any given time and that the number of existing small groups may number in the billions throughout the world.[2]

Symbiotic Relationships   The business of living, from the simplest tribe to the most complex civilization, is dependent upon the commitment of people to invest energy in collective efforts—to work together in a social contract for the common good. Ours is not a nation of individuals but of interpersonal, *interdependent* (often called symbiotic) relationships. Organizations are generally not pyramids of individuals alone, but a combination of many small groups.

Male and female bonding is an example of a symbiotic relationship. The physically and psychically distinct roles of a male and female are often not complete alone—not that each cannot "sing" alone, but alone there could be no "duet." Without the commitment and combination of many different instrumentalists, there could be no symphony orchestra, a much larger symbiotic group. That different people with various skills can do together what they cannot do alone, is a sufficiently good reason for forming groups.

Consensual Groups   Yet others of similar characteristics and talents gravitate into groups *consensually* either because they need recognition, companionship, or security; or circumstances of job or residence pull them together. Society grants approval of major shifts in our personal groupings (graduation, marriage, divorce, awards, retirement) by ceremonies conducted by official groups (see ritual communication in Chapter 2).

What then is a small group? *A small group is a collection of two or more people who frequently communicate and interact in the hopes of achieving interdependently what they cannot achieve singly.* They define themselves and are defined by others as members. They take on a group personality, think in terms of "we" and "they," and speak as a body to outsiders.[3] These groups are not mere street corner aggregates, nor are they members of large organizations to whom they pay dues, nor are they total organizations, nor are they corporations, though within aggregates and organizations there may be many small groups.

A *small group* is one in which the members each interact with the others. Group interaction centers among proportionately fewer people as the size of the group increases. In groups of seven or more, for example, the less talkative tend to talk to only the more important members. In groups of 13 or more, five to seven people do most of the talking. Subgroups tend to form and satisfaction decreases as size increases.[4] But let us consider the smallest group first.

Small Groups

THE DYAD

There are certain characteristics that two people communicating alone can be seen to exhibit. The qualities of such an experience are only visible in *dyads* (a two-person communication transaction), and they are important to understanding day-to-day interactions with friends as well as improving the ability to deal with all people in interpersonal situations. Since the main difference between the dyad and larger groups is the number of people in the transaction, we will first look at what the difference means to the nature of the formation.

When you have a group of three or four participating in a communication transaction, there is a kind of immortality that the group possesses. One person can leave and others may join but the group will continue to exist. In a dyad, as soon as one person leaves, the formation no longer exists. This inability to continue is the first characteristic and it is called *the absence of potential immortality.*[5]

STRUCTURAL CHARACTERISTICS

Another feature that larger groups exhibit is the tendency to assign certain tasks and duties to members of the group. In work groups, people are usually assigned roles that correspond with their talents, resources, and preferences. The specific delegation of duties and responsibilities is typically a function of economy of resources and time, in order to achieve certain goals.

But in the dyad, it is possible for each person to refuse to accept certain duties or responsibilities much easier than in larger groups. Although a person in a large group may not agree with the role or duties assigned him, out of politeness or a sense of privacy, he has a tendency to wait until he is alone with the leader to discuss or negotiate the specifics of the assignment. A married couple is not likely to argue or discuss important matters in front of their children or other family members. In bridge, a team player will act in a certain capacity for the good of the team. But in general, the second structural characteristic of dyads is said to be an *absence of specifically delegated duties or responsibilities.*[6]

The third characteristic of the dyad is the *absence of potential coalition formation.*[7] Because there is only a one-to-one exchange, there is no opportunity for two members to come together against the third. In groups of three or more, as we will see later in the chapter, there is always the potential for coalition.

BEHAVIORAL CHARACTERISTICS

In addition to the three structural features of the dyad, there are certain closely related characteristics that make people's behavior different in dyads than in groups. In the dyad, there is a heightened sense of individuality that promotes a greater sense of responsibility. Because of the increased sense of individuality and shared responsibility, there is also an increase in the level of intimacy that one feels. Sharing responsibility for the efforts of the team often results in sharing a personal uniqueness. This is called *self-disclosure,* and it accounts for a great deal of the intimacy found in one-to-one relationships. In larger groups, there is considerable reluctance to disclose your own feelings but in dyadic relationships, the increased intimacy fosters trust. While there is less trust of others in large groups, in the dyad, this trust is a result of strong dependency, sharing of responsibilities and increased intimacy.

While the dyad contains certain features and qualities that larger groups do not, the dyad does not exist in its own right. However, dyads may be part of a larger group system. In a family of four, there are potentially six dyadic relationships: mother-father, mother-daughter, mother-son, father-son, father-daughter, and sister-brother. Furthermore, the communication system in each dyad is unique unto itself. The relationship of sister-brother is not like any other in the family, and sister and brother together are not the same people we know as individuals.

THE TRIAD AND SMALL GROUPS

When a third person joins a dyad, it becomes a *triad* (threesome) or small group. Small groups can have more than three members, and we will describe that shortly, but for now let us consider the changes that occur when a dyad becomes a triad. The structural change is obvious but the effects may vary. Certainly when one leaves a triad, it does not cause the group to disband, so triads can have a sense of potential immortality. But it is important to remember that a different third member transforms the triad into a new group. Their purpose may remain constant but the addition of a new personality with her own unique psychological set and, perhaps, some other reference groups makes the triad different. The members of the triad, therefore, are not interchangeable. In addition, two may join together to force the third member to take on certain responsibilities.

Interaction in this group increases significantly. Now, instead of a two-way message exchange, there is a possible six-way exchange. In addition to three one-to-one relationships, there are now three two-to-one relationships. The formulation of agreements is likely to take longer because of the additional point of view but chances for exploring new ideas are increased because of the additional personality, background information and psychological set of the new member.

There are certain features that dyads and triads do share. They are both usually formed for some purpose or function and they may dissolve when that function has been accomplished. Both may be part of a larger group system and may perform some duty or even make changes in the larger group. They may also, in return, both be influenced by the larger group or the individuals may be separately influenced. Lastly, the triad, like the dyad, is capable of producing an effect that is greater than the sum of the inputs from individual members.

Small groups share a lot of the same characteristics as triads, except for structure and the larger range of possible communication transactions. When members of a small group (more than three but few enough to communicate face-to-face and simultaneously) begin interacting, the possible number of exchanges that can occur increases well beyond what is possible in dyads and triads. Also, the interaction in a small group can become so intense and dynamic that the group may take on its own personality and behavior patterns. This is partly due to the phenomenon known as "group-think." When a group works together over a long period of time, they tend to develop common attitudes and opinions. When faced with certain decisions, then, there is the tendency to go along with the group either because we fear disapproval for disagreeing or we share the group's feelings and see no reason not to support the decision. We will discuss "group-think" in more detail in Chapter 7, but for now it is important to recognize that it is one of the characteristics of small groups.

TYPES OF GROUPS

Earlier in the chapter, we discussed the ways groups are formed and some of the reasons we have for joining them. In most instances, we join groups for some purpose and that purpose will largely determine the type of group it is. In addition to our family (a primary group), there are four general types of small groups we can identify. And although purpose will largely determine the activity of the group, it is important to keep in mind that all the groups share the characteristics mentioned above, and all of them may have overlapping functions at one time or another.

TYPES

I	II	III	IV
Casual-Social	Interpersonally Supportive	Learning	Decision and Policy Making
Examples	*Examples*	*Examples*	*Examples*
Street corner gang	Divorce Anonymous	Great books discussion group	Committees and task groups
Gourmet club	Weight Watchers	Classroom	General Motors Board of Directors
A group who bowls together	Religious workshop	Photography club	

The first and most important group in our life is the *family*. Our relationships with our parents, brothers and sisters provide us with the first and most influential feedback on who we are and might become, and condition many of the ways we interact with others. To a very large extent, our personalities are formed in the early years when the family is our primary source of human interaction.

The family is a unique group, not only in its importance, but because we have no control over joining it. As such, it does not fall into the categories listed. Nevertheless, the family provides us with our first experience of unity and prepares us for later participation in other groups. It is not surprising, then, that many of the characteristics of other types are copied from the family group.

THE FAMILY GROUP

The comforts of belonging found in the family are, in later years, somewhat taken up by *casual-social* groups. We enter into such groups primarily for companionship and the exchange of ideas and feelings. We often look for the support of others in this group and may model certain behaviors of an admired member.

These groups do not usually center around a specific activity or goal and there is rarely a set or structured agenda. However, such groups do tend to show certain patterns of member communication and may have leaders or high status members. To be "one of the guys" often involves a code of behavior peculiar to the group. The motorcycle gang has its uniforms, lifestyle, and language—much in the same way the jet-setters have theirs. In more formal groups, these codes and patterns are more structured and institutionalized.

THE CASUAL-SOCIAL GROUP

The *interpersonally supportive* group is characterized by a personally significant goal or characteristic its members share. Participation in such a group helps to strengthen the members in their attempts to achieve a goal or improve the quality of their life. The interpersonally supportive group may be informal, but more often an organized structure exists to attract and integrate new members. Also, there is usually a clear-cut leader present to direct the members and ensure maintenance of unity.

THE INTERPERSONALLY SUPPORTIVE GROUP

In the *learning* group, members often have nothing more in common than a desire (or a requirement) to become educated in the same area. For some, that may imply learning certain skills;

THE LEARNING GROUP

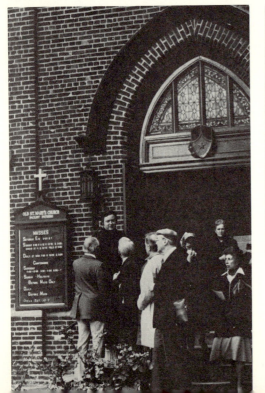

for others, it may simply mean becoming acquainted with facts in a certain area. Because of the somewhat ambiguous nature of the learning process, these groups are not characterized by any one set of structures. Learning may take place in a classroom, in the field, or in the lecture hall. Teachers may lecture, interact with students, provide programmed materials, or encourage class discussion. As a result, the kinds of communicative interactions that are significant vary according to the type of learning structure used.

This group is distinguished by its specific goals. While all types of groups exhibit goal-directed behavior, this group exists *only* to develop some plan or decision. Furthermore, this type of group is usually concerned with objectives that are community oriented; that is, unlike the interpersonally supportive group, they do not deal with the problems members have as individuals.

THE DECISION-AND POLICY-MAKING GROUP

These groups generally have well defined structures and incorporate a set of procedures to facilitate the decision-making process. They may be disorganized but in any kind of decision-making group, some procedure must be established (or tacitly accepted) as to how final decisions are made.

Before looking at how the groups function, we will consider how we behave in groups as individuals and the behavior of the groups themselves.

INDIVIDUAL AND GROUP BEHAVIORS

The interaction of people in groups is not altogether random, although it often is surprising. Social psychologists, sociologists and scholars of communicative behavior have examined the life of continuing groups. Their studies have led to a number of observations about the phases in the interaction. Not all groups exhibit the same behaviors in their development, but most exhibit some of those we will cover here. First, we will discuss the interpersonal needs of people in groups which show themselves in a number of ways. Second, we will describe the development of standards in the life of groups. And lastly, we will describe the communicative interaction within a group.

INTERPERSONAL NEEDS   A group, providing it is rewarding to its members, evolves from a loose, informal activity toward permanent structures. If the activity is particularly rewarding, an organization may be formed. Over a period of time, organizations codify policies with respect to such items as membership, attendance, officers, responsibilities, goals and actions. In business organizations, lines of authority are charted and the managerial and lower-level employees are assigned to divisions, departments and crews, according to tasks. Formally designated leaders are assigned responsibility for these functions and may utilize group decision-making. Whether the group is volunteer or business, the members carry common interpersonal needs for *inclusion, control,* and *affection.*[8]

Inclusion   The intensity for these three needs may vary but each member has a paramount concern for whether he is included. Particularly in the early stages of formation, belonging, membership and acceptance take on primary importance.

Control   The concern about control is shown in the efforts of a group to find structure and leadership. If a leader is assigned, the struggle to resolve "who's in charge" and "who's supposed to" take responsibility is much less pronounced than in groups that have no assigned or elected leader. But the struggle for controlling the interaction, nevertheless, is present even when a leader is assigned. It is natural to be concerned about how well the leader is performing his job and how well the group likes his style of leadership.

Affection   The liking and disliking of other members in a group is the third common interpersonal concern. Attraction to a group is traceable to a number of causes, but high among these is how well one likes and is liked by its members. It is particularly important that a member finds other members in the group to be likable and attractive people.

The expression of interpersonal needs of group members may be thought of as *socio-emotional* communication. Signs of socio-emotional concerns are visible in such positive communications as showing agreement, giving support and expressions of friendliness; or in negative expressions such as unfriendliness, disagreement and nervous laughter. Socio-emotional tension is not always visible, but it is not far from the surface as a group works on a task.

NORM DEVELOPMENT   It is difficult to describe the phases through which a group progresses. Rarely do we find a group that makes no progress at all in decision-making and rarely does a group move in a strictly linear progression.

Let us suppose, for a moment, that is is the first in a series of *Process* meetings of a newly formed group. Such a group would be concerned about inception and identity—what were its reasons for being and what will it be known as. After that and at subsequent meetings, attention increasingly turns to other concerns such as structure, roles, rules and management of its members. Tacitly at first, then more explicitly, a group formalizes its organization, rules, duties, division of labor and techniques for controlling its membership. When the group has established its structure and management, all of these *process* concerns intermingle with the task content.

The specific tasks to be achieved are the *content* business of *Task (Content)* the group. After a group has gained a concept of its own identity, developed a structure and arrived at its mission, it naturally becomes concerned about its *image.* And after a group has gained some history, it inevitably *evaluates* its success. Phase movements should be viewed as fluctuating and overlapping rather than as distinct and sequential.

We should expect groups to have many problems. Orientation *Relationship Concerns* problems and organizational functions take time and patience. Merging individual member's goals and hopes can also be a matter of considerable confusion and anxiety. Conflict over direction and decisions will invariably arise.

Groups within organizations exhibit similar phase movement to that of newly formed groups. They do not, however, have to give as much attention to such issues as identity and leadership selection. During times of stress, these concerns do arise again and become important. Frequently, during a group's life history within an organization, members will be concerned about its relationship to units above, parallel and subordinate to them.

Discussion in groups does not progress in linear fashion as it **COMMUNICATIVE** may in dyads. Rather, interaction proceeds in a reach-test spiral. **INTERACTION** One member makes a suggestion. The others may ask questions and comment on the suggestion. Group members tend to circle about a suggestion, clarifying, modifying, elaborating, sharing their ideas and feelings about it. It is a time in which the members seek to discover common values and meaningful relationships.

After a period of circling the suggestion, the group may accept or reject it and then someone else will bring forth another idea.

PHASES IN GROUP LIFE

PHASE	Inception Identity	Structure Roles & Norms	Management Action & Evaluation

PROCESS CONCERNS	Rules of
	  membership
	
	Selection of
	  leadership
		Organizational
		policies evolve
		
		Some explicitly
		  stated. Others
		  implicitly under-
		  stood
			Application of sanctions
			to those not adhering
			  to norms.
			
			Assignment of responsi-
			  bilities
			
			Performance reviewed

TASK (CONTENT) CONCERNS	Expressions of felt
	  needs
	
	Definitions of
	  problems
	
	Information sought
		Analysis of causes
		  and proposals
		  debated and
		  decided
		
		Mission assigned
			Proposals implemented
			
			Public relations
			  strategies
			
			Feedback sought

RELATION-SHIP CONCERNS	Tension over degree
	  of involvement
	  and acceptance
	
	Leadership choice
	  tensions
	
	Personal expecta-
	  tions, tensions
		Tensions over leader-
		  ship behavior and
		  style
		
		Tensions over
		  decisions and
		  values as repre-
		  sented by develop-
		  ment of norms &
		  rules
			Tensions over control
			  and fairness of appli-
			  cation of sanctions
			
			Tension over load assign-
			  ments and performance
			  evaluations
			
			Tensions over external
			  feedback

The process is then repeated and the group again will circle about, then double back to rediscover an anchor in the common values and reasons for their relationship. This backward and lateral movement serves as both a time for reestablishing the group's interpersonal relationship and for deliberating on the pros and cons of each idea.[9]

Approximately one-half of all contributions in discussion groups, according to the findings of Robert F. Bales, consists of answers and the other half of questions and reactions. He suggests that if enough time is not allowed for asking questions

TURN-TAKING AND INTERRUPTIONS

Taking turns at talking is the accepted basic rule during conversations. Yet yielding to another is often the result of being interrupted.

Basic Question: In one study, group discussions were observed in a high school and university settings (the numbers in groups ranged from four to six). The researchers were interested in determining how many times persons talked at the same time. A total of six hours of conversation was observed.

Results: Simultaneous talking was observed in 625 of 3362 utterances or 18.67%. Men were observed to talk simultaneously 388 of 2152 utterances compared to 237 of 1210 utterances for the women.

Implications: Men tend to dominate in group conversation in our society. When women and men are in a group, the women have a harder time getting the floor and they are more likely to lose it by interruptions from the men.

Men talk more at the same time (simultaneously) when a woman is talking than when another man is talking. The reverse is not true.

Men tend to disagree more with women than they agree with them (4 times more). On the other hand, women tend to agree with men more than they disagree.

Talking while another is talking generally is considered somewhat impolite, if not rude, and boorish. But simultaneous talk also may be a measure of dominance, and particularly, a subtle clue as to how one views a social relationship as in the relationship of men to women, child to parent, or superior to subordinate.

Abstract of Frank N. Willis and Sharon J. Williams,
"Simultaneous Talking in Conversation and Sex of
Speakers," *Perceptual and Motor Skills*, Vol. 43, 1976. pp. 1067–1070.

and expressing opinions and reactions, members will carry away tensions that eventually will ruin an apparently successful, but actually superficial, decision. Bales also established that within the course of a group meeting, no matter whether it be the beginning, middle, or end, the verbal and nonverbal interaction involved both task and socio-emotional communications. Productive and cohesive groups average two task types of contributions to one socio-emotional.[10]

These observations about group behavior are partly explained by the tasks and structure of the groups. Ultimately, the socio-emotional communication and the group interaction must be considered in light of the members' personalities too. Although the study of personality is more properly the domain of psychologists, there are a few reliable personality traits we can observe in most people working in groups and they often affect the group's composition.

GROUP COMPOSITION

Two personality characteristics have been found to be present in people who seem particularly suited to groups: *extroversion* and *tolerance for ambiguity.*

LEADERSHIP By definition, extroverts like to work with people and in groups. Their extroversion is apparent in a willingness to talk, laugh and to choose seats that encourage interaction (opposite others, central, head positions and close to others).[11] Extroversion appears to be related to the amount of participation a member engages in. One study, in which the most talkative member of a group is given the solution to a problem resulted in the group's acceptance of it; but when the solution is given to the least talkative member, who subsequently reveals it, the group more often rejects it.[12] Talkative participants do seem to have their ideas accepted more than less talkative members, and the highly energetic, outgoing participator frequently is perceived as the group's leader.[13] Overly talkative people who dominate and dog-

RESEARCH FINDINGS ON LEADERSHIP

People are eliminated from leadership who appear uninformed, unparticipative, rigid, who talk too little or too much.

Persons emerge as leaders who exhibit greater total activity, the time talked is greater, response is quicker, speed of response faster when interrupted, and ability to speed up interaction. Leaders are those with the best ideas. They initiate structure in interaction. They address specific individuals. They talk to the group as a whole. They are talked to more. They are more tolerant of the deviate and give low status members attention and encouragement. Leaders are perceived as self-confident, capable of the task, and friendly. They score high on dominance, exhibiting both more controlling behavior and agreeing behavior than the submissive individual.

Leaders generally avoid expression of negative feelings and behavior destructive to the group and organization. Leaders permit freedom for participation and expression of feelings.

Leaders of effective groups differ from ineffective by being less severe in evaluation of members with low achievement and in their encouragement of those with marginal behavior.

Based on Ralph M. Stogdill, *Handbook of Leadership: A Survey of Theory and Research.* (New York: The Free Press, 1974) chapter 20.

matically take far-out positions, however, are rejected from leadership positions after a time. Introverts can also make strong group members, especially when the reward of belonging to a group is high and their particular skills are needed.

FLEXIBILITY

A second characteristic that is present in people who are particularly suited to groups is a *tolerance for ambiguity.* Ambiguity and uncertainty obviously are part of all group deliberations. Michael Burgoon found that people with a tolerance for ambiguity react more favorably to group tasks that involved processing conflicting information.[14]

To be effective in group discussions, we should develop a tolerance for dealing with uncertainty and disputable issues, and we must learn to expect differences and conflict. People who see issues in "black or white" will have difficulty in functioning effectively. How does a group go about finding people who are extroverts and have a tolerance for ambiguity? In the formation of a group, we can hardly administer tests as do social scientists but we can ask a potential task group member if he prefers to work with people or alone. Next we can question whether he thinks there is a right and wrong way to do almost everything. People who respond that there are few absolute right and wrongs are more apt to be tolerant of a group's struggle to arrive at compromise and consensus. A productive task group does not just happen. It results from first, the lucky combination of a wise choice of members with skills suited to the task; second, the training for working in groups; and third, the personality characteristics of extroversion and tolerance for ambiguity. Finally, if there is sufficient motivation, a group may find it is compatible and productive in spite of personality differences.

SEATING ARRANGEMENTS

How individuals seat themselves in groups is not entirely accidental. The place, room, furnishings, and the size of the group influence whether the arrangement is formal or informal—rows, circle or rectangle; hard chairs or soft; on the floor or on the grass, etc. A group's purpose influences its setting. Sensitivity and encounter groups are more likely to lounge on pillows or a rug. A board of directors usually is seated about a long rectangular table. Formal arrangements will arouse feelings of anxiety if informal arrangements are expected, and vice versa.

The influence of seating has not been carefully field–tested. We

Power

do know from laboratory research and observation, however, that a number of factors influence choice of seats. People who feel on the fringe of a group tend to sit on the fringe. Leaders and more dominant people tend to choose head or central positions. Leaders apparently select positions where they can more easily see everyone. Dominance in animals is related to the eye space controlled. Submissive birds look away when dominant birds give them the eye. When crowded, birds in a cage tend to look outward, apparently to avoid the stress generated by visual contact. A similar behavior may be seen in people. People who desire little involvement frequently sit behind others. They avoid the head seat or positions opposite the leader, where they could easily be seen. We do know that nearby seating is the rule when people like one another, distance is more common when people dislike one another, and opposite seating is more common when people are competing.

Interaction

Spatial arrangements reflect the flow of the interaction. When seated in a circle, people tend to communicate with people across from them more than with the person next to them. People in end positions at rectangular tables usually participate more and are seen as having more influence. The position itself tends to influence the role; that is, if one sits opposite the leader, he is likely to be more involved than others. One experiment discovered, for example, that when five-person groups were seated two on one side and three on the other, more people emerged as leaders on the two-person side than on the three-person side.[15] There is power in the spatial arrangement, whether it be a throne or a long table.

Territory

People tend to carry territorial concerns into groups. They tend to sit in the same seats and may be upset if someone sits in their usual chair. With such awareness of the influence of position, a conscious effort might be made to vary a group's seating positions. Obviously, participants should avoid intrusion upon each other's territory. Assuming that maximum participation is desired, the group should arrange itself in a circle. Such conscious efforts in seating arrangements will help broaden the friendships within the group and tend to avoid cliquishness. Wise leaders might well avoid sitting opposite antagonists and overly assertive members. Changing the location of meetings from time to time will also help minimize the negative effects of seating.

When considering the personality traits of members, it is important to remember that predicting human behavior is difficult for even the most highly trained psychologists. We can use our observations about group composition as guides but we must be prepared for surprises and disappointments. We must not assign specific roles for members merely based on their seating position around a table. As an example of the dangers of this procedure, I am reminded of the story about an elderly gentleman whose family was admonishing him not to sit in the middle of the table during a family gathering and dinner. Several members insisted that he sit at the head but he replied, "It really doesn't matter; wherever I sit is the head of the table."

Now that we have covered group characteristics, types of groups, and the importance of group behavior, we are ready to examine interpersonal and group behavior more closely. In the next chapter, we will use some of the principles we have described to show how they apply in various settings: teaching or offering instructions, problem-solving and decision-making.

SUMMARY

In this chapter, we have examined many of the dynamics present when individuals become members of groups. Reference groups are important to the socialization process and to the development of our personality and self-image. A group consists of many individuals who interact in hopes of achieving together what they cannot achieve singly and a small group is one in which all members interact with all the other members.

A dyad is a small group of two people. Dyads have certain qualities that triads and small groups do not share: the need for all (both) members to continue, the inability to form a coalition, and the lack of specifically designated responsibilities and duties. Trust and intimacy are more easily attainable in dyads than in triads or small groups. Dyads are similar to triads in their ability to be part of larger group systems and in the fact that members are not interchangeable without the group's changing its identity.

Triads and small groups have three or more members who interact frequently on a firsthand basis. They have the ability to communicate simultaneously, as do dyads, but there is always the potential for coalitions. The communication interaction is greater in triads and small groups but the formulation of agreements is likely to take longer. However, the points of view expressed are more varied, and the chances of arriving at more suitable solutions are increased.

In addition to the family (the primary group) there are four general types of groups. They are arranged according to purpose or function, and the functions are overlapping. They are called: casual-social, interpersonally supportive, learning, and decision- or policy-making groups.

The interaction of groups centers in content (task) and socioemotional concerns. Productive and cohesive groups tend to fluctuate between task-type contributions and socioemotional in approximately a 2:1 ratio. The interaction tends to follow a reach-test spiral in which a group circles back from a new idea to find an anchor in the common values agreed to in previous discussions. Interpersonal concerns common to individuals in groups are inclusion, control and affection. The intensity of these needs varies, of course, depending on the personalities of the individuals and the composition of the group. Groups must address identity issues, leadership roles, management, public image, rhetorical concerns and performance evaluation. These issues are not always met in this sequence but are normal phases in the life of a group.

A small group is a particularly important social unit in a complex organization that helps to relieve the alienation which appears to spring from largeness. People who are by nature extrovertive and who have a tolerance for ambiguity find working in groups more pleasant than those with opposite personality characteristics.

Seating arrangement can affect interaction. People in key seating positions tend to take on or are given leadership roles. This may be due partially to more dominant people naturally choosing these seats and also because we attribute to key seats certain leadership roles. People seated opposite each other tend to talk more to each other. We also carry territorial concerns into group relationships. Not only do individuals become possessive of certain chairs, but groups tend to prefer certain locations. Changing seating positions and meeting places can sometimes break up the negative effects of position.

INITIATIVES

INITIATING ACTION 1 *Twos, Threes and Small Groups.* Pair off to discuss the question, "Is marriage a failure?" After five minutes, have each member of the dyad score himself on the following items:

Uncomfortable	1 2 3 4 5 6 7	Comfortable
Personal	1 2 3 4 5 6 7	Impersonal
Not forced to Take a Stand	1 2 3 4 5 6 7	Forced to Take a Stand

Discuss your feelings about the encounter. What about the brief conversation made you feel the way you do? Now, add another dyad to some of the dyads forming small groups of four; and to the others, add just one member, forming triads. Have at least two dyads continue in the same pairing without disturbances. Continue to discuss the topic for ten more minutes. Again each student should score himself. Compare the feelings of the experience among the three sizes of groupings: dyad, triad and small groups.

INITIATING ACTION 2 *Group vs. Individual.* Bring a jar of peanuts or candy to class. *Step One:* Have each class member write his name and estimate the number of peanuts or candies in the sealed container. *Step Two:* Group in clusters of threes and discuss and compare your estimates. Each group should make an estimate. *Step Three:* Each member should write on the bottom of his card a Final Estimate. Compare the results of the experiment on the board. Perhaps two class members would volunteer to count the nuts or candies. Were more initial individual estimates nearer the correct count than the group estimates? Were more final estimates closer to the correct answer than the initial estimates? How do you explain the results of this exercise? Is it more than a matter of averaging estimates?

INITIATING ACTION 3 *Structural Influence.* The instructor should randomly divide the class into groups of five each, two on one side of a table and three opposite. Ten minutes should be allowed for each group to formulate as many words as they can from the letters in a long word, such as "disappointments." After the time is up, each member should rank-order the other four members of the group according to who in his opinion displayed the most, second most, third most and fourth most leadership (excluding himself). Tally the results on the chalkboard; names are not important. What should be made known is where the person who was ranked highest in displaying leadership was sitting. Note on which side of the table that individual was seated. Discuss why the results worked out as they did. Was it a matter of personality because of the special mix of personalities, or did the seating influence the results? What were the signs of leadership exhibited in the group?

Observing Process. A sociomatrix provides a way to ascertain who talks to whom. Such information enables researchers to describe group interaction more objectively. It also provides data for individual members to reflect upon their own contributions. Learning to use a sociomatrix is not complicated but does necessitate some practice.

INITIATING ACTION 4

Step 1. Prepare a chart with the members' names arranged both across the top and along the left side of the chart:

Person Speaking:	Person Spoken to:						
	John	Dale	Sue	Beth	Les	All	Totals
John							
Dale							
Sue							
Beth							
Les							
TOTAL							

This is just an example. The chart should be a whole page in order to give enough room to keep a tally of contributions in each box.

Step 2. Assign yourself a code for marking a contribution. For example, you might work out the following: a slash (/) will be placed in the column of the member who is spoken to on the row of the person speaking. The sign that a person is addressed is that his name is used or that the speaker looks at him more than any other person in the course of his remarks. If he looks at several people, the slash will be placed in the "All" category. A more detailed tally may be used. For example, a smile ($\smile$) might designate a contribution that attempts to build harmony. A frown ($\frown$) might designate a contribution that belittles an idea or another member. A question mark (?) might designate a contribution that asks for information or an opinion.

Step 3. Tally the contributions for each member and the total for the group. Then calculate percentages. You can then produce data which demonstrates who talked most, who talked least, and who was spoken to from most to least.

Step 4. Discuss what communication patterns are revealed by the matrix and why. What *feelings* do each of the group members have about the data? Does the data tell you something you did not know about yourself and others? How might you change the interaction?

INITIATING ACTION 5   Play a game of three-dimensional Tic Tac Toe with one other person. Next, play the game in a group of three. How does one additional person change the activity with respect to:

    (a) Your feelings about winning;

    (b) Your ability to control the actions of the other;

    (c) Your ability to predict and execute a strategy?

Remember comparatively that twos are more direct, intimate, easily predictable; threes are less direct, intimate, predictable.

INITIATING ACTION 6   In twos, discover a topic about which you differ. Discover why. Now add a third person. What happens? Does the third person try to avoid taking sides? Does one of you urge him to take a position? If he does, how do you, who are now the minority, feel? In one sense, you are now less important and in another, more important, because your position is singular.

INITIATING ACTION 7   In twos, bet a milkshake, pizza, or beer with another class member about who will win a coming sports event. Would you like for someone to know the terms of the bet? Why?

INITIATING ACTION 8   *Role Play Mistrust.* Characters: Father, Mother, Daughter. Situation: Eleven o'clock in the evening in the family car. The parents have just picked up the fifteen-year-old daughter from the skating rink. Earlier in the evening, the parents had come to the skating rink but the daughter was not there. She had asked to go skating. The parents know that the daughter has previously been truant

from school and tried to lie her way out of it. The daughter
believes she should not have to tell her parents where she goes.
Role play this situation. After the scene has been played for five to
seven minutes, discuss the following questions:

How realistically were the roles played?
Was there any resolution to the situation?
What influence did past behavior have upon this event?
How can trust be reestablished?
What would trust mean?

Posting. One of the most effective techniques for providing assembling member's concerns and questions about a topic is to
write all questions or items on a chalkboard. Such participative
agenda building is time consuming, but does promote involvement. Practice the technique of Posting with such a topic as
''course evaluation.''

INITIATING ACTION 9

NOTES

1. H. H. Hyman, "The Psychology of Status." *Archives of Psychology,* 1942, No.
   269.

2. Theodore M. Mills, *The Sociology of Small Groups* (Englewood Cliffs, N.J.:
   Prentice-Hall, 1967), p. 2. Mills bases the figure upon a world population of
   3,200,000,000 individuals and upon the rough estimate that each one belongs
   to five or six groups, allowing for overlap. Of course, families, the primary group,
   are figured into this estimate.

3. Some works deliberate at length concerning definition such as Marvin E.
   Shaw, *Group Dynamics: The Psychology of Small Group Behavior* (New York:
   McGraw-Hill, 1971), Chapter 1; also Doran Cartwright and A. Zander (Eds.),
   Group Dynamics Research and Theory, 3rd ed., (New York: Harper and Row,
   1968), Chapter 3, pp. 45–73.

4. Edwin J. Thomas and Clinton F. Fink, "Effects of Group Size," in Hare *et al.*
   (Eds.), *Small Groups Studies in Social Interactions* (New York: Alfred A.
   Knopf, 1968 revised), pp. 525–36.

5. George Simmel, *The Sociology of George Simmel,* Translated, edited and with
   an introduction by Kurt H. Wolff (New York: The Free Press, 1950), p. 124.

6. W. J. Lederer and D. D. Jackson, *The Mirages of Marriage* (New York: W. W.
   Norton, 1968), p. 180.

7. T. Caplow, *Two Against One: Coalitions in Triads* (Englewood Cliffs, N.J.:
   Prentice-Hall, 1968).

8. William C. Schutz, *FIRO: A Three Dimensional Theory of Interpersonal Behavior* (New York: Rinehart, 1968).

9. Thomas M. Scheidel and Laura Crowell, "Idea Development in Small Discussion Groups," *Quarterly Journal of Speech,* Vol. L (April, 1964), pp. 140–45; and "Feedback in Small Group Communication," *Quarterly Journal of Speech,* Vol. LII (Oct., 1966), pp. 273–278.

10. Robert F. Bales, *Interaction Process Analysis* (Homewood, Mass.: Addison-Wesley, 1950); and Robert F. Bales, "In Conference," *Harvard Business Review,* Vol. 32 (March–April, 1954), p. 45.

11. Mark Cook, "Experiments on Orientation and Proxemics," *Human Relations,* Vol. 23 (Feb., 1964), pp. 61–76.

12. H. W. Recken, "The Effect of Talkativeness on Ability to Influence Group Solutions of Problems," *Sociometry,* Vol. 21 (Dec., 1958), pp. 309–321.

13. E. J. Thomas and C. F. Fink, "Models of Group Problem-Solving," *Journal of Abnormal and Social Psychology,* Vol. 68, No. 1 (1961), pp. 53–63.

14. Michael Burgoon, "Amount of Conflicting Information in a Group Discussion and Tolerance for Ambiguity as Predictors of Task Attractiveness," *Speech Monographs,* Vol. 28 (June, 1971), pp. 121–124.

15. Lowell T. Howells and Selwyn W. Becker, "Seating Arrangement and Leadership Emergence," *Journal of Abnormal and Social Psychology,* **64,** No. 2 (1962), pp. 148–150.

SUGGESTED READINGS

Applbaum, Ronald L., Edward M. Bodaken, Kenneth K. Sereno, and Karl W. Anatol, *The Process of Group Communication.* Chicago: Science Research Associates, Inc., 1974.

Barnlund, Dean C., and Franklyn S. Haiman, *The Dynamics of Discussion.* Boston: Houghton Mifflin Co., 1970.

Bormann, Ernest G., *Discussion and Group Methods: Theory and Practice,* 2nd Ed. New York: Harper & Row, Inc., 1969, 1975.

Brilhart, John K., *Effective Group Discussion,* 2nd ed. Dubuque, Iowa: Wm. C. Brown, 1974.

Burgoon, Michael, Judee K. Heston, and James McCroskey, *Small Group Communication: A Functional Approach.* New York: Holt, Rinehart and Winston, 1974.

Cartwright, Dorwin, and Alvin Zander, *Group Dynamics: Research and Theory,* 3rd ed. New York: Harper and Row, 1968.

Cathcart, Robert S., and Larry A. Samovar (Eds.), *Small Group Communication: A Reader,* 2nd ed. Dubuque, Iowa: Wm. C. Brown Co., 1974.

Douglass, Paul F., *The Group Workshop Way in the Church.* New York: National Board of Young Men's Christian Associations Press, 1956.

Egan, Gerard (Ed.), *Encounter Groups: Basic Readings.* Belmont, Calif.: Wadsworth Publishing Co., 1971.

Goldberg, Alvin A., and Carl E. Larson. *Group Communication Discussion: Process and Applications.* Englewood Cliffs, N.J. Prentice-Hall, 1975.

Golembiewski, Robert T., and Arthur Blumberg (Eds.), *Sensitivity Training and the Laboratory Approach: Readings About Concepts and Applications.* Itasca, Illinois: F. E. Peacock Publishers, 1970.

Jandt, Fred E., *Conflict Resolution Through Communication.* New York: Harper and Row, 1973.

Johnson, Kenneth G., John J. Senatore, Mark C. Liebig, and Gene Minor, *Nothing Ever Happens: Exercises to Trigger Group Discussions and Promote Self-Discovery.* Beverly Hills, Calif.: Glencoe Press, 1974.

Kruper, Karen R., *Communication Games: Participants' Manual.* New York: The Free Press, 1973.

McCroskey, James C., Carl E. Larson, and Mark L. Knapp, *An Introduction to Interpersonal Communication.* Englewood Cliffs, N.J.: Prentice-Hall, 1971.

Miles, Matthew B., *Learning to Work in Groups: A Program Guide for Educational Leaders.* New York: Columbia University Teachers College Press, 1971.

Mills, Theodore M., *The Sociology of Small Groups.* Englewood Cliffs, N.J.: Prentice-Hall, 1967.

Mills, Theodore S., and Stan Rosenberg (Eds.), *Readings on the Sociology of Small Groups.* Englewood Cliffs, N.J.: Prentice-Hall, 1970.

Monroe, Alan H., *Principles and Types of Speech Communication,* 8th ed., Chapter 19. Glencoe, Illinois: Scott, Foresman and Co., 1971.

Phillips, Gerald M., and Eugene C. Erickson, *Interpersonal Dynamics in the Small Group.* New York: Random House, 1970.

Rosenfeld, Lawrence B., *Human Interaction in the Small Group Setting.* Columbus, Ohio: Charles E. Merrill Publishing Co., 1973.

Schmuck, Richard A., and Patricia A. Schmuck, *Group Processes in the Classroom.* Dubuque, Iowa: Wm. C. Brown, 1971.

Secord, Paul F., and Carl W. Backman, *Social Psychology.* New York: McGraw-Hill, 1964.

Shaw, Marvin E., *Group Dynamics: The Psychology of Small Group Behavior.* New York: McGraw-Hill, 1971.

Stanford, Gene, and Barbara Dodds Stanford, *Learning Discussion Skills Through Games.* New York: Citation Press, 1969.

Stewart, Charles J., and William B. Cash, *Interviewing: Principles and Practice.* Dubuque, Iowa: Wm. C. Brown, 1974.

Verderber, Rudolph F., *The Challenge of Effective Speaking,* 2nd ed., Chapter 4. Belmont, Calif.: Wadsworth Publishing Co., 1973.

7 problem solving & decision making

Recalling our discussion in Chapter 6 of group characteristics and individual behavior in groups, we know that it is in groups that we share most of our ideas and it is in groups that we reveal much of ourselves to others.

We also said in Chapter 6 that groups are often formed for purposes of accomplishing some task or making some decision. This is usually the setting in which the characteristic we described as the ability to produce an effect that is greater than the sum of the inputs from the individual members can be observed. The decision-making process of a group becomes much more important than the personal concerns of any one individual. First, we will look more closely at the value of group decisions and the processes for arriving at them. Following that, we discuss the processes and approaches to problem-solving and decision-making. In the conclusion of this chapter, barriers to working effectively in groups is examined.

VALUE OF GROUP DECISIONS

Group activity is quite different from individual activity. Obviously, certain tasks are better handled economically, aesthetically and emotionally by individuals than groups, e.g., math problems, routine typing and artistic creations. Groups, likewise, are superior to individual deliberations in other tasks.[1]

People in groups doing motor tasks such as running or bicycle riding appear to accomplish more than when exercising alone. People tend to learn faster with greater economy of instructional facilities in groups. Groups tend to produce higher quality and more accurate solutions to various kinds of problems (industrial and social) than do individuals working alone.

People in groups tend to be more highly committed to new ideas, behaviors and projects after group deliberations than when appealed to singly. During World War II, lectures as compared to discussions, were tested to discover which was more effective in persuading mothers to feed their families organ meats, such as kidneys, because of the shortage of beef. Discussions proved far more persuasive than lectures. The impact of others on us to do that which we decide is right has been demonstrated again and again by such organizations as Alcoholics Anonymous and Weight Watchers. Individuals in small groups planned the nonvio-

ARE GROUPS MORE CORRECT THAN INDIVIDUALS?

Basic Question: Do groups make better decisions because the less intelligent capitulate to the more intelligent members?

Test: 143 students enrolled in freshmen discussion courses at Northwestern University were assigned to small discussion groups. They and a control group completed as individuals a 30-item test for logical conclusions given about two months earlier. The students were put into groups which received the same number of correct answers. The groups were, therefore, considered alike in intelligence. A second form of the test was given and often the group scores rivaled the performance of the most brilliant members working alone.

An example of the type of question (which sometimes has more than one correct answer) on the Bradley Test of Formal Validity in Problem–Solving is:

Some Communists are advocates of heavy taxes; and advocates of heavy taxes are conservative Republicans. Therefore:

    A. Some advocates of heavy taxes are not Communists.
    B. Some Communists are conservative Republicans.
    C. Some conservative Republicans are Communists.
    D. Some Communists are advocates of heavy taxes.
    E. None of these conclusions follow.

Average Correct of 30 Item Test:
Individual Decision—16.5 / Group Decision—21.9

Implications: Groups are not superior to individuals because the less intelligent side with the more intelligent but because of certain factors inherent in diagnostic discussions: (1) members in groups get more interested and involved in successful completion of a task, (2) members in groups are more self-critical and have more critical resources, and (3) they deal more objectively with individual biases that get in the way of logical reasoning. Even better answers might have been obtained if groups had been trained not to consider initial unanimous agreement as a sign of *correctness*, and instead, had someone play the devil's advocate causing more careful deliberations. The same might be true for deadlocks because when they occurred, a poor compromise alternative often resulted. Training might have taught them to give in and go with one or the other of the two best answers.

We can safely say that there are certain inherent psychological and logical factors at work when people work in groups and that these produce positive results.

Dean C. Barnlund, "A Comparative Study of Individual, Majority and Group Judgment," *Journal of Abnormal and Social Psychology,* 1959, Vol. 58, pp. 55-60.

lent campaigns for civil rights as well as the equal rights struggles for women, Indians and homosexuals.

Large organizations find that as size increases, greater specialization occurs. The greater the specialization, the less satisfying the job; the less satisfying the job, the greater the absenteeism and alienation. Workers on assembly lines have been known to cheer when there is a breakdown and sometimes even cause them deliberately. The inherent consequence of bigness appears to be a lessening loyalty to the organization. All this suggests that the larger the organization, the more important it is that individuals have a small group which satisfies their interpersonal needs and allows them to meaningfully participate in formulating policy, procedures and practices. Later in the chapter we will point out some of the disadvantages of group problem-solving.

THE PROCESSES OF PROBLEM-SOLVING

Any group that meets to solve a problem or make a decision does not automatically know how to go about it. Certain matters of members' roles, procedures for accomplishing the goals of the group, and the norms of expected behavior all may have to be arrived at through group discussion. After this, the group exchanges information and ideas. The discussion may be characterized by free interaction among the members in which specific objectives are decided on by the group, and information and ideas evaluated. The group task is usually directed toward the movement of an idea or suggestion from conception to resolution. All of these activities are more smoothly accomplished if group members adopt some kind of format for conducting their business.

REFLECTIVE THINKING   Near the turn of the century, John Dewey promoted the application of science to social problem–solving; he described what has come to be known as the *reflective thinking process*.[2] This process involves five sequential steps that begin with knowing a problem exists to determining what to do about it: (1) recognizing the problem, (2) describing the problem, (3) suggesting possible solutions, (4) evaluating the solutions, and (5) developing a plan of action.

Recognition of the problem involves agreement by the group that something is wrong and needs to be changed. Not all members may see the problem until someone points it out. Often the problem is an internal one, centering around procedures for discussion, activity or policy that concern goals and values. Externally, the possibilities are infinite, from deciding on a theme for a homecoming dance to determining what strategy to use in a political campaign.

Describing the problem usually involves studying its effects. If no information can be gathered about the effects, it may indicate the problem has diminished or been eliminated, or perhaps never existed at all. In this stage, the problem has to be defined so that it is within the group's ability to solve it. A plan for a political campaign for the entire country, for example, may be beyond reach for the group but determining local campaign strategy may not be. Limiting the problem usually occurs early in the sequence of steps, but it can often be repeated in later stages and is a good idea when the group's time, authority, or resources are limited.

Describing the problem of strategy in a political campaign or the theme of a homecoming dance are problems of policy or process. Policy is the most typical question a small group discusses. In process cases, information about the cause of a problem may be needed in order to adequately describe it. Recommending

"I will now affix the deciding button."

what to do about the increase in crime against the elderly will require data concerning the causes, who commits it, why the elderly are victimized more often than others, where the crimes occur, and what police protection is now offered in those settings. Learning about the causes of a problem is essential when the group begins offering solutions.

Finding the solution to a problem is often the most exciting and creative of the steps in the reflective thinking process. It is here that brainstorming pays off. At times, the most far fetched idea becomes the most valuable. Members have opportunities to express themselves, discover new information about each other, identify smaller problems and resolve them, and become more strongly attached to the group. The exchange in this stage is sometimes described as *ventilation* because it allows members to air out their problems, suggest new information, and seek out solutions.

Evaluating the solution continues the intense exchange of ideas and requires that members feel free to express themselves. This is the place where disagreement is important and should be welcomed. This is also the time when waiting for all the information and suggestions before arriving at solutions is essential. There are times when all the solutions suggested contain partial value and a multistage solution is required.

Despite the unpredictable factors that arise in the evaluation phase, there are certain reliable measures we know are useful. We should always ask if a solution appears reasonable. Just as we test numbers for reasonableness when working math problems, so should reasonableness apply to social problems. Another question to ask is, "Does the solution create new, unanticipated problems?" And finally, "How much will the solution cost in terms of time, money, and other resources?" By asking these questions of all solutions, we can spare the group considerable time and devote more effort to working directly on the problem itself.

The solution may be selected by several methods. Sometimes majority vote will be used. For more important or difficult problems, a group consensus may be required. Whatever method is used to choose a solution, the group must now develop a plan of action. The plan is where the solution is tested. For this reason, decisions on who will carry out the plan and how barriers will be overcome are very important. If the group's best efforts are not used to implement the plan, the solution will not have been tested.

Several problem-solving formats have been developed since **USING A FORMAT**
Dewey's reflective thinking process came into use. Most of them
are refinements of Dewey's work but some of them came about as
a result of tailoring the process to a specific kind of problem.[3]

FORMATS FOR TASK GROUPS

A. Problem-Solution to Action Sequence—an Expansion of John Dewey's Ideas*

1. Location of "felt need." Physical location of the problem. Psychological and Social signs of a problem. History of the growth of the difficulty.
2. Causes of the problem(s).
3. Standards a solution should meet to be acceptable to those concerned.
4. Listing solutions available and testing these against the criteria above.
5. Selection of best solution.
6. Development of that best proposal and securing approval.
7. Implementation, assignments, deadlines, review.

B. Ideation-Evaluation adapted from John Brilhart†

1. What is the nature of the problem facing us (present state, obstacles, goals)?
2. What might be done to solve the problem (or subproblems)? List all ideas which group members suggest without evaluation.
3. By what criteria shall we judge among our possible solutions? Rank order from the most important to the least important.
4. How do these solutions compare? Combine and then decide which best meets the criteria.
5. How will we put our decision into effect? Deadlines, assignments and review.

C. Ideal Solution—Carl Larson‡

1. Are we all agreed on the nature of the problem?
2. What would be the ideal solution from the point of view of all parties involved?
3. What conditions within the problem could be changed so that the ideal solution might be achieved?
4. Of the solutions available to us, which one best approximates the ideal solution?

D. Single Question—see Carl Larson**

1. What is the single question, the answer to which is all the group needs to know to accomplish its purpose?
2. What subquestions must be answered before we can answer the single question we have formulated?
3. Do we have sufficient information to answer confidently the subquestions? (If yes, then answer them. If not, continue below.)
4. What are the most reasonable answers to the subquestions?
5. Assuming that our answers to the subquestions are correct, what is the best solution to the problem?

E.   Work Chart—based upon Programmed Evaluation Review Technique††

   1.   What is it we wish to get done and when, i.e., how many product units sold and delivered within a target date?
   2.   Work backward from that point. Chart the jobs that must be done, their sequence, deadlines, and assignments to personnel.
   3.   Draw a red line and number this sequence—a critical path to completion.
   4.   Prepare contingencies and alternate routes.

F.   Inductive Leadership—based upon Maier's training‡‡ for discovery and acceptance of solutions.

   1.   Do not present *the problem,* but instead ask the group whether they have any problems.
   2.   Recognize all suggestions, but influence direction in thinking by asking for further suggestions.
   3.   Protect individuals from criticism of the group members by interpreting all remarks in a favorable light. Avoid blame for anyone.
   4.   List all suggestions. Do not get bogged down on early simplistic remedies. Seek to combine.
   5.   Do not reveal your preference.
   6.   Keep good leads before the group by asking probing questions about them.
   7.   Work to eliminate undesirable features from a solution.
   8.   Make your objectives that of resolving group differences.

*John Dewey, *How We Think,* Lexington, Mass.:
D. C. Heath & Co., 1910.

†John K. Brilhart, *Effective Group Discussion,* Dubuque, Iowa: Wm. C.
Brown Co., 1974 (Second Edition), pp. 110–111.

‡Carl E. Larson, "Forms of Analysis and Small Group Problem
Solving." *Speech Monographs,* volume XXXVI, November, 1969, pp. 452–455.

**Ibid.*

††Gerald M. Phillips and Eugene C. Erickson, *Interpersonal Dynamics
in the Small Group* (New York: Random House, 1973), pp. 12–24.

‡‡Norman F. Maier, "The Quality of Group Decisions as Influenced by
the Discussion Leader." In Maier (Ed.), *Problem Solving and Creativity*
(Belmont, Calif.: Wadsworth Publishing, 1970), p. 361.

Whatever the format we use for seeking solutions to our problems, there are certain general principles that seem to be reliable:

1   Some order enhances the quality of group problem-solving.
2   Formats that encourage analysis prevent an impulsive rush to shallow decisions.

DOES A FORMAT OF PROCEDURES HELP?

Basic Question: Do some problem–solving formats produce more correct answers than others?

Test: 32 groups composed of four or five college men each discussed four different short industrial relations problems. Each discussion was limited to 20 minutes. Experts had identified a best solution for each problem. The four different analysis forms were: (1) *No Pattern.* (2) *Single Question.* The analytic procedure was to discover what is the single question, the answer to which all the group needs to know to accomplish its purpose. And following this the group examines subquestions and their answers. (3) *Ideal Solution Form.* This analytic procedure asks (*a*) Are we agreed on the nature of the problem? (*b*) What would be the ideal solution from the viewpoint of all parties concerned? (*c*) What conditions within the problem could be changed so that the ideal solution might be achieved? and (*d*) Of the solutions available to us, which one approximates the ideal solution? (4) *Reflective Thinking.* This form considered the following: (*a*) What are the limits and specific nature of the problem? (*b*) Causes and consequences of the problem. (*c*) What things must an acceptable solution accomplish? (*d*) What solutions are available to us? and (*e*) What is the best solution?

Results: Number of correct answers arrived at:

	No Pattern	Single Question	Ideal Solution	Reflective Thinking
On Four Problems	15	24	26	19

The Single Question and the Ideal Solution forms were superior to the Reflective Thinking and No Pattern. The Reflective Thinking form also produced more correct answers than did the No Pattern.

Implications: People tend to function more logically and possibly more amicably when they have a structure. One must be cautious in generalizing from this one study that longer-term problems will be solved more accurately or more creatively by these forms.

Carl E. Larson, "Forms of Analysis and Small Group Solving." *Speech Monographs,* Vol. XXXVI (November 1969), pp. 452–455.

3 Formats that discourage hasty acceptance or rejection of ideas promote a climate more satisfying to members.

4 When a leader encourages a group to discover its own problems, higher quality and greater acceptance of solutions results.

Perhaps the single most characteristic behavior of effective participation in group deliberation is questioning. Questioning symbolizes an attitude of inquiry and of joint research for a solution. The formulation of problems into questions that should be

ASKING QUESTIONS

answered focuses the search towards rational, efficient analysis. In addition, discovering what the member's questions are tends to merge individual goals into group concerns. Anyone who wishes to develop skills in problem–solving and decision–making must first acquire the technique for questioning.

ASK THAT QUESTION

Questions seeking information and clarification:

> What was it you said about . . .
> Please elaborate on . . .
> When you say . . . do you mean . . .
> I want to learn more about . . .
> How do you . . .

Questions seeking support:

> Isn't it great that . . .
> Do you agree that . . .
> Do you know that . . .
> Is it not a fact that . . .
> Don't you feel that . . .

Questions weighing, testing, seeking opinions:

> Are you sure about that . . .
> How can you claim that . . .
> What do you think of . . .

Questions about procedures and transition:

> What should be on our agenda . . .
> What should we do first . . .
> What are our goals . . .
> What should we accomplish . . .
> Who is allowed to vote . . .
> Who should do what . . .
> What can we say about that . . .
> What next . . .

In Chapter 5, we developed seven principles that effectively aid the listener in understanding the views of others. Those principles can be equally useful in group discussions and problem–solving. Now we can look at Dewey's notion of reflective thinking and formulate additional questions that are useful in group discussions. When we discussed listening critically, we said that the critical listener had to be both analytical and able to synthesize many different pieces of data and information. In a group discussion, it also helps to formulate questions of analysis and synthesis. These would be the questions you ask during the first stages of the reflective thinking process.

Dewey suggested that the beginning point for examination of a problem is when someone is lost, someone hurts, or when alternative choices are present. That is the time, for instance, when someone scales a tree to examine some unknown terrain. When someone is ill, he begins to describe what and where it hurts, and traces with his physician the possible causes. When someone arrives at a fork in the road, he must weigh the possible consequences of his alternate choices.

When we are trying to recognize the problem, we ask the following kinds of questions, just as a doctor or therapist might. First, there are *questions of analysis:*

1 What exactly is the problem? Where does it hurt?   *Questions of Anaylsis*
2 What evidence do we have for the cause of the pain?
3 What evidence do we have of psychological pain? Of social pain?
4 Is the pain severe, recent, long–standing, or imaginary?
5 Are there examples, testimonies, and statistical evidence of the pain?
6 What are the possible causes? What can we rule out? Does it matter what caused it? Is finding a cure more important than looking for the cause? (This last question is both one of substance and process.)

Once we have recognized the problem and described it, we must then suggest solutions or remedies. In this stage we are asking *questions of synthesis:*

7 What are our goals? What kind of behavior or degree of   *Questions of Synthesis*
health are we seeking?
8 Have we considered all the possible alternative solutions? (This is a question of substance and process.)
9 Have we measured the alternatives against our agreed-upon standards and goals?
10 Is the alternative selected the best of those available?
11 What are its benefits, costs, and possible ill effects?
12 Will it be acceptable to the parties involved?

Obviously, this list of synthesis questions cannot be asked all at once. But active members should be constantly asking themselves these questions so that when the opportunity arises, they are ready to critically respond. These members play the role of testers and checkers. They critically look at ideas, evidence, relationships and proposals. Such members are essential to the proper and successful functioning of any group.

Before a group gets too deeply involved in solving a task or deciding alternatives, the members might well consider *questions of process.* What are the questions of procedure? They are questions regarding personnel involved, order, and how the decision will be arrived at:

1 Who has a stake in this issue? Of those people and groups   *Questions of Process*
involved, is the representation sufficient and efficient? Are there too many, too few, or enough involved? Who selected whom to consider this issue?
2 How often should we meet? When and where?

3 Do we need a leader? If so, who might best lead? What do we want the leader to do?

4 What do we want the result to be from this and future occasions?

5 By what method should we make decisions? Who should have a say? When do we have a quorum?

Questions of process are essential questions running through the minds of discriminating listeners and voiced when appropriate. They usually spring from a sense of fairness and must be answered for those wanting to work together for any period of time.

Parliamentary procedure grew out of the need to work together in larger groups efficiently. Process does not mean a group ought to take on such formalities as a matter of course, but rather that process should be considered to the degree that it may facilitate working on a task. When it gets in the way, the rules should be shelved and new and less encumbering procedures found. A successful group arrives at solutions to process questions quickly. When important policy questions arise, a time delay between discussion of the procedure, analysis, synthesis and choosing a solution is wise.

INTERPERSONAL RELATIONSHIPS

Members should not be oblivious to the "people" side of accomplishing a task. Therefore, intelligent questions should consider intent, motivation and socio–emotional payoffs. Here are some questions that enable a member to understand the subtle interactions that are sometimes involved in group discussions. They are not questions to ask but rather to ponder. Generally, only when interpersonal conflict frustrates task accomplishment should such questions be openly deliberated.

1 What does the advocate really want? Is there a "hidden agenda" of goals that is below the surface of the stated goals? What are the motivations of the advocate? Is it power?

2 Is there a power struggle involved? Is there an in–group and an out–group?

3 What relationships exist between the advocate and people outside this audience who have a stake in the issue?

4 Are there secret agreements which the advocate has with certain members? Is there a public image which differs from the real face of the group?

The critical member, then, is one who asks probing evaluation questions in the areas of analysis, synthesis, process and interpersonal relationships. He is always examining his own hidden agendas while dealing as openly as possible with others.

BARRIERS TO GROUP PROCESS

So far in this chapter, we have presented group process as a favorable and effective way to solve problems. Before we can consider our discussion complete, we will look at some of the factors that can frustrate group processes.

ATTITUDES

In this section of the book, we have referred to the value of keeping an open mind and being receptive to new ideas. In Chapter 4, we discussed it related to psychological set; in Chapter 5, we observed the importance of open-mindedness in being an effective listener; and in Chapter 6, we referred to it in regard to group composition and the need for tolerance for ambiguity. But on occasion, group members exhibit attitudes that are resistant to new ideas or change. Three such attitudes may be described as: (1) *hypercritical negativism,* (2) *dogmatism,* and (3) *mental inertia.* Here are brief descriptions of them so they may be easily recognized.

Negativism is demonstrated by insistance that nothing can be decided until *all* the evidence is gathered. As seemingly well-motivated as such a plea may be, in reality it is rarely possible. Negativism often is exhibited in intellectual fence sitting. People who take such positions are usually those who do not feel the pain of a situation.

Dogmatism seems to be related to authoritarianism. Dogmatic people refuse to question their personal biases. They think basically in terms of either–or. They ignore assumptions, tend to stereotype, act impulsively out of prejudice and self-interest. Last, they are rigid and seem most satisfied under strong leaders.

Mental inertia is characterized by a lack of curiosity, acceptance of hasty generalizations, diversion to irrelevant topics, and general uncritical acceptance of shallow analysis and solutions.

Although these attitudes may be troublesome, there is something to do about them. Being involved encourages the practice of positive elements of group behavior for all members. Regular problem–solving training can raise sensitivity to attitudes and behaviors antagonistic to effective group process. And just by being a participant in group decisions persuades those with poor attitudes to observe the benefits of critical thinking and open–mindedness.

CONFORMITY AND GROUP-THINK

A second important barrier to group process is the tendency of group members to conform in the face of a problem. In Chapter 6 we mentioned group-think as a behavioral characteristic of small groups. We said there was a tendency of members to develop common opinions or attitudes and that when faced with decisions, would go along with the group out of fear of disapproval or because if the group thinks it right, it must be so.

Social scientists have demonstrated that some individuals go along with judgments that their own eyes tell them is wrong and take risks that are contrary to decisions they would make when alone. This suggests that in many instances, individuals rely on others' opinions over their own. To be forewarned of this tendency to bow to social pressure is to be partially armed against it.[4]

But being forewarned about the tendency to bow to social pressure may not be enough. Social psychologists have been observing group problem–solving for many years and their findings do not always support the widespread use of groups to solve important problems, as the above study points out. Here is another example from recent American history.

In January of 1961, the outgoing Eisenhower administration left the new President Kennedy with a highly important and pressing problem: A force of Cuban exiles, secretly trained by the CIA, was preparing to invade their homeland in an attempt to overthrow the Castro government. Kennedy was faced with the problem of approving or rejecting the plan of invasion. The Joint Chiefs of Staff thought the operation would succeed. The Secretary of State thought the political aspects of the plan were feasible and, naturally, the CIA supported it. Despite the objections of a few outsiders, after a few weeks of deliberation and consultation with his inner circle of advisors, the President approved the plan. In April, the brigade of 1,400 exiles struck at the Bay of Pigs in Cuba. The invaders were soundly defeated after three days of fighting. Nearly 1,200 of their number were captured and their small fleet of support ships were scattered or sunk by Castro's air force.

About a decade later, psychologist Irving Janis of Yale blamed the Kennedy administration's mistake on group-think. Janis argued that the cohesiveness in the Kennedy group caused the members to not think clearly. Some of the participants were reluctant to express their dissenting view for fear of incurring disapproval; they did not want to risk losing their new membership in a

DO BACKBONES TURN TO NOODLES IN A GROUP?

Basic Question: Can a minority strategy move a majority to agree with them?

Method: Twenty groups of mostly college freshmen, averaging six subjects each, discussed a case that actually happened at a university concerning a student named Betty who struck a teacher with a ruler. The teacher, attempting to dodge the blow, fell and suffered some brain damage, making it impossible to continue teaching. Each group's task was to come to an agreement on how the university administration should handle the matter. Alternatives ranged from one extreme (#1) give her counseling, to the other extreme (#7) suspension. Most students elected middle positions.

Two plants (confederates with the experimenter) were in each group. One was to play the Deviate role. He was to take a position at one extreme (#1 or #7), hold that position but act as though he felt awkward about being different than the others. He was instructed to be pleasant and show every deference possible. The other plant was instructed to play a Mode role. He would take a position similar to what most of the others took. His instructions were to attack the Deviate intermittently for 10 minutes.

The Mode's behavior was designed to alienate the rest of the group from himself personally. He was to avoid objective arguments against the Deviate and use such comments as, "The rest of us are trying to solve this problem and you are just being stubborn." "What are you trying to do—split up the group?" After 10 minutes of such attacks, the Mode was to remain thoughtfully quiet until some 10 minutes of discussion time remained and then hesitantly say, "Wait a minute. You've been saying that . . . (repeats an argument the Deviate has offered). Yes, I think I see what you're driving at, but #7 (or #1) is rather tough, don't you think? Would you be willing to come down to #6?" The Mode then suggests the rest of the group might also reconsider their first hasty impressions. The Deviate was programmed to reluctantly shift down from the original extreme position.

Results: The 80 naive subjects in the 20 groups shifted 148 out of a possible 218 from their previous pre-discussion positions.

Implications: The pressure to come to an agreement in a group, at least on a subject which does not involve loss of money appears to make a majority move in the direction designed by a tenacious minority. It *is* possible to manipulate a group. The experiment suggests that interpersonal liking and disliking apparently influences a group's reasoning. Perhaps one should guard against pressures to compromise toward positions tenaciously held and reluctantly compromised by only a fraction of the membership, particularly under the pressure for reaching a conclusion.

R. Victor Harnack, "A Study of the Effect of an Organized Minority Upon a Discussion Group," *The Journal of Communication,* Vol. XIII (March, 1963), pp. 12-24.

very special and attractive group. Others, not so concerned, adopted the group's shared belief that large numbers of Cubans were very dissatisfied with Castro and failed to gather or consider information that went counter to this opinion. Loyalty also brought about a self-imposed censorship that restricted opposing views. As a result, no one in the inner circle raised strenuous objections and the apparent agreement led members to an even greater confidence in the correctness of their views.

In his 1972 book on the subject, Janis presents other instances of errors caused by group-think (the Japanese attack on Pearl Harbor and the escalation of the Vietnam war) in which group processes resulted in narrowing the thoughts and information available. Janis concludes:

> The more amiability and *esprit de corps* there is among members of a policy–making group, the greater the danger that independent critical thinking will be replaced by group thinking, which is likely to result in irrational and dehumanizing actions directed against out–groups.[5]

Individuals in such groups tend to become yes–men. They not only seek to anticipate and please their leader but to insulate him against criticism. Janis suggests the following structural safeguards:

1 The leader should adopt an impartial position and probe many possibilities.
2 Playing the devil's advocate should be an accepted norm.
3 Invite outside independent experts to react to ideas and plans.
4 Write scenarios of how out–groups may respond to a course of action.
5 Hold second–chance meetings in which decisions may be changed.
6 Avoid irrational decision making such as tossing a coin, quick majority votes and bargaining.
7 If someone loses, do not feel he must get his way next time.[6]

Not all of these group-think safeguards can be used on every occasion, but even the use of one of them may prevent a "groupie" decision. Conformity is inevitable and necessary to groups. Yet, unless members become aware of the very real social pressures to conform to others, the quality of group decisions will suffer. Individuals in groups also are more subject to the persuasive influence of articulate people. Sometimes this means making decisions that are more risky or conservative than one would make if alone.

The word of Janis has made us aware that group-think is especially likely in highly cohesive groups. However, structures and policies may be instituted to ensure more careful decision-making, such as encouraging members to play devil's advocate, seeking outside review of decisions, and holding second-chance meetings.

SUMMARY

This chapter on problem-solving and decision-making contains information concerning the value of group decisions, the reflective thinking process, the various formats task groups may adopt in the procedural side of their work, the value of asking questions and the barriers to group process.

The reflective thinking process contains five steps: (1) recognizing the problem, (2) describing the problem, (3) finding solutions to the problem, (4) evaluating the solutions, and (5) choosing a plan of action. The various formats of group process include: (1) The Dewey Problem-Solution to Action Sequence, (2) Ideation-Evaluation, (3) Ideal Solution, (4) Single Question, (5) Work Chart, and (6) Inductive Leadership.

Asking questions is important for determining the answers to all steps in the reflective thinking process. Questions of analysis help us to recognize the problem and describe it. Questions of process help us suggest and evaluate solutions and they are important for implementing a plan of action. There are some questions that originate in the interpersonal relations of the members. These usually deal with the socio-emotional payoff for certain members and they can be useful in clearing the air or uncovering any hidden agendas.

Barriers to group process are attitudes, groupthink and conformity. Hypercritical negativism, dogmatism, and mental inertia are three attitudes that can frustrate the group's process. Groupthink and conformity are dangerous because they reduce the creativity and flow of new ideas into the group process. Maintaining an open mind and playing the devil's advocate can help reduce the chances for groupthink or conformity from disrupting the group process.

INITIATIVES

Observation. Observe a coach of some team sport and a dancing instructor of a group. Write a report on the similar and contrasting use of reinforcement by the coach and the instructor.

Compatibility. Have a member of the class record the characteristics of one member of an *ideal* work team on the board. Among others, the traits that should be considered are personableness, assertiveness and intelligence. High, low or medium should be assessed for each of these traits. Other members of the class should take turns adding a second, third, fourth and fifth member to the *ideal* grouping. The chart might look like this:

	Personableness	Assertiveness	Intelligence
First Member			
Second Member			
Third Member			
Fourth Member			
Fifth Member			

Discuss why such a grouping might or might not result in a compatible, productive group.

See how close the class can come in forming compatible task groups. Work on an assigned topic given by the instructor. Afterwards, ask others in the class to judge the results of the task groups. Each team should review its experience by talking over the following questions: (1) Did we have a compatible grouping? Why? Why not? (2) How did the personalities and abilities of the members mesh or clash? (3) If there was a conflict, and there usually is, what brought it about and how was it resolved? (4) What did each of the members learn about themselves working in combination with others in a group? (5) Who in each group served mostly as the task leader? Why? (6) How satisfied was each member with the group result?

INITIATING ACTION 3 *Productivity—Letters to the Editor.* Divide into work groups of seven to nine members. See how many different letters to the editor your group can write and have published. Certain rules should be observed:

1 All letters should be typed and must be signed by a majority of the members in the group who are responsible for its contents.
2 Group members should be responsible for postage costs and stamps.
3 No mention should be made in any letter that this is a class project.
4 Carbon or xerox copies of all letters must be turned into the instructor at the completion of the assignment. The instructor will then rate each letter from one to five points based upon style and rhetorical strategy. In addition, every letter published will earn the group one point per member.

At the termination of the project, each group should reflect on the experience. Consider the following questions together: How satisfactorily was the problem of leadership resolved? Was the leadership too permissive or too authoritarian? What other roles were evident: catalyst, opinion giver, prober, tester of ideas, morale builder, blocker, playboy/playgirl? What norms were developed? What attention was given to process, i.e., developing an agenda, agreeing on a schedule and deadlines, voting on ideas, reviewing progress? How important were interpersonal concerns: inclusion, control, affection? Why were or weren't members satisfied with their working relationship and productivity?

INITIATING ACTION 4 *Participant Observer.* Develop criteria such as those suggested by Chris Argyris below.[7] Use these criteria as standards for writing a log of your membership in a group. Be introspective in asking the question, "Do we work as a team?"

1 Contributions made within the group are additive.
2 The group moves forward as a unit; there is a sense of team spirit and high involvement.
3 Decisions are made by consensus.

4 Commitment to decisions by most members is strong.
5 The group continually evaluates itself.
6 The group is clear about its goals.
7 Conflict is brought out into the open and dealt with.
8 Alternative ways of thinking about solutions are generated.
9 Leadership tends to go to the individual best qualified.
10 Feelings are dealt with openly.

Do your best to build team spirit in your group and then keep a record of how successful you are.

Meet the Press. Role play interrogation by the press. Begin by announcing two or three areas of a topic about which you are prepared to answer questions. For example, one might say: I am prepared to respond to questions on the topic of pollution. The two areas in which I am most able to answer questions are (1) industrial pollution of our rivers and air, and (2) work of the Environmental Protection Agency. A panel representing the press then probes with questions seeking information, interpretation and evaluation. A variation of this exercise involves a panel of four or five persons each listing one facet of a topic for which he or she is prepared to answer questions. An opposing panel role playing the press then takes turns with the interrogation.

INITIATING ACTION 5

Consciousness Groups. Women and men's consciousness raising groups have become popular in the seventies. They usually meet once a week for a two-hour session and vary in size from eight to twelve members. Membership is usually limited to members of the same sex. Their purposes for meeting are many, yet the common concern of all C-R groups appears to be personal growth via the experience of continuing dialogue. Rarely are they social action groups. Often the content is unstructured. The first sessions may begin with shared biographies. Each person may take turns telling the group whatever information he or she feels the group should know. Some may begin by each member answering, why have you come? Others may need more probing questions to get started, such as, who do you live with and how do you like it? Or, what do you like or dislike about your living arrangements? Following sessions may center on other questions such as, whom do you confide in? Do you feel like a grown-up? Some sessions may be centered on subjects such as parents, children, food, money, jealousy, sex, discrimination, growing up male or female, becoming comfortable with our bodies. The tendency is for the

INITIATING ACTION 6

group to become increasingly open and candid. In so doing, we learn to know the worst about one another but to care for and to want the best for each other. Ground rules usually state that: (1) a person who is talking should not be interrupted except for clarification; (2) no one has to participate; (3) the order of participation is random rather than in the order of seating; (4) all information is confidential; and (5) no one is wrong because each person speaks from his own frame of reference. (See *MS.,* July 1972, for a basic guide to consciousness raising.) Join or form a C-R group if you would like to achieve the experience briefly suggested by this Initiative.

INITIATING ACTION 7 *Audience Panel.* Prepare a discussion to be presented before an audience. Use the guide below to structure your discussion.

PANEL PARTICIPANT GUIDE SHEET FOR PREPARING FOR A PROBLEM-SOLVING DISCUSSION

I. Locating the Problem
  A. When did the problem first come to your attention? Is it troubling you now? Will it likely get worse?
  B. Who is affected? How many? How seriously?

II. Discovery
  A. Why did the problem arise?
  B. What are the possible causes?
  C. What are the principal causes?

III. Criteria
  A. What would it be like if there were no problem?
  B. How will we know if the problem is solved?
  C. By what standards should we measure the success of the solution?

IV. Ideation
  A. How many possible solutions (both serious and wild) can we list?
  B. How many can be combined?
  C. How much do we know about them?

V. Evaluation
  A. Which of the solutions best cures the symptoms and deals with the causes of the problem?
  B. How well do the solutions compare costwise?
  C. Which will be most easily implemented and be most acceptable?

Members of the class may use the form below to evaluate the panel discussion.

EVALUATION INSTRUMENT FOR GROUPS USING
THE REFLECTIVE THINKING FORMAT

Group Interaction

Task Level

a) located ill	Efficient	5	4	3	2	1	Inefficient
b) agreed upon question	Thorough	5	4	3	2	1	Shallow
c) defined terms and criteria	Creative	5	4	3	2	1	Dull
d) located blame	Productive	5	4	3	2	1	Unproductive
e) considered major cures							
f) considered costs							
g) made decision							

Process—Sensitivity

a) worked out procedures	Orderly	5	4	3	2	1	Disorderly
b) talked conversationally	Conscious of	5	4	3	2	1	Unaware of
c) asked questions	Procedures						Procedures
d) summarized when needed	Balanced	5	4	3	2	1	Unbalanced
e) sought others' opinions	Dealt with	5	4	3	2	1	Ignored
f) progressed at an agreed upon rate	feelings						feelings
g) shared negative feelings	Worked out						Struggled
h) shared positive feelings	power	5	4	3	2	1	for power
i) worked out power relationships	relationships						
j) demonstrated concern for morale	Morale high	5	4	3	2	1	Morale low

Individual Interaction

	Task Accomplishment	5	4	3	2	1
1. _____	Process Awareness	5	4	3	2	1
	Sensitive of Others	5	4	3	2	1
	Task Accomplishment	5	4	3	2	1
2. _____	Process Awareness	5	4	3	2	1
	Sensitive of Others	5	4	3	2	1
	Task Accomplishment	5	4	3	2	1
3. _____	Process Awareness	5	4	3	2	1
	Sensitive of Others	5	4	3	2	1
	Task Accomplishment	5	4	3	2	1
4. _____	Process Awareness	5	4	3	2	1
	Sensitive of Others	5	4	3	2	1
	Task Accomplishment	5	4	3	2	1
5. _____	Process Awareness	5	4	3	2	1
	Sensitive of Others	5	4	3	2	1

Comments:

NOTES

1. M. E. Shaw, *Group Dynamics: The Psychology of Small Group Behavior (New York: McGraw-Hill, 1971), pp. 80-83.*

2. John Dewey, *How We Think.* (Boston: D. C. Heath and Co., 1910), pp. 68-78.

3. These ideas are based in part upon the ideas and/or research of: James J. McBurney and Kenneth G. Hance, *Principles and Methods of Discussion* (New York: Harper and Row, 1950); Alma Johnson, "An Experimental Study in the Analysis and Measurement of Reflective Thinking," *Speech Monographs, X* (1943), pp. 83–96; Dean C. Barnlund, "A Comparative Study of Individual, Majority and Group Judgment," *Journal of Abnormal and Social Psychology,* **58** (1959), pp. 55–60; Harry Sharp and Joyce Milliken, "Reflective Thinking and the Product of Problem-Solving Discussion," *Speech Monographs,* **31** (1964), pp. 124–127; H. Charles Pryor, "An Experimental Study of the Role of Reflective Thinking and Professional Conferences and Discussion," *Speech Monographs,* **31** (1964), pp. 158–161.

4. Solomon Asch, "Studies in Independence and Conformity: I a Minority of One Against a Unanimous Majority," *Psychological Monographs,* **70,** 16 (1956); Robert D. Mead and William A. Barnard, "Conformity and Anticonformity Among Americans and Chinese," *The Journal of Social Psychology,* **89** (Feb., 1973), pp. 15–24.

5. Irving L. Janis, *Victims of Groupthink: A Psychological Study of Foreign Policy Decisions and Fiascos.* (New York: Houghton-Mifflin, 1972).

6. *Ibid.*

7. Chris Argyris, *Organization and Innovation* (Homewood, Illinois: Richard D. Irwin, Inc., 1965), p. 264.

SUGGESTED READINGS

Davis, James H., *Group Performance.* Reading, Mass.: Addison-Wesley, 1969.

Ewbank, Henry L., and J. Jeffery Auer, *Discussion and Debate: Tools of a Democracy.* New York: F. S. Crofts and Co., 1947.

Fisher, B. Aubrey, *Small Group Decision Making: Communication and the Group Process.* New York: McGraw-Hill, 1974.

Gouran, Dennis S., *Discussion: The Process of Group Decision Making.* New York: Harper and Row, 1974.

Kiesler, Charles A., and Sara B. Kiesler, *Conformity.* Reading, Mass.: Addison-Wesley, 1970.

Maier, Norman R. F., *Problem Solving and Creativity: In Individuals and Groups.* Belmont, Calif.: Cole Publishing Co., 1970.

Patton, Bobby R., and Kim Griffin, *Problem Solving Group Interaction.* New York: Harper and Row, 1973.

part three

public
expectations

8 the speech: a unique event

Now that we have looked at the process of communication in groups and on the interpersonal level, we move toward the public setting and consider what ideas are important to understanding our expectations of communication in more public situations. In beginning this section on public expectations we will consider the process of information exchange and the components of the basic speaker-audience transaction. The remaining chapter will address designing the speech, preparing for the presentation of the speech, the process of influence, our responsibilities in the use of persuasion and ethics, and the importance of the media.

In this chapter we will address information exchange first on an instructional level—teaching another person how to do something. After we establish the basic ideas of transferring information, we move to the speech itself and examine examples of simple speeches. The chapter ends with a discussion of the audience—how to consider your audience and how to determine your approach to it.

INFORMATION EXCHANGE

In the preindustrial age, the main energies of mankind were expended in the forest and on the soil. Fathers taught their sons to hunt and farm. Mothers shared their domestic skills with daughters. Then came the industrial age and almost everything changed. A career in agriculture or hunting was no longer automatically expected. There were jobs outside the home that women could pursue. Instead of the natural power of wind, water, draft animals and people, the transforming resources became coal, gas, oil and electricity. Machine technology and productivity became the order of the day and organizations grew in size and international influence.

Today a new age is upon us. The transforming resources now also include *information exchange*. This information can be stored in people's brains, files, journals, books, but increasing amounts are being stored and processed by computers, then to be transferred through data transmission systems. Knowledge of a complex and theoretical nature accentuates the need for communicative skills. The service occupations have become increasingly important and they have become more and more dependent upon the transfer of information. Consider the importance of information exchange in transportation (pilot to control tower), in finance (financial analyst to investor), in government (legislators' dependence on committee meetings and reports), in health (doctors' dependence on the instructions to a nurse or drug dispensary). These are just a few examples of our great dependence on information exchange.

Much of the business of living is dependent on the passage of know-how from one generation to the next and increasingly upon the everyday exchange of information. All of us are, depending on the occasion, either senders or receivers of information. In a way, we are sometimes teachers and at other times students. Before we look at some actual cases of transferring information, let us consider the types of information we are likely to exchange, some guiding principles in information exchange that may be useful, and the process of presenting information in a dyad or small group.

TYPES

Communicating information sometimes centers on *process,* at other times on *description,* and still other times, on *policy.* There are situations, though, when all three are equally important. *Process* largely refers to "how-to-do-it" activity; *description* details explaining "what-it-was-(or is)-like", communicating *policy* in forms of regulations or procedures and usually refers to a principle, plan, or course of action. Although our attention will first focus on description because it is the most frequent type of information exchange, we will also make some general observations about all three types. Process and policy, however, will be discussed more fully later.

A presentation of process, description and policy frequently involves an interpretation of *why.* Whenever *why* or *should* becomes more important than *what,* the presentation has shifted emphasis to instrumental-persuasive communication. We have touched on persuasive communication in Chapters 2, 4 and 6. At this time, we are concerned only with the persuasive nature of establishing credibility but we will discuss persuasion more thoroughly in Chapter 11 when we cover influence. For now we can say that all informative communication is persuasive to some degree, even the how-to-do-it variety. Anyone presuming to show us "how to" must ultimately establish his credibility. Similarly, a witness in a court case who describes an accident places his ability to observe on the line as does a scientist who attempts to describe some physical phenomenon. The inevitable question of *why* lurks near any communication of information, particularly a communication of policy. Consequently, the teacher (or presenter) and the student (or learner) are concerned about both information gain and information justification. Establishing expertise and a rationale, obviously, involves persuasion.

The same is true when setting forth policy. Managers, directors and coordinators frequently must explain policies of their organization. Clarity and understanding are the first objectives of such explanations. A secondary and equally important objective is to provide a persuasive rationale for the policy. For example, the governor's assistant may be called upon to explain to the staff their duties and schedule. Such an explanation stands to have much greater chance for compliance if it is not only clear but also reasonable.

Students participate in similar information exchanges each time their instructors hand out a syllabus. In that syllabus, the course may be outlined, examinations scheduled and grading explained. The instructor not only seeks a clear understanding of his policies, but also an acceptance of them. Should any of the students speak out for modification of the syllabus, they shall have entered into persuasive communication. Here again, informative and persuasive communication share the stage.

COMMUNICATION AND LEARNING

Experimental psychologists tell us that animals and man may learn to respond by *classical conditioning* and by *reinforcement*. In classical conditioning, when an organism is exposed simultaneously to two stimuli, one which is known to produce a response and one which is neutral, after a time the positive stimulus may be withdrawn and the neutral one will result in the same response. Moreover, we know that a reward following a behavior tends to make that behavior recur and, conversely, a punishment after a behavior tends to make that behavior occur less frequently. When learning new behaviors, the closer the reward is to the correct performance, the more likely the behavior will be tried again. After we have learned the behavior, we are more able to wait for rewards. Such learning is called *operant learning*. It should also be noted that organisms sometimes learn not to respond when there is a lack of reward or punishment. For example, a snail that is tapped withdraws, but may fail to withdraw after habitual tapping if no reward or punishment for the behavior occurs. This behavior is said to be *extinguished*.

Learning to recall and reproduce information depends on how closely it is linked to rewards, punishments, and/or other positive stimuli; therefore, when presenting instructions, it is wise to use stimuli that are rewarding, punishing, or were previously effective. I once took a graduate course in voice science which de-

Rewarding

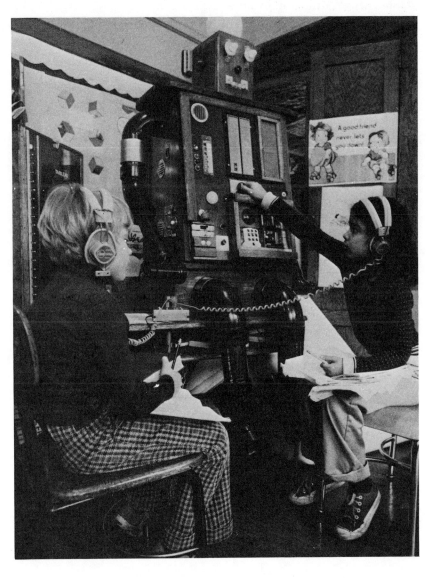

The curious robot-type device these children are using, is an innovative learning machine. The machine, like other similar devices, teaches various skills and facts by asking specific questions and giving direct and immediate feedback to the child's answers.

manded knowledge of higher mathematics and physiology. At the conclusion of the first examination, I wrote, "This is the answer, but I can't see why I need to know it." When reviewing the exam, the professor said to me, "I'm here to teach voice science, not to justify it to every Tom, Dick and Harry." In so answering, he was both right and wrong. My enrollment was sign enough I was there to learn, even though it was to satisfy a minor requirement. But the professor failed to link his body of instruction with my career goals, or should that be impossible, redirect my enrollment into another course. My interest dropped as I could see no personal benefit (reward) in the course.

Consider another example of how a manager linked rewards to learning sales methods. In order to motivate employees of a hotel to use suggestive selling, the manager allowed them to stay overnight in the hotel during the orientation period. He provided other rewards as well, such as purchasing name identification tags, piping in closed circuit television to the employee cafeteria and insisting that any performer appearing in the hotel nightclub must do his first show for the employees. In some cases, giving attention and recognition is ample reward to reinforce and increase desired behavior.

Successful Playback

Learning is dependent upon the listener's successful accomplishment of the task. One frequent mistake of a teacher is that after presenting a task or process to an audience, he assumes it is understood. He often fails to check it out by observing and testing. Real learning demands that the learner can recall or reproduce on his own. The effective communicator checks out comprehension and abilities to complete the assignment. Checking for understanding during a communication, therefore, is an important component of teaching. In presenting a sequence of several learning levels, the teacher should get a positive feedback from the preceding step before moving to a more advanced one.

Teacher–Student Relationship

When do we learn? Is it when we participate in a communication event that learning takes on a special meaning for us? This can occur by reading instructions, but most often we learn when we want to imitate behavior or when we find the completion of a task is beneficial to ourselves and to those for whom we care. We are turned on by those who are concerned for us and turned off by those who show little interest. We associate with those who are interested in our happiness and success, and when we are convinced that another has our welfare at heart, we will listen to their advice.

When we try to hide our ignorance, we cannot learn. We may use such words as "I know" even when we do not to cover any threat to our status. Learning must be an active, candid exchange between the teacher and the student—one in which feedback is plentiful and there is a feeling of mutual appreciation.

Here are questions designed to focus on the important steps within an information exchange:

GUIDING PRINCIPLES

1 Did the teacher specify what behavior would be learned within the allotted time period? Did he check with his students whether the end behavior suited them?

2 Did the teacher link the content with anticipated rewards, punishments or other positive stimuli?

3 Did the teacher establish his credibility? Did he with self-assurance and modesty demonstrate his know-how?

4 Was the instruction clearly arranged? Did the teacher provide an overview, and did he utilize guides and summaries?

5 Was the teacher receptive to periodic feedback? Did he appear willing to repeat and rephrase? Was the teacher alert to nonverbal signals of fatigue or confusion?

6 Was there ample reinforcement of successful responses? Did the teacher express genuine praise appropriate to the levels of accomplishment?

7 Did the teacher use all appropriate channels—oral, visual, touch, taste and smell?

8 Did the teacher demonstrate a friendly concern for the student as a person? Was he friendly but not nosy about other aspects of the student's life? Was there a serious interest coupled with a sense of humor in the exchange?

9 Was the teacher honest and candid about failures, both his own and his student's? Did he deal frankly with problems of low motivation and/or careless performance?

10 Did he ask for a trial performance, first to reflect his own example of how to perform the task and secondly, to test what is correctly or incorrectly performed?

One of the best ways to develop our informative communication skills is to practice them and to examine that practice. Perhaps the most enjoyed and beneficial assignment I have given during my years of teaching has been one I call "Each One Teach One." The first phase of this assignment begins by each class member revealing several things he is able to teach and several things he would like to learn. These things are usually limited to what can be taught in one to three lessons. Next, the "teacher-student" teams pair off and set dates for the lessons. After the lessons are completed in out–of–class time, both teacher and student do an analysis of the learning experience. The questions we just asked about information exchange serve as a framework in the analysis.

The following reports[1] of students who participated in an "Each One Teach One" venture are revealing. Take special notice of the use each one makes of the guiding principles discussed above.

CANOEING

Perceived competence

I was the pupil and my teacher was Andy. First of all, Andy provided me with a list of basic things to know about canoeing. He showed me two books which had pictures of the different types of canoes. He also explained proper carrying and docking procedures. He convinced me that he was experienced with canoeing when he said he's been doing it for about two years now. He made it seem a lot easier than I thought it would be when he told me he learned how to canoe by going out in one without knowing anything about it. Also, his family owns a canoe and lives near the Cuyahoga River, so he has the chance to do a lot of canoeing.

Logical organization: 1st— equipment; 2nd— rules; 3rd— practice

He told me about the basic equipment needed: a canoe, which is usually aluminum, but can also be fiberglas or redwood; two light, wooden paddles, one for the front and one for the back; life jackets for each person, floatable seat cushions, which can also be used to hold onto if the canoe capsizes. I was a little wary about the safety of a canoe, but he assured me that a canoe will never sink, even if it overturns or fills with water.

Perceived concern for safety and comfort

Andy also has gone canoeing in the winter, so he knows you've got to make sure you're warm enough by wearing loose-fitting clothing, plus warm gloves and shoes.

Concerned to check for accuracy of his teaching by repeating and summarizing the message

Then, so I could actually experience canoeing and learn more about it, we went out on the Cuyahoga River in his family's 17 foot, 85 pound canoe. As we went downstream, I paddled in the front and Andy paddled in the back. He showed me the different ways to position the paddle according to what you want to do. The person in the back has to do all of the steering, which is a harder job and which takes a lot of practice to do well. Then we docked and switched positions so that I could try steering for awhile. It takes a while to get the feel of it, so when I did anything wrong, Andy would keep showing me how to do it right. While we were on the river, he told about past experiences he's had while canoeing, some good and some bad. This helped make the lesson even more interesting.

He asked if I had any questions about anything we were doing so that I would understand it better. He explained everything in simple terms and did it more than once if I didn't understand the first time.

Canoeing was something I had never done before so it was quite an experience for me. But now I think I'm more interested in it since I learned how to paddle and steer one, how to dock one correctly, and how to turn one around in midstream, which has a lot to do with knowing how to steer. I know I'd be a lot more anxious to go canoeing again sometime since I've had the lessons. It was fun to do and learn about something new.

TECHNICAL ROCK CLIMBING

To begin with, I had never climbed anything before these lessons that required any more skill than it takes to climb a ladder. Randy and I had three lessons that were culminated in a successful climb on Saturday morning. The first lesson dealt mainly with general information and basic equipment that is essential to mountain climbing. During the first lesson, Randy explained how he was going to go about teaching me to climb, showed me a basic outline, and loaned me a book on basic mountaineering. The book was easy to understand with illustrations that were very helpful.

Perceived credibility:

The instructor provided an overview of his lesson

The second lesson was centered around the equipment and its use. I learned how we were going to use it, why, and when to use certain equipment and not others. For example, in climbing steep cliffs where there is a danger factor, it is necessary to drive pitons (pronounced pee-tons), little spike-like objects, which the climbers hook their rope into so that in case of a fall, the climber will only fall as far as the distance from the previously driven piton. These pitons come in many shapes and sizes, and are used depending on how big and where the crack in the cliff is. In the climb on Saturday, we used more than ten pitons and at least half of them were different.

The student learned the whys *for the how–to–do–it*

Saturday morning, we had our third and final lesson. The first thing Randy taught me to do was to rappel. Rappeling is descending from a height by sliding, with the aid of a harness, down a rope. To be frank, I was very hesitant and skeptical about leaning backwards over a 30 foot cliff, but with Randy's example and assurance, I succeeded in performing it without too much difficulty. I am now positive that this subject was the most exciting and could have been the most dangerous subject of all the "Each One Teach One" projects. After rappeling, we set about making the climb. Randy picked out a climb that would end about 60 feet up the side of a cliff in the Cuyahoga River Gorge in Cuyahoga Falls. Randy would start out first, and I would control the safety line. About half way up, Randy stopped on an overhang and controlled the safety line while I began the ascent. When I reached him, we switched positions, and Randy climbed again. When he reached the top, I started my climb. About ¾ of the way up, I had to climb over an overhang and became very frightened. Randy was out of sight, and I became scared and nearly panicked. Randy told me to relax, wait a minute, and calm down. Randy kept talking to me, which calmed me down and I made it to the top. Randy was very competent and gave me confidence that everything was all right. After a few minutes at the top, we then

Notice how the learner depends upon the example of the teacher

The learning experience has progressed to being put on one's own

rappeled down the 60 foot cliff to the bottom. Later we practiced falling off a 30 foot cliff to get the feeling and the experience of what to do in case of a fall.

Randy seemed to care whether he was doing a good job as a teacher, making the lessons interesting as well as factual, and he repeated many of the important parts and anything that I asked him to repeat. We got along well and had a good time. All in all, the lessons were a complete success, not only because they satisfied a class assignment, but also because I got to do something I had always wanted to try. It was truly a great experience.

Perceived good will

LEARNING THE PHOTOGRAPHIC PROCESS

Outline of the photographic process:

Notice how a clear outline may guide both the instructor and the learner.

I. Operating the actual camera
  A. Parts
    1. Focus—turn until clear picture is in lens
    2. Aperture setting
      a. controls amount of light let into camera
      b. is listed in *f*/scale
    3. Speed Control
      a. how long shutter stays open
      b. settings from 1/1000 of a second to B (i.e., as long as you hold Button down)

This outline follows a logical sequence from shooting to the finished product.

      c. how to use speed control for specific effects
        (1) stop action
        (2) blur action
        (3) panning (one object in focus, the rest blurred)
    4. Light meter—measures correct aperture and speed control
  B. Film
    1. Tri-X—set at 400—needs no extra light
    2. Plus-X
    3. Panatomic-X
    4. Emulsion on films
      a. is sensitive to light
      b. developing chemicals build on emulsion

II. Developing
  A. Tools
    1. Reels
    2. Cans—containers for reels of film
    3. Developing chemicals
  B. Steps
    1. Roll film onto reel
    2. Place reel in can and add developing chemicals
    3. Rinse
    4. Fix
    5. Rinse and Dry

III. Printing
    A. Equipment
        1. Enlarger
        2. Photographic Paper
    B. Steps
        1. Place film in enlarger and focus to desired size
        2. Put paper in position and turn on enlarger
        3. Develop, rinse and fix paper
        4. Dry

I decided to have Bob teach me some photography for two reasons: (1) Because I knew nothing about photography and thought it would be fun to learn a little about it; (2) I knew I would have to take an introduction photography course before I completed my studies at Kent State University. *[Motivation to Learn]*

Bob's first step was to establish his credibility. He did this by informing me of some of his jobs in photography. I learned that he works for *The Chestnut Burr* [Yearbook], and that he was chief photographer for his high school newspaper. He further established his competence in my eyes by showing me some of the equipment he used, including a $400 camera of his own and a rather expensive–looking camera that the *Burr* lets him use. The next step he took was to show me some of his previous photographic shots. They were beautiful and probably impressed me the most of all his supports. *[Credibility established]*

Before our first meeting Bob showed me a prepared outline of exactly what we would cover. This told me that he had put thought and preparation into the project. He had broken down the project into three main steps: the shooting of the film, developing, and printing. *[Organization reviewed]*

Showing me the workings of the camera and how to use it was Bob's next step. He explained the various dials and settings to me. He also let me focus the camera. To accomplish this I had to set the focus dial, the speed control, and the aperture setting. Next we went to my room where he let me pick the subjects I wanted to shoot. My roommate was photographed twice and I shot a special effect piece using glass bottles. Bob then showed me the delay switch on the camera so I could take a self-portrait. When we finished shooting we set a date to develop the film and finish up.

We developed the film in the *Chestnut Burr*'s darkroom in Taylor Hall. Bob showed me the steps by first lecturing on how it was done, letting me ask questions, and then by making me do it myself with him observing me. He applauded my steps and answered any questions I had cheerfully. He seemed really interested in my understanding of the subject. *[Feedback/ reinforcement]*

Finally, we took some film that had already been dried (we couldn't print the actual film that I shot because it was still developing) and he let me print that. He demonstrated the techniques used for special effects, and showed me how to do a test strip. The test strip showed how long to leave the print in the developer.

Bob seemed more interested in my getting a basic understanding of photography for my future use in journalism-photography courses than in getting a good grade in our class out of the teaching experiment. That

Demonstrated goodwill

was very relaxing for me and perhaps it was the reason why our lesson went so smoothly. I could tell from Bob's nonverbal actions that he enjoyed giving the lesson. He always seemed to be smiling and I'm sure the lesson was nicer for both of us than we'd thought it would be when the assignment was first given.

THE BASIC SPEECH

Although they are not exactly the same thing, giving a speech in public is similar to teaching someone how to do something. The speaker must decide what he wants to say, organize his ideas, and determine how to make them clear and interesting to his listeners. Giving a speech in public can be a rewarding and exhilarating experience. Speaker-meets-audience dates back to ancient civilization, and even in this age of radio and television, the live public address is a familiar sight in every culture and community. The ancient scholars labeled the study of this process *rhetoric*: the communicative art of influence. In modern times, the art of moving people to belief and action has come to be thought of as *public speaking*.

A speech may, of course, serve either individual or organizational purposes, be motivated by profit or charity, and be by invitation or self-initiated. The subject matter may be broadly classified as educational, economic, political, spiritual, or recreational. When a speaker addresses an audience, he seeks to draw the audience closer to certain ideas, feelings, or actions. The purpose, for example, may appear to be to entertain, as is true of an after-dinner speech for the college football team. Yet humorous after-dinner remarks may also be intended to arouse good feelings about the team so that financial support for the school's athletic program can be more easily obtained from school board members attending the dinner. Members of the audience—players, coaches, parents and school boosters—all have unspoken reasons for being at the dinner but, in all probability, are there mainly to play supportive roles for the speaker. A speaker–audience occasion may be more clearly understood when the relationship of those present is examined.

In courtrooms, we have lawyers pleading cases; in churches, clergymen promoting the faith; in classrooms, teachers explaining concepts; and in business, representatives selling products and company image. If we are to understand fully the purpose of public speeches, we should *not* think of them as isolated events. Rather, we should see them as events linking individuals and organizations. Speeches may reinforce established loyalties or promote new ones; they may entertain, inform, impress, convince, or any combination of these that serves the purposes of the speaker to influence his audience. But they always contain an element of the speaker's history and the audience's expectations.

Although the purpose for which a speech may be given is not always immediately known, there usually is at least one. The way a speech is delivered and the occasion on which it is given tell us much about the speaker's purpose. Before going on to the general concerns of the speech event, let us consider the simplest kind of speech: the story. Long before Gutenberg invented the printing press, the ability to tell a good story was highly valued, and it still is a basic element in giving a good speech.

In the summer between my freshman and sophomore years at college, I worked at a drill press in a factory. For eight hours a day, five days a week, I pulled down a lever and oiled a hot bit that burrowed into metal. In the fall when I returned to college, I wrote a speech attacking mass production. I gathered statistics about strikes and described sociological studies about the dehumanizing aspects of the industrial revolution. After reading the manuscript, my professor wrote, "Everything you explain here would be ten times more interesting if you had told it with stories."

The advice paid off. The following year, using a narrative description of my growing anger over the high cost of dying, I won first place in the state and advanced to the national oratorical finals. In addition to statistics, testimonies, and explanations, I used examples. Two of the stories I used in that speech, titled "Buried Treasure," expressed my feelings about modern funeral customs. The first was a true story, and the second was hypothetical:

> Before I was in grade school, my grandfather died. I don't even remember the funeral, but I do remember that, when one of the children would ask, "Where's Grandpa?" we'd receive the answer, "Grandfather's in heaven." If one of us would follow with, "What if Daddy'd die?" the quick answer from mother would be, "Let's not think about such things."
>
> My grandmother paid for my grandfather's funeral in installments. Each month I saw a portion of Grandma's few dollars go to the funeral director. All I knew then was that it seemed we'd never get Grandpa paid for.

Suppose, my friends, that someone in your family should die. Let's say it might be someone like Bruce, my redheaded, freckle-faced brother, who is in high school. Of course, we would want to show our love for Bruce by selecting a beautiful casket and grave marker. Friends would show their sympathy by sending basket after basket of flowers. Then Mom, Dad, and all of us children would go to the funeral home, there to have the rigid, lifeless form of Bruce stamped indelibly upon our memories. Forgotten is the warm vigor of his life—the sparkle that would light his eyes when the coach would send him in the game; the broad grin that would break out when mom would ask about the missing cookies.

When Bruce is buried, it never occurs to me that I might not be in school next year. None of us ever thinks about the fact that with the hundreds of dollars we bury in Bruce's funeral, we are also burying the treasure of my education and weeks of my father's labor. We are burying more than money. We are sacrificing to the pagan gods of waste the possibilities of bettering our lives. We are placing our gifts on the altar of ancestor worship. We are, in fact, denying the words of Christ, who evaluated the unimportance of the dead when He said, "Let the dead bury the dead."[2]

To be effective, any public presentation involving information exchange must incorporate the statement-example format. In training military personnel in the use of computers, the instructor reinforces his commentary with concrete examples and audio-visual aids.

We can embody a message in a story. Almost anything that is worth saying grows out of an experience. Stories alone, however, cannot satisfy rational people. Facts, testimonies, and scientific experiments must also support the emotions and conclusions that grow out of experience.

In the simplest form, a short speech is a statement and a story. **STATEMENT AND**
For instance, a speaker may assert that football is a dangerous **EXAMPLE**
sport. Then, in an accompanying story, he may describe an event
in which a player incurs a lifelong injury. A student who masters
that simple pattern may not win a debate, become a professional
lecturer, or be asked to present the keynote address at a political
convention, but he will possess the *key* to public speaking.

Read the following speech, which won first place in a contest
sponsored by a savings and loan company for its employees. See
how cleverly the stories are entwined with the purpose of the
speech and how it holds your interest to the very end.

YOU HAVE TO SEE IT FIRST

THIS is a marvelous place, this auditorium
where we sit in warmth and comfort, isn't it?
For a moment, let's not take it for granted—
let's look at it. Those lights—tubes of glass,
apparently empty, yet they glow! That
ceiling—what a load it can carry, yet how
easily. How nicely this room fits into the rest
of the building. Now, let me ask you a
question about this room: When did it first
exist? Was it when the roof and walls first
enclosed this space? Or was it when the
stone and steel and wood and plaster to
make it were gathered together? Or was it
perhaps when the architect completed his
plans and specifications? Now we are getting
nearer. I'm sure the architect *saw* this room
in his mind's eye before he was ready to
commence drawing his plans—and that's
when this room first existed. It couldn't have
been built if somebody hadn't seen it, splendid as it is now, when this ground was just a
vacant lot.

Several years ago—I think I was in the
fourth grade—there was a red-headed kid in
our block who had a red pushmobile, and
was he ever cocky! I remember looking at
him in his red pushmobile and being burned
up. Then I saw another pushmobile, a *blue*
one, and this one was bigger than his, and
faster, and it had ball-bearing wheels—and it
was *mine*. So I got busy and mowed lawns,

ran errands, and started filling the piggy-
bank with pennies, nickels, dimes, and once
in awhile a quarter. You know, ball-bearing
wheels cost money! I got the wood and the
axles, found a steering wheel in a junk
yard—off a *real automobile*—and pretty
soon there was a blue pushmobile. It was
faster than Red's, and it was wonderful. You
know, there wouldn't have been any blue
pushmobile if I hadn't seen it first. All the
time I was saving up to buy those ball-
bearing wheels, that vision was in front of
me whenever I went past the ice cream
parlor. It didn't hurt me much to save
money when I could see what I was saving it
for. And Mom was sympathetic—she made
chocolate syrup for me and kept it in the
icebox next to the milk.

In our neighborhood in Chicago, every-
body who was anybody saved his money in
some building and loan association. The one
we put our money in had a meeting every
Thursday night, and I used to go there once
in a while with Mother and Dad. I didn't
much like to go because they stood around
and talked and talked and talked—and I had
things to do. But Dad was annoyed if I
interrupted. Then one night I caught on;
Dad was listening to a friend of his who was
telling about his new home. He described
every room in it—color, furnishings, and all.

Afterwards I said to him, "I thought the Duffys lived in the flat over Novak's grocery store." And Dad said, "They do, Mr. Duffy was talking about the new house he is saving up to build. He thinks he will have the money in about a year and a half more, but to hear him talk you would think he is living in it!" "So that's it," I thought, "just like my blue pushmobile." Mr. Duffy built his house! I've always liked Mr. Duffy ever since I found out he could see the house he was saving for.

When you work in a savings and loan association, especially in the loan department as I do, you meet lots of people like Duffy and me, and you understand why those two words, "savings" and "loan," go together the way they do. Folks come in to see me every day and talk about the homes they want and lots of other dreams. When it's a close case and I'm not sure whether to recommend the loan or not, I ask them to describe the house to me. Some can't do it at all, but lots of times it comes sharp and clear and detailed, just like Duffy's. Then I smile, think of Duffy's house and my blue pushmobile, and recommend the loan if I possibly can. If they haven't enough money yet, I take them over to the savings department and say, "It won't take long now. That home of yours is so real the way you describe it. When you have enough in your savings account to swing the deal, bring your passbook with you so that you can show it to any loan officer. I might be tied up with someone else. That savings passbook shows more than just how much money you have, it shows how you saved it, and that's the finest recommendation you could bring!"

And it is, folks! You have to *see* it *first*. You have to see it *clear*, and *sharp* and *clean* and *splendid*—then you'll start to *save* for it, and then you'll *get* it. It *never fails*.

—Bernard A. Polek

Winner of the 1948 Five-Minute Speech Contest of the American Savings and Loan Institute, a nation-wide educational organization for the savings and loan business.

The speech you have just read is brief and only covers one major point. It is an excellent example of limiting the topic and illustrating a statement with a story. All speeches are not this simple, however. In the following pages we'll examine a slightly more complex speech given under more difficult circumstances.

A SPEECH IS A UNIQUE EVENT

Every effective address is a unique event. The speaker, the audience, the occasion—all come together at a specific time, usually for the better but occasionally for the worse. There are any number of reasons on the part of both speaker and listeners that bring about the meeting. Sometimes, the reputation of the speaker prompts an invitation to speak. On other occasions, his occupation or position is the determining factor; for example, it is expected that the president of a company will address the annual stockholder's meeting.

In a very real sense, an invitation to speak poses a challenge. It dares the speaker to be as good as his reputation. The audience has certain expectations based on the speaker's expertise. The speaker, in turn, must share part of his knowledge and experience with the audience, at least to show the audience their faith in him is justified.

OCCASION AND PURPOSE

The creative interaction of the social environment and a rhetorical event is illustrated by the acceptance speech of a winner of the Gold Key award presented by the Avenue of the Americas Association. This association is a group of neighborhood businessmen in New York City. They took their name from a street called the Avenue of the Americas. Formerly Sixth Avenue, it was in a rundown section of town. The business community spurred its renovation by changing its name and initiating plans for renewal. In 1972, Shelton Fisher, President of McGraw-Hill, was named as a recipient of the association's annual award along with Miguel Aleman, ambassador from Mexico.

The events that prompted the committee to select Fisher for the award were interesting. McGraw-Hill had recently made a decision to stay in New York at a time when the press had given front-page coverage to another firm who chose to move away. Mr. Fisher's topic for his acceptance speech grew out of his decision to stay in town. Moreover, McGraw-Hill had just completed a detailed study of conditions in several other communities to aid them in making their decision. This study convinced Mr. Fisher and his top executives that other communities also had severe problems, and while some of them were not as serious as New York's, these alternate cities could not hope to match New York's advantages. These were the circumstances that led to the award and inspired the message Mr. Fisher prepared for its acceptance.

Mr. Fisher's speech was scheduled at the end of a long evening. Ambassador Aleman's speech, which preceded Mr. Fisher's, was lengthy and required simultaneous translation, so an already restless audience grew uneasy and noisy.[3] When Fisher began, he was forced to ask for attention. He began, "I cannot compete with 900 of you. If you will take 10 minutes to listen to me, I will stay behind to listen to anything you have to say, even if it takes all night!" The request was effective, and after the speech was over, he was greeted with a tremendous ovation. In the next few days, there were hundreds of requests for copies of the speech. The *New York Times*, which had relegated the earlier news that McGraw-Hill had decided to stay in town to page 58, asked permission to reprint the speech in a promotional brochure it was issuing.

An effective address is a unique rhetorical event melding together the occasion, the speaker(s), and the audience. Bear this in mind as you read Shelton Fisher's acceptance speech. Notice, too, the way he identifies with the audience through the frequent use of such words as we, our, and us. But even more important than his use of pronouns, he talks about his company's people as New Yorkers whose homes are there. He describes the McGraw-Hill employees as talented, creative resources who are drawn from the city, just as his listeners are. His whole address is a personal narrative about why he and his McGraw-Hill staff like New York well enough to stay. Lines of the speech are numbered so they can be referred to in the commentary that follows it.

1	Thank you very much for this special recognition.
2	I am accepting it tonight on behalf of my company, and I intend to
3	share this award with my colleagues in our new headquarters just four
4	blocks south of here on the Avenue.
5	Sharing this award with the McGraw-Hill staff is not a grand gesture,
6	for they are the real reason we are located in your midst instead of
7	some other city, or the suburbs, or even some more remote rural
8	retreat. And thus, they deserve the credit given the company and its
9	officers for contributing to the stability of New York City. I know
10	that's the real reason why I am one of your honorees tonight.
11	You might like to know why our decision to stay in New York with
12	3,000 people (featured on page 58 of one of our local papers) was in
13	contradiction of a trend of some corporations to leave the city with, for
14	example, a headquarters of 250 people (featured on page one of one of
15	our local papers).
16	In the early Sixties it became apparent that we had outgrown our
17	building on West 42nd Street. We had already spilled over into eight
18	other buildings. What to do? Should we consolidate in New York City?
19	Or should we move out?
20	We considered both alternatives—and in doing so, discovered some
21	interesting things about ourselves. One, especially, led to our decision
22	to stay. We early realized that a company like ours—a company which
23	has no manufacturing facilities but relies for its fortunes on the creativ-
24	ity of many people—such a company simply does not have a real option
25	to leave this city.
26	If we had moved away, our human loss might well have been
27	crippling. Much of our talent, particularly the younger ones, would
28	have balked at being closer to the solitude of some remote spot than to

other editors, artists, writers and sales, promotional, and other creative people of their own kind.

In things spiritual, as well as in things material, there is considerable truth in the maxim that "only diamond can cut diamond." Talents develop and grow when exposed to other talents. In New York, and in particular in this, our new neighborhood, we are rubbing shoulders with all sorts of talent, and some of the best in the world. Why should we want to escape that fraternity? Think of our neighbors . . . *Time–Life, The New York Times, Newsweek* and *Esquire* and other major magazines are only steps away. This city is the center of *book publishing* activity. And all along our Avenue are the *television* networks—and *TV* is McGraw-Hill's *newest* endeavor.

In short, the comfort, productivity, and growth of our employees depend more on their proximity to their fellow professionals than to their proximity to green pastures.

Moreover, we publish for all ages and all strata of American society. It takes a plentiful supply from all ethnic groups and all creeds to do that. Only here could we be sure of finding enough of *this* talent.

In a word, our people—rather than economic or sociological factors—were our first and determining consideration.

To be absolutely certain of our decision, however, we took a long look at the advantages and disadvantages of the city versus the suburbs. Our conclusion: There's not a great deal wrong with the suburbs; there *is* a great deal right with the city. People talk of New York's problems—perhaps they overstate them because *everything* in New York is bigger and better illuminated, including the problems. And while people talk of the advantages of the suburbs—it's just possible they overstate those, too.

As for crime, New York does not have a monopoly on it, as lurid as our published record is. F.B.I. figures *do* show that crime rose by 3 percent in cities of over a million population in 1971. But the crime rate was up 10 percent in rural areas, 11 percent in the suburbs, and 12 percent in small towns. You can lose your wallet in Westchester, too, and drugs today are no respecter of geography. If you think so, talk to the Police Chief, as I have, in Bakersfield, California.

Transportation is something of a standoff. It's bad here, but at least a vast system is in place and new rolling stock is coming. Washington is digging its first subway, and Denver doesn't have *any* public transportation. On the other hand, driving to work in the smaller cities and suburbs—while it favors some employees—is absolutely impossible for others, particularly those who can't afford two cars.

As we continued examining the relative merits of the city and the countryside, an interesting thing happened. We realized that you don't really appreciate something you have until you consider the possibility of giving it up.

For example, we reawoke to the fact that New York is the commercial and financial center of the country, the hub of its communications and the heart of our cultural activity. With our involvement in all these fields, we just could not be anywhere else.

In addition, even as we discovered that life can be difficult in New York, we discovered that this wasn't necessarily a disadvantage. Some

80 folks tried to tell us that life was too competitive here, that you had to
81 scramble too hard to overcome transportation and other problems, that
82 you have to be tough to be a New Yorker. And we asked ourselves:
83 What's wrong with building your *business* with people who are com-
84 petitive, who are used to scrambling, and are accustomed to overcom-
85 ing problems? Do you build success with *non*competitors?
86 Moreover, as we looked closer at New York, we discovered that it
87 isn't just a "big city." New York is a small world, with all the
88 cosmopolitan advantages that implies. Nor is our new neighborhood
89 just a neighborhood—Rockefellar Center is a city within a city. Within
90 its limits are shops, restaurants, services, and facilities that even some
91 of our *large cities* cannot boast.
92 Finally, we believe New York has been through the valley. It
93 inherited a bad press, but has retained many great people and that
94 means great business enterprises. Some time, on a clear day or night—
95 (and *they* are getting more numerous)—go to the top of your favorite
96 building, look out and try to imagine all this force of human energy
97 drying up and blowing away.
98 I have done that and felt the full force of its impact—economic,
99 social, and personal. This city is forever . . . and I hope my company
100 will be.
101 Thank you, Mr. Salomone, for New York and for McGraw-Hill.

COMMENTARY In analyzing how Mr. Fisher developed such an effective address, we will divide it into three basic parts: opening, development, and closing.

Opening In his first sentence, Mr. Fisher thanks those who made the
award. Following this greeting, he demonstrates goodwill toward
his colleagues by stressing that they (line 6) are the ones who
deserve the award because they were the real reason McGraw-Hill
decided to stay in New York City. The subject of the speech—
"Keeping Business in New York"—was of high interest to those
who belonged to the association, and the bad press served as a
stimulus to justify the choice of topic (lines 13–16). In a modest
way, Mr. Fisher quickly establishes his competence to speak: by
reference to McGraw-Hill's new headquarters building and the
problem in the early sixties of whether to consolidate in New York
(lines 17–21); by reference to his position as a publisher in a city
of publishers (lines 32–41); and by references to a recent study of
other areas for a suitable location (lines 51–58).

Development The development of the speech was a narrative description of
the advantages New York City has over the suburbs, such as a
greater number of creative people to draw from (lines 23–50). Mr.
Fisher sums up his feelings in the phrases "There *is* a great deal
right with the city" (line 54) and "*everything* in New York is bigger

and better illuminated, including the problems" (lines 55–56), and both serve to introduce his comparison of New York's problems with those of other cities and suburbs (lines 59–73). Here statistics reported by the FBI are used to support his argument that other places have increasing problems with crime (lines 59–64). A conversation with a police chief is recalled to argue that drug problems exist elsewhere (lines 64–66). To illustrate that New York's transportation system is no worse and potentially better than others, Mr. Fisher points out that Washington, D.C., is just digging its first subway while Denver has no public transportation at all (lines 67–73). After listing the difficulties New York has but others have also, Mr. Fisher shifts to the offense, suggesting that one does not value what he has until he is faced with the possibility of having to give it up (lines 74–77). He moves dynamically from problems to the advantages of having to scramble and compete (lines 82–90) in this exciting "small world" of New York (lines 91–96).

In concluding his address, Mr. Fisher becomes eloquent though *Closing* his style is still direct and plain. He pictures New York as having been "through the valley" (line 97) and does not believe its "force of human energy" will dry up and blow away (lines 97–102). Thus he expresses the kernel of his message symbolically. His closing paragraph is poetic and personal, as he affirms dramatically "This city is forever . . . " (lines 103–105), and closes with a final word of gratitude (line 106). By praising New York, Shelton Fisher urged those 900 business neighbors to affirm anew their determination to keep their headquarters in the city.

So far in this chapter, we have examined the purposes for which you might give a speech. The speeches analyzed help us see that a speech is not necessarily a strong political statement or a call to action for solving a social problem. The occasions for speaking publicly vary infinitely, and all of us, at one time or another, can expect to be invited to address an audience on a topic of personal interest.

It is important to notice that, in both speeches above, the speakers used an even tone and everyday language. A public speech does not need to contain lofty-sounding phrases and literary references for the audience to appreciate its message. Choice of language and examples are important for establishing rapport with an audience, and it is wise to keep your audience in mind from the beginning. In the following section, we will look more carefully at the audience.

THE AUDIENCE

In Chapters 4–6, we discussed the importance of the listener to the message process. Without the listener, some would argue, no message is being delivered at all. For the communication transaction to be complete, the listener must perceive the message, decode its meaning, and provide feedback to the sender. In the public speaking situation, the audience is the listener. Although there may not be an opportunity for immediate and intimate feedback, there is an interaction between speaker and listener which is extremely important to the effectiveness of the message. Just as the occasion for presenting a speech may determine the content and format of the message, so will the kind of audience and how you relate determine the ultimate results of the speech. In the following pages, we will consider some of the methods we can use to ensure that the interaction with the audience will be helpful in planning the speech, useful while delivering the speech, and instructive in planning for future speeches.

TYPES OF AUDIENCES There is a classic categorization of audiences that was first suggested by H. L. Hollingworth; and although some of his categories are for small group and interpersonal settings, they are all worth looking at. The five audiences he labeled are: (1) pedestrian or casual, (2) discussion group or passive, (3) selected, (4) concerted, and (5) organized.[4]

1 The *pedestrian* or *casual* audience has no common group purpose for being together and usually is not together in one spot for very long. A crowd waiting to cross the street of a busy corner or a group of people waiting to enter a movie or sports event would be an example of this kind of audience. Getting and maintaining attention are essential for the speaker to address this type of audience for very long.

2 The *discussion* or *passive* audience usually has come together for purposes other than just to hear the speaker, and establishing interest is high on the list of priorities for the speaker. The

Each of these photos illustrate different audience-speaker relationships. It is the speaker's responsibility to analyse the type of audience and whether its attitude toward the speaker is positive, indifferent or negative. The presentation should then be adjusted accordingly.

town meeting, the social organization, and the after-dinner audience are examples.

3 Members of the *selected* audience have usually been asked to attend a gathering or meeting because they have a common interest in the subject being discussed. Although they may not share the same opinion, the speaker knows she will have their interest, and her first task will be to establish credibility and authority for speaking.

4 Members of the *concerted* audience usually have mutual interests and a specified purpose for being together. Although they may have shared interests, they have no clear direction or lines of authority for achieving their purpose. The speaker's responsibilities will be to recommend action, suggest solid plans for achieving goals, and generally organize audience momentum. A special task or training group and a political rally are concerted audiences.

5 The *organized* audience is usually made up of persons having a common purpose, a system of authority and leadership, and considerable sympathy for the subject to be addressed. The speaker has a high degree of control over the audience and need only speak to direct what action should be taken.

You may recall that in the chapter on listening (chapter 5) we decided that there were certain purposes for which we listen to a message and that these purposes overlap or shift from time to time. So also do the kinds of audiences overlap and change. The pedestrian audience that is captured by an unexpected rain shower may discover they have a shared interest in the dynamic speaker's message and continue to listen, at least as long as it rains. Or a selected audience may be so influenced by a speaker's message that they indicate their willingness to take some kind of action. Under these circumstances, that audience could be re-labeled as concerted.

Hollingworth used the orientation of audience members toward the speaker in his classification system. While the degree of predisposition toward the speaker is certainly helpful in planning a speech, we must not rely on it exclusively. There may be a time, for example, when we are asked to speak to an audience that is totally unsympathetic to our message (discussed in Chapter 10). The reason for classifying audiences is to narrow the factors we must consider when preparing a speech. The process by which we assess a potential audience is called the audience audit and is the first step in speech planning.

THE AUDIENCE AUDIT

As we looked at the types of audiences suggested by Hollingworth, we observed that each one required a certain action by the speaker. We said, for example, that getting attention was the first thing a speaker had to do when addressing a pedestrian audience. Your analysis of an audience will largely determine how you plan your speech. There are two questions you must ask as you begin your audit: (1) What more can I know about the audience that will help make my speech more effective? (2) What does the audience know about me and about my message? If you know about the audience you will be facing, you already know a considerable amount. If you do not, you must begin by acquiring more information.

ACQUIRING INFORMATION

There are two reliable methods for acquiring audience information, and when used together, these can be extremely useful in the planning stage of your speech.[5] The first is to organize the information you already know and the second is to acquire additional information from those who are familiar with the group. Information you may already know concerns such variables as age, sex, occupation, education, ethnic background, race, religion, and political affiliation, and this information can help in determining how you can relate to the audience. If any one or more of these variables separates you from the audience, you may want to consider ways to emphasize your similarities and minimize your differences.

KNOWN INFORMATION

Political candidates, public relations experts, and representatives for large corporations have the means for acquiring considerable data about their audiences before they address them. Through the use of surveys, questionnaires, and random interviews, they gather information that will help them give a smooth and effective presentation. Most of us do not, however, have the luxury of sophisticated information services and must rely on informal observations, personal relations, and experience to draw inferences. The minister of a church grows familiar with his congregation, and the social club member gets to know the members' preferences. In any community we live in, we learn at least one or two facts that can be useful. We know what recent local event will get a humorous reaction, and we know what historic event will receive a sober, patriotic response.

Unknown Information   But what can we do when we have no personal experiences to help us? The second method for acquiring audience information is to discover as much as possible through anyone who has had contact with the audience. If a representative of a group asked us to speak, we can ask that person about the group's characteristics. Perhaps we can get in touch with a former speaker who could tell us what received a warm reaction and what was ignored. If we have a friend or business associate who is a member, we can call on him or her to share information with us. Asking group members about their group will show the seriousness with which we view the presentation and illustrate our appreciation for the opportunity to speak.

Audience Information   Especially important in acquiring information is the question, "What does the audience already know about my topic?" To speak on the value of public transportation to a society of automotive engineers would probably be a disappointment to them and a disaster for you. If they are experts in their field, you will have to reveal your credentials in a modest, pleasing but informative manner. Earlier in this chapter we discussed the after-dinner speech to gather support for the college athletic program. It would be of little use for such a speaker to have a breakdown of the audience's political affiliations; but information regarding their ages, whether they had school-age children, their educational backgrounds, and how many among them were school athletes would be very helpful. If we can identify the predisposition of the audience toward our topic, we can decide what to emphasize. For audiences with school-age children, the rewards for developing strong bodies, the benefits of teamwork, and the need for good sportsmanship as preparation for life will probably be highlighted. For audiences with no children living at home, the importance of community pride and tradition, the continued development of good citizens, and the opportunity for childless persons to become active in a challenging and rewarding youth program can be emphasized.

Related Information   Finally, while you are conducting the audience audit, you should be asking some related questions that can help in planning your speech. Are you the only speaker for the evening? Is there a limit to how long you can talk? Will your speech be given indoors or outdoors? How many people are expected to attend? Will amplification be required, and who is responsible for obtaining and checking it? Where and when will the audience be seated? Is the site easily accessible at the time you are due, or will you need to allow extra travel time? Is the occasion formal or informal, and how should you dress? Will your speech be given after a large dinner? Should you eat before you arrive? The answers to all these questions will influence how you prepare for making a public speech.

Collecting information about the audience is only valuable to the extent that the speaker can draw inferences on how well his message will be received. A second important method of analysis is to determine your purpose in speaking. As was true of the college athletic program, the speaker may want members of the audience to show their support by voting to allocate more funds. When you have specific goals in mind for your audience, it is important to state them to yourself as you plan your speech. Doing so can help you focus on the important questions you need to answer if you are to be persuasive. Several examples of how a speaker's goals might be more specifically stated are:

BEHAVIORAL GOALS

1 I want my audience to laugh at my stories of how our company came into being. I want them to tell these stories to their friends. I want the chamber of commerce and the company employees to have a personal identity with the company by knowing its humble beginnings.
2 After hearing my presentation, I want the research and development board to allocate $25,000 toward a more economical and safer process for . . . .
3 After my address to the City Club, I want 25 people to give a pint of blood in the current Red Cross drive.
4 After my speech to the class, there will be a discussion about why the women's athletic program receives only a fraction of the amount budgeted for the men's program. I want at least half of the class to sign my letter to the campus paper requesting a change.

A behavioral goal includes *what* behavior you want to happen, *who* you want to perform it, and *when*. A good audience audit will include a careful consideration of the answers to what, who, and when. In combination with the other information you have acquired about your audience, your goals will help you plan a memorable and persuasive message.

ADAPTING TO THE AUDIENCE

Even though you have prepared as much as possible to understand the setting and audience you will face, you must still be flexible and willing to change your material and style of delivery. All the audience analysis beforehand will not be nearly so useful if you do not continue your analysis while you are speaking. For it is during the presentation that you have the last chance to adjust your message as you observe how it is being received. Audience feedback plays the same role as listener feedback in dyadic communication: it helps a speaker be better understood.

Even the most detailed plan for a speech can require modification during delivery. As you gain experience in speaking, you will read audience cues more accurately and develop the ability to adjust your delivery and message to meet audience responses. During the presentation, you can watch the audience for signs of interest. Shuffling feet, expressions of puzzlement, staring out of windows, and yawning or fidgeting tell you to adjust your message. Are you being easily heard in all parts of the room, or is the high volume of the amplification system causing discomfort? Are you being too expansive in sections where the audience appears to have little interest? A more aggressive (or slower) delivery style or condensation (or expansion) of material may be in order.

You need to be discriminating in your interpretation of audience feedback. The frown or furrowed brow may be someone concentrating very intently on the message, not necessarily disagreeing with you. Or the listener with the nodding head may not be agreeing with you, but only understanding what he thinks you said.

The planning and advance work you do is not lost if you change at some point. To adhere stubbornly to a plan that is getting negative feedback just because you rehearsed it that way is more damaging than to abandon some portion of your prepared speech. The experienced speaker not only knows when his audience is signaling for a change but also prepares the speech with an awareness of places where change or shift can be easily made. Because the audience is the final judge of the success or failure of your message, the analysis you perform during the planning stages and your willingness to adapt while you are speaking are two key factors in having a positive interaction with the audience and presenting an effective speech.

EVALUATING YOUR SPEECH

A final word about the audience and how you interact with them concerns the time right after you have completed your speech. This may be the most important time for audience analysis and may be your first indication of your effectiveness. If yours was a speech to influence the audience to take action, you will know soon enough how effective you were. You must be cautious, however, in attributing certain group action to your influence without other confirming data. If you have urged three groups to protest land development on the lakefront and only one takes action, you have reason to be skeptical and may want to investigate other factors about the group before taking responsibility for their action.

Applause, compliments, the way the press reports your speech, and criticism from others provide good feedback as to how your message was received. All these signs can indicate places where you may want to change or adjust your message the next time you have occasion to speak. If there is time, trying out your speech on friends or family is an excellent way to gain an evaluation prior to the actual event. If you are in a class where you will deliver several speeches to the same audience, you have an excellent opportu-

"That concludes my prepared remarks. I will now fend off questions from the audience."

nity to use the evaluation of each one to improve the next. Just as we learn what communication techniques are effective for us in interpersonal settings, so may we also discover how to develop effective public speaking techniques by seeking out information about our audience, keeping an open mind during the speech, and inviting feedback to help us refine our presentation of ideas to others.

Most of all, remember when evaluating a speech, that communication is a complex process. The symbols we must use are inexact and fragile. The odds, therefore, are high that we will be misunderstood. We must also remember that many factors may influence how favorably a speaker and his message will be received. An audience is not putty in the hands of even the most accomplished speaker; but it is rather an assembly of individuals with diverse interests, loyalties and pressures. More often than not an effort to persuade another fails or achieves only part of what the speaker intended. The key to evaluating even the simplest public speech is the question, "Why?" "Why was the message persuasive, or why was it not?" Looking on evaluation in this inquisitive fashion, can give the beginning speaker the tools he needs to improve.

SUMMARY

In the first part of this chapter, we described the different types of information exchange: *description, process,* and *policy.* By concentrating on description, we explored the relationship between communication and learning. The need for reinforcement and the uses of punishment in operant learning were related to the process of giving another person instructions on how to do something. This discussion was aimed at the principles involved in transferring information.

The rest of the chapter deals with the speech and the audience, we have surveyed the general speech event. The occasion and purpose for giving a speech can vary widely, and the speaker must take that into consideration. When preparing a talk in its simplest form a speech is one person telling a story to another. When we extend that a little, we can say a short speech is a statement and a story. As an example, we suggested that football can be a dangerous sport and then told of a player's receiving a serious injury.

Not to oversimplify what a short speech is, we then examined two speeches in light of the occasions on which they were given and the reasons the speakers gave them. Establishing rapport with the audience by careful use of language and examples and keeping the audience in mind from the beginning will generally result in a more effective statement.

In the second part of this chapter, we discussed the audience. The types of audiences Hollingworth classified were (1) pedestrian or casual, (2) discussion or passive, (3) selected, (4) concerted, and (5) organized. The audience audit is the first step in planning a successful speech event. In it the speaker acquires information about, and determines his behavioral goals for, the audience. Drawing on personal experience and interviewing members of the audience, as well as persons who have had contact with them, are two ways of acquiring information. Data such as age, sex, occupation, education, ethnic background, race, religion, and political affiliation can all be helpful in determining what kind of message to bring to an audience. In combination with the knowledge we have of the occasion and purpose for speaking, the information we acquire about an audience can help us select an approach to the topic and a method for presenting it.

Adapting to our audience is as important as our analysis of them. We must be ready to adjust our message when we see signs that our audience is not receiving our message. Many of the same sensitivities we discussed in the section on interpersonal communication are useful in reading audience feedback and altering our message while our speech is in progress.

Evaluating our speech is also a part of audience analysis. When we know we will be speaking to an audience on subsequent occasions, we can use their feedback to improve our next message. Trying out our speech on friends and family ahead of time is an excellent way to get preliminary audience feedback and evaluation. And most importantly we must always remember that communication is a complex event. The odds of failure are great, and the appropriate attitude for the evaluation of a speaker/audience event is an inquisitive one. We should always ask why a message was received favorably or not.

INITIATIVES

INITIATING ACTION 1   *Each One Teach One.* Each student presents to the class several skills he has and several skills he would like. Pair off the class so that half the students may learn a new skill from someone else. If time permits, reverse the teacher-student pairs. Topics may range from academic skills which lend themselves to a session or two of tutoring to very practical skills such as tuning a car. Avoid dangerous skills and topics which demand long weeks of instruction. Each party should do a short analysis of the learning experience. Use the *Guiding Principles* in this chapter to reflect upon the process.

Each class member schedules two sessions to: (a) teach another class member, or (b) be taught. BONUS: REVERSE THE PROCESS.

Prepare a step-by-step design of how you will teach it or outline how it was taught to you. Don't choose a project which is too difficult such as learning how to speak a foreign language or too easy such as how to tie a knot. Select topics you genuinely want to learn whenever possible.

Participants in the lessons should present separate reports for teaching or learning, based on indicated items which follow:

Report Due: _____

1. Your name: State whether you were instructor or pupil and give the name of the other person, and the subject or item taught.
2. Specify end behavior. List the things the pupil should be able to do or know after the lessons.
3. Step-by-step outline. For example, list equipment necessary and where to buy it. Indicate what the pupil should do, and how many times.
4. What was done to build credibility? How did the student-instructor convince the pupil he or she was competent?
5. Did the student-instructor present an overview or preliminary outline of what was to be covered? How organized was the presentation?
6. Did the pupil know exactly what he or she was supposed to learn?
7. How important was feedback? Was understanding checked from time to time? How?
8. Was friendly concern shown for the pupil's interests and welfare? How?
9. How could you tell from your pupil's nonverbal behavior how well he understood? What could you read in the teacher's nonverbal behavior?
10. Were accomplishments praised?
11. Was there redundancy? That is, was the same thing said in several ways or several times?

12 Was more than one channel used? That is, were visual aids or physical demonstrations utilized?

13 Was playback asked for? How successful was the experience?

Do not simply answer each of these questions, but rather organize your report into paragraphs dealing with topics suggested by the above questions. Particularly, examine such elements as credibility, organization, feedback, and interpersonal relationships. Approximate length of the report—two pages, double-spaced typed.

Speak Out. Speak for two or three minutes on a topic you would like the class to look at more closely. Select a topic that needs, but does not have, the concern of your classmates. The topic may be intellectually provocative, socially controversial, or politically current. You may gauge your effectiveness by your ability to enlist your class in presenting a symposium on the topic. A number of sample topics (either pro or con) follow: **INITIATING ACTION 2**

1 The family should be the most important unit in a healthy society.

2 Peaceful use of nuclear energy should be expanded.

3 Big families are superior to small families.

4 Women do not have equal rights and opportunities.

5 Tax reform is needed.

6 Ecology is overemphasized.

7 Every young person should serve his country for some period in the military or alternative service

8 Hunting is outdated for a humane society.

9 Busing as a means of integration is unwise and impractical.

10 Prostitution should not be legalized.

11 Trial marriage would make for happier homes.

12 The United States should not supply armaments to any country in the Middle East.

13 Universities should dissociate themselves from military-supported research.

14 A volunteer army is superior to a drafted army.

15 Socialized medicine is the answer to high medical bills.

Symposia. The symposium presents an excellent vehicle for gaining experience both in delivering a short formal speech and in answering questions. Speeches should be three to five minutes in length and a 20-minute question period (forum) should follow. **INITIATING ACTION 3**

INITIATING ACTION 4   *Home*. Present a speech applauding your hometown or the place where you now live, such as the university. Study Shelton Fisher's address to the Avenue of the Americas Association in which he affirmed his company's faith in New York City.

INITIATING ACTION 5   *The Inspirational Speech*. Reread Bernard A. Polek's speech, "You Have to See It First." Construct a speech based on this model that speaks affirmatively about how your chosen vocation is able to help people. Do your best to use the same style Polek used, but draw from your own experiences.

INITIATING ACTION 6   *Conveying Conceptual and Factual Information*. Prepare and present a speech on some subject that is new to you. First, read about the subject in a general way. Then, interview persons knowledgeable about the topic. Next, analyze what your audience knows and what you think they should know. Design your introduction to recognize and possibly test the audience's knowledge and interest. Reserve some of your information for a question-and-answer period after your presentation. Perhaps there will be time for you to conclude your presentation with a short test of what you have taught. Have a student jot down the questions asked. Reflect upon them. They are pretty good indicators of what facts are remembered and what concepts are and are not understood.

NOTES

1. These Each One Teach One reports were written by students in the author's Introductory Speech class. Annette Dagil reported her experience in learning canoeing, Andy Fisher on technical rock climbing and Ron Modic on learning the photographic process.

2. William I. Gorden, "Buried Treasure," *Winning Orations* (Evanston, Ill.: Interstate Oratorical Association, 1950), pp. 51–52.

3. Theodore S. Weber, Jr., personal letter to the author, July 22, 1974. Mr. Weber is senior vice president of McGraw-Hill, Inc.

4. H. L. Hollingworth, *The Psychology of the Audience* (New York: American Book Company, 1935), pp. 20–22.

5. Theodore Clevenger, Jr., *Audience Analysis* (Indianapolis: Bobbs-Merrill, 1966), pp. 43–50.

SUGGESTED READINGS

Campbell, John Angus, *An Overview of Speech Preparation*. Chicago: Science Research Associates, 1976.

Colburn, C. William and Sanford B. Weinberg, *An Orientation to Listening and Audience Analysis*. Chicago: Science Research Associates, 1976.

McCabe, Bernard P., Jr., and Coleman C. Bender, *Speaking Is A Practical Matter.* 2nd ed. Boston: Holbrook Press, 1973.

Mills, Glen E., *Composing the Speech.* Englewood Cliffs, N.J.: Prentice-Hall, 1952.

Monroe, Alan H., and Douglas Ehninger, *Principles and Types of Speech Communication.* 7th ed. Glenview, Ill.: Scott, Foresman, 1974.

Zacharis, John C., and Coleman C. Bender, *Speech Communication: A Rational Approach.* New York: Wiley and Sons, 1976.

9 designing the speech

A few people may be intuitive in their speaking abilities. Instinctively, they organize their thoughts, support their points, and deliver them persuasively. But for most people, delivering a persuasive speech takes more than intuition or instinct. The long-time editor of the *Saturday Review of Literature*, Norman Cousins, had little patience with intuitive writing. He was fond of saying that writing is not neat and quick, and that teachers, rather than rewarding nice handwriting, should encourage students to strike through, substitute, and rewrite and rewrite. The same is true of speech preparation.

In the previous chapter, we focused on the importance of analyzing the audience and adjusting the message to the listeners during a speech. In this chapter, we will continue our description of the creative process, the process that is going on in the speaker's mind in defining the core idea and developing strategy to influence listeners. We will study the steps in speech preparation: (1) choosing a topic, (2) researching the topic and acquiring information about it, (3) organizing information, and (4) developing forms of support.

CHOOSING A TOPIC

In the beginning of Chapter 8, we looked at two speeches given on typical but very special occasions. Classroom speaking differs from this type of speaking in that no special occasion will suggest a topic for you. You will need to choose a topic and decide what you intend your speech to accomplish.

In Chapter 8, we said that communicating information usually centers on *description* (telling what something is like), *process* (telling how something is done), or *policy* (telling of regulations and usually referring to a principle, plan, or course of action). We also said that this kind of information falls into the category of *instrumental* or *persuasive* communication whenever the purpose for telling it is to communicate what it *should* be in addition to what it is. As you consider your purpose for giving a speech, you must decide whether you want to inform or persuade your audience. Determining your purpose will be closely linked to selecting your topic and organizing your speech.

INTEREST

Two preliminary questions to ask yourself as you consider a topic are: "Am I genuinely interested in this topic?" and "What do I want to say about it?" Look for something that interests you. Such broad issues as inflation, environmental problems, and energy conservation are important, but it would be difficult to cover them adequately in a five- or 10-minute talk. These subjects are perhaps best left for discussion groups. Your interest level is important to the speech for several reasons. You share many ideas and experiences with your classmates, and if a subject does not appeal to you, there is no reason to expect that it will appeal to them. Also, if you are not interested in a subject, your lack of enthusiasm will affect the way you present the speech and, consequently, the way your audience receives it.

One way to search for a topic is to reflect on your own interests. How do you spend your time? Do you enjoy needlepoint, ceramics, or some other craft? Perhaps you worked in a pizza restaurant or an ice cream parlor last summer and became an expert at making something. Have you discovered a way to cut your study time in half? Can you keep plants thriving indoors during the cold winter months? Do you make your own clothes? If you work in the library, you have much information that can be useful to your classmates. Your own experience can be the starting point for an informative and interesting speech.

If your interests genuinely take you to the broad issues being discussed in the press, you may want to narrow the topic and research some specific aspect of it. For example, you may be interested in gun control but find the topic too broad to cover in a five-minute talk. But gun safety or the status of gun laws in your state may lend itself more easily to the time you have and may satisfy your own personal interests, as well as provide useful information to your class. It may even persuade some of your classmates to take notice of an issue they have been ignoring.

After you have thought of several topics on which to speak, place yourself in the position of being a member of the audience. Now as a member of your future audience decide which topic would be of real interest to you and what you would like to know about it. Try your idea out on some friends and see how they react. If the topic is controversial, decide which position you feel in agreement with but also consider whether or not you want to share your feelings with others. Finally, ask yourself if information about the topic is easily obtainable. If you have to write letters to Paris or Peking, for example, you are not likely to get the facts in time.

RESEARCHING THE TOPIC

Once you have chosen a topic, you are ready to start the process of finding out more about it. You probably know something already, but to acquire the kind of facts needed to discuss the topic publicly, you will have to tap a variety of information sources.

SOURCES Just as your own experiences are useful in selecting a topic to speak on, so are they helpful in acquiring information. You may have (or know someone who has) a personal story about your topic that will not only help your audience feel closer to you, but will enhance your credibility as well. Remember our discussion at the beginning of Chapter 8 where we described the effectiveness of making a statement and following it with a short story? If you do not know anyone who can provide background for this part of your talk, you may want to look outside your own circle of friends.

Your hometown or even your own neighborhood can be a good source of information. Public officials, members of the chamber of commerce, and civil servants can all provide facts based on their experiences and training. Members of your school faculty can also give expert advice. Before going to experts, however, it is important to learn as much as possible on your own. Then, when you are interviewing someone, you will be able to ask meaningful questions and not waste her time in providing basic information you can acquire elsewhere. You will do most of this preliminary research in the library.

Although you have probably been using libraries for most of your life, you may not be aware of all the services and facilities they offer. The library has two main sources of information: the reference section and the card catalog. In the reference section alone, you will find volumes of information and sources for still more information. Encyclopedias, such as the *Britannica* and the

International Encyclopedia of the Social Sciences, provide general background information and excellent bibliographies of other sources. *The Statistical Abstract of the United States* or *The World Almanac and Book of Facts* can help you identify useful statistics or short factual statements about your topic. *Who's Who in America, The Dictionary of American Biography*, and other biographical dictionaries are filled with information about special people. The *Reader's Guide to Periodical Literature* can help you locate current news and magazine articles that discuss your topic. There are, of course, hundreds of other sources not mentioned here; and in your preliminary research, a few hours spent in the reference section are certain to be rewarding.

The card catalog of the library is the other main source of information. Every book or document in the library is listed here. In addition to the location of the volume, the cards contain information that can help you decide if the book will be useful. If you know little about your topic, it can be very helpful to begin your search for more information by looking under the subject, where cards for all the books the library has on your topic are located. Also, a browse through the section of the stacks where the books on your topic are located may reveal surprising information. The reference section and the card catalog are two places you can start your search, but a talk with the librarian can be of infinite value as you begin. The time you save and the effort you expend acquiring information will be largely determined by how organized you are. Note taking is a good method of becoming organized, and it will be essential as you plan your speech.

NOTE TAKING

As you go through the sources you have located, you need to decide which information will be useful. Some can be eliminated early. There will be other data you are uncertain about and, of course, much that you will want. To locate the important information, it is helpful to devise some system for categorizing information. You may want to arrange it by statistical data, opinion, expert testimony, or personal experience; or you may want to keep it according to the sources in which it is found. You may devise other systems, but whichever one you use, the system must allow you to locate any information you have filed easily. Taking your notes on cards (3'' × 5'' or 4'' × 6'') will allow you to retrieve information easily and to change filing systems if another turns out to be better suited to your purposes. Using note cards can help you keep all your sources in order and organize your speech more effectively.

The secret to useful note cards is to put only a small amount of information on each one and to record fully the date, author, title, page number, and other important data about the source. Always place quotation marks around material quoted from any document, and circle or bracket your own words if added within so you do not confuse them later. Once you have exhausted your sources and recorded the important data on cards, you can classify and subclassify in many different ways by shuffling the cards. As you begin organizing your speech, you will then find it easy to relate specific cards to certain sections.

ORGANIZING THE TOPIC

GESTATION   Somehow the expression, "to make a speech," got started and has stuck. To say, "make a speech" implies that a speaker constructs something outside himself, as when a chef mixes together ingredients in a recipe to make a pie. We usually think of "having a conversation" rather than of "making a conversation." And this idea of "having" something seems to say it is truly a part of the person or persons having it. And having, like having a baby, tells us that something happens in us, grows inside until it must give birth. A person who merely *makes* a speech probably will be thought of as someone who is not completely into what he is saying. He is giving a performance rather than sharing something that happened to him. The way it should be is to "have a speech."

In "having a speech," as in having a baby, there is a gestation period during which the components of the speech take form. During this period of gestation you will need to consider how to organize all of the data you have collected to make a knowledgeable presentation. The way you organize the speech is one of the most important determinants of how effective it will be. It begins by showing your attitude toward your listeners.

Your stance toward the listener comes across in the design of your presentation. For example, when I hear someone "suggest several alternatives," I see him as one who thinks of me as an adult able "to consider." On the other hand, if I hear someone outline a course of action as the "*only* reasonable way," I hear him telling me he has wisdom superior to mine and that I should acquiesce to his decision.

The approach reveals the attitude a speaker has about himself and about his audience. As presenters, we model our message. If our organization is confusing, we will never sell our customers a course in straight thinking. Most of all, listeners want to buy ideas from presenters who think straight. Therefore, the speech preparation period, or perhaps more correctly put, the gestation period, is an important time for reflection and nourishing that message yet to be born.

There are probably unlimited ways to organize a speech, and usually it is only after you have delivered it that you find the best way. Your purpose for giving the speech will have some bearing on how you organize your speech. For example, if you are making a presentation that is intended to inform your audience of certain facts and ideas, you may arrange them in order of importance or from the least to the most complex. But if your purpose is to influence a decision, you may choose to point out advantages and disadvantages of the proposal under consideration. Whatever the occasion or the purpose for the speech, organization is important for establishing credibility and for delivering the message efficiently.

In the following paragraphs we will look at some methods for organizing your information into a speech. The figure below is a preview of the methods we shall discuss.

DESIGN FORMATS

Speeches and houses have some basic similarities. Among the most important is that they should suit the needs of the owner. To cater to these needs, there are a number of models or stock designs from which to choose. They offer the home buyer a structure that is more economical and more readily available than one for which plans must be created. And stock designs offer the

---

DEVELOP A STRUCTURE FROM THE LISTENER'S PERSPECTIVE

I am not a complex minded person, so organize your message in familiar patterns.
Topical Patterns: Divide your message into topics I can remember and keep in order.
Questions and Answers: Answer the questions I have about this topic.

Problem and Solution: Identify the problem and suggest a solution for me to consider.
Process of Elimination: Help me to consider several alternatives for dealing with an issue, and tell me why you prefer a certain one.

speaker a basic structure within which he is free to exercise his imagination and creativity.

Usually, speech texts are divided into three parts: the introduction, the body, and the conclusion. While these terms have served speakers well as aids to organizing a speech, I prefer to use the terms *opening, development,* and *closing* to describe the functions which are accomplished by these three parts of the speech. Psychologically, when a speaker begins his presentation, he is trying to open up the audience to a new relationship and a new idea or way of looking at an idea. Next he develops that idea, and finally, he seeks to bring the topic and the audience to a sense of completeness or closure. Later, in Chapter Ten, we will look at this process more closely. For the moment we will examine some standard design formats for organizing a speech. In the opening the communicator (1) gets the attention of the audience, (2) establishes a common ground and creates interest, and (3) prepares the audience for the message that follows.

The development of the speech is where the main point of the message is delivered. The body contains the information and material that will support the main point. It is the longest part of the speech, and it may be arranged according to any one of a number of stock designs, which we will discuss in a moment.

Finally, the closing is used to summarize and highlight what has just been said. Sometimes it is a good place to arouse the audience emotionally and make them willing to do something, such as donate their time or money, or vote. It is also the place to let your audience know you have finished.

Although all speeches may be arranged in the general order of introduction, body, and conclusion, the stock designs we mentioned can be employed within the speech and especially in the body of the speech. Your imagination is the only limit to the number of ways you can arrange your material within these formats.

There are four commonly used designs for organizing a speech: (1) *topical*, according to the topics that will be covered; (2) *question and answer*, according to the questions the audience may have about the subject; (3) *problem and solution*, by describing the problem and offering a solution; and (4) *process of elimination*, by presenting the options or courses of action that are available and eliminating all but the one you want to suggest.

Topical   The topical solution is well suited to the brief, informative speech, but may be used in persuasive speeches as well. In this design, the three or four most important ideas form the framework for the speech. For example, in a speech explaining the role of the symphony conductor, the speaker might decide that the conductor's analysis of a musical piece, the rehearsal, and the conductor's actions on the night of the performance are the three topics that will adequately describe what a symphony conductor does. Or in a speech to persuade, a speaker might list and elaborate on three or four major reasons for supporting a certain position.

Question and Answer

Any speaker using this format must discover what questions the audience is most likely to have in mind. Some preliminary research about the group to whom the speaker will present the speech is essential to using the question-and-answer format effectively.

Problem and Solution

This format is especially useful in presenting persuasive speeches. The speaker describes the problem and presents a possible solution. For example, in a speech that identifies the dangers of hazing and discriminatory pledging practices of social fraternities and sororities, the speaker may recommend the abolishment of those organizations on campus, or may outline a plan for more stringent codes of conduct and governing boards to control the incidence of abuses.

Process of Elimination

This format is similar to the problem-and-solution format, except that the speaker identifies the problem and then discusses several alternatives. Gradually, all are eliminated except the one the speaker is recommending. For example, in a speech that discusses air pollution in our cities, you might suggest that (1) we ban private transportation, (2) we ration gasoline to private individuals, (3) we increase taxes on gasoline, or (4) we have the government adopt a "hands off" policy. After discussing each alternative and pointing out its drawbacks, you would come to the one you feel offers the best solution to the problem.

*The Motivated
Sequence*

There is another design format called the *motivated sequence*. Not really a stock design, it is based on the universal principles of learning, such as human needs and motivation. Alan H. Monroe designed this approach with five steps which he labeled: *attention, need, satisfaction, visualization,* and *action*. Briefly, the steps follow the psychological behavior of the individual. First, his interest is aroused by some startling or alarming statement. Next, a need or comparative deprivation is generated in the listener. For example, he may not know the degree to which alcohol or tobacco is harming him, and the speaker may give him some facts and statistics to make him aware of the effects of these products. Once aware of the potential danger, he needs the speaker's suggestions.

To enhance the acceptance of these suggestions, the listener is projected into the future and asked to imagine or visualize himself suffering from his ignorance. Startling statements, such as, "There are 20 million alcoholics in the United States," are used to attract his attention. Through projection the listener's choice is made crystal clear: he can be a fortunate person who enjoys happiness and success, or an unfortunate person who suffers heartbreaking tragedy.

Finally, the time is right for action. In our example, if the speaker is successful, the listener will stop drinking alcohol and contribute time, effort, and money to Alcoholics Anonymous.

The *motivated sequence* is designed to manipulate the audience psychologically. At its best, it recommends solutions to an audience's real problems. At its worst, it is condescending in tone and based on assumptions that are invalid.

There are good reasons for using organizational models. Not only do they help the speaker structure what she says, but they also help the audience interpret what it hears. When the form of the speech is familiar, the listeners can concentrate more closely on what may be unfamiliar or unkown to them: the meaning of the message.

Time spent composing a speech is a period of invention, a period of discovery. The speaker arranges his materials, tests the logic of his ideas, and uses the organizational model he has chosen to help him quickly detect any deficiencies. He also seeks to impose on his ideas a design that is attractive to the audience and appropriate for the occasion.

This period of planning then, is a time for generating new ideas and creative solutions. It is a period I enjoy immensely. I design and redesign major addresses several times. I talk about my ideas with friends. I try to find a symbol that is consistent with my values and appealing to the audience. I examine my major headings to discover if there is a way to make them parallel and more memorable. I seek illustrations that force me to look at my problems and solutions differently. Planning has always been, for me, a very challenging and delightful part of the art of rhetoric.

CONTINGENCY   Before we leave this section, let us think for a few moments about the "what ifs" of a speech situation. Ponder these possibilities: What if the person who speaks before you uses the same humorous story you planned to use? What if the chairman for the evening announces that the organization has just voted

not to contribute to the United Fund and you are one of its
directors? What if you notice that some members of the audience
are rubbing their foreheads as though they do not understand
you? What if others yawn and appear restless?

Wise speakers prepare contingency plans, that is, they have
alternative material and options to which they can turn if appropriate. When a preceding speaker has used similar material, the
most obvious choices are: (1) To repeat the material and appear
unaware it has been used. Such a choice is insensitive and
boring. (2) To repeat the material acknowledging it has been used
previously but paraphrasing it with greater emphasis on one
aspect or a different interpretation. Such a choice might be
considered sensitive and even clever. (3) To drop out the repeti-
tious material and substitute something previously prepared.

An experienced speaker, sensitive to the varying interests of
audiences, may begin by saying, "Today I can talk about any one
of several topics, such as government regulations, union negotia-

tions, organizational innovation, or the concern of business for the quality of life. Do you have a preference?'' He may then take a straw vote to see which topic interests the most members or he may base his choice on someone's expression of strong interest. This principle of multiple contingencies may be applied not only to the entire speech but also to its individual sections as well.

At various points, the speaker may ask the audience questions. For example, when talking about changes the future will bring, he may ask, ''How many of you believe in flying saucers? How many do not believe flying saucers exist?'' Such questions both involve members of the audience and provide the speaker with an instant audit of their beliefs. Before using an important word with which the audience may be unfamiliar, a speaker might ask, ''How many are well acquainted with the word *triage*? How many are not?'' If a sizable number are not familiar with the term, the speaker needs to define it clearly before using it frequently.

Although most speaking events are not debates, we may learn from the careful preparation practices of accomplished debaters. They plan how they will respond to different arguments and outline counterarguments. Speeches that really matter to an audience will spark questions and comments. One of the most important aspects of contingency planning, therefore, involves preparation of additional supporting materials for major points during the speech and for the questions that follow. The goal of contingency planning is to anticipate so that the material presented will receive a fair hearing.

FORMS OF SUPPORT

We all tell stories or describe events we have seen in terms of the experiences of our listeners. Very often, when we are at a loss to explain a certain idea or item, we will find an *example* of it and show or tell it to our listener. At other times, we explain an idea by *comparing* it with something with which our listener has experienced. These are just a few of the devices we use every day to communicate with others, and there is no reason not to use them in a speech. We explain and we illustrate all the time, and the formality of a speaking occasion should not inhibit our use of these communication techniques.

Before going on to the next chapter, where we will outline a speech and describe what takes place when we deliver it, we should take stock of the various means we have for communicating an idea. When applied to the data and information we gathered in the research process, these methods of expressing our ideas become our *forms of support.*

Forms of support may be given many different labels, but for our purposes, we shall broadly classify them as *explanations, illustrations,* and *evidence.* The speaker uses supports to generate interest, establish rapport with the audience, and to lend a sense of credibility and reasonableness to the message. Although supports come in many forms, you will be likely to use all of them at one time or another.

EXPLANATION

An explanation is a statement that clarifies a meaning or shows the relationship between certain ideas, but an explanation alone is seldom sufficient support. Explanations are improved by the use of a story, a description, an analogy, a metaphor, or a simile. While you are probably familiar with how effective a story and a description can be (recall the speech on saving in Chapter 8), you may be less familiar with the other techniques.

Analogy

When something is explained by comparing it point by point with something else, an analogy has been made. In academia, a typical analogy compares getting a PhD to courtship and marriage. Beginning a master's program is like going steady. Selecting a chairman for a thesis committee is like proposing. The comprehensive examinations may be compared to the wedding ceremony. And the writing of the dissertation (with all of it trials and rewards) may be likened to a long marriage. Analogies come in varied species and sizes. They are often fun to use and display measure of creativity.

Metaphors

Metaphors are similar to analogies in that they make use of the similarities between certain ideas or objects. A metaphor is a figure of speech that implies comparison by calling one thing another, thereby giving a new meaning to a familiar word or phrase. "The curtain of night," or Shakespeare's famous, "All the world's a stage," are typical metaphors.

A popular metaphor used to organize speeches is the *medical metaphor.* This metaphor positions the speaker in the role of a wise doctor, able to both diagnose the illness and prescribe the remedy. The doctor-speaker (1) observes the symptoms, (2) names the illness, (3) analyzes the causes, and (4) prescribes the cure. For this metaphor to be effective, the audience must perceive the speaker as being very informed on the topic. If members of the audience doubt the speaker's knowledge, they may be reluctant to take his prescription. The medical metaphor's strength lies in its familiarity: the four-step sequence is easy for the audience to follow. It is often used by speakers seeking to persuade the audience to follow a certain course of action. The medical metaphor may also serve as a design for the whole speech.

Simile   A simile makes a comparison but does not assign the meaning of one idea to another, as is done when the world is called a stage. In similes, the comparison is often introduced by the words *as* or *like;* for example, "tears flowed like rain," "as dark as night," "as cold as ice," or "as quiet as a mouse."

ILLUSTRATIONS

Illustrations are usually detailed examples that serve to clarify meaning. The best illustrations are those drawn from your own experiences. The more personal the examples you use, the more enjoyable and believable they will be to the audience. If you do not have a firsthand experience, you may cite someone else's or use a hypothetical illustration (invented stories that probably could have happened). If the latter, be certain that your audience knows they are made up and also be sure they are relevant to the discussion. An illustration that does not contain a lot of detail, but is only referred to, is called a *specific instance*. To indicate that people can endure extreme hardship and still survive, you may mention the bombing of London during World War II. You need only mention the bombing, as the details are sufficiently well known by most people.

Be they factual accounts of something that actually happened or hypothetical stories, illustrations are the most effective means of dramatizing your meaning. A factual illustration consists of a story (narrative) of an event. As in the first line of a news article, it should include the who, what, when, and where; and in the rest of the story, there should be enough description of the interaction so that the audience can infer some reasonable explanation of why. Imagery, movement across a period of time, and actual or paraphrased dialogue may be used liberally.

Observe how illustration is used to intensify interest in this excerpt from a speech made to a Rotary Club by Roger Deer, vice president of Lamb Electric.

We have been able to maintain a fairly stable workforce and the company has grown in spite of some difficult periods—including the Great Depression of the '30s and various periods of labor unrest. As a matter of fact, we were about the first industry in the community to be organized by labor back in the '30s. The initial organization effort is remembered by many in the community as the "War on Lake Street," and unfortunately our company is known by many for this event rather than for the products we make. The strike was so heated and the controversy so great that it was said that this water tower looked much like a large sieve from the bullet holes that it contained. I know it must have been a rough period for when I first came to the company there were still file cabinets being used that contained bullet holes. . . .[2]

This illustration affected the speaker as well as the audience. He verbally relived the experience, and in so doing, was caught up again in the tonal and muscular tension of the event. Members of the audience saw and heard the nonverbal cues and shared Mr. Deer's emotions. At that moment, identifying with the early difficulties of the company, they became sympathetic toward his forthcoming message.

In speeches to inform, illustrations may take the form of visual aids. Comparing a camera and a model of the human eye will make apparent the similarities between the two. Sometimes the real thing is useful as a visual aid. If, for example, you are explaining something fairly uncomplicated, such as the theory of stress behind the workings of a bow and arrow, you may want to bring one along to enhance your presentation. But in most instances, a diagram or mock-up is more suitable and allows the speaker more flexibility.

EVIDENCE

Evidence is also called proof. This supporting material is usually made up of information that comes from external sources and/or from internal reasoning. It is not normally found in personal stories or in a specific instance. Therefore, we may think of evidence (proof) as being either *extrinsic* (coming from facts, observable data, statistics, testimony of an expert, etc.) or *intrinsic* (application of logic and reasoning, or causal relationships, to arrive at some truth).

Observable Data

Observable data is made up of the things we can see around us and know to be true. If you were to go to the Rose Bowl and count 103,236 people there, the number in attendance would be a fact you would have observed. On the other hand, if the official attendance counter were to report that number to the press and it was published in the newspaper, you could probably consider that a fact, too. Now it is possible for the counter to make a mistake or for the typographer to make an error, but in most instances, observable data can be verified by someone else's

In defending 1975 grain sales to the Soviet Union, then Secretary of Agriculture, Earl L. Butz used a loaf of bread to aid his economic arguments.

seeing the same thing. When observable data become measure-able in numbers, they become statistically significant.

Statistics   Statistics are probably the most commonly used type of extrin-sic proof. Using statistics we can summarize, show averages and abnormalities, and examine the relationship between certain measurable phenomena. Because statistics usually refer to abstractions (that is, they may be percentages, ratios, or numbers of great size such as the national debt or national population) audience members may find them difficult to visualize; therefore, the careful speaker uses them sparingly. A long list of numbers can quickly become meaningless to an audience when there is no identifiable idea to which they relate. The speaker should try to translate statistics into understandable terms for the audience. Round numbers can replace exact figures; pie or bar graphs are very useful; and stating the numbers in a different way can make them more easily understood. In addition to saying, for example, that 50,000 people are killed and several hundred thousand are injured annually on American highways, a speaker can say that three out of every five persons in the audience will at sometime in their life be involved in an auto accident.

In a speech to the Society of Automotive Engineers, Semon E. "Bunky" Knudsen, chairman and chief executive officer of White Motor Company, used hypothetical illustration to make statistical data meaningful:

> Let me give you a hypothetical illustration of what I mean. On the Alaskan North Slope in the Prudhoe Bay area, there are proven reserves of about 10 billion barrels of oil. That sounds impressive, and many of us have been comforting ourselves with the thought that this great oil find will solve our energy problem if we can only get the oil piped out. But let's take another look.
>
> At the present time, we are consuming—in the United States alone—between six and seven billion barrels of oil a year. And our consumption of oil is increasing at an annual rate of six or seven percent. Now, suppose we had all that Alaskan oil pumped out of the ground, shipped, refined and in storage tanks. And suppose we decided to use it up so as not to deplete our reserves in the lower 48 states, and that we quit importing oil so as to improve our balance of payments to strengthen the dollar, all of that Alaskan oil would be gone in 18 months.
>
> So, even if we get that Alaskan oil out, and even if we find other equally big fields on the North Slope, in off-shore areas, and in other parts of the world, the rate of use throughout the world is so high and growing so fast that we must ultimately find other sources of energy to take over much of the energy load now being carried by petroleum.[3]

Knudsen used the comparison between new availability and quantity consumed to show how small the figure of 10 billion barrels is when placed in context with present and future U.S. oil consumption.

Testimony is the opinion of someone who should know, possibly an authority in the field, or a person who witnessed an event. In a speech, as in court, the validity and admissibility of the testimony depends upon the credibility of the witness; therefore,

Testimony of an Expert

when using a witness care should be given to establishing his or her credentials. I once listened to a most unusual use of expert testimony at a funeral sermon. The clergyman read brief statements from 40 famous people affirming their belief in immortality. The event was moving and persuasive because of the credibility of the famous people, despite the fact they had no proof to support their opinions.

Inductive Reasoning

There are two general kinds of reasoning: inductive and deductive. *Inductive reasoning* is the basis for most scientific knowledge because it enables us to move from specific observations or experiments to general laws or theories (inducing from the specific to the general). It is subject to error, however. We may infer a generalization from an insufficient number of examples and so draw an incorrect conclusion. For example, we may reasonably conclude from our personal experience that all birds can fly. In fact, though, there are several species, such as the Kiwi, that cannot. One must always be careful to test an inductively derived theory as much as possible before stating it as fact.

Deductive Reasoning

Reasoning from known facts or generalizations is known as *deductive reasoning*. We deduce from the general to the specific. For example, from the fact that all men and women are mortal, we deduce that a particular woman is mortal. Or we deduce from the general to the general, that since $2 + 2 = 4$ and $3 + 1 = 4$, then $2 + 2 = 3 + 1$. Generally, we use a combination of inductive and deductive reasoning. We may notice, for example, that many advertising executives have stomach ulcers and *induce* that all such executives have or will have ulcers. We then *deduce* that, because all advertising executives have or will have ulcers, working in advertising causes ulcers. Our error in drawing this conclusion is twofold. First, we incorrectly induced that *all* advertising executives have or will have ulcers because our experiences are not broad enough to bear out this generalization. Furthermore, we incorrectly deduced from the common association between advertising and ulcers that advertising *causes* ulcers. To prove a causal relation, we must not only show that advertising executives commonly have ulcers but that an advertising executive *must* have ulcers. Finally, we must show that it is advertising and not some other factor that is causing the ulcers. Speakers sometimes intentionally make subtle errors in deductive reasoning to mislead naive audiences; but conscientious speakers—and their listeners—take care in drawing conclusions from the available evidence.

As you prepare your materials, you will want to keep in mind certain ideas that will help you test your supports and evidence. If your explanations are from your own experience, you will want to ask:

1 How accurately did I observe?
2 What kinds of inaccuracies could have been caused by my mood or attitude, my physical condition, or the setting?
3 Was what I saw typical? Could it possibly have been the exception rather than the rule?

If the supporting materials come from another person's experience and observation, you should ask (in addition to those questions asked of yourself):

1 Did the person who reported to me observe the occurrence himself?
2 Is the reporter's reputation reliable? Is he known for the accuracy of his accounts? Is he regarded as a careful observer? Is he an expert in the field?
3 Is there more than one observation of the event available and do the witnesses agree?

If the supporting materials come from a book, magazine article, or television program, you will want to ask yourself:

1 How consistent is this piece of information with my own experience or what I know to be true?
2 Does it seem reasonable?
3 Is the source considered reputable and impartial? If it is biased, how would this have affected the reporting?
4 How careful are the writers? Do they provide details such as names and places? Do they make statements that seem broad or oversimplified?
5 Does the source refer to research methods used? What geographical area did the study cover? How many samples were taken? Would occupation, age, or political affiliation have influenced the answers to the questions asked in the survey? If so, how?

No doubt you will think of other questions to ask yourself as you research your topic. The more you ask, the more accurate your information will be.

FORMS OF SUPPORT

Explanation	Description Analogies Metaphors Similes	*Tend to generate New Images*
Illustrations	Actual examples Hypothetical examples Specific instances Visual aids	*Tend to generate Feelings and Identification*
Evidence	Observable data Statistical data Expert testimony Inductive reasoning Deductive reasoning	*Tend to generate Logical Analysis and Reflective Judgment*
Total		*Belief in the core assertion and credibility of the speaker*

SUMMARY

In this chapter we have covered four important processes for designing the speech: choosing the topic, researching the topic, organizing the topic, and understanding forms of support. The two essential questions one must ask in choosing the topic are: (1) "Am I genuinely interested in this topic?" and (2) "What do I want to say about it?"

While researching the topic, the speaker should learn to identify sources of information and should devise a good system for recording the information. It is important to classify information according to various levels of importance, so it will be readily available when you begin to organize the speech.

Speeches are traditionally divided into three parts: the introduction, the body, and the conclusion. But I prefer to describe the parts of the speech as the opening, development, and closing phase of the speech. This way the functions of the parts are more clearly labeled. Within this general format there may be many different patterns or designs for organizing the material in a speech. The designs identified in this chapter are: topical, question and answer, problem and solution, and process of elimination. The *motivated sequence*, developed by Alan Monroe, is often used in speeches to persuade, but it can sometimes suffer from overgeneralization about human behavior and appears condescending to the attentive listener.

Forms of support may be divided into three broad categories: explanations, illustrations, and evidence. Explanations can be made through stories, analogies, or descriptions, or we can use the everyday communication techniques of simile and metaphor to draw a comparison and thus make a point. Evidence includes observable data, statistics, expert testimony, and reasoning. All supports should be tested. As the speaker is organizing material for his speech, he will ask questions about the reasonableness of certain information. He should examine carefully any information obtained from sources outside his experience, questioning especially the reliability and expertise of the source, the recency of the events, the objectivity of the report, and its relevance to the point he wishes to make. In every case, to the degree that it is possible, supporting material should be chosen for how well it will be understood and believed by the audience to whom it will be presented.

In the next chapter we will examine the steps leading up to the presentation of the speech and—more important—what actually happens during the delivery of the speech itself.

INITIATIVES

INITIATING ACTION 1 *Finding a Topic.* The topics listed in this initiative ask the question, "What's happening?" Scan the list and search out your answer to one that will interest both you and the audience. Your investigation may result in your coming to a position about what happened, and possibly what was right or wrong about what happened.

TOPICS—WHAT'S HAPPENING?
or
Up Against the Wall, Apathy!

ECOLOGY: What's happening to our world?
      pollution
      population
      pesticides
      natural resources

MINORITIES: What's happening to our brothers and enemies?

Blacks	South Asians
American Indians	Chinese
Eskimos	Russians
Mexican-Americans	Israeli
Puerto Ricans	Arabs
South Americans	Europeans

DEMOCRACY: What's happening to the "American Dream?"
      the radical Right
      the radical Left
      the "Silent Majority"
      freedom of speech
      dissent/protests/desegregation/violence/riots
      taxes/inflation
      bugging
      X-rated movies/smut for children
      militarism

LIFE STYLES: What's happening to our culture?

drugs	
music	communes
morality	health foods
mass media	

EDUCATION: What's happening to our schools?
      student rights

    quality of teaching
    grading system
    relevance of education

CITIES: What's happening to our cities?
    crime   education
    housing   poverty
    urban renewal

LIFE CRISES AND CHOICES:
    parent-child discipline
    vocational choice
    marriage/divorce/bachelor/children/childless
    suicide/natural death
    faith/religion/non-religious
    aging

Clear and Cloudy. The test of any speech is how well it is **INITIATING ACTION 2**
understood and believed by the target audience. Your own class-
room is a laboratory which should provide you feedback on your
speaking effectiveness. Ask a listener (perhaps several class
members would be willing) to use the Clear and Cloudy, Believable and Unbelievable questionnaire below to give you feedback
on one of your speeches. The listener can rate how clear or
unclear your speech is by placing a check in the space that most
represents his feeling for each category.

AUDITOR IMPRESSIONS OF THE PRESENTER

Cloudy message	___: ___: ___:	___: ___: ___:	Clear message
Unbelievable message	___: ___: ___:	___: ___: ___:	Credible message
Uncaring about me	___: ___: ___:	___: ___: ___:	Caring about me
Passive	___: ___: ___:	___: ___: ___:	Enthusiastic
Uninteresting	___: ___: ___:	___: ___: ___:	Interesting

Comments:

Instructor feedback. Your instructor is trained in helping you **INITIATING ACTION 3**
improve your speaking. He/she has probably listened to hundreds
(or perhaps thousands) of speeches. He may have designed a
form for the purposes of evaluating speeches. The form below is
designed to help you evaluate your speeches based on the ideas
in this book. Use it to record your impressions of your own
speeches.

INSTRUCTOR'S EVALUATION FORM A
Profile of Student Presentations

KEY: − = Leaves something to be desired or remedied ✓ = Satisfactory + = Creative

PRESENTATIONS

	First	Second	Third	Fourth
Opening				
Statement of Thesis				
Message Organization				
Credibility of Supports				
Vocabulary				
Emotional Involvement				
Closing				
Overall Effectiveness				
Notation of Problem Areas				

Items noted below may suggest problem areas of a presentation.

1. fidgeting
2. slouching
3. stiffness
4. pacing
5. weak gestures
6. little eye contact
7. sloppy pronunciation
8. too low volume
9. too loud volume
10. overuse of notes
11. halting (uh's)
12. overuse of slang
13. inappropriate dress
14. overexplanation
15. position unclear
16. needed cues or signposts or previews
17. needed summary (internal or final)
18. needed more illustration
19. needed evidence which was credible to audience
20. lacked enthusiasm

NOTES

1. Alan H. Monroe, *Principles and Types of Speech* (Chicago: Scott, Foresman, 1935.)

2. Roger Deer, "The Lamb Electric Story," Rotary Club Address, February 5, 1974 (mimeographed).

3. Semon E. Knudsen, "The Interchange of Technical Information," presented at the West Coast Meeting of the Society of Automotive Engineers in Portland, Oregon, August 22, 1973. Printed in *Vital Speeches*, vol. 40 (November 1, 1973), pp. 40–42.

SUGGESTED READINGS

Anderson, Martin P., Ray E. Nichols, Jr., and Herbert W. Booth, *The Speaker and His Audience: Dynamic Interpersonal Communication*, 2nd ed. New York: Harper and Row, 1974.

Arnold, Carroll C., Douglas Ehninger, and John C. Gerber, *The Speaker's Resource Book: An Anthology, Handbook and Glossary*. Chicago: Scott, Foresman, 1961.

Bradley, Bert E., *Fundamentals of Speech Communication: The Credibility of Ideas*. Dubuque, Iowa: Wm. C. Brown, 1974.

Clevenger, Theodore, Jr., and Jack Matthews, *The Speech Communication Process*. College Speech Series. Glenview, Ill.: Scott, Foresman, 1971.

Dickens, Milton, *Speech: Dynamic Communication*, 3rd ed. New York: Harcourt, Brace, Jovanovich, 1974.

Gibson, James W., *Speech Organization: A Programmed Approach*. San Francisco: Rinehart Press, 1971.

Haynes, Judy L., *Organizing a Speech: A Programmed Guide*. Englewood Cliffs, N.J.: Prentice-Hall, 1973.

10 outlining & delivery

Just as deciding what you want to say and gathering information about the topic require planning and organization, so does the actual presentation. All of us like to think that what we say is more important than the way we say it, and in the final analysis, that may be true. But researchers have found that the delivery or manner in which we give our speech is strongly related to the way the message is received. Delivery (1) affects credibility and persuasiveness, (2) influences audience comprehension and retention, and (3) determines overall effectiveness.

In the previous chapter we spent considerable time discussing the importance of organization and preparation for the speech. In this chapter we shall look at outlining information, developing the speech, and choosing the method of delivery.

OUTLINING

A good way to organize the material you have gathered is to construct an outline of the message you intend to deliver. Your outline will serve several purposes. In the beginning it will guide and stimulate your thinking. Later, it will help you test your organization and consider alternative plans. As you think about the points you want to make and gather your supports, it will help you keep track of your data and judge how well it works together. And finally, your outline will help you decide which data you must use and which data are not really pertinent to the purpose of your speech.

BEGINNING THE OUTLINE   In a general sense, outlining is nothing more than dividing your speech into organized parts and deciding what points you want to make in each part. Because all speeches have an opening, development, and closing (or beginning, middle, and end), three very important parts of any speech are already identified for you.

One way to begin outlining is to make a list of the important points you intend to discuss, and then to arrange them in the order in which you think you will want to present them. As an example, suppose you were planning a speech to tell an audience how to begin playing the harmonica. Your first task would be to state your reason for giving the speech. You might write: "My purpose is to tell the audience how to begin playing the harmonica." And without concentrating very hard you might decide you need to cover the different kinds of harmonicas, the type of music played on the instrument, the history of the harmonica, how to practice the harmonica, how to play the instrument, how to take care of it, and how it works. Your general list of things to cover might look like this:

```
kinds of harmonicas
type of music
history of the harmonica
practicing the harmonica
playing the instrument
taking care of it
how the harmonica works
```

TYPES OF OUTLINES

As you examined this list, you might think of other ideas about the harmonica and combine them with the research and reading you have done on the topic. Going through this process, you might also decide to drop others; you might even rearrange the list into an order that is easier for you to discuss and for the audience to follow. After a few rearrangements, your list would become what is called a *working* or *thumbnail outline*.

A working outline is a list of topics to be covered which reflects deliberate thought concerning priorities, sequence of events, or reasoned determination as to what should be presented and at what time. It will help keep you oriented during the lengthy planning job. A working outline for your speech on the harmonica might look like this:

BEGINNING THE HARMONICA

```
History of the harmonica
     Origins of the instrument
     Popularity in the United States
What the harmonica is
     Actual description
     Types
     How to choose one
     How it works
```

Playing simple songs
    Single blow notes
    Single draw notes
Special techniques
    Bending notes
    Vibrato
    Blues riffs
    Talking
Care of the instrument
    Durability
    Breaking in
Tips on practicing
    Books
    Listening to others
    Playing in groups

After you have identified your main points and subordinate topics, you might evaluate your plan again. If you were satisfied with the order and kinds of topics you had decided to discuss, you could begin to construct a *topic outline*. The purpose of the topic outline is to help you identify in detail all the information you will need to cover the subject adequately. The following topic outline lists the ideas your working outline has generated:

BEGINNING THE HARMONICA

   I. History of the harmonica
     A. Origins of the instrument
       1. Invention
       2. Early manufacturers
     B. Popularity in the United States
       1. Role on the frontier
       2. Contemporary popularity
  II. What the harmonica is
     A. Actual description
       1. Materials and shape
       2. Free reed principle
     B. Types of harmonicas
       1. Chromatic
       2. Diatonic
     C. How to choose one
       1. Different keys
       2. Size and number of holes

      D. How it works
         1. Holding the instrument
         2. Blowing and drawing
III. Playing simple songs
      A. Single blow notes
         1. Tonguing
         2. Puckering
      B. Single draw notes
         1. Tonguing
         2. Puckering
IV. Special Techniques
      A. Bending notes
         1. For tonguers
         2. For puckerers
      B. Vibrato
         1. Pivoting on the palm
         2. Opening and closing the cup
      C. Blues riffs
      D. Talking
V. Care of the instrument
      A. Durability
         1. How much wind the reeds can take
         2. Resiliance of wood and metal
      B. Breaking in
         1. Soaking
         2. Cleaning
VI. Tips on practicing
      Λ. Playing from books
         1. Books on technique
         2. Anthologies of songs
      B. Listening to other artists
         1. Sources of information
         2. Choosing a model
      C. Playing in groups
         1. Locating the right group
         2. Carrying the melody, playing lead and solos

In constructing a working outline, we evaluated the reasonableness of our general plan. We were concerned primarily about the sequence of ideas (Does it make sense to discuss techniques for special sounds before or after we have explained and demonstrated how to play a simple song?) and about what we needed to say about those ideas. In the topic outline we identify and evaluate each item we plan to cover in the speech. This more detailed outline helps us see how and where specific data fit and whether they are relevant.

Of course, the information in the topic outline could be given in greater detail, or even arranged as a *sentence outline*. The topic outline contains only phrases, and is less time-consuming to construct. It does not require us to decide exactly what we intend to say about each point. In the sentence outline, each point is expanded into a statement about the point we are discussing. For example, a sentence outline of the opening of your harmonica speech might look like this:

I. I will begin with a brief history of the harmonica.
   A. First, I will mention the origins of the instrument.
      1. There is some controversy about who the first inventor was.
         a. Sir Charles Wheatstone, who invented the concertina and is called the actual inventor of the electric telegraph is said to have invented the harmonica, in 1829.
         b. It is also claimed that in 1827 the Chr. Messner firm started manufacturing the instrument at Trossingen, Wurttemberg (Ger.).
      2. Other early manufacturers are the Fr. Holtz Company, which started in 1825 in Knittlingen, Germany, and the Klingenthal Company, founded by J. W. Glier in 1829.
   B. The harmonica has always been popular in the United States.
      1. In the settlement days of the frontier, it was common to most communities because it is easily carried and learned.
      2. With the rise in the popularity of folk songs in the fifties and sixties and the stronger-than-ever interest in country music, the harmonica is as popular now as before.

Writing a sentence outline forces us to think out completely what we will say to the audience. It allows us one more check on the completeness and reasonableness of our information, and becomes the first rehearsal of the speech.

In the section on delivery we shall look at the advantages of speaking from a topic or sentence outline. For now it is important to keep in mind that the outline is a tool for developing our ideas. As you progress from the general list of things you want to cover to the sentence outline, you will constantly initiate new ideas, refine old ones, and strengthen the general plan of your speech.

After you have gained some practice developing outlines, you may let the thoroughness with which you know a subject and the amount of time you have available to rehearse determine how complete an outline you want to make. Although mixing a topic outline with a sentence outline violates strict outlining convention, when you are speaking about a subject with which you are very familiar, you may wish to write complete sentences for the main points and list the subtopics briefly.

NOTATION

Outline notation is standardized so that anyone looking at it can follow it, but the system may seem a little mysterious at first. The idea behind the notation is not simply to impose a structure on a list of ideas, but also to make clear the relationships between them. In our example, main points are written first with subordinate points following. The symbols beside each topic or sentence (*I, A, 1, a*) indicate the importance of each idea. A main idea is preceded by a roman numeral. A supporting point under that main idea takes a capital letter, and lesser points are designated by arabic numerals, then lower case letters. The number of levels you need will be determined by the complexity of your subject and how deeply you intend to go into it.

Each outline symbol carries only one idea. If a topic is divided, it should have at least two parts. That is to say, if you are going to have an *A* you should also have a *B*, or if you are going to have a *1*, you should also have a *2*. If a topic cannot be divided into at least two subtopics, it should not be divided at all. For example, if all you had to say about the history of the harmonica was something about its origins, the beginning of your topic outline might look like this:

I. Origins of the harmonica
    A. Invention
    B. Early manufacturers
II. What the harmonica is
    A. Actual description
    B. Types of harmonicas
    C. and so on

The only time you should list a single subtopic is when it is an example.

Of course, each main point does not divide easily into the same number of subtopics. If you look back at your topic outline, you can see that, although there are four subordinate ideas under the main point, "What the harmonica is," there are only two subordinate ideas under, "History of the harmonica."

The final point to remember about outline notation concerns assigning levels of importance. The three or four main points of a speech should be of equal weight or importance. The subordinate points should be equal to each other, and so on. In our example, the history, the description, the methods of learning to play, special techniques, care of the instrument, and tips on practicing are all considered equally important. Each point is treated as a separate discussion, and together they achieve the purpose of the speech: to tell the audience how to begin playing the harmonica.

OUTLINING FOR AUDIENCE EXPECTATIONS   In addition to the reasons we suggested at the beginning of the discussion, there is another, more general, purpose for outlining. An outline can help us meet the needs and expectations of the audience more effectively, especially if we develop it from the audience's perspective. (See list on page 261.)

People are not always logical beings who will accept a logical argument, nor are they emotional children who can be moved if properly praised; but as we observed in the discussion on learning (Chapter 8), response to information is favorably affected by positive stimuli. A speech should be designed to meet the rational and emotional expectations of an audience. While you are busy arranging the subject matter of your speech into an outline, you may not have time to think much about your listeners. After you have completed your outline, you should consider your audience. The list below is divided into three parts, corresponding to the parts of a speech: the introduction, the body, and the conclusion. Within each part is shown what the audience might reasonably expect from you, the speaker, during that phase of your speech. Use this list as a reminder that you will be talking to a particular audience with specific needs. Of course, there are some things that are not always easily accounted for in an outline (e.g., expressions of goodwill, or cues that a new topic is about to be introduced); but if you keep them in mind while you practice, you will be more likely to use them in an actual presentation.

SAMPLE SPEECH   Study the student speech that follows. The general pattern of the speech is *problem and solution*. Pay particular attention to the speaker's strategy. The design of the speech fits the typical

AN OUTLINE OF AUDIENCE EXPECTATIONS

Opening Phase

We, the audience, expect

- to be recognized in greeting.
- some expression of goodwill, friendliness, and concern for common ground.
- attention to what interests us.
- an announcement of the subject.
- sound reasons for the selection of the subject.
- a modest explanation of why you, the speaker, are competent to speak in this area.

Development Phase

We, the audience, expect

- a core idea, a clear, concise statement of your position.
- a preview, a partition of the major areas or points you will cover. We expect structure and order.
- cues or signposts signaling when you begin a new point.
- explanation, illustration, and evidence to support each point.
- internal summaries of lengthy or complex ideas and transitions to the next point.
- to be honestly and ethically treated as equals.
- to have a solution offered in problem speeches and recommendations for how to best use information in an informative speech.

Closing Phase

We, the audience, expect

- to have the highlights of the message recapped quickly.
- to hear again the core thesis.
- to hear a clinching argument.
- to be invited to talk back, to question, and to test the thesis, to be treated as people who have something to offer and say about this matter.

introduction-body-conclusion form we have been using throughout the chapter. Within this form the speaker states the problem, describes and defines it, and discusses and evaluates solutions. Finally, after showing why standard solutions are not acceptable, she makes her recommendation and asks the audience to support it.

Two outlines precede the speech. One is a topic outline and the other, a sentence outline. Reading these outlines before you read the speech should give you a sense of the development of the subject. As you read the speech, notice the comments in the margin. They point out the speaker's concern for the audience's expectations and how she attempts to satisfy them. Notice also that this speaker prepared an alternative ending for her speech to use in the event questions were asked or more information about the topic was required.

TOPIC OUTLINE FOR SAMPLE SPEECH

Opening: Statement of the problem
  I. Indians' rights restricted
  II. Imagine living under government agency
Development: Problem defined
  I. Bureau of Indian Affairs
    A. Unchallengeable power of agency
    B. Three levels of power
      1. Political
      2. Judicial
      3. Administrative
  II. Unsuccessful attempts for solution
    A. Disband Bureau of Indian Affairs
    B. American Indian Chicago Conference
Closing: Solution
  I. Initiative for change
  II. General equal rights movement

SENTENCE OUTLINE FOR SAMPLE SPEECH

Opening: What is the problem?
  I. Indians on reservations are denied rights that the rest of us take for granted.
  II. Imagine having your everyday activities regulated by a government agency.
Development: How is the problem defined?
  I. The Bureau of Indian Affairs controls the lives of American Indians on reservations.
    A. The power of the agency is practically unchallengeable for the Indians.
    B. Indians lack power on three levels.
      1. They are politically weak because they do not represent a strong voting constituency.
      2. They are judicially weak because of the poor legal counsel that is afforded them.
      3. They are administratively weak because they have to deal with a large bureaucracy.
  II. Unsuccessful attempts to arrive at a solution have been made.
    A. In the 1950s the government tried a policy called "termination."
    B. In 1961 the American Indian Chicago Conference issued a Declaration of Purpose.

Closing: What is the solution?
  I. The initiative for change should be placed with the Indians.
  II. The Indians should be included by those of us who are fighting for equal rights for all peoples at all levels.

THE VOICE OF THE AMERICAN INDIAN?

"Although the normal expectation in American society is that a private individual may do anything unless it is specifically prohibited by the government, on the reservation Indians may not do anything unless it is specifically permitted by the government." This is a quote from the *Harvard Law Review* summing up the plight of the American Indian today. Stop and think about the magnitude of that statement for a moment. You and I find enough to complain about when we consider the guidelines set for us by the government. Try to imagine what it would be like to have your home, land, schools, jobs, stores where you shop, the opportunities available to you, and the way you spend your money all determined by a separate agency of the government set up just for you.

Opening—Statement of Problem: Brings classmates into speech by showing that the problem concerns everyone.

Additional statement: Includes audience in concern for problem; helps to strengthen statement of problem.

This is the way of life for 600,000 descendants of the original Americans. The Indians' controller is the Bureau of Indian Affairs, an agency of the U.S. Department of the Interior. BIA power is virtually unchallengeable. As normal citizens, we are able to challenge government power three ways—politically, administratively, and judicially. Politically, the Indians lack significant voting power, as they constitute not even one-half of one percent of the total population in the United States. Administratively, the Indian has to deal with more than 2,000 regulations, 389 treaties, 5,000 statutes, 2,000 federal court decisions, 500 Attorney General opinions, and 33 volumes of the Indian Affairs Manual—all in addition to the regulations governing him as a U.S. citizen. Judicially, few lawyers are provided for the Indians, although federal law requires that they be provided with legal representation. No tribe can hire a lawyer without federal approval and there are times when the lawyer representing them has been barred from the reservation.

Development—Shows that standard solutions to this kind of problem do not work now.

Uses data to describe problem more fully. Rejects standard solutions.

The most dramatic example of the BIA's authority is that of its power over Indian trust property. The BIA controls the use, sale, exchange, and other transactions of Indian land. Between 1887 and 1966, Indian land acreage has decreased from 138 million acres to 55 million. In the name of progress, Indian land has been taken for construction, roads, and dams. Those carrying out the work have found that Indian land is cheaper, easier, and less dangerous politically to take. The BIA allows some states to treat Indian trust land as a disposable and available resource, although the Indian cannot sell or mortgage his trust property himself. Many of these states will not let anyone holding such assets qualify for welfare. So the BIA allows the Indians to sell the land in order to qualify. He must then spend the money from the sale in a manner acceptable to the BIA, which holds the money and gives him installments equal to what the Indian would receive on welfare. And then the Indian may qualify for welfare— now that he has no land as an asset.

Uses example to show effects of problem.

States most severe consequences of the problem. Describes how problem affects the people involved and what the ends results are.

Presents the most extreme solution and, by use of example, describes the results when it was tried.

To those of us who do not understand the Indians' problems, the most obvious solution to the problem is to do away with the BIA and "free" the Indian. This was done in a policy adopted by the federal government in the 1950s in the form of termination. Typically, Indians were not given any choice concerning the policy. Termination did away with the special status of the Indian and disavowed his trusteeship and protection with the U.S. government. This proved to be tragic to the tribes that experienced it. The reservation of the Menominee Tribe of Wisconsin became a county after termination. However, the tax base was too small to support decent schools and health services. The county is the most poverty-stricken in Wisconsin today. The termination policy was officially abandoned in 1961.

Suggests solution to problem.

If neither goverment control nor termination are sensitive to the rights of the American Indian, what *can* be done? In 1961 at the American Indian Chicago Conference, the Indians published their own Declaration of Purpose. It rejected the termination policy and suggested Indians be allowed to participate "in developing their own programs with help and guidance as needed and requested from a local decentralized staff." The declaration was ignored.

Closing—Involves audience again.
Restates solution.
Invites classmates to help solve problem. Appeals to their sense of what is "good" and "right."

You and I covet our belief that we know what in general is best for us and expect the right to participate in determining our futures. The American Indian has the right to make these same demands. The initiative must be placed in their hands and the help in reaching the level to maintain full control must be given. While we are fighting for equality on all levels for all peoples, let's remember the Indian situation and help the voice of the American Indian—the original Americans—to be heard.

CONTINGENCY PLAN

Credibility Establishment: My credibility is largely dependent upon the quality of the information. In the question period, I will have an opportunity to add that I took a course about the American Indian at Heidelberg College. During the semester a group of Indians came to present a program, and they met with our class for discussion.

In preparation for the speech, I spoke with Jim Buchanon, who worked with the Indians through the Teacher Corps Team. He has also participated with the United Native Americans and the American Indian Movement.

Additional Information: Demonstrating BIA power over Indian trust property, in Fort Berthold, North Dakota, the Indians fought to keep the U.S. Army Corps of Engineers from building Garrison Dam and flooding one-fourth of their reservation (154,000 acres of fertile land). Experts from the Bureau of Reclamation drew up an alternate plan that was feasible and used less valuable land. The alternate plan was not accepted. The Indians then scraped together money, hired their own expert, and devised a third plan, even offering to donate the lands they would lose. The BIA would not endorse the plan. The government finally promised 150,000 substitute acres of equally valuable land to the Indians, but after the area was flooded in 1953, the government did not keep the promise.

In Palm Springs, California, the Agua Caliente Indians own major properties. State officials declared nearly two-thirds of the Indians incompetent to manage their own affairs and provided trustees to act for them. In 1968 the Secretary of the Interior revealed that these trustees had been pocketing an average of one-third of the land proceeds for "legal fees."

Pamela K. Stone

No speaker should try to meet each of the predictable expectations in one-two-three order. To do so slavishly would result in a tedious, lackluster presentation. Several of the expectations may be satisified with one sentence or a well-placed example. Composing and delivering a speech is an art. Art is usually not formula, but rather the product of an artist's using his tools and creative imagination. Moreover, public speaking is a transient art: the speech's design and presentation depend on the unique interplay of speaker, occasion, and audience. The Outline of Audience Expectations only points out what should be planned for. The decision of what to say and how to say it in order to meet those needs is a matter of personal style and judgment for which no exact and unvarying prescription can be written.

TRANSITIONS

Before we leave the section on outlines, there is one last item to be planned for: *transitions.* Preparing the speech in clearly identified parts is a reliable way to ensure that we have covered the topic thoroughly and that our audience will be able to follow the presentation easily. But a problem that is common to both experienced speakers and beginners is how to get from one point to another.

The groups of words we use to move from one main point to another are called *transitions*. For example, if you are talking about "Business as a Career" and you want to move from the rewards of business to how someone gets started, you might say something like, "Now that we have seen how exciting and challenging a career in business can be, let's look at how you can get started in your own program." This kind of remark cues the audience that you are about to introduce a new topic.

Depending on your message content and speaking style, transitions will come more easily at certain times than at others. The organization of your speech will help you determine where they are needed. As you prepare the outline, ask yourself what connection there is between one point and the next. In the above example, the speaker has just finished describing the rewards of a business career and why members of the audience should consider it. The next obvious item to be covered is how they can get started. If you do not see any connection between the ideas that follow one another in your speech, you should consider rearranging the order of presentation. When you are satisfied, link your main points with transitions and practice them when you rehearse.

FUNCTIONAL PHASES OF THE SPEECH

In the discussion of design formats in Chapter 9 and throughout this chapter, we have concentrated mostly on the body of the speech. It is important to remember the functions of the introduction and conclusion also and to keep in mind that the three parts of the speech work together to form one unit. You might wish to think of the three parts of the speech as functional phases, each flowing into the next, related to each other by your purpose. And as you rehearse these phases, you should consider what you will actually do in each one.

OPENING PHASE   In designing the opening phase of your speech, you need to consider your greeting and how you recognize the audience, and your credibility or the way the audience perceives you. Most expectations of the opening are in keeping with the social norms of civility; that is, when we are spoken to, we like to be recognized. The audience has gathered to attend your presentation. The effort on their part should be recognized, and some small sign or greeting is usually enough. The sincerity of the speaker in expressing goodwill indicates his own recognition of the audience's efforts. A friendly greeting, expression of goodwill, and sincere tone help establish a common ground between speaker and audience.

Graphically the opening phase of the speech might look like this:

Opening Phase

Greeting
Recognition
Goodwill
Common ground
Qualifications (credibility)

Every speech setting does not demand that you establish credibility by describing your qualifications. Very often your occupation or experience qualifies you in the eyes of the audience. As a student you are qualified to talk about student life. As an avid skier you may be qualified to discuss most aspects of recreational skiing. But on some occasions, you may have to speak on a topic that your audience does not readily identify as within your expertise. In such instances, you will want to demonstrate that you have the knowledge to discuss the subject of your speech.

It takes some thought to present qualifications in a modest manner without resorting to self-glorification or technical jargon. While there are many ways to approach the problem, here are some suggestions to consider: (1) You can plunge right into the subject and let the content of your speech demonstrate your ability. (2) You can announce your qualifications in a brief opening statement. (3) You can humorously refer to your experiences ("I have had as many as 50 skiing falls in an hour, and I think I have learned something about ski safety."). (4) You can briefly describe how you prepared for this speaking occasion ("I have just read three books, eight articles, and interviewed fifteen people."). Where time permits, a careful audience audit can help you decide which approach would be most effective.

DEVELOPMENT PHASE

The development phase or body of the speech is where the bulk of your presentation will occur. We talked about this part of the speech in the previous chapter when we looked at patterns of development and forms of support, and earlier in this chapter when we talked about outlining. Let us review quickly the main ingredients of this part of the speech.

If you have not mentioned it before, the body of the speech is the place to make your core statement or main point. You may not wish to begin the section with it, but someplace in this part your audience expects to hear why you are making this speech. They also expect to be informed of where you are going in the speech. A preview of the broad areas to be covered and the main questions to be answered will help them hear the cues and signposts you employ along the way. And, of course, the body of your speech is where the forms of support we discussed in Chapter 9 (illustrations, explanations, and evidence) should be used.

Our developing speech, which now includes both opening and development phases, might be represented graphically in this way:

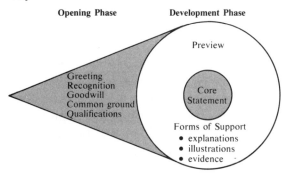

CLOSING PHASE   The closing phase is the final stage of development. It is where the speaker ends the speech, but it should not be considered unimportant or less significant than the other parts. In a speech to persuade, the speaker makes her last appeal for action in the closing phase. In a speech to inform, the speaker will use the closing phase to summarize or shape into a memorable format the information that has gone before. And in any speech, the closing phase is the time to signal the audience that the speech is nearly finished.

Looking again at our Outline of Audience Expectations, we can see that several items should be included in the closing. You will probably want to restate your thesis or core idea. Doing so will remind the audience what has been the point or purpose of your speech and, at the same time, will indicate that you are drawing to a close.

The closing is also the place to summarize your main points. A good summary will help audience members get their notes together and form any questions they may want to ask. Some speakers have trouble ending the speech. Choosing an appropriate ending is important so that your message will not seem to end abruptly. If, in the course of your research, you have found a quotation that sums up the way you feel about the subject, you may want to use it as the final appeal to persuade. Such phrases as "in conclusion" or "finally" will signal the audience that your speech is ending and provide a transition to your last statement.

Inviting questions from the audience is certainly an obvious indication that you have finished speaking. Question-and-answer sessions are normally arranged ahead of time. Some programs do not permit time for question-and-answer sessions, and the alert planner will cover this option in the beginning stages of the speech.

A final element found in the closing is a *thank you* or expression of the speaker's willingness to speak again. There is some controversy about the appropriateness of the thank you. "If the speech is any good," some scholars will say, then "the audience should thank the speaker." But there is no standard rule. If you have interrupted an especially busy schedule to share your knowledge about something with the audience, then indeed, you should be thanked. On the other hand, if you have used this time to present a special idea to members of a group with the expectation that they will adopt your recommendation or take a particular course of action, you may want to thank them for their time and consideration. Politicians' speeches typically end with a thank you because they are usually asking audience members for their time, their money, and their vote.

Although the closing phase is almost always shorter than the others, it is important for a sense of completeness in the speech, and you should plan it with care and attention. When we add the closing phase of our speech, the graphic model looks like this:

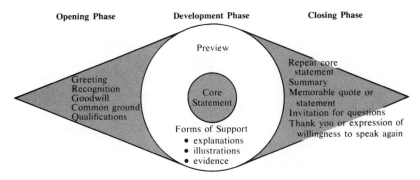

Opening Phase   Development Phase   Closing Phase

Preview

Greeting
Recognition
Goodwill
Common ground
Qualifications

Core
Statement

Repeat core
statement
Summary
Memorable quote or
statement
Invitation for questions
Thank you or expression of
willingness to speak again

Forms of Support
• explanations
• illustrations
• evidence

THE DELIVERY

Now that we have organized our materials for the speech from our perspective (so as to make clear the purpose for giving the speech) and the audience's perspective (so as to meet its needs and expectations), there is nothing left to do but rehearse. The rehearsal is the time to iron out any problems you may find in your organization or delivery, and although your first practice may be faltering, you should deliver the speech in rehearsal as though you were giving it to the audience. In the final stages of rehearsal having a friend listen is a good way to check out your speech; but if no listener is available, you can practice in front of a mirror.

TYPES OF DELIVERY

You can deliver your speech (1) from memory, (2) from manuscript, or (3) from notes. Your purpose, the occasion, the length of the speech, and the audience may all be factors in determining what method you choose. Most classroom speeches are given from notes, and we shall have the most to say about that method; but let's look first at the other two types of delivery.

From Memory

Occasionally we hear a speech delivered from memory. Usually it is short because tremendous effort is required to memorize word for word. Introducing an important celebrity or speaker may require you to state certain biographical information about that person. Because you may not want to carry notes cards around on a busy evening, you may decide to memorize your remarks. But most of the time, any speech you give is likely to be longer and more involved than the ones just cited, and giving a long speech from memory poses particular dangers. If your memory should fail in the middle of the speech, you would have no recourse but to start over or to skip what you had forgotten and go on to the next part you could remember. The first choice would be annoying to your audience and time consuming, and the second would force you to leave out information. In either event, your speech would probably be less effective.

Even when you plan to speak from manuscript or notes, you may want to memorize parts of your speech. If you are beginning or ending with a special quotation that you think captures the essence of your message, you may find that memorizing it enables you to deliver it with emphasis and style, and without breaking eye contact with your audience.

From Manuscript   The manuscript speech is the type given most often for important political statements. There are several reasons for this. One is that a speech written out in full leaves little chance for error, for misstatement or misquote. Complete copies can be given to members of the press ahead of time so they can print the entire text or excerpts from it in the next edition of the paper. Copies can also be made available to media news commentators and political analysts. In speeches concerning important policy issues or relations with foreign governments, imprecise language may result in serious misinterpretation and misunderstanding. These speeches must be carefully constructed and their printed texts, rigidly adhered to.

Our feelings influence our thinking. Emotions that are deeply felt may interrupt our thought processes and interfere with or alter our memories. We have all known moments of extreme excitement, joy, or sorrow when we could not find the "right words," when we were left speechless. If you are asked to speak on what may be a highly emotional occasion—to give a eulogy, to dedicate a memorial, to present an award posthumously—you may want to speak from manuscript, rather than from notes or memory, so that the moment's emotional impact cannot leave you—and your audience—speechless.

The manuscript method of speech delivery does have serious drawbacks. The physical manipulation of manuscript pages can be troublesome. If you are speaking out-of-doors on a windy day or if a fan is blowing in your direction, a large manuscript can become a comical struggle, and your message may never reach the audience. To read a manuscript, you will need to look at it, and away from your audience, much of the time. Unless you have practiced the script and become thoroughly familiar with it, interaction with the audience while you deliver your speech from manuscript will be minimal at best. Thus, a manuscript speech will inhibit your ability to read audience feedback to see if your message is getting through or should be changed. Most good manuscript reading requires considerable memorization and practice, so that you may be free to look up at the audience, pause in important places, and emphasize particular points.

Preparation for a manuscript speech is more demanding than for a speech from notes. The way the speech is written must be considered carefully. The language, especially, must be examined for appropriateness. Most people do not write the same way they speak. Written language is usually less direct and more formal. We also tend to write in shorter, more complete sentences than we use when we speak. And when we distribute a written statement, we know the reader can stop and go over our words, use a dictionary, or even leave the material and come back to it later. In a speech we must strive to hold attention and make our message clear at the time of delivery. So the manuscript speech writer must frequently read over the material, ask the question, "How would I say this out loud?" and then rewrite.

Speaking from notes is called *extemporaneous speaking*. It is the kind of public speaking you will do most often in this course. There are some distinct advantages to delivering a speech from notes. Doing so allows you maximum flexibility in your presentation so that you can read and react to audience feedback. Assuming you have rehearsed and gathered sufficient information to discuss the topic, using notes you can change the order of your presentation as you like. You can use certain arguments for one audience and use others to adapt the speech for another group. You can move about the room to make use of charts or other visual aids.

From Notes

Your outline may be on sheets of paper or on note cards. Note cards are preferred by experienced speakers because they are easy to carry and can be held in one hand. Thus a speaker using them does not need to stand behind a podium but is free to move closer to the audience or to his visual aids. Statistics or quotations can also be written on the cards so that they need not be memorized. Although note cards may seem awkward at first, if you rehearse with them, you will feel confident using them. Several rehearsals will enable you to use fewer and fewer notes until only a few key words will be required on each card to help you recall your ideas during the delivery of the speech.

Because much of the knowledge we have of verbal and nonverbal communication in the interpersonal setting applies to the public presentation as well, you may want to review quickly the chapters on verbal and nonverbal cues before reading about using your voice and body.

VOICE   Although you will be using your voice and body together to deliver your message, for the sake of convenience we shall consider them separately. In Chapter 4 we discussed some of the voice characteristics, such as volume and quality. In a public presentation, try to adapt your voice to the setting. Look for cues that indicate you are not being heard clearly (puzzled looks on faces, or people leaning toward you), and increase your volume if you think it necessary. Even though your presentation is public, you need not feel reluctant to sound the way you do in conversational speech. The audience wants to hear the real you. So use pitch naturally, and vary it the way you normally would to make a point, clarify a meaning, or secure attention for an idea you feel is important.

We do not talk at a constant rate of speed. When we are excited, we tend to speak quickly. The rate of our speech may increase when we are nervous or on edge. Thus, beginning speakers have a common tendency to speak more quickly than they would in normal conversation. Our rate of delivery becomes a problem when we speak too quickly for the audience to assimilate our message and place it in a meaningful context (recall our discussion of decoding in Chapter 4). A reliable way to check your rate of delivery is to rehearse in front of someone. If she does not notice the rate, it is probably fine. You can also tape record your speech as you rehearse it.

Pause is an effective device for getting attention and stressing a point. You may want to pause just before an important idea to give your audience time to prepare for it, or you may want to pause just after an important idea to suggest, "This is important. Think about it."

Articulation and pronunciation are important factors for the image we want to present. Just as the correct choice of language can affect the way our message is received (recall the discussion of language in Chapter 4), so can the way we pronounce words influence the identity the audience has with us. The most reliable advice is, "Speak in a manner that is natural for you." But you should also notice and try to eliminate any bad pronunciation habits you might have developed. The most common fault in adults is the omission of sounds from, and addition of sounds to, words. Most sound omissions occur at the ends of words (doin' or goin') and stem from habit, nervousness, or laziness. Additions to words are not as easily attributable to a single cause but may come from carelessness or a poor model. An example of a widely used sound addition is "orientated" for "oriented." Your pronunciation does not have to be perfect (hardly anyone's is) but don't let it detract from your message.

Once in the history of speech communication science there were theories about the best way to use the body to communicate certain meanings. The art of using gestures was called the "elocutionary school." It is a credit to us all that research has taken us beyond that level of communication analysis so that we understand communication behavior in a more natural setting. But we still should take note of certain nonverbal signals that may influence the way our public speech is perceived.

BODY

The Reverend Sun Myung Moon, in this sequence from a large rally, demonstrates the body movements which add dramatic emphasis to his sermons. The importance of these gestures is highlighted by the fact that he spoke in Korean (with simultaneous translation) to an American audience.

Eye contact, facial expressions, and gestures are no less important in the public speech setting than they are in interpersonal settings. Considerable research has been done in the area of eye contact. Most of the findings suggest a strong correlation between the amount of eye contact and the audience's perception of the speaker's credibility (see "Look 'Em in the Eye"). Your facial expression and other gestures reveal your feelings about what you are saying. Your body can also underscore your meaning or add emphasis. Moving toward the audience indicates concern that your message is being received; retreating provides time for relaxation and a return to normal emphasis. Slumping shoulders or a bowed head may imply dejection, while erect posture may indicate pride in what you are saying or enthusiasm for your message. Whatever gestures you use, they should be true reflections of your feelings, not a matter of "going through the motions." As we said in Chapter 3, when gestures and expressions seem to come spontaneously with the verbal message, they confirm the listener's perception of the meaning.

AUDIOVISUAL AIDS

Audiovisual aids, such as a microphone and speaker system, a tape recorder and film or slide projector, charts and graphs, and models and mock-ups, can enhance the meaning and effectiveness of our message.

The beginning speaker sometimes has trouble with the microphone. If you are speaking in a setting that requires a microphone and speaker system, arrive early and check the system ahead of time. A faulty sound system can be distracting to you and your audience. Learn how you sound over the speakers. Practice with the microphone. Adjust it to suit your height. A tendency among many speakers is to lean down to a microphone that is not tall enough for them. Doing so not only inhibits body movement and looks awkward, but also can impair the natural voice mechanisms. If you follow another speaker, do not be reluctant to adjust the microphone to suit yourself before you begin speaking. Members of your audience will be sympathetic to your needs, and they will appreciate your attention to theirs.

If you prepare charts or graphs to aid your message, make them large enough to be seen by the people in the farthest parts of the room. An aid that cannot be seen by everyone is a distraction at best. And if you have models or mock-ups of some items you may be discussing, take them apart and use them as you practice your speech. If you wait until the time of your speech to try them, you may discover they are faulty or you may be fumbling with them

LOOK 'EM IN THE EYE

Basic Question: Is a speaker who has much eye contact more credible to an audience than a speaker with little eye contact?

Treatment: A female, experienced speaker, presented the same 7-minute speech to three different audiences, but she varied her amount of eye contact. Before one audience she constantly fixed her eyes on her notes and lectern. Before the second audience, she maintained direct eye contact with her audience approximately 50 percent of the time and looked at her notes the other half of the time. In the high eye contact condition, she maintained direct eye contact with the audience at least 90 percent of the time, and she did not refer to her notes.

Introductory speech classes in a midwestern university served as the audiences. There were more than 42 persons in each audience.

Results: After the speech was ended, all members of the three audiences completed surveys which rated the speaker on her qualifications, presentation, honesty, and dynamism. The speaker in the high eye contact presentation was evaluated to be more qualified and more honest, although only slightly more dynamic, than in the no or moderate eye contact presentation. The rating scale on the survey questionnaire ran from very *low for positive* reactions to *high for negative* reactions.

Audiences' Perceptions	No Eye Contact	Moderate Eye Contact	High Eye Contact
Qualified	7.60	5.67	4.74
Honesty	9.36	8.71	6.98
Dynamic	9.79	9.67	8.24

Implications: The amount of the speaker's eye contact does make a difference to the audience. Although (as we mentioned in Chapter 3) in interpersonal communication eye contact is not a reliable sign of honesty, audiences tend to perceive speakers in public settings as having high credibility when they maintain a high amount of eye contact with the audience.

Steven A. Beebe, "Eye Contact: A Nonverbal Determinant of Speaker Credibility," *The Speech Teacher* 23 (January 1974), pp. 21–25.

during the speech. In either event, they will not be as useful to you as they would have been had you been able to use them freely and with ease.

All of the ideas we have considered here point to a few basic notions about the public speech. Deciding on our purpose and researching the topic thoroughly help us determine how best to present our ideas. Organizing the speech and outlining the way we want to proceed enable us to present our message in a comfortable time frame and to avoid rambling or talking about irrelevant matters. And practicing the presentation can give us confidence and improve our methods for presenting the message.

TIPS ON DELIVERY   Try the following steps in perfecting the delivery of a message once it has been composed:

1   Begin by reading the central idea and supporting points aloud. Then talk to an imagined audience from the opening to the closing of the speech. Use simple, easy to articulate language. Translate the speech into a keyword outline by using keywords that will aid your recalling whole paragraphs. Next practice before a mirror, using the keyword outline. Talk through the speech once, twice or more using the body movements and gestures that come naturally. If the mirror bothers you, practice without it, but do stand up for your final practices. Do not take your manuscript with you unless you intend to read it. If this is your intention, have it typed in large print and double spaced. Practice reading it until you can look up frequently for half a sentence or more.

2   Approach the platform with confidence. Sometimes, if the mood is one of excitement, you may even hurry to the dias to express your eagerness to greet the audience. Select dress which will be appropriate and comfortable.

3   As you reach the speaker's stand, make contact with the chairman, accept his or her introduction with a handshake or nod and greet any other person on the platform.

4   Next, look over the crowd; and then pause to concentrate upon your verbal greeting and the first words of your message. Don't look at your notes again before you begin. Don't sweep the audience with your eyes. Rather, talk to an *individual* in the center of your audience for a sentence or two, then to another person nearby. After that, you may widen your attention by focusing upon other individuals in various sections of the audience. The platform is yours. It is your responsibility to establish a relationship of respect and goodwill.

5   As your speech moves into the development phase, make your body work for you. Move to demonstrate a transition into a new point. Use your hands, head and eyes to convey feelings or to describe and illustrate. Movement causes the eye to follow. Keep gestures up, make them definite, and do not hurry them. Maintain good posture. Suit your movement to the size of the room.

6   Look for audience signs of confusion, disinterest and fatigue. Adjust appropriately to these cues: perhaps, by rephrasing or adding an illustration; possibly by shifting from your formal presentation to a question and answer period.

7 In the closing phase of a presentation delivery noticeably changes in rate. The climax has been attained and the sense of closure often is felt by a relaxation in the body of the presenter. If the presentation has been particularly energetic and emotional, he may appear weary or exhilarated. If the message has been more informative and less emotional, he may be more interested in moving to a stage of playback in order to discover how clearly it was understood and learned. In any case, the closing phase should, by change of rate, intensity, volume and bodily tension, signal the end—possibly a nod or a thank you, followed by returning to your seat.

SUMMARY

In Chapter 9, we discussed the elements that are important for designing the speech: research, organization, and forms of support. In Chapter 10, we concentrated on the steps you will take in making the speech: outlining, developing the three phases, and actually delivering the speech.

The outline has several functions. It acts as a guide or stimulant to thinking. It also helps test organization and develop alternate plans. And the outline provides a place to examine your data and to consider how well they work together.

There are three types of outlines: (1) the *working* or *thumbnail* outline, (2) the *topic* outline, and (3) the *sentence* outline. The working outline is a list of topics to be covered that reflects deliberate thought concerning priorities, sequence of events, or what should be presented when. The topic outline contains detailed information about each topic and enables you to evaluate the relevance and importance of each item in the speech. The sentence outline is an expanded version of the topic outline. The phrases or key words used in the topic outline are written in complete sentences. Writing out complete sentences about the topics provides an opportunity to further check your organization, and helps you think of what you will actually say to your audience. In some ways the sentence outline is a prerehearsal of the speech.

The importance of the listener or audience has been emphasized throughout the text, and it is no less important where outlining is concerned. Outlining for audience expectations helps to ensure that you meet the needs of the audience, and provides further checks on the completeness and reasonableness of your speech.

Planning for transitions helps you check the organization of your speech (If you do not know how to get from point *A* to point *B*, it may be because they are not at all related) and ensures smooth progression within it.

Much of the planning discussion in this and the previous chapter centered on the body of the speech. When the speech is actually delivered, it is likely to be perceived by the audience as a single experience; therefore, when planning the delivery, you should keep the introduction and conclusion in mind as integral parts of it. You might think of your speech as being made up of three developmental phases that flow, one into the next. For each phase—opening phase (introduction), development phase (body), and closing phase (conclusion)—there are certain audience expectations you must consider.

There are three main types of delivery: (1) from memory, (2) from manuscript, and (3) from notes (extemporaneous). Speaking from notes allows you more flexibility in presentation. Speaking from manuscript may be preferable if you are delivering a speech to be reprinted by the press or speaking on what may be a very emotional occasion. Even when you speak from manuscript, you may wish to memorize sections of your speech so that you can deliver them more effectively.

In Part II, we discussed the roles of voice, body, and language in interpersonal communication. They are important in public communication as well. You should use them naturally and adjust to audience feedback to ensure that your voice is heard and your message is understood.

Appropriate audiovisual aids can make a speech more interesting, more easily understood, and more effective. If you intend to include them in your speech, you should rehearse with them so that you become thoroughly familiar with how they open, pull down, turn on, come apart, sound, and *work*! And you should be certain they are large enough or loud enough to be enjoyed by all members of your audience.

INITIATIVES

INITIATING ACTION 1   *The Major Address*. Select an area of concern and earn your right to speak. Do some investigative preparation. Read, interview, and collect information as though you were writing a television documentary. Decide what is the size of the problem, who is most seriously hurt by the situation, and what are the major causes. Role play what it is like to be one of those hurt by the situation. Think in terms of remedies and prevention. Now organize your information into a narrative account of your investigation. Perhaps your instructor will assign interim presentations such as:

      (a) How I became interested in the topic.
      (b) How serious is the problem?
      (c) What caused the problem?
      (d) Are there any signs that this problem can or will be solved?

NITIATING ACTION 2   *The Stump Speech*. Speak in and out of doors. Climb on top of a bench or bring your own soapbox. Carry a sign for a cause such as "Give Blood," "Support John Doe for Vice President," "Volunteer to Read to the Blind." Your speech may:

      (a) Describe the need.
      (b) Tell what you personally did when you saw the need.
      (c) Challenge and invite your audience to join the cause.

    Remember that even a serious speech may receive better attention if you lace it with humor. Be prepared to respond to hecklers and answer questions. A stump speech is no place for the weak of heart.

INITIATING ACTION 3   *The After-Dinner Speech*. Divide the class into groups of seven to ten and arrange for each group to eat together. Select a place where group members can speak after the meal. Ask each group member to prepare a few after-dinner remarks. The goal of the occasion is to entertain. Speeches should be short and might consist of two or three stories or jokes about campus life or absentminded professors, or a brief satire on "How We Might Increase Taxes" or "The Importance of Treating Our Leaders Like Royalty." Each speaker might close by introducing the next.

INITIATING ACTION 4   *The Key Word Outline*. Using a felt-tipped pen, print the major points and supports of your speech in large letters on sheets of newsprint or wrapping paper. Print only one point on each sheet.

Tack these sheets to the back wall of the room. They will serve as a key word outline for your speech, similar to the "idiot cards" used to prompt television personalities.

Debriefing. After several speeches an audience has sufficient data **INITIATING ACTION 5**
to provide a comparison of live presentations. Too often we tend to evaluate a speaker in good or bad terms generally, but never analyzing why we liked or did not like a speech. A better attitude is to examine *why* a speech succeeds or fails for you and your classmates in the audience. Use the following questions to ask that essential question of *why*.

QUESTIONS FOR DEBRIEFING AFTER SEVERAL STUDENT PRESENTATIONS

I

A. What did the speakers do today to help us feel that they recognized us?
B. How did they express their goodwill and relate it to their subjects?
C. In what did they develop common ground?
D. How did they establish their own credibility?

II

A. What were the positions of the presenters? Where do they appear to stand on the subjects.
B. Were any of their core ideas put into particularly motivating or memorable phrases or propositons?
C. What organizational formats were used? What psychological impression did these organizational patterns convey?
D. What evidence appeared particularly well presented and credible?
E. What evidence was most believable with little substantiation? Why?
F. What illustrations were particularly involving for you?
G. What did the speakers do to demonstrate their concern for ethical principles?
H. What motivational appeals were made?

III

A. Can you remember the major arguments or divisions of the presentations? Why? Why not? Were they well summarized?
B. What for you were the most clinching arguments?
C. What questions were answered most persuasively?
D. When did the audience most and least seem interested?
E. What seemed to arouse the most thought and debate? Why?

Rhetorical Analysis. When determining the reason a certain **INITIATING ACTION 6**
speech succeeds or fails, we must examine a number of variables: 1) the speaker's inventiveness; 2) style and organization; 3) supporting materials and delivery. Use the items suggested in this activity below, to perform a rhetorical analysis of a live speech.

SUGGESTED OUTLINE FOR RHETORICAL ANALYSIS OF A SPEECH

INVENTION:

What was the central message of the speech? To whom was the speaker directing his message—what clues do you have that the speaker was conscious of his audience? Why did the speaker feel that his message would matter to his listeners? Was his analysis accurate? Did his selection of theme "turn on" his listeners? Did his ideas reach the listener's heart (or gut)? Did the speaker's ideas challenge the values of the listener? Did his ideas intellectually stimulate the listener? Could the listener thank the speaker because he presented new information, concepts and/or analysis of an issue?

DISPOSITION AND STYLE:

What was the organizational plot? Was it clear and memorable? Was the organization and language creative? Did the vocabulary speak to the level of a college audience? Was the syntax clear? Was the language esthetically pleasing? Was the language too plain or too flowery?

INTEGRITY OF SUPPORTS:

Did the reasoning follow? Were the supporting materials adequate? Up to date? From reliable sources? Was there a good balance of the abstract with the concrete? Was there a good balance of emotional (pathos) with cognitive logical proof (logos)? What was the message of the man? Did he appeal to the listener characterwise? Did he help the listener realize that he had earned his right to speak on the chosen theme?

DELIVERY:

What did you conclude about the thoughtfulness from the presentation? Did the speaker seem prepared? How did the tone strike you—arrogant, warm, unsure, inconsistent, poised, confident, pleasant?

INITIATING ACTION 7   *What makes a speech listenable and readable?* Sentence length, number of syllables, and the personability of our language are measures of how listenable our speeches are. Some scholars have determined various methods for examining listenability or readability. You might take on a team project of comparing a speech that was transcribed from a video or audio tape with a speech written in manuscript form. The definitions and guidelines below will help you perform a listenability analysis.

LISTENABILITY

One way to measure listenability is to count the number of words per sentence.[2] A sentence is a unit of thought which is grammatically independent of another sentence or clause providing its end is NOT punctuated by a comma. It may be punctuated by a colon, semi-colon, exclamation point, question mark, or period. Incomplete sentences or sentence fragments should be counted as sentences also.

Here is how you may interpret your results:

Description of Style	Typical Magazine	Average Sentence Length
Very Easy	Comics	8
Easy	Pulp Fiction	11
Fairly Easy	Slick Fiction	14
Standard	Digests, *Time*, Mass non-fiction	17
Fairly Difficult	*Harper's, Atlantic*	21
Difficult	Academic, Scholarly	25
Very Difficult	Scientific, Professional	29

Limitations of this instrument:

Short sentences can be filled with difficult words just as long sentences can be filled with simple, monosyllabic words. Either combination can be hard to read, to listen to and understand.

Another way to measure listenability is to count in each sentence the number of syllables above one per word.[3] This is called the easy listening formula (ELF). For example, take these two sentences: (1) He was a magnanimous supervisor; and (2) He was a generous boss. The first sentence has an ELF score of 6 and the second sentence has an ELF score of 3.

Here is how you may interpret your results:

Writing Source	Average ELF score for each sentence
New York Times	17.4
CBS TV NEWS	9.8

No highly rated television news writer had an ELF score above 12.
Television network news writers averaged 10.4.
In general newspapers averaged 15.0

Limitations of the Instrument

ELF measures clarity. A sentence that scores 20 may be perfectly clear and may be the best way to deliver a fact. A series of parallelisms, delivered rhythmically may be perfectly comprehensible, yet it lengthens the sentence and increases the ELF score. Despite these limitations the ELF is much easier to use than Flesch's Reading Ease Formula and takes into consideration the same two variables as Flesch does: average sentence length and average number of syllables per 100 words.

HUMAN INTEREST

Human Interest is measured by the average number of personal words and the average number of personal sentences.

Personal Words are:

(a) All first, second, and third-person pronouns except the neuter pronouns *it, its, itself,* and the pronouns *they, them, their, theirs, themselves,* if referring to things rather than people. For example, count the word *them* in the sentence "When I saw her parents, I hardly recognized them," but not in the sentence "I looked for the books but couldn't find them." However, always count *he, him, his* and *she, her, hers* even where these words refer to animals or inanimate objects.

(b) All words that have masculine or feminine natural gender, e.g. John Jones, Mary, father, sister, iceman, actress. Do not count common gender words like teacher, doctor, employee, assistant, spouse, chairperson, even though the gender may be clear from the context. Count a phrase like President Jimmy Carter as one "personal word" only. (Only the word Jimmy has a natural masculine gender.) Mrs. Gorden contains one "personal word" with natural gender, namely Mrs.; Ms. Gay Gorden contains two, namely Ms. and Gay.

(c) The group words *people* (with the plural verb) and *folks*.

Personal Sentences are:

(a) Spoken sentences (direct quotes). But do not count quoted phrases such as, the senator accused McGovern of being "a hypocrite". Count all sentences included in long quotations, as part b (below).

(b) Questions, commands, requests, and other sentences directly addressed to the reader as: "Does this sound possible?" or "Imagine the implications." Do not count sentences that only vaguely address the reader, like: *"This is typical* of our national character."

(c) Exclamations.

(d) Grammatically incomplete sentences as: "Handsome, though." If a sentence fits under 2 of these classifications count it *only once.*

There are two ways to compute HUMAN INTEREST SCORE: mathematically or visually

Mathematically:

multiply the no. of personal words per 100 words by 3.635 _____
multiply the no. of personal sentences per 100 sentences by .314 _____
add the products of the previous two lines for HUMAN INTEREST SCORE _____

Visually:

Use the chart below:

How do you interpret the HUMAN INTEREST SCORE?
Human Interest Score will put the writing on a scale between 0 (no human interest) and 100 (full of human interest).

HUMAN INTEREST SCORE	DESCRIPTION OF STYLE	TYPICAL MAGAZINE	PERCENT OF PERSONAL WORDS	PERCENT OF PERSONAL SENTENCES
60 to 100	Dramatic	Fiction	17	58
40 to 60	Highly Interesting	*New Yorker*	10	43
20 to 40	Interesting	Digests, *Time*	7	15
10 to 20	Mildly Interesting	Trade	4	5
0 to 10	Dull	Scientific, Professional	2	0

REALISM

Realism or the lack of abstraction may be measured in this way:[4]

1. Count the number of finite verbs per 200 words. Count all verbs of any tense which are the first, second, or third person and which have subjects, either expressed or understood. Do not count nonfinite verb forms or verbals. In verb forms with auxiliary words, count the auxiliary rather than the main verb. Do not count any form of the verb "to be" (is, was, are, were, will be, have been, etc.) when used only as a copula to link the subject with a predicate complement.

2. Count the number of definite articles and their nouns per 200 words. Count both the article THE and the noun it modifies, but only if that noun is a single word not otherwise modified, either by an intervening adjective or by a clause or phrase following the noun. Do not count THE when modifying adjectives or noun-adjectives, as in THE BEST, THE IRISH.

3. Count the number of nouns of abstraction per 200 words. Count all nouns ending in the suffixes -NESS, -MENT, -SHIP, -DOM, -NCE, -ION, and -Y, including the plurals of such nouns. Count nouns ending in -Y even when it is the end of a longer suffix like -ITY or -OLOGY but not when it is used as a diminutive (tiny).

4. Add the numbers found in Steps 1 and 2 and add 36 to this sum.

5. Multiply the number found in Step 3 by 2.

6. From the total found in Step 4, subtract the result of Step 5. The result of this subtraction is the abstraction score.

How are the scores to be interpreted?

0–18	Very Abstract
19–30	Abstract
31–42	Fairly Abstract
43–54	Standard
55–66	Fairly Concrete
67–78	Concrete
79–90	Very Concrete

What scores do different sources get?

True Confessions 68
Reader's Digest 51
Atlantic Monthly 41
A college philosophy text 31

NOTES

1. Robert L. Applbaum *et al*, *Fundamental Concepts in Human Communication* (San Francisco: Canfield Press, 1973), pp. 144–5.

2. See Rudolf Flesch, *How to Write, Speak, and Think More Effectively* (New York: Harper and Row, 1960), pp. 303–307.

3. Irving Fang, "A Computer-Based Analysis of T.V. Newswriting Style for Listening Comprehension," Unpublished Ph.D., University of California (Los Angeles), 1966, pp. 136–7.

4. See Paul J. Gillie, "A Simplified Formula for Measuring Abstraction in Writing", *Journal of Applied Psychology*, XLI, no. 4 1957, pp. 315–320. This formula was validated against the Flesch abstraction formula. It cannot be any more valid than Flesch's. But it is easier to apply than Flesch's.

SUGGESTED READINGS

Anderson, Martin P., Ray E. Nichols, Jr., and Herbert W. Booth, *The Speaker and His Audience: Dynamic Interpersonal Communication*, 2nd ed. New York: Harper and Row, 1974.

Arnold, Carroll C., Douglas Ehninger, and John C. Gerber, *The Speaker's Resource Book: An Anthology, Handbook and Glossary.* Chicago: Scott, Foresman and Co., 1961.

Bradley, Bert E., *Fundamentals of Speech Communication: The Credibility of Ideas*. Dubuque, Iowa: Wm. C. Brown, 1974.

Clevenger, Theodore, Jr., and Jack Matthews, *The Speech Communication Process*. Glenview, Illinois: Scott, Foresman and Co., College Speech Series, 1971.

Dickens, Milton, *Speech: Dynamic Communication*, 3rd ed. New York: Harcourt, Brace, Jovanovich, 1974.

Gibson, James W., *Speech Organization: A Programmed Approach*. San Francisco: Rinehart Press, 1971.

Haynes, Judy L., *Organizing A Speech: A Programmed Guide*. Englewood Cliffs, N.J.: Prentice-Hall, 1973.

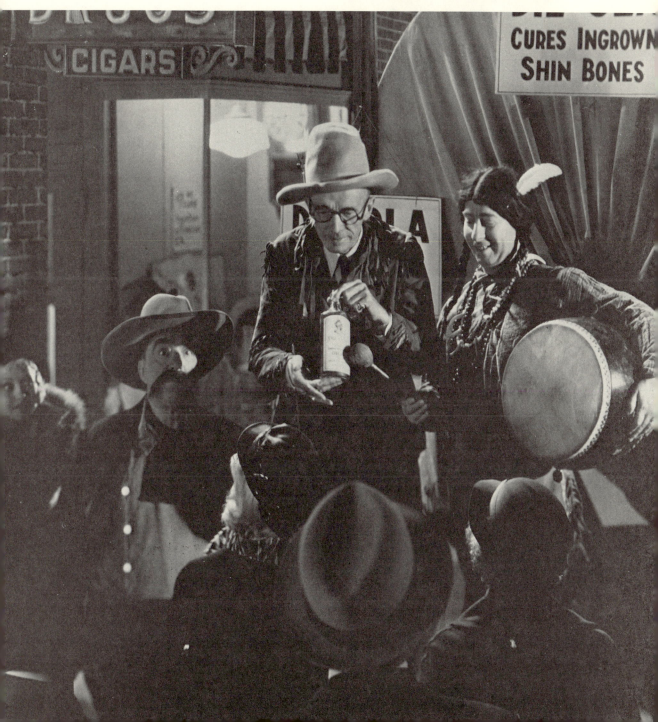

In Chapter 2, we discussed four general kinds of communication based on the functions they serve for us and society. One of those, which we called instrumental or persuasive, we said refers to messages that inform or influence toward a particular end. Because it centers closely on human behavior with all of its complexities and uncertainties, influence is a subject of considerable on-going research and discussion. In this chapter we shall discuss the main ideas about influence and the reasons that understanding influence is important to understanding communication.

BASIC DEFINITIONS

INFLUENCE Generally, influence can be defined as the power of a person or thing to affect others, and it usually is seen through its effects. One reason influence is an area of research and controversy is that much is still unknown about the process of influence and its relationship to communication. For example, some people claim *all* communication involves influence; others disagree. And people on both sides of the issue build strong cases for their positions.

People who contend all communication contains influence point to the situation wherein a person is influenced by a message which was not intended to influence. Those who maintain not all communication contains influence point to the times we are not influenced by an intentionally influential message. In everyday interactions, it is very difficult to tell just what a person's intent is much of the time; therefore, instead of concentrating on what may be the intent of a certain message, I suggest we focus our examination on the aspects of the influence process we can observe and discuss. For example, a fairly reliable indicator of influence is *change*. We can observe a change in someone's behavior, and the behavioral change may reflect a change in that person's attitudes, values, or beliefs. The change in attitudes, values, or beliefs may be the result of some outside influence, a compelling speech the person heard or a persuasive article he read. But people do not always act in ways that are consistent with their beliefs or attitudes, and that is why we must proceed with caution when we use behavioral change as an observable indicator of influence.

Attitude is often used interchangeably with opinion or belief. **ATTITUDE**
Although they are related, it is important to keep some basic distinctions in mind. An attitude is a learned and fairly long-lasting predisposition to evaluate a person, event, or situation in a certain way. On the simplest level it is a feeling or reaction, and on the broadest scale it is a composite of how a person understands, feels about, and acts toward an issue or object. If you feel angry and hostile when you read or hear about child pornography, it is safe to say that your attitude toward it is one of disapproval and intolerance. Your attitude reflects everything you have been taught about sexuality, children, and what is right.

A belief or opinion refers to a cognition, that is, what we know **BELIEF**
or assume to be true. If I think that school desgregation will improve the overall quality of education for children in my city, this belief is based on factual, or what seems to be factual, information. My attitude toward desegregation may be described as tolerant and approving; and you could say it has much more to do with feelings.

The attitude-belief distinction makes a good deal of sense. To say that you have a certain belief about some issue does not guarantee that you feel deeply about it. This distinction is important to keep in mind when you read opinion polls. Thousands may share a belief and still not care very much about an issue. Opinion surveys in America from as far back as 1938 have shown that over two-thirds of the people interviewed favored some form of governmental supervision of private ownership of guns.[1] Yet there has not been any strong public voice about the continued failure of Congress to pass adequate gun-control legislation. Americans have beliefs about the need for gun-control laws, but they don't have very strong feeling about that need.

VALUE   A value may be described as an ethical principle to which people feel a strong, emotional commitment and which they employ in judging others' attitudes, beliefs, and behaviors. Values provide us with our conceptions of good and evil; and they serve as guides to our actions and development of attitudes toward other people, events, and objects. While we may have many attitudes and beliefs, we have only a few values, such as freedom, equality, and wisdom, and they are of a general nature.

All people do not share the same values. Those who have unlike values will probably have unlike beliefs and attitudes. But even people with like values may not agree as to the importance of those values. While you may think equality among people is the most important value to hold, your friend may think wisdom and knowledge are most important; and the difference in the ways you both order your values may have an impact on how you discuss certain issues, such as desegregation or gun control.

BEHAVIOR   Behavior is any action a person chooses to perform or not perform. If you choose to help a stranded motorist on the freeway, that is your behavior. If you choose not to help him, that too is your behavior. The difference, of course, between behavior and attitudes, beliefs, and values is that behavior is observable while the others are not. Furthermore, we know attitudes, beliefs, and values are fairly long-lasting while behavior is fleeting and not always consistent. To compound the issue, behavior does not always reflect true attitudes. Recall the gun-control illustration in which we observed that persons' beliefs are not always as strong as their attitudes. We can infer from that knowledge that it is unsafe to predict a person's attitude just because we know his or her beliefs about a certain issue. Behavior is equally unreliable. There is a growing body of research that indicates that attitudes are not all-important in predicting behavior.[2]

The findings of a classic study by Richard T. La Piere are frequently cited as an example of the discrepancy between the attitudes people express and the actions they will take.[3] In 1934, La Piere and a young Chinese couple traveled extensively across the United States, stopping at 66 hotels, auto camps, and tourist homes (there were no motels as we know them today) and at 184 restaurants and cafes. The travelers were refused service only once. Sometime later though, when La Piere wrote to some establishments asking if they would "accept members of the Chinese race as guests," over 91 percent of the 128 responses were negative. The attitudes proprietors expressed in response to the questionnaire did not reflect how proprietors actually behaved when confronted with the specific situation. (Although La Piere did not know whether all of his respondents were the same persons with whom he and his companions had spoken, the study still illustrates our point—people do not behave consistent with their expressed attitudes.)

THEORIES OF INFLUENCE

Because we have discovered there is more to predicting or changing behavior than knowing or changing attitudes, and because the manner in which people are influenced is more complex than just the power of suggestion, various theories of influence have grown up from various points of view. The two theories from which all others are derived are learning theory and consistency theory. You may recall our brief discussion of learning theory in Chapter 8.

Learning theory is also known as reinforcement theory. Essentially, it states that we tend to repeat behavior that is rewarding to us and avoid behavior that is harmful or unrewarding. One reason attitudes and behavior are so difficult to influence is because people tend to seek out communicative relationships that support their attitudes, beliefs, and values and to avoid communication that is not supportive. This notion is especially important to advertisers who seek to have people become regular users of some new product. If the new product results in a smoother running car, less dandruff, or whiter teeth, the likelihood of its being used again is increased. But the first time the product fails us, we may try another.

Whenever we communicate with others, we exhibit reinforcing or nonreinforcing behavior. As a result, we influence, to some degree, their attitudes, their beliefs, and their values. We use reinforcement in our everyday communications, and it can be seen in the public speech setting as well. Verbal and nonverbal messages, such as expressing agreement or nodding in approval, are typical. If we receive these kinds of responses from many persons to whom we express a certain idea, we will be influenced

LEARNING THEORY

to maintain that idea and to continue expressing it. Conversely, if our listeners withhold reinforcement from us by remaining silent, or if they nod negatively or verbally express disagreement, we may decide to rethink our idea.

The source of the reinforcement is important. Sources viewed in a favorable light have greater potential for reinforcing and nonreinforcing impact than sources viewed in an unfavorable light. Most of us like to associate ourselves with persons whom we think are attractive, intelligent, and influential; and if such persons condone our behavior or a statement we make, we feel strongly reinforced. Conversely, if these persons respond negatively to our statements or behavior, we may try to change our behavior or to qualify our statements. When reinforcement or nonreinforcement for our behavior is provided by positive or negative responses to it from those whom we highly respect, it is more likely to influence us to alter our behavior.

In summary, learning theory explains our behavior in terms of others' responses to it and how we value the source or sources of these responses, that is, whether these responses are mildly or strongly reinforcing or nonreinforcing. Its critics point out that it is based on a simplistic, cause-effect view of human behavior and does not account for such variables as preexisting attitudes, beliefs, and values. Their reservations about the exclusive use of learning theory to explain human behavior has given rise to other theories.

CONSISTENCY THEORY   Imagine you have recently purchased a new car. You began by saving your hard-earned money and foregoing other purchases over a long period of time. You considered several makes available in your price range and read various consumer reports concerning them. You then spent many hours over a period of weeks test driving and comparing the cars you were considering. Finally you decided on a particular make and model. Now a close friend, whose opinion you usually respect, has informed you that, in his opinion, you bought a lemon and that the manufacturer has determined the car does not sell well enough to justify his continuing to manufacture it. How do you feel?

Your first reaction may be to challenge the source of your friend's information. You may tell yourself that sales on the model you bought are slow because not many people are as astute as you in recognizing a good value. You may also decide that your friend is not as knowledgable about cars as you had previously thought. Finally, when the manufacturer's decision to discontinue production is officially announced, you may tell yourself that your car will soon be a collector's item, and it will be even more valuable than before.

Whatever your thoughts, chances are you will adjust your thinking to some extent; however, you will probably not see your car as unworthy of your ownership, and you will probably not allow others' comments to undermine your own opinion. There is a very good reason for this. We all strive to make our behaviors consistent with our attitudes. In spite of La Piere's findings that we are not always consistent in our attitude toward an issue and our behavior concerning it, we all are comfortable when our behavior reflects our attitudes and beliefs.

Regarding your purchase, you believe you are an intelligent shopper and that you have made a good buy. It would be very difficult for you to reconcile the effort that went into your decision with having made a bad purchase. Doing so would be inconsistent. Although most of us claim to be flexible and open to change, the greater the commitment we make to an idea or activity in time and money, the more reluctant we are to change our attitude concerning it. When we receive information that contradicts our attitude, we experience discomfort or tension and we try to reduce that discomfort.[4]

More common examples of the difficulties that arise because of our tendency for consistency can be seen in the way we deal with current issues. Assume that you are strongly in favor of abortion. You believe a woman should have the right to terminate her own pregnancy. Perhaps you believe so strongly about the matter that you have gotten involved in community pro-abortion activities, including supporting pending legislation and political candidates who are for it and raising funds for the local abortion clinic. But also suppose that you discover your best friend vigorously opposes abortion and believes it is an act of murder. How can you possibly have a close relationship with someone whose opinion on this issue is so different from your own? Should you immediately call a halt to the friendship? Probably not. But you may reexamine your beliefs about abortion legislation and decide you do not feel as strongly about it as you had originally thought; or you may decide you are not really as close to your friend as you thought; or you may tell yourself that your friend does not really understand the issue. In any event, chances are that you will change some attitude in an attempt to reconcile your feelings about your friend with your feelings about abortion.

From these examples it is clear that behavior can involve more variables than one's seeking out rewarding and avoiding unrewarding experiences. Consistency theory helps us look more closely at human behavior. There is, however, more than one variety of consistency theory. *Balance theory, congruity theory,* and *cognitive dissonance theory* were each developed to help explain additional observed aspects of human behavior.

Balance Theory   Balance theory was initially developed by Fritz Heider in his attempts to better understand attitude consistency.[5] He felt that the scientific study of human behavior could progress by first understanding and then systematizing common sense. For his analysis he borrowed some simple ideas from formal logic and the algebra of sets and relations. In studying balance theory and attitude change, Heider was concerned with three elements involved in attitude change: (1) the person who is the focus of attention, (2) some other person, and (3) an interpersonal entity (some idea, issue, or event) that has the focus or attention of both persons. Heider labled the first person, P; the other person, O; and the idea or issue, X. Heider's goal was to discover how relations among P, O, and X are arranged by the person, P.

In the abortion illustration, you would be P, your friend would be O, and support for abortion legislation would be X. The situation might be diagrammed as follows:

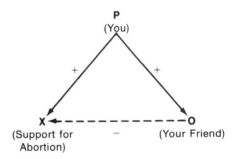

Because you favor abortion, the link between you and abortion has a positive value and can be indicated by a plus sign. Because you and your friend also have a close relationship, the link between the two of you has a positive value. But because your friend opposes abortion, the link between your friend and abortion has a negative value. In mathematics the product of two positives and a negative is negative.

$$+ \times + \times - = -$$

Heider terms a negative situation one that is imbalanced. In such a state you will likely feel anxiety, discomfort, or stress, and according to Heider you will be motivated to reduce the anxiety. To do so you might change *your* attitude toward abortion.

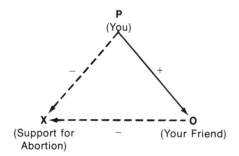

When you multiply two negatives and a positive, the product is positive.

$$+ \times - \times - = +$$

Because the product is now positive, we can say balance has been restored.

But you may decide on another course of action. Instead of changing your attitude toward abortion, you could reject your friend.

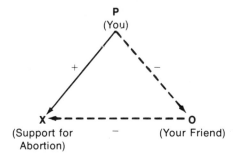

In this way you will also restore balance or reconcile your feelings.

$$- \times - \times + = +$$

Looking back on the diagrams you are sure to have noticed that a balanced state exists when there are an even number of negative values or no negatives at all, and an imbalanced state exists when there is an uneven number of negatives. An imbalanced state is characterized by discomfort and unpleasantness. Accordingly, the individual is under pressure to reduce imbalance, which means changing one's attitude toward either the person or the impersonal entity (object, idea, or event).

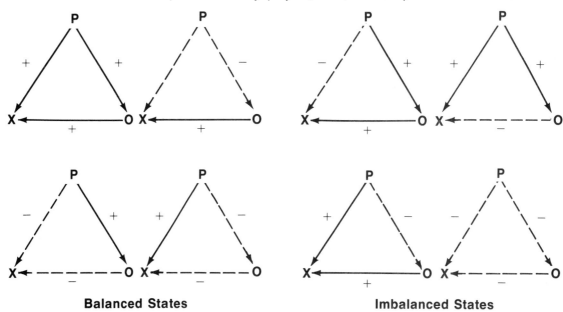

Balanced States   **Imbalanced States**

Congruity Theory   Congruity theory grew out of balance theory. Essentially, it is the same as balance theory, but goes a step further in determining a way to predict how attitudes and behavior will change.[6] Osgood and Tannenbaum, the developers of this theory, recognized that we hold a great many attitudes some of which are consistent with one another and some of which are not. Inconsistent attitudes are not usually a problem unless they are brought into relation with one another. Imagine that we hold a negative attitude toward a certain public official and also toward the idea that all guns should be registered. The two matters remain unrelated unless the official expresses an opinion on gun-control legislation. Should the official indicate support for gun legislation, the two attitudes are congruent. That is to say they are in agreement or harmony. If the official opposes gun legislation, our attitudes about the official and the issue will be incongruent, out of agreement.

So far this sounds like balance theory all over again. But Osgood and Tannenbaum developed a scheme in which something is evaluated on a scale from +3 to −3. On the scale +3 means that we have a maximum positive evaluation of something, and −3 means a maximum negative evaluation. 0 means we are neutral or have not evaluated the issue. Predictions involving the degree and direction of attitude change are based on the recognition that we do not feel equally strongly about all matters. One of the difficulties with the balance theory is that it only assumes one change in a situation. But congruity theory allows for more than one change and changes of varying degrees.

Assume that our attitude toward the public official is at the moderate scale value of −2 and we learn that he or she supports gun control. Remembering that we are in favor of gun control, let us say that we support that position to the highest scale value of +3. On the basis of the observation that extreme attitudes are more resistant to change than moderate ones, Osgood and Tannenbaum would predict that our attitude toward the public official would be more likely to change than our attitude toward gun control. The even greater likelihood is that we will change in two ways, but not by the same amount. First we are likely to grow more favorable toward the public official because he or she agrees with us; and at the same time our position on gun control will probably soften.

If we assume that our attitude toward the anti-gun legislation position would probably change more than our attitude toward the public official, we might illustrate the shift in our feelings with the following scales.

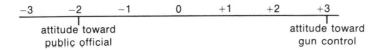

Our feelings about the public official and the anti-gun control position before they were brought into relation with each other.

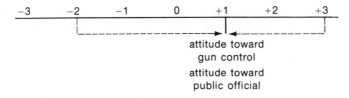

Our feelings about the public official and the anti-gun control position after they were brought into relation with each other.

Few theories in the study of behavior and attitudes have had the impact of Leon Festinger's theory of cognitive dissonance.[7] In this theory the concept of consonance replaces balance, and disso-

Cognitive Dissonance Theory

nance takes the place of imbalance. Viewed this way Festinger claims "there is pressure to produce consonant relations among cognitions and to avoid dissonance."[8] Recall that earlier in the chapter we said a cognition refers to something we know or assume to be true.

The theory developed as a means of interpreting some strange rumors that started after an earthquake in India. The rumors carried threats of cyclones, floods, and more earthquakes. They arose in an area where tremors had been felt but where there had been no destruction of property or personal injury. The existence of the rumors seemed to contradict the prevalent idea of learning theorists that people try to avoid unpleasant things, such as pain or anxiety at the prospect of pain or suffering. After all, why would people create anxiety for themselves? And even more curiously, comparable data indicated that people who lived at the actual disaster site and who had suffered injury or property loss did *not* create rumors of further destruction.

Festinger concluded that the rumors in the undamaged community came about as a result of the inhabitants' cognitive dissonance. The people had a strong fear reaction to the tremors; yet because no disaster seemed forthcoming, they could see nothing to fear. Experiencing fear in the absence of an adequate reason for fear created a feeling of dissonance or imbalance in the citizens of the undamaged community. The rumors of impending disaster provided explanations that were consonant with feelings of fear; the rumors functioned to justify the fear and thereby reduce the dissonance. In other words, we could say that the people attempted to reduce dissonance by adding to their cognition new consonant elements (the fear-inducing rumors) that were in balance with being afraid.

Another method of reducing dissonance is to change given cognitions. Festinger used the example of people who believe that cigarette smoking causes cancer but continue to smoke. Such people experience dissonance. The most efficient way to reduce the dissonance would be to stop smoking, but that would also be the most difficult for many people. Instead of quitting cigarettes, most people choose to undermine their own cognition, that cigarette smoking causes cancer. They may belittle the evidence that smoking causes cancer.[9] Or they may switch to filter-tipped cigarettes, deluding themselves that all the cancer-producing materials will be trapped in the tips. Or they might even convince themselves that smoking is worth the price, adopting the idea that they would rather have a short, enjoyable life than a long unenjoyable one without cigarettes. In adopting any of these stances, the individuals are seeking to reduce the dissonance by reducing the absurdity involved in making themselves cancer-prone.[10]

As a result of additional research, a few qualifications have been appended to Festinger's original theory. One of the most notable of these is the idea that the theory holds only under certain conditions, and two key conditions are commitment and volition.[11] *Commitment* is the decision to do or not to do something. It is a choice that requires active participation or the rejection of some alternative action. The implication of commitment is that, by closing the door to alternative actions, people must live with their decision. As a result, when they make an irreversible commitment to a certain idea, they must reduce the dissonance that arises as a result. *Volition* is the degree of freedom we feel we possess in making a choice or decision. To experience dissonance we must feel that we acted voluntarily so that we are responsible for the outcome of the decision. If we feel we have been forced to act contrary to our beliefs, we can avoid dissonance by telling oursleves we had no control over the matter.

For example, assume Jim and Barbara have been renting in the city since their marriage but now are looking for a home to buy. In the past, they have praised the advantages of living "close in" to the city, and they have ridiculed suburban living, calling it mediocre and tacky. They discover that they cannot find a house to their liking and in their price range in the city, so they decide to buy in the suburbs. According to dissonance theory, it can be predicted that they will reduce dissonance by bringing their attitudes in line with their behavior: their attitude toward suburban living will become more favorable, and possibly, their attitude toward urban living will grow more negative.[12] If Jim and Barbara feel as though they acted voluntarily, they may experience considerable dissonance. But if they believe they really had no choice except to buy a home and they bought the best they could find for their budget, they can reason that they were compelled to their decision. In this instance they will feel less dissonance and less pressure to change their attitudes.[13]

A further refinement of dissonance theory reveals an even more interesting aspect of commitment and attitude change. This time the prediction runs counter to common sense: the smaller the reward for engaging in a behavior that is contrary to an attitude, the greater will be the resultant attitude change. What is more, the

WHEN PROPHECY FAILS

Some years ago the following story appeared in a midwestern newspaper.

*PROPHECY FROM PLANET
CLARION CALL TO CITY:
FLEE THAT FLOOD
IT'LL SWAMP US ON DEC. 21,
OUTER SPACE TELLS SUBURBANITE*
Lake City will be destroyed by a flood from Great Lake just before dawn, December 21, according to a suburban housewife, Mrs. Marion Keech, of 847 West School Street. . . . It is the purport of many messages she has received by automatic writing, she says. . . . The messages, according to Mrs. Keech, are sent to her by superior beings from a planet called "Clarion." These beings have been visiting the earth, she says, in . . . flying saucers. . . . Mrs. Keech reports she was told the flood will spread to form an inland sea stretching from the Arctic Circle to the Gulf of Mexico. At the same time, she says, a cataclysm will submerge the West Coast from Seattle, Washington, to Chile in South America [Festinger, Riecken, and Schachter, 1956: 30–31].

Mrs. Keech told her friends about the message and attracted a small following of believers. Leon Festinger, Henry W. Riecken, and Stanley Schachter (1956), three social psychologists, joined the movement for research purposes, concealing their identity as social scientists. Many of the members of the doomsday sect made considerable financial sacrifices in committing themselves to the group, resigning from jobs and giving away their belongings. Thus the way was prepared for a monumental instance of cognitive dissonance between prophecy and outcome.

Mrs. Keech set the hour (midnight, December 21st) for the arrival of a visitor from outer space who would escort group members to safety by a flying saucer; at the appointed hour, however, nothing happened. When the visitor failed to arrive and the earth was not destroyed, the believers found themselves in intense confusion, apprehension, and despair. They checked and rechecked their watches in disbelief. Two facts were in dissonance—the members believed in their prophet and her prophecy had failed.

About five hours later, Mrs. Keech called the members together and announced that she had received a message: God had saved the world from destruction because of the faith spread throughout the world by the believers' actions. In so doing, Mrs. Keech offered a way by which dissonance could be reduced. Rather than reject their prophet, the members undertook to alter the other cognition—the doomsday belief. They reinterpreted the events and redirected their cause, finding a justification for their considerable commitment and investment. This illustrates how attitudes can be resistant to change even in the face of strong disconfirming evidence.

This article is adapted from the study, *When Prophecy Fails* by Leon Festinger, Henry W. Reicken, and Stanley Schachter. Minneapolis: University of Minnesota Press.

less coercion used to force the commitment, the greater will be the chance of attitude change.

This observation was illustrated in a classic experiment by Leon Festinger and J. Merrill Carlsmith.[14] They asked a group of subjects to perform a tedious and boring task for two hours. When they had completed the task, part of the group was asked to lie by telling the subjects who replaced them that the task was fun and exciting. The rest of the group was not asked to lie. Some of the subjects who lied were paid $1 for cooperating; others received $20. All of the group was then referred to the psychology department office where they were informed the experiment was ended and were asked to evaluate it. In truth, their evaluation was also a part of the experiment.

Among the questions the students were asked on the evaluation was the degree to which they had enjoyed the task they had performed. In the results the subjects who had been paid $1 for their compliance rated the task more positively than those who had been paid $20. The findings are in keeping with dissonance theory. Presumably, persons who, by virtue of a large reward or by force, behave in a way that conflicts with their attitudes can deny responsibility for their behavior by reasoning, "How could I refuse such a large reward," or "They made me do it." But in Festinger's experiment the subjects who received only $1 found it necessary to rationalize their lie. They had been dishonest for a trivial sum, and so they undertook to resolve the dissonance by coming to believe that they had really liked the dull task. In contrast, the subjects who received $20 experienced little dissonance and had little reason to alter their unfavorable attitude toward the boring tasks.

Amount of reward and attitude change. The experiment by Festinger and Carlsmith bears out the theory that the less the reward for engaging in behavior contrary to an attitude, the greater will be the accompanying change in attitude; the greater the reward, the less the change in attitude.

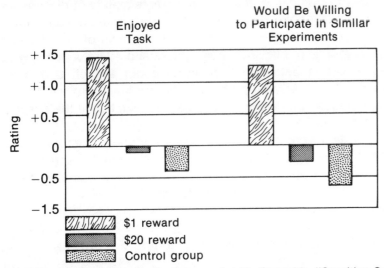

SOURCE: Adapted from L. Festinger and J. M. Carlsmith, "Cognitive Consequences of Forced Compliance." *Journal of Abnormal and Social Psychology* 58 (1959).

Since the Festinger study there have been several enlightening findings that have helped refine the dissonance idea. Aronson suggests that Festinger mislocated the source of the dissonance.[15] He argues that the source of the dissonance is the conflict between a person's self-conceptions and his cognitions about a behavior that violates these self-conceptions. According to this view, dissonance does not emanate from any two cognitions; rather, it occurs when one's behavior threatens the positive feelings one has about one's self.

In the experiment we just examined, Aronson argues the dissonance did not occur between the cognition, "I believe the task is dull," and the cognition, "I said the task is interesting." Instead, what Aronson says is dissonant is the cognition, "I am a good and decent human being" and the cognition, "I have committed an indecent act; I have misled someone."[16]

PERSUASION AND ATTITUDE CHANGE

The theories of influence are helpful to us in understanding why people have had certain attitude or opinion changes. Indeed, they can shed light on some of our own behavior. But how do we apply these ideas to the speech situation? Do we formulate a persuasive speech with the idea in mind, "I will create a state of dissonance in the minds of the listeners?" Perhaps. Certainly some more experienced speakers may do that; but for most of us, who give only occasional public speeches, understanding influence may be more useful in helping us to evaluate our speech before we present it. By examining the points we intend to cover and considering the audience, we can partly predict what the effect of our speech will be.

It is evident from the studies discussed in the preceding section that influence and attitude change are fairly complex and difficult to control, and they do not always reflect what common sense tells us should be. If the ability to influence the listener is so difficult to predict, you may ask, "What *can* I do to influence attitude change?" While you cannot directly measure or control audience attitude change, you *can* control the two elements of

Advertising is a form of persuasive communication that relies on a few short messages to influence our purchasing attitudes.

THERE IS ONLY ONE JOY...
THE COSTLIEST PERFUME IN THE WORLD

PENNY GIVE-AWAY

In a student-designed experiment to show the verbal and nonverbal reactions of people to stereotyped roles we can gain an interesting look at how others' perceptions of us will influence their behavior toward us. Six members of a fundamentals of speech class disguised themselves in various readily identifiable roles: 1) a young clergyman, 2) a pregnant woman, 3) an average, middle-class housewife, 4) a Hell's Angel gang member, 5) a streetwalker, and 6) a confidence man.

The stereotypes placed themselves in the flow of pedestrian traffic at a busy shopping mall. As people passed by, each of the stereotypes would randomly attempt to give certain individuals a penny, saying, "I'd like to give you this penny." Other class members situated themselves in places where they could observe and record the reactions of the passersby. Below are some of the reactions the class recorded for each of the stereotyped roles.

CLERGYMAN

Two young teenage girls accepted penny and laughed as they moved on.

Well-dressed elderly couple kept moving, refused penny.

Late middle-aged woman, well-dressed, immediately accepted, smiled, and said, "Thank you."

HOUSEWIFE

Well-dressed couple, middle-aged: Woman paused, man walked on, shook his head, then acted as if he were looking into store window. Woman turned away, said, "No thank you" and quickly moved to catch up with her companion.

Middle-aged, couple: Man veered away, continued walking. Woman accepted penny with a courteous, "Thank you."

STREETWALKER

Man, probably in 50's, in business suit, accepted penny, laughed.

Youngster alone, about four years old, looked around, grabbed penny and quickly walked into nearby store.

Six men, business suits, one accepted penny, all grinned.

Middle-aged woman in fur coat, refused saying, "I don't accept what I don't understand."

PREGNANT WOMAN

Woman, possibly in 60's, plainly dressed, shook head, refused, smiled and walked on.

Woman, nothing unusual about her dress, quickly checked to see if the penny was real, accepted it, smiled, walked on, and both she and her male companion examined the penny.

GANG MEMBER

Two middle-aged, fashionably dressed women laughed, avoided eye contact, walked by.

Two elderly women looked away as they passed.

Elderly man, grabbed hand of small boy companion, hurried past.

Two teenagers, hesitated, one put out hand and accepted penny, moved on quickly.

Businessman, looked Hell's Angel up and down, turned away.

CONFIDENCE MAN

Woman in 50's, plainly attired, replied in tone which appeared annoyed, "Keep your penny, you might need it someday."

Man, perhaps in 70's in old workclothes, shook finger, in angry voice said, "Keep your penny." Walked on mumbling.

This experiment was designed and carried out by members of a class at the Kent State University Stark County Regional Campus in 1975. The instructor, Rex Damron and the author assisted with the activity.

your speech that are most likely to bring it about: the communicator and the message.

THE COMMUNICATOR

Aristotle observed that persuasion is achieved by the speaker's personal character when the speech is spoken so as to make us think him credible. We believe good men more fully and more readily than others.[17] This conclusion is in keeping with commonsense notions, but it is a little more difficult to identify in careful research.

Credibility is not a tangible or finite reality. It is a *perception* of one communicator on the part of another.[18] A person may be extremely competent, but if that person is not perceived as being competent by the listener, then he lacks credibility on that dimension; and if he cannot establish credibility through some other means, he will not be seen as credible at all.

Results of studies in the area of credibility are mixed, but there are certain elements that we know affect it. The four most often considered are: (1) trustworthiness, (2) expertise, (3) sociability, and (4) similarity.

Trustworthiness

Trustworthiness refers to the degree of honesty with which the speaker is perceived. Conventional wisdom suggests that untrustworthy communicators are not as effective as trustworthy ones. Presumably, if we think that a speaker is attempting to advance his or her own best interest, we view the person as biased, as having ulterior motives; therefore, we are less inclined to be influenced by that speaker. Yet research on this matter has produced mixed results. While high-credibility sources often produce more *opinion change* than low-credibility sources, credibility has not been found to affect *message learning* (new information gained from a message intended strictly to inform). Neutral sources produce an amount of opinion change halfway between that produced by high- and low-credibility sources, but neutral sources produce more learning of message content.[19] When people know that the source is untrustworthy, they can evaluate the conclusion without considering the argument; when people are unable to evaluate the source, they must evaluate the arguments themselves.[20]

Further, when the communicator is seen as arguing against his or her own best interests, the person's influence may increase. In one study it was found that when a criminal argued in favor of more individual freedom and against greater police powers, he produced little attitude change in his listeners; but when he argued in favor of a stronger police force, he produced considerable attitude change.[21]

Expertise   Expertise is not so easily defined as trustworthiness. Your perception of another's degree of expertise is greatly influenced by the amount of experience you have had in the same or a related area. If you have considerable experience and competence at doing something, say cooking, you may not think a certain chef is particularly good; but your friend, who rarely opens the refrigerator except for ice cubes, may find the same chef's meal quite satisfying. We do tend to accept the opinions of persons whom we judge to be more competent than ourselves, and research indicates that experts are more persuasive than nonexperts.

Two groups of students had negatively evaluated nine stanzas of poetry. Each group was then asked to read an evaluation of the poetry by someone who praised it. The favorable evaluation read by one group of students had been written by the distinguished poet, T. S. Eliot; the one read by the other group was by Agnes Stearns, a student at Mississippi State Teachers College. The subjects then reevaluated the poetry. Perhaps it is not surprising that considerably more attitude change occurred among those students who had read the evaluation by Eliot than among those who had read the one by Agnes Stearns, the nonexpert.[22]

Sociability   Sociability is determined by how likable or friendly a speaker appears to be. For the most part, the more we like the source of a persuasive message, the more likely we are to change our belief in accordance with the idea advocated by the source. This fact probably is not surprising to any of us. The discussion on balance and congruity theory presented earlier in this chapter should help us understand why we behave this way. In some studies based on dissonance theory, however, the rule has not held up. The explanation given by the dissonance theorists is that people who agree to listen to a disreputable or unsociable speaker can find little justification for agreeing with that person; and so, just as the students who performed the boring task and then lied to others about it needed to convince themselves that the task was not all that dull, these listeners may feel compelled to justify their attention by saying that the message itself was worthy of a hearing. And they may be more influenced by it than one would have predicted.[23]

Similarity   Similarity is the degree to which the speaker is perceived to share his listeners' interests and concerns. We tend to be influenced more by people who are similar to us than by people who are different. We may conclude that what a source advocates is good for "our kind of people" and change our attitude accordingly. Furthermore, similarity tends to produce liking for a source, and liking enhances our perceptions that a person is similar to us.[24]

THE MESSAGE

The other element over which we said we can have some control is the message. Four of the most frequently asked questions about persuasive messages are: (1) How effective is fear appeal? (2) Is it better to draw conclusions for the audience or to let them decide on their own? (3) Are one-sided messages better than two-sided ones? and (4) Do people differ in their levels of susceptibility?

Arousing Fear

Early studies on fear appeals indicated that there was an inverse relationship between the amount of fear appeal and the amount of attitude change. In one study, three groups of high school students were exposed to different forms of communication on dental hygiene. The first group received a strong fear appeal that emphasized the pain caused by tooth decay and gum disease; the second group received a more moderate appeal; and the third group received an appeal that focused on completely healthy teeth. Eight percent of the students who had been exposed to the fear appeal changed their dental practices, compared with 22 percent of those who had been exposed to the more moderate appeal, and 36 percent of those who received the low fear appeal. In short, as the amount of fear-arousing material increased, the conformity to recommended actions decreased.[25]

As a result of the early studies, further research has been done on a wide variety of actions, such as giving up smoking, obtaining tetanus injections, and using auto seat belts. In most of the later studies, the findings have *contradicted* the earlier studies: the higher the fear level of the appeal, the greater the acceptance of the recommendations.[26]

On the basis of this contradiction in research results, scholars have concluded there must be other factors that account for the effect of fear-arousing communication, specifically, the circumstances under which fear facilitates or inhibits persuasion. Subsequent study suggests that fear arousal produces two parallel but independent reactions. One is the strong emotional response of fear; the other is a readiness to cope with danger. The arousal of fear in and of itself (the emotion) does not guarantee that people will undertake action to cope with the danger. Instead, they may think up counterarguments to the fear appeal, stop thinking about the danger, or develop various rationalizations for not worrying. One researcher indicates that high-fear-arousing messages result in greater persuasiveness than low-fear-arousing messages *if* the high-fear messages contain recommendations for reducing fear, that is, coping with danger by ceasing to smoke, getting a tetanus injection, or wearing a seat belt.[27]

Drawing Conclusions   The question of whether to draw a conclusion in the speech for the audience or to let the audience draw its own conclusion based on the case you present is not easily answered. Studies have been mostly inconclusive on this matter. If the conclusion is stated, the possibility for misinterpreting the argument is greatly reduced. On the other hand, if a speaker does not state a conclusion, she may appear unbiased and, therefore, more credible. Furthermore, if the audience members reach the conclusion themselves, they may be more strongly persuaded than if the conclusion is handed to them.

In general, most speakers believe it is not sufficient to simply state the case; they must also force the audience to reach the same conclusion.[28] But there does seem to be an exception to this notion. With relatively well-informed, sophisticated audiences or where the issue is a very simple one, it appears more effective to allow audience members to reach their own conclusions.[29]

One-sided versus
Two-sided Messages   Is it more effective to acknowledge the opposing arguments and refute them or simply to ignore them? If the message includes mention of arguments in support of the opposing view, the speaker has the advantage of appearing less biased, more knowledgeable, and less intent on trying to persuade. In brief, the speaker appears more credible because his message sounds less like propaganda and more like an objective account. On the other hand, a one-sided message is less complicated and easier for the listener to grasp.

Research suggests that the relative effectiveness of one-sided and two-sided messages is partly dependent on the audience. The one-sided communication appears more effective when the audience is poorly informed and poorly educated. To present members of such an audience with both sides of a complicated issue merely confuses them and provides them with counterarguments they would not have thought of otherwise. One-sided communications appear to be more effective also when members of an audience already agree with the message, and the speaker is trying to reinforce their thinking, to strengthen existing attitudes.

IMMUNIZATION AGAINST ATTITUDE CHANGE

Following the Korean War, Senate investigators were alarmed by the lack of resistance to Chinese Communist "brainwashing" that had been displayed by American prisoners of war. A congressional committee concluded that if Americans received more instruction in "Americanism" at home and at school, they would be less vulnerable to enemy propaganda in future wars. Various church groups have adopted a similar stance, calling for stepped-up training of young people in various moral precepts. Research by William McGuire (1964), a psychologist, and his associates suggests, however, that a more effective approach would be to expose people to opposing viewpoints as an immunization device.

When we wish to develop people's biological resistance to disease agents, we inoculate them with a weakened form of the infectious material so as to stimulate their defense mechanisms prior to massive exposure. McGuire suggests that, analogously, individuals can be made immune to propaganda by being exposed to weakened forms of the opposition's arguments before they experience the main attack.

To test this hypothesis, McGuire had subjects participate in two experimental sessions. During the first session, they were exposed to four cultural truisms regarding various health measures, including frequent tooth brushing to prevent dental decay and the use of X-rays to detect tuberculosis. For example, the subjects were told that "Everyone should brush his teeth after every meal if at all possible."

In the initial session, one of the truisms was accompanied by *supportive information*—for example, that brushing teeth improves their appearance and eliminates decay-causing bacteria. A second truism was followed by the equivalent of inoculation—a weak counterargument and its refutation: some people say that brushing injures the gums, but dental evidence suggests that brushing stimulates and improves gum condition. The counterargument was designed to be strong enough to threaten the individuals slightly and so stir up resistance, but not so strong as to overcome their weak defenses. The other two truisms were control truisms and were neither attacked nor supported.

In another experimental session a few days later, subjects were confronted with a strong attack against three of the truisms—the truism receiving supportive information, the truism with which inoculation was provided, and one control truism. A follow-up assessment of the subjects' attitudes revealed that the undefended truisms were highly vulnerable to the subsequent attack. In contrast, both supportive defense and inoculation defense helped subjects to resist the counterattitudinal propaganda. But of most interest is that the inoculation defense conferred considerably more immunity than did the supportive defense. Apparently, as in the case of medical inoculation, people who experience an earlier weak attack bolster their defenses: they prepare arguments to support their position, construct counterarguments, belittle opposing views, and so on.

This article is adapted from the study, "Inducing Resistence to Persuastion" in Berkowitz, L. (ed.), *Advances in Experimental Social Psychology*. Vol. I. New York: Academic Press.

Where members of an audience are well informed and well educated or are initially opposed to the message, a two-sided communication is more effective.[30]

You may recall our discussion in Chapter 4 regarding a person's ability to defend his or her beliefs when they are mildly attacked or attacked often. "Immunization against attitude change" goes beyond the notion of practice and points out that it is possible to inoculate listeners to certain arguments. When deciding to use a one- or two-sided presentation, you may want to determine how much your audience already knows about your topic before you present it.

Susceptibility   Our daily observations suggest that some people are gullible "pushovers" while others stubbornly "stick to their guns." Do people in fact differ in their susceptibility to persuasive communications? Evidence suggests that there is such a trait as general persuadability, that there is some consistency in the degree to which a person can be persuaded by certain kinds of appeals and on certain kinds of issues.[31] Although there is such a trait as general susceptibility, a host of situational factors moderate the impact of any particular appeal. Thus the relationship between personality and persuadability cannot be determined without taking into account the source and nature of the appeal and the nature of the issue.

A sampling of the research reveals the following findings on the nature of susceptibility:

> The more a person's attitude is founded on logically related beliefs, the more resistant is the person to change.[32]
>
> Under some circumstances, role playing seems to be an effective device for altering attitudes and behavior. A group of young women who were heavy cigarette smokers played the role of cancer patients in an experimental study. After an 18-month interval, these young women smoked significantly less than a control who had not acted in the play.
>
> Making public one's opinion on an issue tends to make a person more resistant to counterpropaganda and more dedicated to the cause. In one study, women who favored dissemination of birth control information and who signed a petition in support of such a program were sent a flyer attacking their stand. Follow-up investigation revealed that these women—when compared with a control group who had signed the petition but had not received the leaflet—increased their commitment to the cause and were even willing to do volunteer work on its behalf.[33]

Clearly, the effectiveness of communications that are designed to persuade depends on situational factors; reliable generalizations regarding a person's susceptibility to persuasion are difficult to make.

SUMMARY

Influence is one of the most interesting aspects of the communication process. Understanding how it is achieved or exerted is difficult, but some elements of human behavior and some personality characteristics are important to the process. A fundamental understanding of these elements can be useful in predicting the impact of communication and in understanding our own behavior.

Attitudes, beliefs, and values are components of our lives that determine the relationship between influence and behavior. Although people sometimes use them interchangeably, there are differences among the three concepts. An *attitude* is a learned and fairly long-lasting predisposition to evaluate a person, event, or situation in a certain way. There may be a large discrepancy between the attitudes people express and their actions. A *belief* refers to a cognition or something we know to be true. And a *value* is an ethical principle or conviction to which we feel a strong emotional commitment. It is the premise we use in judging others' attitudes and beliefs. Values provide us with our conception of what is good and bad in the world.

Considerable research has been done in the area of attitudes and influence, and some controversial but extremely interesting theories of influence have been developed. Learning theory and consistency theory are the most highly developed explanations of the influence process. *Learning theory* is based on the idea that people tend to repeat rewarding behavior and avoid unrewarding behavior. Whenever we communicate with others, we exhibit reinforcing or nonreinforcing behavior; and as a result, we have an influence on other people. Because learning theory emphasizes feedback and interaction, both the source and the message are important.

Consistency theory grew out of the criticism of learning theory. Critics point out the shortcoming of learning theory as its apparent lack of attention to attitudes, values, beliefs, and other variables that exist in the mind of the listener and affect his persuadability and his behavior.

The essential idea behind consistency theory is that people try to keep their behavior consistent with their attitudes, values, and beliefs; and when it is not, they feel uncomfortable and compelled to change one or the other (behavior or attitude) to bring them into balance. The three basic consistency theories are: (1) balance theory, (2) congruity theory, and (3) cognitive dissonance theory.

Balance theory was initially developed by Fritz Heider. He used simple letter notation (P, O, X) and a combination of plus and minus signs to examine all possible relations among (1) the person who is the focus of attention, (2) some other person, and (3) an interpersonal entity (some idea, issue, or event) that has their attention.

Congruity theory is an extension of balance theory. It holds that people have countless attitudes, values, and beliefs, and some are consistent while others are not. Further, the inconsistent attitudes are not troublesome until they come into relation with one another through some communication or other kind of experience.

Cognitive dissonance theory was delevoped as a means of understanding contradictory behavior, behavior that defies commonsense explanations. Continuing to smoke cigarettes in the face of the knowledge that smoking is harmful to health and may very well cause cancer, or spreading rumors of danger when no apparent danger is present are examples of the contradictory behavior this theory may be used to explain.

Degree of commitment and whether or not an individual feels as though he acted freely are two important aspects of cognitive dissonance theory. One study in the area showed that, when people are given a very small reward for acting in a manner contradictory to their own values, they may actually change their thinking rather than face the reality that they accepted a small reward for behaving inconsistently with their values.

While influence cannot be predicted and can be measured only indirectly, through expressed changes in attitude or observable changes in behavior, we do know it is directly affected by the two basic components of the communication process: the *communicator* and the *message*. For speaking to be persuasive, the communicator must be perceived as credible. The four basic elements of credibility are: (1) trustworthiness, (2) expertise, (3) sociability, and (4) similarity.

Four commonly expressed concerns about persuasive messages are: (1) How effective is fear appeal? (2) Is it better to draw conclusions for members of an audience or to let them decide for themselves? (3) Are one-sided messages better than two-sided ones? and (4) Do people differ in their levels of susceptibility?

The answers to these questions depend on certain characteristics of the audience and of the message. Fear messages are effective when they contain recommendations for reducing fear, that is, when they offer an alternative course of action. Drawing conclusions is usually a safe technique, but may not be required with a sophisticated audience or a simple topic. Two-sided messages enhance credibility but raise questions in the minds of the listener. One-sided messages work better with complex topics or when the audience is poorly educated or already in agreement with the speaker's position. Although susceptibility is difficult to measure, some persons are more persuadable than others. The more a person's beliefs are founded on logic and reasoning, the more difficult it is to change his thinking. A public commitment to a position increases resistance to change, and role playing can result in more change.

INITIATIVES

POX Positive. Reread the section on balance theory and then make some triangles of your own. Label the three corners of a triangle with *your name* and a *friend's name* and an *issue* upon which you both agree. Then on each side of the triangle label all of these relations with a + sign. Reflect upon *if*, and *why* agreement makes you feel good. Does knowing that someone you like and respect holds an opinion like yours confirm that you are sensible, that you are "ok"?

INITIATING ACTION 1

POX Negative. Now place at the three corners of another triangle your own name, a parent's and an issue upon which you disagree strongly with that parent. Next place the appropriate positive and negative signs. For example, the issue may be smoking, material wealth, or one of your friends whom a parent dislikes. Reflect upon how this made you feel. What did you do or did your parent do once the difference in feelings about this issue were acknowledged? Did one of you slightly change your attitude toward the issue? Or did one of you lose respect or liking for the other? Or might one or both of you have decided the issue was not so important?

INITIATING ACTION 2

City-Country. Ask one of your acquaintances how he feels about living in the country. If you discover that your preferences are different discuss what it would take for each of you to change? Was there some value or change in circumstance which would make the change tolerable or even attractive. Now, think for a moment about how difficult it is to change another person's attitude.

INITIATING ACTION 3

Relationships. A speaker and an audience usually begin their relationship before a word is uttered. Observe a forthcoming speaker. Ask someone who wants to hear this speaker why he plans to do so. What about the speaker has generated an initial credibility? During the speech trace how the speaker's credibility rises, remains even, or goes down for you. Consider such factors as: Trustworthiness, Expertise, and Sociability.

INITIATING ACTION 4

Fear. Studies show that people often do things they know are harmful to themselves such as consuming too much chocolate

INITIATING ACTION 5

candy. Or they don't do things that are important to their well being such as wearing a helmet while riding a motorcycle. Pick such an item and work out a list of increasingly frightful consequences. Also list the increasingly high probability of these consequences occurring. For example, perhaps the most frightening consequence you could imagine to not buckling your seat belt would be to be in a vegetable-like coma for two years after an accident. Now suppose that the odds of this happening were the highest possible, i.e., that the next time you got into your car such an accident would occur. Consider how strong a fear must be for you to do something which you presently recognize as good for you but do not do, or vice versa. Also consider how fear might be legitimately used by a speaker to motivate.

INITIATING ACTION 6   *Your Campaign.* To influence most often requires more than a speech. The United Fund, for example, requires more than a few advertisements. Plan a campaign. First select an accomplishable goal that is worthy of your energy and time. Here are some ideas: To increase the funds to the women's athletic program, to have your classmates give blood to the Red Cross, to persuade some of your classmates to stop smoking, or to promote the use of a new word such as "che" to be used instead of he and she. Second, analyze what your target group believes or feels about the goal you have selected. What is their level of interest and commitment? Are they apathetic, hostile, or concerned? Third, what are the interests, attitudes, and values of the target audience? Fourth, how might you link your campaign to the interests, attitudes, and values of your audience? Fifth, map out a campaign strategy which extends across several weeks. Do not overlook any appropriate media, such as posters and hand bills, radio or television spots, symbols and buttons, letters to the editor, and class demonstrators.

INITIATING ACTION 7   *There Are Two Sides.* Review what this chapter says about one sided vs. two sided messages. Now prepare two manuscript speeches, one with as persuasive a message as you can muster in behalf of the cause. Now prepare a second speech which adds arguments of opponents. Do not include your own conclusion. Video or audio tape a presentation of each of the two speeches. Play the first for one audience and the second for a different audience. Before and after each speech ask the audiences to indicate their position on the topic on the following scales:

	The Core Idea							
Stupid	−3	−2	−1	0	+1	+2	+3	Brilliant
Impossible	−3	−2	−1	0	+1	+2	+3	Possible
Worthless	−3	−2	−1	0	+1	+2	+3	Worthwhile

Now for each audience compare the responses people gave you before they heard the speech with the ones they gave you after the speech. Which audience seems to have more change in the direction of the speaker's opinion?

Disorganization. Select a well-organized speech. Xerox a second copy to use in this exercise. Remove any preview, summary, and signposts. Now cut the speech up and rearrange the paragraphs. Tape both speeches: the organized and disorganized. Play them to different audiences. Have them rate the speeches on:

INITIATING ACTION 8

Unbelievable	1	2	3	4	5	6	7	Believable
Uninteresting	1	2	3	4	5	6	7	Interesting
Bad	1	2	3	4	5	6	7	Good
Cloudy	1	2	3	4	5	6	7	Clear

Compare the results. Afterwards interview both audiences. Ask them to outline the speeches and to describe their impression of the author of the speech.

NOTES

1. Hazel G. Erskine, "The Polls: Gun Control," *Public Opinion Quarterly*, 1972, vol. 36, pp. 455–69.

2. Allan W. Wicker, "Attitudes versus Actions: The Relationship of Verbal and Overt Behavioral Responses to Attitude Objects," *Journal of Social Issues*, 1969, vol. 25, pp. 41–78.

3. Richard T. La Piere, "Attitudes versus Actions," *Social Forces*, 1934, vol. 13, pp. 230–237.

4. Robert B. Zajonc, "The Concepts of Balance, Congruity and Dissonance," *Public Opinion Quarterly*, 1960, vol. 24, pp. 280–96.

5. Fritz Heider, "Attitudes and Cognitive Organization," *Psychology*, 1946, vol. 21, pp. 107–22.

6. Charles E. Osgood and Percy A. Tannenbaum, "The Principle of Congruity in the Prediction of Attitude Change," *Psychological Review*, 1955, vol. 62, pp. 42–55.

7. Leon Festinger, *A Theory of Cognitive Dissonance* (Stanford, Calif.: Stanford University Press, 1957).

8. Ibid.

9. Ibid.

10. Elliot Aronson, "The Theory of Cognitive Dissonance: A Current Perspective." In Leonard Berkowitz (ed.), *Advances in Experimental Social Psychology*. vol. 4, (New York: Academic Press, 1969, pp. 1–34).

11. J. W. Brehm and A. R. Cohen, *Explorations in Cognitive Dissonance*, (New York: John Wiley & Sons, 1962).

12. J. J. Sherwood, J. W. Banon, and H. G. Fitch, "Cognitive Dissonance: Theory and Research" in R. V. Wagner and J. J. Sherwood (eds.), *The Study of Attitude Change*, (Belmont Calif.: Brooks-Cole 1969).

13. Ibid.

14. Leon Festinger and J. M. Carlsmith, "Cognitive Consequences of Force Compliance", *Journal of Abnormal and Social Psychology*, 1959, vol. 58, pp. 203–10.

15. Aronson, op. cit.

16. E. Nel, Robert L. Helmreich, and Elliot Aronson, "Opinion Change in the Advocate as a Function of the Persuasibility of His Audience: A Classification of the Meaning of Cognitive Dissonance", *Journal of Personality and Social Psychology*, 1969, vol. 12, pp. 117–124.

17. Aristotle, *The Rhetoric and the Poetics*, (New York: Random House, 1954).

18. James C. McCroskey and Lawrence R. Wheelers, *Introduction to Human Communication*, (Boston: Allyn and Bacon, 1976), pp. 101–6.

19. William J. McGuire, "The Nature of Attitudes and Attitude Change," In G. Lindzey and E. Aronson (eds.), *Handbook of Social Psychology*, vol. 3, 2nd ed., (Reading, Mass.: Addison-Wesley, 1969), pp. 136–314.

20. Raymond A. Bauer, "A Revised Model of Source Effect." *Presidential Address to the Division of Consumer Psychology*, American Psychological Association Annual Meeting, Chicago, 1965.

21. Elaine C. Walster, E. Aronson and D. Abrahams, "On Increasing the Persuasiveness of a Law Prestige Communicator," *Journal of Experimental Psychology*, 1966, vol. 2, pp. 325–42.

22. Elliot Aronson, J. Turner, and J. M. Carlsmith, "*Communicators Credibility and Communicators Discrepancy*," *Journal of Abnormal and Social Psychology*, 1963, vol. 67, pp. 31–6.

23. McGuire, op. cit.

24. Ibid.

25. Irving Janis and S. Feshbach, "Effects of Fear Arousing Communications," *Journal of Abnormal and Social Psychology*, vol. 48, pp. 78–92.

26. Howard Leventhal, "Findings and Theory in the Study of Fear Communications," In Leonard Berkowitz, (ed.), *Advances in Experimental Social Psychology*, vol. 5, (New York: Academic Press, 1970), pp. 120–86.

27. Ibid.

28. McGuire, op. cit.

29. Donald L. Thistlewaite and J. Kamenetz by, "Attitude Change Through Refutation and Elaboration of Audience Counterarguments," *Journal of Abnormal and Social Psychology*, 1955, vol. 51, pp. 3–9.

30. Elliot M. McGinnies, "Studies in Persuasion: III. Reactions of Japanese Students to One-sided and Two-sided Communications," *Journal of Social Psychology*, 1966, vol. 70, pp. 87–95.

31. McGuire, op. cit.

32. J. E. Holt, "Resistance to Persuasion on Explicit Beliefs as a Function of Commitment to and Desirability of Logically Related Beliefs," *Journal of Personality and Social Psychology*, 1970, vol. 16, pp. 583–91.

33. Charles Kiesler, *The Psychology of Commitment: Experiments Linking Behavior to Belief*, (New York: Academic Press, 1971)

SUGGESTED READINGS

Aronson, E., "Dissonance Theory: Progress and Problems," In Abelson, R., Aronson, E., McGuire, W., Newcomb, T., Rosenber, M., and Tannenbaum, P. (eds.) *Theories of Cognitive Consistency: A Source Book*, Chicago: Rand McNally, 1968.

Bettinghaus, Erwin P., *Persuasive Communication*, 2nd ed., New York: Holt, Rinehart and Winston, 1973.

Festinger, Leon, Riecken, Henry W., and Schachter, Stanley, *When Prophecy Fails*, Minneapolis: University of Minnesota Press, 1956.

Hovland, Carl I., ed. *The Order of Presentation in Persuasion.* New Haven: Yale University Press, 1957.

Hovland, C. I., Janis, I., and Kelly, H. H., *Communication and Persuasion*, New Haven: Yale Universtiy Press, 1953.

Kiesler, Charles A., Collins, Barry E., and Miller, Norman, *Attitude Change*, New York. John Wiley & Sons, 1969.

Langer, Ellen J., and Dweck, Carol S., *Personal Politics: The Psychology of Making It*, Englewood Cliffs: Prentice-Hall, 1973.

Miller, G. K., and Burgoon, M., *New Techniques of Persuasion*, New York: Harper & Row, 1973.

Skinner, B. F., *Beyond Freedom and Dignity*, New York: Knopf, 1971.

12 ethics & freedom of speech

Congress OF THE United States

begun and held at the City of New-York, on

Wednesday the fourth of March, one thousand seven hundred and eighty nine.

THE Conventions of a number of the States, having at the time of their adopting the Constitution, expressed a desire, in order to prevent misconstruction or abuse of its powers, that further declaratory and restrictive clauses should be added: And as extending the ground of public confidence in the Government, will best ensure the beneficent ends of its institution.

RESOLVED by the Senate and House of Representatives of the United States of America, in Congress assembled, two thirds of both Houses concurring, that the following Articles be proposed to the Legislatures of the several States, as amendments to the Constitution of the United States, all, or any of which Articles, when ratified by three fourths of the said Legislatures, to be valid to all intents and purposes, as part of the said Constitution; viz.

ARTICLES in addition to, and Amendment of the Constitution of the United States of America, proposed by Congress, and ratified by the Legislatures of the several States, pursuant to the fifth Article of the original Constitution.

Article the first... After the first enumeration required by the first Article of the Constitution, there shall be one Representative for every thirty thousand, until the number shall amount to one hundred, after which the proportion shall be so regulated by Congress, that there shall be not less than one hundred Representatives, nor less than one Representative for every forty thousand persons, until the number of Representatives shall amount to two hundred, after which the proportion shall be so regulated by Congress, that there shall not be less than two hundred Representatives, nor more than one Representative for every fifty thousand persons.

Article the second... No law, varying the compensation for the services of the Senators and Representatives, shall take effect, until an election of Representatives shall have intervened.

Article the third... Congress shall make no law respecting an establishment of religion, or prohibiting the free exercise thereof; or abridging the freedom of speech, or of the press; or the right of the people peaceably to assemble, and to petition the Government for a redress of grievances.

Article the fourth... A well regulated militia, being necessary to the security of a free State, the right of the people to keep and bear arms, shall not be infringed.

Article the fifth... No Soldier shall, in time of peace be quartered in any house, without the consent of the owner, nor in time of war, but in a manner to be prescribed by law.

Article the sixth... The right of the people to be secure in their persons, houses, papers, and effects, against unreasonable searches and seizures, shall not be violated, and no warrants shall issue, but upon probable cause, supported by oath or affirmation, and particularly describing the place to be searched, and the persons or things to be seized.

Article the seventh... No person shall be held to answer for a capital, or otherwise infamous crime, unless on a presentment or indictment of a Grand Jury, except in cases arising in the land or naval forces, or in the militia, when in actual service in time of War or public danger; nor shall any person be subject for the same offence to be twice put in jeopardy of life or limb, nor shall be compelled in any criminal case to be a witness against himself, nor be deprived of life, liberty, or property, without due process of law; nor shall private property be taken for public use, without just compensation.

Article the eighth... In all criminal prosecutions, the accused shall enjoy the right to a speedy and public trial, by an impartial jury of the State and district wherein the crime shall have been committed, which district shall have been previously ascertained by law, and to be informed of the nature and cause of the accusation; to be confronted with the witnesses against him; to have compulsory process for obtaining witnesses in his favor, and to have the assistance of counsel for his defence.

Article the ninth... In suits at common law, where the value in controversy shall exceed twenty dollars, the right of trial by jury shall be preserved, and no fact tried by a jury, shall be otherwise re-examined in any court of the United States, than according to the rules of the common law.

Article the tenth... Excessive bail shall not be required, nor excessive fines imposed, nor cruel and unusual punishments inflicted.

Article the eleventh... The enumeration in the Constitution, of certain rights, shall not be construed to deny or disparage others retained by the people.

Article the twelfth... The powers not delegated to the United States by the Constitution, nor prohibited by it to the States, are reserved to the States respectively, or to the people.

ATTEST,

Frederick Augustus Muhlenberg, Speaker of the House of Representatives.

John Adams, Vice-President of the United States, and President of the Senate.

Influence involves not only persuasive strategy, but also the question of ethics and freedom of speech. A machine may process information amorally, but people, as they communicate, make choices based on what works and what is right. In the previous chapter we discussed the behavioral underpinnings of the influence process. In this chapter, we will look at some of the ethical questions a speaker should consider in light of our cultural and social values; and we will examine some of the problems that arise from our constitutional commitment to freedom of speech.

THE ETHICAL QUESTIONS

One of the central by-products of preparing a speech on any subject is that the speaker may become more aware of his feelings and attitudes toward that subject. This is even more true when the speaker interacts with others who respond to his ideas. Speaking and listening provide an arena for examination and testing of opinions, beliefs, attitudes, and values. You may recall in the previous chapter we described values as ethical principles to which people feel a strong, emotional commitment and which they employ in judging others' attitudes, beliefs, and behavior. We said they provide us with our conception of what is good and bad in the world. The ethical principles on which those values are based affect the way we conduct our lives, and apply equally to how we behave and how we judge others.

Ethics have been a part of the study of communication since the time of the ancient rhetoricians. Although we do not treat them here as a separate, theoretical question, there are several ideas based on ethics for which all communicators are responsible. Whenever a speaker prepares a message to persuade, the question of ethics arises; for we must consider whether the means we are using to make our argument convincing are ethical. As a speaker you can meet the obligation to evaluate those means by asking these questions: (1) Have I placed the welfare of the audience above my self-interests? (2) Am I sharing all that I know about this topic in the time I have, and is the same information equally available to the audience members? (3) Is my reporting of data and factual information honest and accurate? (4) Have I mistakenly imposed my own personal values on the listeners for the sake of the argument of a broader issue on which there is room for more than one right answer?

Placing our own interests above the best interests of the group or the community can lead to ethical problems in presenting a persuasive speech. The land developer who speaks to the citizens of a community about the creation of a new housing development in their town but fails to mention the costs of providing water to the inhabitants and the impact that will have on the water supply of the community, is probably more concerned with the personal monetary rewards of the project than the welfare and future of the community. In such an instance, the speaker is also guilty of not sharing all the information there is about the project with the audience members. By ignoring the first ethical principle the speaker becomes involved in other unethical practices.

SELF INTEREST

The question of honesty and accuracy occurs in interpersonal interactions all the time. The publisher who tells a writer a certain kind of book will sell more copies than the publisher really knows to be possible is practicing a similar technique for the sake of getting the author to write. In our first example, information was being withheld; and in the second, data are being manufactured to achieve the speaker's goal.

HONESTY AND ACCURACY

Another way these messages might have been handled would be for the land developer to show his audience how the cost of water will be offset by the infusion of new people and money into the community; and the publisher might have mentioned to the author other benefits of writing (recognition, movie rights, opportunity to develop new talent and areas of interest) to be gained as well as the real profit picture. Under these terms, everyone's welfare is being cared for.

Since a speaker may often have special information available, or discover more information as a result of the research and preparation he or she may have done for the presentation, it is unreal-

SOURCES AND INFORMATION

istic to expect the audience to be as informed on the topic. But the ethical speaker will keep records of all the sources of information and share those sources when it is appropriate. When time allows for it in a speech, showing the relationship between certain data or how you arrived at a conclusion based on certain information is not only a more credible way to make your point, but it can also be a highly persuasive technique.

IMPOSED VALUES   The question of imposing values is not so easily answered as the others we have been discussing. Certainly you would not choose a topic to dicuss or speak on that you did not have some feelings about. And those feelings will be affected by your values. In interpersonal settings there are countless times you may discuss a question for which there is no single "right answer." The solution you would choose to resolve a problem may be quite different from the one your neighbor may select. In our first example, some of the citizens of the community where the land developer is speaking may feel their land is already over-burdened with the requirements of people. They may strongly support recent environmental causes and view increased development as harmful to the goals of good environmental management. Others may see the opportunity for building better schools and roads, attracting more talented citizens, and establishing power as a community in the state political organizations, and thereby gaining more public works projects for the good of the community. In both instances the people have the good of the community in mind, but each group values different aspects more highly. The hope is that a solution can be developed through communication and discussion and the goal is for all to be satisfied with the solution.

If the speaker has the welfare of the audience members in mind, he or she is more likely to conform to the principle of not imposing his or her own values on the listeners. But some care not to presume that you know best what is good for the audience must be constantly applied. A presumptuous attitude may result in much less influence than a more even handed, informative one; and it is not likely to help the speaker establish credibility or empathy.

A considerable portion of communication is a matter of trust. Trust is a matter of perceived goodwill, belief in competence, and reason to believe in the character of the advocate. The honesty of a communicator may be measured by the visibility of his or her purposes, the rationale of the argument, and reasonableness of the supports. I am fond of Max Ehrmann's advice:

> As far as possible without surrender be on good terms with all persons. Speak the truth quietly and clearly; and listen to others, even the dull and ignorant; they too have their story.[1]

FREEDOM OF SPEECH

The question of values and ethics (especially the notion of imposed values) inevitably leads to a discussion of freedom of speech. For although the constitution guarantees us the right to free speech, the definition of what is free speech and the limits of the constitution are constantly challenged as a result of our changing values and ethics. Technology, the changing environment, and the need for greater social interaction have all added to the social change that presses us to reconsider our values and definitions of what is right and wrong in the world.

LIMITS OF PUBLIC SPEECH

The ancient Greek forum served as the marketplace of both commerce and ideas. In our complex society, which weathered the civil rights demonstrations of the sixties and the antiwar protests of the seventies, considerable debate has been raised over two essential questions: (1) What are the legal limits of public protest? and (2) What is the individual's responsibility to him or herself and to the public?

The open air or public forum is of particular importance for a free society because frequently the poor cannot hire a hall[2] to publicize their causes or pay for radio and television time. The streets, too, belong to the people. Consequently, the courts have ruled that any group may get a permit to march in demonstrations so long as the time and frequency of the demonstrations do not occur during peak traffic or when it might prove difficult to protect the demonstrators, such as at night in certain neighborhoods opposed to the demonstrators.

The State reserves the right to protect the property entrusted to it as it does the property held by the private sector. Therefore the individual who would take a message to the public park or street may be required to get a permit. Blocking an entrance or obstructing sidewalk or street traffic, harrassing a speaker (such as chanting during commencement exercises) and gathering too near a courthouse (especially during business hours) may result in arrest. In 1961, some 2,000 black students marched to a point 101 feet across from the courthouse and jail in Baton Rouge and sang along with fellow protestors who had been arrested for picketing and imprisoned the day before. They sang "God Bless America" and several hymns, pledged allegiance to the flag, prayed while some seventy to eighty policemen and a crowd of one hundred to three hundred whites watched. When the blacks refused the Sheriff's order to disperse, policemen threw tear gas canisters which exploded in the crowd.

Four years later the Supreme Court ruled the Baton Rouge demonstration had been peaceful and was unjustly dispersed. However, at the same time it cautioned that groups could not take decisions into their own hands about when and where to demonstrate anymore than one could decide to ignore a traffic signal or call a meeting in the middle of Times Square at rush hour as a form of freedom of speech or assembly.[3] In a subsequent case—in fact, one very similar jailhouse protest, this time at night in Tallahassee—the arrested and convicted protestors lost their appeal to the High Court.[4]

Today in some parts of the country the marketplace has shifted from the center of town to the shopping plaza. Reaching the public with a message is not so easy here. Union picketing outside a supermarket has been upheld;[5] but passing out antiwar leaflets upon the premises, the court ruled, may be selectively prohibited.[6]

The very real concerns of any civilized people are that protest, on the one hand may break into riot, or that, on the other, the police might brutally put down a peaceful assembly. History is scarred with such incidents, from our own Boston protests prior to the American Revolution, the Chicago Haymarket slaughter, the Washington, D.C. routing of the ragged veteran's bonus army, and more recently the tragic, fatal shooting into the crowd of students at Kent State University.

This society, therefore, has set forth certain standards to prevent speakers from setting fire to reason. We cannot publicly advocate violent action. It is unlawful to shout "fire" in a crowded theater and it is unlawful to urge a crowd to burn, lynch, and kill. Inciting to riot should not be confused with advocacy of another form of government or of revolution. During times of war and other periods of national stress it has not always been safe to

Picketing and the right to assemble continue to be disputed issues. Striking farm workers, led by Cesar Chavez, are shown being arrested after violating court orders restricting picketing at struck ranches.

advocate revolution, even in theory. During World War I, socialists were convicted for publishing and distributing leaflets opposing the war.

There are yet other issues when trying to discover what limits should be placed upon speech in public places. Examine for a moment the following two overlapping questions about the roles of two public servants:

INDIVIDUAL RESPONSIBILITY

1 Should a policeman participate in a political campaign?
2 Should a teacher post his central beliefs on his classroom door?

All of us probably subscribe to freedom of speech. But how free should the policeman or teacher be to push for a particular candidate? How free should they be to publicly advocate their religious beliefs? How free should they be to speak their personal opinions about controversial topics such as birth control, drugs, and American foreign policy?

Should not the policeman or teacher remain neutral? Can anyone really be neutral? Won't a policeman's beliefs show up in the way he treats persons who have a lifestyle which he abhors? Would not a teacher favor those students whose ideas coincide with his own? If a teacher avoids taking a position on controversial political matters, what message does that failure to take a position communicate?[7] In many states recently teachers have had to swear their loyalty to this country and to disclaim any sympathy, theoretical or real, to any other form of government. Several landmark cases have reinstated teachers who were fired for refusal to take such loyalty oaths.[8] But such cases do not really answer the question. The danger that a teacher might spread propaganda is real if a school board cannot dismiss him no matter what he says. Is there likewise danger if a policeman talks politics. Does belief in freedom of speech provide a simple answer to the limits of free speech? Is there not something healthy about knowing where a policeman or a teacher stands? Should they not be encouraged, even required, to post their credo? There is no neat answer.

Open debate of public issues has been held to be so important to the political process that candidates may have to suffer abusive attacks. The Courts have reasoned the public interest suffers more if a citizen fears expressing his opinion lest he be subject to arrest or suit. *The New York Times* vs. Sullivan is a landmark case in this respect. An Alabama judge had awarded a half-million dollars to L. B. Sullivan, a sheriff, and to other city officials of Montgomery to be paid by four Negro clergymen and the *Times* which published a paid advertisement attacking the city's handling of civil rights demonstrations. However, the clergymen and *The New York Times* won a reversal of that judgment in the Supreme Court. The issue centered on the accuracy of some of the descriptions and statements in the ad. Justice Brennan summed up the Court's point of view in this sentence: "A rule compelling the critic of official conduct to guarantee the truth of all his factual assertions—and to do so on pain of libel judgments virtually unlimited in amount—leads to a comparable 'self-censorship.' "[9]

But we should not think there are no limits to what we may say, however false, about one another. The High Court just three years after *Times* v. Sullivan, upheld a three million dollar suit by Wallace Butts, a Georgia University football coach, against the Curtis Publishing Company (publishers of the *Saturday Evening Post* magazine). The *Post* had printed an article which alleged that Butts had helped fix a game between the Universities of Georgia and Alabama. The Supreme Court decided the fix charge was not well supported by the evidence and the editors of the magazine had failed to check out the allegation.[10] Public figures apparently were not subject to suffer the same abuse as public officials or candidates for public office.

More recently the Court has reaffirmed the more flexible standard for debate, permitting seemingly defamatory statements at least in the case of labor disputes. In 1970, the National Association of Letter Carriers in Richmond, Virginia, with a membership of 420, launched a campaign to force the fifteen non-union carriers to join up. Each month in the union's newsletter the names of the fifteen were printed under the heading, "List of Scabs." In one of these letters the following definiton of a scab appeared; its authorship is generally attributed to Jack London:

"The Scab"

After God had finished the rattlesnake, the toad and the vampire, He had some awful substance left with which He made a Scab.

A scab is a two-legged animal with a corkscrew soul, a water brain, a combination backbone of jelly and glue. Where others have hearts, he carries a tumor of rotten principles.

When a scab comes down the street, men turn their backs and Angels weep in Heaven, and the Devil shuts the gates of hell to keep him out.

No man (or woman) has a right to scab so long as there is a pool of water to drown his carcass in, or a rope long enough to hang his body with. Judas was a gentleman compared with a scab. For betraying his Master, he had character enough to hang himself. A scab has not.

Esau sold his birthright for a mess of pottage. Judas sold his Savior for 30 pieces of silver. Benedict Arnold sold his country for a promise of a commission in the British Army. *The scab sells his birthright, country, his wife, his children and his fellowmen for an unfulfilled promise from his employer.*

Esau was a traitor to himself; Judas was a traitor to his God; Benedict Arnold was a traitor to his country; a scab is a traitor to his God, his country, his family and his class.[11]

Virginia courts awarded $55,000 in damages to three nonunion members who brought suit. In overturning that award, Justice Marshall, writing for the six-man majority of the Supreme Court, said: "Vigorous exercise of [the] right 'to persuade other employees to join' must not be stifled by the threat of liability for the over-enthusiastic use of rhetoric or the innocent mistake of fact."[12]

Obviously, in a society which prizes the First Amendment, there will be rhetoric which inflames and defames. Balancing the public interest in a vigorous exchange of ideas against private injury is not an easy task and may, as the late Justice Black declared in his dissent, be:

> that the court is getting itself in the same quagmire in the field of libel in which it is now helplessly struggling in the field of obscenity. No one, including this Court, can know what is and what is not constitutionally obscene or libelous under this Court's rulings.[13]

In a complex open society our trust, when conflict among individuals or parties arises, is in the judgment of, we hope, wise men whom we have elected to our courts. We must preserve by law and moral suasion the place for vigorous interaction (short of violence) between and among parties in dispute. While at the same time preserving that right for rhetorical confrontation, we who would play reconciling roles must seek to prevent polarization and refusal to interact.

The press seems to seek out that rhetorical behavior which is most different and overt. The hunger of the public for excitement and conflict seems to lure the demonstrators into more and more bizarre behavior and the opposition into also demonstrating its power. In such conflict mistrust and alienation thrive. Trust can only be regenerated, if and when the dissonant voices are given a fair hearing, and the stabilizing forces of a community respond to just demands.

When we are a part of a group or movement, let us be aware that the more antisocial our rhetoric, the more defensive will be the reaction. The issues, thesis, and antithesis must be granted a hearing before an adoption of a solution or an agreement can grow out of the conflict. This is not to suggest that all rhetoric must be rational and polite. Sometimes in order to get a hearing, someone must be annoyed or publicly confronted. Such tactics, however, tend to limit the degree of freedom a person at the eye of the target may have. To save face or to protect himself, he may dodge or lash out, rather than to seek a mutually acceptable solution. Not all problems can be resolved by communication and responsible deliberations. But very few problems can be resolved without both open channels and persistent deliberations.

ELECTRONIC MEDIA

In 1934 Congress passed the Federal Communications Act, which later was modified to include television. The Federal Communications Commission (FCC) under this act issues licenses if "the public convenience, interest, or necessity will be served thereby." One obvious criterion considered whenever an application for a license is received is whether the frequency, power (wattage), and direction of the station will seriously interfere with an existing station. Such a license, like staking out and registering a claim to mine a deep vein of ore, entitles the holder to mine the rich resources of public opinion.

Under the 1960 Communications Act the FCC has power to exact fines, to put a station on probation, or to revoke a license if it finds after reviewing the programming of a station that it is not serving the public interest.

Almost every breakthrough in technology brings with it great changes for a society and sometimes difficult ethical questions. This has been particularly true for radio and television. Two important questions concern the distribution of justice and the shaping of public opinion.

1   Should the electronic media, like the press, be allowed to cover criminal trials?
2   Should the radio and television station be required to grant free time to comment upon its reporting or editorials when the press is not?

JUSTICE AND THE MEDIA

The pretrial publicity of Billie Sol Estes of West Texas totaled some eleven volumes of press clippings. Such pretrial notoriety in itself is cause for a change of venue. Now, with the advent of the television media, which can make any local event national or even international in audience, the conflict is even more intensified between the public's right to know how our justice system works and the individual's right to privacy.

Billie Sol Estes objected to the televised broadcasting of his trial and consequently the Court permitted no coverage, still photos, or television of the defense counsel. Only the State's statements were actually televised. There were many pro and con arguments also posed by the broadcast of portions of the trial. Crucial questions, aside from the hassle of cameramen and clutter of cables in the courtroom were: Which trials (if any) should be broadcast and which should not? Would a man who had a televised trial get as fair a trial as one who did not? Would judges running for office render as impartial a decision when seeking to please the television audience as when not on television? What would a judge or prosecutor who was running for office do to get television exposure?

Moreover, could not the way the cameramen and producer select certain dramatic testimony and ignore other portions distort public opinion? All of this is different from the coverage of a trial by the printed media because few, if any, trials could be covered by more than one channel. The ethical issue raised is a matter of trusting or not trusting the communicators. In this case, could the defendent trust the television media? And in a new relationship with the politicians, who would have the say over televising trials? But there also were arguments on the side of televising such proceedings.

"The free press," one Justice argued, "has been a mighty catalyst in awakening public interest in governmental affairs, exposing corruption among public officers and employees. . ."[14] However, in a five to four decision the Court ruled that the notoriety of the trial and televising the proceedings denied the defendant his

"And here to bend the news a little is Jim Cravanaugh."

right to due process. In a case that raised similar issues, Dr. Samuel Sheppard had been convicted of murdering his wife in their home in a Cleveland suburb and the Court ruled similarly with only one Justice dissenting. In that case the large majority of the High Court held that an earlier trial judge had failed to protect Sheppard from massive prejudicial publicity and thus deprived him of a fair trial. This decision modified the long standing faith in justice in the open. Justice Clark, however, raised another issue: "The principle that justice cannot survive behind walls of silence has long been reflected in the Anglo-American distrust for secret trials."[15] How much information should be shared with the public and the point at which that sharing becomes an invasion of privacy or affects the fairness of a trial or the shaping of public opinion is not an easy question to answer. As citizens though, we should be sensitive to the rights of others and judge second hand or reported information by using some of the same principles we discussed in the first part of this chapter.

The Codes of Good Practice of the National Association of Broadcasters support the FCC call for a discussion of public issues. Time allowed for such discussion usually does not get commercial support and, moreover, presentation of controversial issues is bound to offend some of the publics served. Consequently, the motivations not to discuss public issues conflict with those idealistic urgings of the FCC and the Codes.

SHAPING PUBLIC OPINION

For example, some years ago the FCC incurred the wrath of a segment of Congress and the general public by suggesting that atheistic points of view should be aired in addition to orthodox religious programs.[16] The private owners of radio and television argue the press is not expected to publicize the many spokesmen for innumerable causes. This argument appeals to the free enterprise system. It is essentially economic. Time is money to a station; but the issue becomes more complicated. If a station is expected to give up time to a representative of an opposing view, possibly a station will tend to avoid public issues which might spark a response.

In 1969, the Supreme Court ruled that FCC equal time rules were not an abridgement of freedom of speech or the press. Billy James Hargis, as part of his "Christian Crusade" series on November 12, 1964, attacked Fred J. Cook who had authored the paperback book, *Goldwater—Extremist on the Right.* Cook demanded free time to reply, but the Red Lion Broadcasting Company denied him that right. The station argued that the First Amendment protects their desire to use their allotted frequencies continuously to broadcast whatever they choose and to exclude whomever they choose from using it. But the Court held that a "... licensee must offer to make available a reasonable amount of broadcast time to those who have a view different from that which has already been expressed on his station."[17]

The issue is not dead. Will such an FCC ruling cause a form of self-censorship that avoids coverage of controversial issues? The FCC's 1941 statement provided that stations should have a balanced presentation of viewpoints. To do so requires a genuine effort to find representative spokespersons and not to make a one-sided presentation. Such a nobly motivated FCC rule may explain why "safe" positions are often taken, when any position is taken at all, by many stations.

A society which trusts in itself will protect the precious constitutional guarantee that specifies there shall be no law abridging freedom of speech or of the press. Such a guarantee is indispensible to a free people. An open society cannot merely trust in the basic goodness of all its people; it must develop laws and practices designed to ensure that its citizens can freely deliberate and exchange ideas and stay abreast of how its representatives conduct the business of the government.

The Speech Communication Association (SCA) has adopted the Credo which follows. Members of the organization support the ideas in the statement; but they are equally appropriate for all of us, as citizens in a free society, to consider and encourage in the name of free and responsible communication.

CREDO FOR FREE AND RESPONSIBLE COMMUNICATION IN A DEMOCRATIC SOCIETY

Recognizing the essential place of free and responsible communication in a democratic society, and recognizing the distinction between the freedoms our legal system should respect and the responsibilities our educational system should cultivate, we members of the Speech Communication Association endorse the following statement of principles:

We believe that freedom of speech and assembly must hold a central position among American constitutional principles, and we express our determined support for the right of peaceful expression by any communicative means available.

We support the proposition that a free society can absorb with equanimity speech which exceeds the boundaries of generally accepted beliefs and mores; that much good and little harm can ensue if we err on the side of freedom, whereas much harm and little good may follow if we err on the side of suppression.

We criticize as misguided those who believe that the justice of their cause confers license to interfere physically and coercively with the speech of others, and we condémn intimidation, whether by powerful majorities or strident minorities, which attempts to restrict free expression.

We accept the responsibility of cultivating by precept and example, in our classrooms and in our communities, enlightened uses of communication; of developing in our students a respect for precision and accuracy in communication, and for reasoning based upon evidence and a judicious discrimination among values.

We encourage our students to accept the role of well-informed and articulate citizens, to defend the communication rights of those with whom they may disagree, and to expose abuses of the communication process.

We dedicate ourselves fully to these principles, confident in the belief that reason will ultimately prevail in a free marketplace of ideas.

Endorsed by the Speech Communication Association,
December, 1972.

SUMMARY

Although influence is a subtle and often evasive process and it is not always easy to tell when it is deliberate or not, all of us have certain responsibilities to ourselves and others in both interpersonal and public speaking settings. The responsibilities are based on the ethics of our society and the values of freedom of expression and the right to privacy in an open society.

Four principal ideas that all speakers should keep in mind are:

1 Do not place self-interest above the interest of your listeners.
2 Do not impose your values on others; and remember that for many issues there may be no single, correct answer.
3 Use information with honesty and accuracy.
4 Use information that is equally available to others so they may pursue the question further on their own and they can reassure themselves of your credibility.

The ethical ideas behind good speech are closely linked with our society's notion of free speech. Although guaranteed by the constitution, freedom of speech and freedom of the press are not always easily defined or recognized. Pressure from the changing values in our culture combine with new problems of the changing environment and advanced technology to create settings and experiences that require us to reexamine our values on a continuing basis.

One result of our constant appraisal is the changing limits of public speech and what is considered lawful or unlawful communication behavior in public. Individual responsibilities to ourselves and others are also important and often difficult to discern. What may be considered defamatory rhetoric in one setting may only be viewed as within the rights of free speech in another.

The electronic media play an increasing role in the question of free speech, and the issues are no less complicated than those surrounding individual behavior. There are three especially exasperating questions. The first concerns freedom of the press as opposed to an individual's right to privacy. The second, related issue is the public's right to know and the press' obligation to keep it informed. And finally, we are concerned with the way in which the press meets its obligations to the public, and how it shapes public opinion.

Because it often concerns the criminal justice process, the first question is a particularly knotty one. Individual courts have ruled on the limits of electronic media coverage for specific cases; but no binding legislation has been passed that adequately protects the rights of accused individuals to trials which are free of the threat of faulty, incomplete, or biased reporting over the highly influential electronic media. Nor has any accommodation been made to prevent individuals' businesses from suffering as a result of public sentiment shaped by the media before the accused has been found guilty of a crime.

Another question which concerns the media and is closely linked to free speech, concerns the right of radio and television stations to select for broadcast whatever information they wish and the obligation of the stations to allow conflicting opinion to be expressed on the air. With some reason private owners dispair of the burden to publicize all spokespersons of opposing viewpoints on various issues. And if a Federal agency (such as the FCC) were to force station owners to grant time for all opposing opinions to be aired, the prevailing fear is that owners will refuse to air any controversial material at all. The result of such a situation would be the waste of an important disseminator of information to the public and the loss of an opportunity to exercise our constitutional rights.

INITIATIVES

INITIATING ACTION 1   *Accomplished Lying.* Prepare a debate in which a ground rule permits fabrication of evidence. See if it can be pulled off without the other side detecting the authentic from the fabricated evidence. After the debate discuss: (a) What did or did not make the evidence credible? (b) Whether any good can result from an exchange of ideas in which falsity is present.

INITIATING ACTION 2   *Free Speech and Police.* List the pro and con arguments for permitting law officers to openly support political issues and candidates.

INITIATING ACTION 3   *Historic Free Speech Battles.* Do a study of struggles for freedom of expression. Prepare a series of cases in which free speech won and a second series in which free speech lost.

INITIATING ACTION 4   *First Amendment Speak Out.* It is obvious that thinking people differ on major free speech issues. There is more than one side to any free speech issue. Pair with another class member who differs with you on one of the following statements. A round of debates may be scheduled on the following issues.

1. Free speech should be absolute.
2. Children should be protected from pornography.
3. Smut should be banned from the news stands.
4. Public school teachers should be screened for loyalty to this country.
5. Employers should be permitted to prohibit union organizers on their plant's premises.
6. Employees should have the right to speak disrespectfully of their employers.
7. Religious activities should be prohibited from public schools.
8. Radio and television stations should be required to make a small share of their air time available for the public.
9. Those who treat the flag disrespectfully should be arrested.
10. Those who have incited a crowd to violence should be banned from the public platform.

INITIATING ACTION 5   *Personal Credo.* Write your credo of communication. Consider both what is trust destroying and trust building.

NOTES

1. Max Ehrman, *Poems of Desiderata*. (Boston: Crescendo, 1948).

2. Frank Hague vs. CIO, 307 U.S. 496 (June 5, 1939) and Dick Gregory vs. City of Chicago, 394 U.S. 111 (March 10, 1969).

3. Cox vs. Louisiana, 379 U.S. 536 (January 18, 1965).

4. Atterley vs. Florida, 385 U.S. 39 (November 14, 1966).

5. Amalgamated Food Employees Union Local 590 vs. Logan Valley Plaza, 391 U.S. 308 (May 20, 1968).

6. Lloyd vs. Tanner, 33 L Ed. 2d 131 (June 22, 1972).

7. William I. Gorden, "The Message of the Classroom," *Western Speech*, Vol. XXXIII (Spring, 1969), pp. 74–80.

8. Keyishan vs. Board of Regents of the State of New York, 385 U.S. 589 (January 23, 1967).

9. *New York Times* vs. Sullivan, 376 U.S. 54 (March 9, 1964).

10. Curtis Publishing Company vs. Wallace Butts, 388 U.S. 130 (June 12, 1967).

11. Old Dominion Branch No. 496, National Association of Letter Carriers AFL-CIO vs. Henry M. Austin, 41 L Ed. 2d 745 (June 25, 1974).

12. *Ibid.*

13. *Ibid.*

14. Billie Sol Estes vs. State of Texas, 381 U.S. 532 (June 7, 1965).

15. Samuel H. Sheppard vs. E. L. Maxwell, 384 U.S. 333 (June 6, 1966).

16. Robert M. O'Neil, *Free Speech: Responsible Communication Under Law* (Indianapolis: Bobbs-Merrill Co., 1966), p. 69.

17. Red Lion vs. FCC, 395 U.S. 367 (June 9, 1969).

SUGGESTED READINGS

Bosmajian, Haig A., ed. *Dissent: Symbolic Behavior and Rhetorical Strategies*. Boston: Allyn and Bacon, 1972.

Bosmajian, Haig A., ed. *The Principles and Practices of Freedom of Speech*. Boston: Houghton Mifflin Co., 1971.

The Civil Liberties Review. New York: An Independent Quarterly Analysis, Opinion, Record, and Debate sponsored by the American Civil Liberties Union and John Wiley & Sons, Inc.

"CREDO for Free and Responsible Communication in a Democratic Society," reprinted with permission by the Speech Communication Association, New York, N.Y.

Dorsen, Norman. *Frontiers of Civil Liberties*. New York: Pantheon Books, 1968.

Fortas, Abe. *Concerning Dissent and Civil Disobedience*. New York: The New American Library, 1968.

Free Speech Yearbook. University of Denver: A Publication of The Commission on Freedom of Speech of the Speech Communication Association, Annually.

Gorden, William I. *Nine Men Plus: Supreme Court Opinions on Free Speech and Free Press. An Academic Game-Simulation*. Dubuque, Iowa: Wm. C. Brown, 1971.

Haiman, Franklyn S. *Freedom of Speech: Issues and Cases*. New York: Random House, 1965.

Hartogs, Renatus, M.D., Ph.D., and Fantel, Hans. *Four-Letter Word Games: The Psychology of Obscenity*. New York: Dell Publishing Co., 1968.

Hovland, Carl I., ed. *The Order of Presentation in Persuasion*. New Haven, Conn.: Yale University Press, 1957.

Jacobson, Wally J. *Power and Interpersonal Relations*. Belmont, Calif.: Wadsworth Publishing Co., 1972.

Johannesen, Richard L., ed. *Ethics and Persuasion: Selected Readings*. New York: Random House, 1967.

Levy, Leonard W. *Freedom of Speech and Press in Early American History: Legacy of Suppression*. New York: Harper and Row, 1963.

Nussbaum, Michael. *Student Legal Rights: What They Are and How to Protect Them*. New York: Harper and Row, 1970.

O'Neil, Robert M. *Free Speech: Responsible Communication Under Law*. New York: The Bobbs-Merrill Co., 1972.

Packard, Vance. *The Hidden Persuaders*. New York: Pocket Books, Inc., 1957.

Reitman, Alan, ed. *The Price of Liberty*. New York: W. W. Norton and Co., 1968.

Scheidel, Thomas M. *Persuasive Speaking*. Glenview, Illinois: Scott, Foresman and Co., 1967.

Shapiro, Martin M., ed. *The Supreme Court and Constitutional Rights: Readings in Constitutional Law*. Palo Alto, Calif.: Scott, Foresman and Co., 1967.

Skolnick, Jerome H. *The Politics of Protest: Report to the National Commission on the Causes and Prevention of Violence.* New York: Ballantine Books, 1969.

Strouse, Jean. *Up Against the Law: The Legal Rights of People Under 21*. New York: The New American Library, 1970.

Wheeler, Ladd. *Interpersonal Influence*. Boston: Allyn and Bacon, 1970.

Wirt, Frederick M., and Hawley, Willis D., eds. *New Dimensions of Freedom in America*. San Francisco: Chandler Publishing Co., 1969.

Zinn, Howard. *Disobedience and Democracy: Nine Fallacies on Law and Order*. New York: Random House, 1968.

13 mass communication

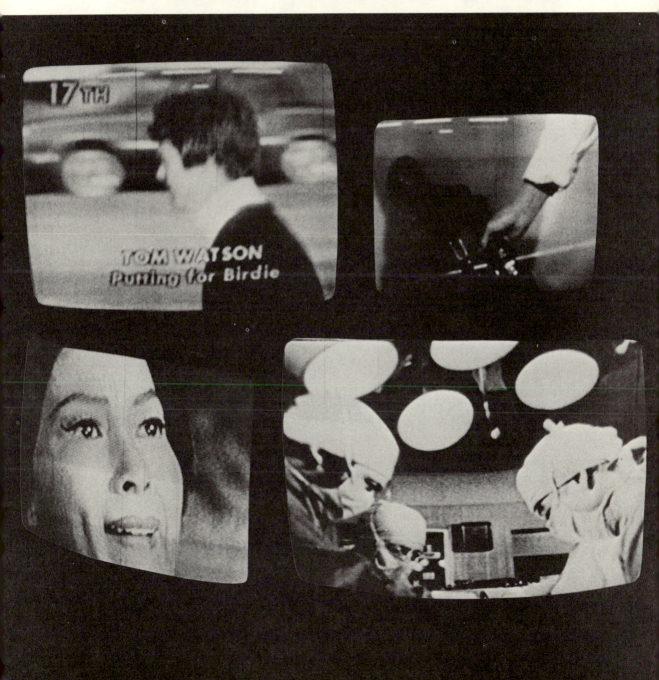

THE MASS MEDIA ARE KING

Wolfgang Amadeus Mozart, working before the Industrial Revolution, churned out four or five compositions a month and received barely enough money to survive. But Picasso was lucky enough to live on into the media era. And because he did, after the blue and pink of his younger years, he enjoyed and died in a green period. His estate with some 800 paintings was worth nearly one billion dollars! In his later years, whatever he wished could be his. One still life picture bought him a house in the South of France. As Marshall McLuhan contends, the media explosion increases the value of one's wares. Publicity made Picasso rich. Mozart's being born in an age before the mass distribution of information resulted in fortune's eluding him and his not becoming famous until long after his death.

Today pop stars such as Elton John may gross $50 million a year because of mass media promotion of their records and concerts. A movie like *Jaws* can make $10 to $20 million for its author Peter Benchley. A prize fight in Africa can mean $10 million to Muhammed Ali because of television. A scoop on a political crime like Watergate can mean millions to the Washington Post. Even the "Bad Guys of Watergate," because of the mass media, have been able to turn infamy into profits with books and television appearances. Staging a benefit concert can make the difference between having enough money to run a political campaign and having to quit, as it did at one point in Jimmy Carter's run for the presidency.

Half of the new hot stocks on Wall Street have such prefixes as *data, tele, techni,* or *compu* in their titles.

The press is big in Washington, D.C. It needs government to make headlines, and the politicians need the press to get into the headlines. Tom Bethell suggests that their relationship is symbiotic: "One group gets headlines, the other bylines. Both enjoy the same daily 'fix.'" And so the journalist plays an ex officio policy role.

"In the decade of the 1970s, 30 to 40 percent of the United States gross national product is accounted for by the production, consumption, and dissemination of knowledge," says Kevin Phillips, who writes the column "News Watch" for *TV Guide.*

Based upon Tom Bethell, "The Myth of an Adversary Press Journalist As Bureaucrat," and Kevin Phillips, "A Matter of Privilege," *Harper's* 254 (January 1977), pp. 33–40 and 95–96, respectively. Phillips's book *Mediacracy: American Parties and Politics in the Communications Age* elaborates on his thesis.

Which of the following activities have you done today: (1) watched television, (2) listened to the radio, (3) listened to records, (4) read part of a newspaper, (5) read part of a magazine, or (6) read part of a book? The last option is, of course, a natural, but you probably checked two or three other options also. For, if you are an average student, you have spent more time attending to mass media than you have going to school.[1] In fact, your home is more likely to be equipped with a TV or radio than with a bathtub or flush toilet.[2]

In a day, the average American spends 3 hours and 17 minutes watching TV, 2 hours and 28 minutes listening to radio, 11 minutes listening to records and tapes, 35 minutes reading newspapers, 28 minutes reading magazines, and 2 minutes reading books.[3] This adds up to a grand total of 7 hours and 1 minute. So even allowing for overlapping consumption (for example, reading the newspaper while listening to the radio), sleeping is the only other single activity that takes up more of your life.

WHAT ARE MASS MEDIA?

Mass media are usually distinguished by their methods of sending messages and by the nature of the audience that receives these messages. A mass media message is one that is: (1) transmitted through some sort of organization, (2) with the use of machinery, (3) in a rapid fashion, and (4) at a relatively low cost *per capita*.

LIVE FROM THE MOON

The audience receiving these messages is: (1) relatively large, (2) dispersed geographically, (3) mainly unknown to each other, and (4) self-selected.

ORGANIZATION   When you sit back to watch Walter Cronkite, for example, you should remember that an entire organization of people has been involved in reporting, selecting, editing, and ordering the stories he is presenting to you; that machines, such as cameras and transmitters, are needed to send the message to you, that this use of machinery allows you to keep abreast of same-day events occurring all over the world; and that this entire program comes to you for a few pennies' worth of electricity.

Furthermore, you are not the only one watching Walter. On any one day an estimated 25 million people, who are spread throughout the entire country, and most of whom you don't know, choose to switch on CBS news to find out what has happened during the day.[4]

Organizations are needed because individuals rarely possess the skills or capital needed to prepare and distribute messages to large groups of people. For example, this book would never have gotten to you if it were not for the Alfred Publishing Company. I had little awareness of their skills in format design and marketing. Even more important, they possessed money to help subsidize the authors, purchase the raw materials, take care of the printing, and promote the book through advertising: advance costs of a textbook can run as high as $100,000.[5]

Because organizations are involved, many people act as gatekeepers. That is, many people have the power to determine the fate of a potential message. By studying the following diagram of the travel route of news and features, for example, you should be able to spot several gatekeepers.

In just the top line, there are three: reporters decide what facts to include in their stories, members of the rewrite staff decide what stories need reworking, and the city editor decides what stories he wants to use.

Gatekeepers usually are conscientious, and they are right more often than they are wrong; but they tend to make conservative judgments, and they sometimes use strange criteria. For example, Harry Cohn, the shrewd and successful President of Columbia Pictures for thirty years, said that he evaluated each picture he previewed by how much his rump itched: presumably, the more itching, the more scenes he had cut from the final print.[6]

TRAVEL ROUTE OF NEWS AND FEATURES ON A METROPOLITAN NEWSPAPER

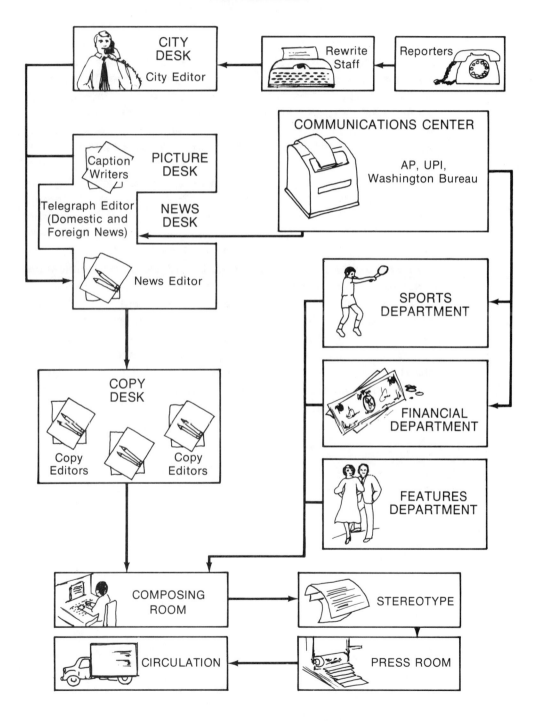

MACHINERY, SPEED, AND COST

Machines are needed because individuals by themselves just do not possess the abilities to transmit quick, cheap messages to large, geographically dispersed audiences. Before the invention of the printing press, it took months for a monk to transcribe one book. For example, before printing from movable type began, one Italian prince hired 45 copyists to produce a private library for him. But in two years of constant work, they finished only 200 volumes.[7] Today, type can be set at the rate of over 15,000 lines (more than are in this book) a minute and tens of thousands of copies can be run off each day.[8] Three weeks after the Israelis' daring raid at Entebbe, it had been written up as a book, printed, and distributed to bookstores across the United States.[9]

Even more rapid, of course, are the electronic media of radio and television, which have made worldwide communication almost instantaneous. For example, in 1776 the news of the signing of the Declaration of Independence required a month to travel the distance of 750 miles from Philadelphia, Pennsylvania, to Savannah, Georgia.[10] But if the signing took place today, the same news could be beamed around the world, by the use of communication satellites, in only 2 seconds.[11]

Machines also reduce labor costs to the extent that the chapters in this book, which each took the author somewhere between two to six weeks to produce, can be read by you for less than a dollar apiece. Indeed, at least one expert argues that the reason the Renaissance flourished when earlier revivals had failed is that the technological breakthroughs in printing greatly reduced the unit cost of storing and transmitting information.[12]

IMPLICATIONS OF INSTANTANEOUS COMMUNICATIONS
IT'S A SMALL WORLD, AFTER ALL

Donne's poetic metaphor, "No man is an island entire of itself," is now writ large on the surface of the planet. The most abrupt and significant aspect of the twentieth century transition has been from a plurality of remote and relatively autonomous national societies to a complexly interdependent world community.

In a few generations, man's world has shrunk from a vast expanse, whose area was still incompletely known and whose peoples were relatively distant from one another, to a continuous neighborhood. No man is more than a few hours journey from all other men, and communications between men may be almost instantaneous. Man-made satellites circle this neighborhood many times in one day, and the repercussions of major events affecting any part of the human family are swiftly felt throughout the whole world.

John McHale, *The Future of the Future* (New York: Ballantine Books, 1969), p. 65.

To support the costs of organizations and machinery, however, mass media need large audiences. Producing this book for just a few classes would be ridiculous: the audience is too small. For a limited audience, the lecture is a cheaper way to transmit knowledge. But for 500 courses around the country, it is cheaper to produce the book than it is to bus lecturers. Once the audience reaches a certain size, mass media transmit messages at a much lower cost per person than other systems do. Naturally, critical size depends upon the medium chosen. Presently, TV programs and movies need the largest audiences, while hardbound books and records or tapes need the smallest.[13]

Obviously, large, geographically dispersed audiences cannot have immediate personal contact with the source of the message. So the ability of the message to be adapted to the feedback of the audience is delayed and diminished, and the probability that the message may be misunderstood is increased. One example of mass misunderstanding occurred on the evening of October 30, 1938. Orson Wells presented a radio dramatization of *The War of the Worlds,* and almost a million people, including such eminent listeners as Steve Allen, "went squawking off into the night like startled chickens" because they believed they were hearing actual news bulletins of a Martian invasion.[14]

But the problem of mass misunderstanding is not as frequent or widespread as one might expect because many media organizations pretest the clarity and effectiveness of potential messages on carefully selected sample audiences.

Because audiences are large and geographically dispersed,

PRETESTING POTENTIAL PROGRAMS
SHOOTING YOUR WAY INTO THE HEARTS OF AMERICA

Why violence? Simple. "Every time you have violence the needle goes up."

Roy Huggins gave that direct explanation to King Features Syndicate columnist Nicholas Von Hoffman. The needle Huggins was talking about is the meter that registers response from experimental audiences watching test films. If they like what they see they twist their dial to "good," which pushes up the needle.

Enthusiastic audience reaction plus competition makes it hard for television producers to provide anything but violence. Huggins said it this way: "The man who finds the way to get around the standards will beat you in the ratings."

Not too complicated, is it? Producers know audiences like violence. If one producer does not provide it another one will, and whoever does it will get the audiences.

Robert Murphy, *Mass Communication and Human Interaction* (Boston: Houghton-Mifflin, 1977), pp. 366-367.

individual members are, for the most part, unknown to each other. That is, you do not know, and therefore would not usually talk to, most of the people who have read this book that you are now reading. As a result, ideas that appear in the mass media spread through society more quickly than they would by simple word of mouth. For example, 90 percent of those surveyed in a Michigan maximum security prison reported learning new criminal skills as a result of watching TV crime programs.[15] And some individuals are given ideas they would never have thought of by themselves. Thus the mother of one 7-year-old boy found him "sprinkling ground glass into the family's food in order to find out [so he said] whether it would work as well as it did on television."[16]

Finally, the audiences of mass media are usually self-selected. People are not forced to attend. They do so because they want to. If you think you won't like "Happy Days," and you aren't curious about it, you won't turn it on. If you give it a try and decide it is uninteresting, or you don't like it, you can change channels. So audience size can be used as a rough index of appeal, and gatekeepers can be expected to emphasize audience appeal in their selection and presentation of messages.[17]

Although we may usually think of news programs as mainly informative and serving the public good, they have a major responsibility where audience appeal is concerned. Because they begin the period of prime time viewing, there is considerable pressure on the evening news shows to attract and maintain a large audience. In his description of the mission of the nightly news, Ben H. Bagdikian presents an insightful picture of the pressures on news programs to go beyond the responsibility of the press to inform the public.

> But another technical factor influences the nature of broadcast news. It is a one-thing-at-a-time medium. Since it survives by collecting large audiences for sale to advertising sponsors, great emphasis is placed on any program that can collect and maintain a maximum audience not only for its own economic value but for carry-over to the next program. This is especially true for the main televised news, at 6 P.M., since this is the start of prime time when television makes most of its money. So news programs are under pressure not only to be exciting enough to attract specific sponsors for the news itself but also to maintain interest throughout for delivery to the next sponsor's program on the same station. Competent but unexciting news can fail this mission. So whatever the professional journalistic standards that operate on a national and regional level for evening newscasts, the station is penalized if the news does not have both mass appeal and excitement to the very end.[18]

THE EFFECT OF THE MASS MEDIA

From what you have read so far, some of you may have concluded that I have a dim view of mass media. Not so. To me it seems obvious that the many benefits they bring us far outweigh the problems they create. For example, books allow us easy access to the experience of our predecessors so that we are not condemned to make their same mistakes over and over again. But in this section you will see that I do have a DIM view of how we are affected by mass media. That is, I believe we are affected *D*irectly, *I*ndirectly, and *M*ediately: through the message itself, through background or incidental factors, and through messages relayed by others.

THE WISE ONES WHOSE STARS HAVE RISEN

A reliable survey tells us that approximately 36 percent of the American public get *all* of their news from television, and 64 percent get most of their news in this way. On any weekday evening 25 million households tune into the network news. We have come to know the anchormen and women who daily come into our homes.

Who are these news sages and how have they earned the right to an audience of millions? Let's consider the commentator's commentators: David Brinkley of NBC, Harry Reasoner and Howard K. Smith of ABC, and Eric Sevareid of CBS. These are the commentators who do a special two- to three-minute news analysis. They don't just report the news. Each began his career in print journalism at least two decades ago, and each still considers himself a writer of words rather than simply a baritone employed to read prepared copy. And each earned his stripes by special duty. Brinkley is the only one of the four who started in television, in 1943, and co-anchored the NBC news for years before he developed a short snippet of news analysis which was titled "David Brinkley's Journal." Smith was stationed as a reporter in Europe twenty years. Reasoner worked for the *Minneapolis*

Star, was drama critic, radio newsman, did a stint in public relations for an airline company, and worked for the Voice of America in Manila. Sevareid spent most of the war years in Europe and later served for thirteen years in the nation's capital.

How do these persons see their roles? Before his mandatory semi-retirement in September, 1977, Sevareid, whose commentaries averaged about 400 words, said, "I try to illuminate some dark corner in the news that needs explaining." He admits that his own opinions become inescapably a part of that explanation, but his intent is not open advocacy. His intent, rather, is to prod and to raise questions more than to give answers about what government has done or failed to do, or even what journalists have done or failed to do. Once he referred to his work as "notations of a puzzled man on the margins of time."

Brinkley also declares that he is not interested in evangelizing, but rather tries to tell something of how Americans live. In addition, he says it is his job to criticize Congress and tell the taxpayers how their money is being spent. Reasoner, with a gift for wry humor, says that he selects for comment, topics over which he feels the viewer has some control. He also insists that he is not an advocate. Smith says his aim as a news analyst is to "provoke thought," "to cast events in a different light," in such a way that people will say, "Well, I never thought of that." Smith, unlike his fellow sages, considers himself a sympathetic adversary to the President, who he feels often is treated badly by the press in its negative tradition.

These news analysts believe that the typical television news watcher is a poor listener, more interested in hearing the views of a father figure than in thinking for him or herself. None of them wishes to be placed in this role. They have reason to feel that their critics only accuse them of bias when disagreeing with them.

How does the general public view the television newsroom? One study found that most viewers believe that they are better served by the local news operations than by the networks. Younger adults place television news in a lower priority than other shows in their family viewing. Some of the most frequent criticisms of the network news were too much "analysis" and "personal opinion." After studying the reasons people watch TV news, one television critic concluded, "Being informed is only a secondary motive for most viewers; most people watch TV news to be amused and diverted or to make sure that their homes and families are safe and secure." Many say that they watch because they like the anchorman.

This abstract was prepared by Richard Breiner and the author based on Mr. Breiner's doctoral study of news analysts. Sources for this essay include "The Roper Survey," *Broadcasting Magazine*, April 4, 1977, p. 44; April 11, 1977, p. 38; and June 6, 1977, p. 36.

DIRECT EFFECTS   Some messages make straightforward attempts to persuade us. For example, in our country advertisers spend over $26 billion a year to sell us products.[19] Still, we are not swayed as much as you may think. On the average we selectively attend to only about 5 percent of the 1,500 advertising messages we are exposed to each day.[20] Furthermore, even when we pay attention to an ad, we may not believe what it tells us. Like other types of persuasive messages, advertising tends to be most successful for topics we consider of little importance, such as the brand of deodorant we use, and least successful for topics we consider of great importance, such as our views about religion.[21]

On the other hand, messages from the mass media that we perceive to be informative have a profound influence on our lives. They account for many of our skills and much of our knowledge about the world. Newspapers give us recipes for new dishes, books tell us what happened in the Civil War, and Walter Cronkite tells us what has happened during the day. Most of these messages we accept because we consider them to be trustworthy and authoritative: trustworthy because we don't see them as attempts

THE WIZARD OF ID by Brant parker and Johnny hart

to influence us and authoritative because we tend to believe only experts appear in the mass media.[22] In the following story a life is saved as a result of information gained through the mass media.

London—Nurse Maitland sat next to the dying child's hospital bed reading a murder mystery—Agatha Christie's *The Pale Horse.*

She was nearly to the end and amateur detective Mark Easterbrook was explaining to Inspector Lejeune how the murders had been committed.

"I read an article on thallium poisoning when I was in America," Easterbrook was saying in the narrative. "A lot of workers in a factory died one after the other. Their deaths were put down to astonishingly varied causes. But one thing always happens sooner or later. The hair falls out."

Miss Christie then began to explain that thallium had not been suspected in the Pale Horse murders, because it is a poison not used much in Britain. It is, however, used a great deal in the Middle East to kill rats and other vermin.

Nurse Marsha Maitland put her book down and looked at the 19-month-old girl on the bed. The girl had been brought to England from her home in Qatar on the Persian Gulf, suffering from a mystery disease. All of Harley Street's vaunted specialists had been unable to diagnose her illness.

The little girl had shown all the same symptoms of the murder victims in the Christie thriller—high blood pressure, difficulty in breathing, unresponsiveness to speech or commands. And, finally, her hair had begun to fall out.

Nurse Maitland hesitated. Then, she made up her mind and went to see the doctor.

"We were at the state where almost any suggestions were welcome," said Dr. Victor Dubowitz, professor of pediatrics at the Royal Medical School, who wrote about the case, which occurred 18 months ago, in the June issue of the *British Journal of Hospital Medicine.*

The doctors went to Scotland Yard and asked for help in testing for thallium poisoning.

Scotland Yard detectives suggested that the doctors contact a thallium expert—one Graham Young, serving a life sentence at Wormwood Scrubs jail, next door to Hammersmith Hospital, where the girl was under observation.

Young knew about thallium because he kept detailed notes on the effects of the chemical as he poisoned his pet rabbits, his family and some of his coworkers.

The doctors never consulted Young. They didn't have to. Their test quickly confirmed Nurse Maitland's suspicions—the child's body contained more than 10 times the permitted maximum of the poison.

Dubowitz, who was in charge of the case, said recovery began after three weeks of treatment and the child was discharged after four months of "remarkable" improvement.[23]

INDIRECT EFFECTS   Entertaining messages amuse us and help pass the time of day pleasantly. And, as with informative messages, we usually don't perceive this material to be persuasive, so we relax our guard and are often affected more intensely.

Still, entertaining messages are an even more important source of indirect influence. For example, in one scene of the classic picture *It Happened One Night*, Clark Gable took off his shirt. That he was wearing no undershirt had nothing to do with the rest of the film. Yet thousands of fans apparently concluded this was he-man behavior, because the sales of men's undershirts promptly took a nose dive.[24] Or take the previously mentioned case of violence on TV. It is injected primarily to sustain interest or create drama, but the end result is a wildly exaggerated portrayal: violence occurs in 7 of 10 programs, homicides are 22 times more common than in real life, and aggressive acts exceed prosocial (helping) acts by a ratio of 4 to 1.[25] Consequently, some viewers come to believe the world is a much more violent place than it actually is while others become much more prone to commit violence.[26]

The following account hints at the breadth of coverage that indirect effects of the media can have on people throughout the world.

... in the early 1960's when at least half of the screen time throughout the world and a substantial amount of television time was taken up with American films and tapes, the USIA sponsored a survey in eleven countries which found out that, on the average, 28 percent of the people in those countries considered American movies a major source of their information about this country. In 1962, 40 percent of the people surveyed in four NATO countries said that they felt American films gave a true picture of American life. A survey in Santiago, Chile, in 1964 found that 56 percent of the movie-goers in that city believed that the films from the United States and Mexico, the countries that provide a high percentage of the movies in Chile, faithfully represented everyday life in those two countries. Holaday and Stoddard found that American children, too, believed that films about foreign countries were factually true and used the films as sources for their answers to questions of fact about those countries. Visitors to Bangkok have sometimes reported that they can walk down a street in the evening and hear gunfire on both sides—from the sound tracks of American westerns being shown on Thai television! It is not entirely surprising, then, that we should hear of foreign visitors landing in New York or San Francisco and looking for frontier scenery and cowboys riding into the sunset.[27]

But indirect influence is not limited to entertaining messages. It can also occur in persuasive and informative messages, as we can see by returning for a closer examination of the CBS evening news. Obviously, in a half hour, only a comparatively few stories can be covered. Those that are chosen become, to most people, the important news of the day, while those not chosen are considered less important, or unimportant news. Yet when you consider, as Walter Cronkite himself has said, that the entire content of his program adds up to less than one-half page of the *New York Times*, you realize that not all of the most important news can be included.[28] Furthermore, as we have seen, gatekeepers tend to choose stories that are dramatic and have strong visual appeal.[29] Thus one might readily conclude, as the Palestinian Liberation Organization did, that terrorism is the quickest path to media attention.[30] Indeed, dramatic events appear to have become the poor man's press conference.

Some historians argue that the sensationalistic "yellow journalism" of the 1890s helped spark the Spanish-American War: an example of the unethical application of the media's impact.

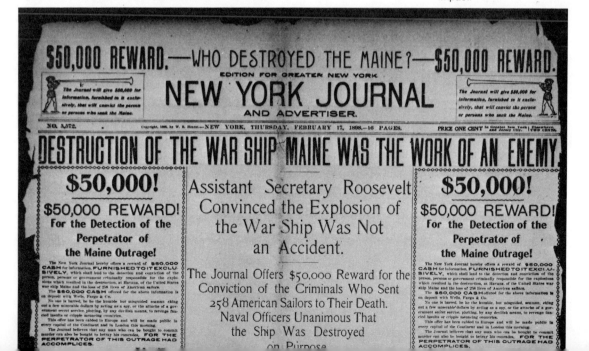

THE MEDIA GOLIATH

The Media conglomerates are big industry. Ten of them are high in the list of the *Fortune* 500 largest corporations. In 1976, for example, CBS ranked 102 with a sales of $2.23 billion. The *New York Times*, 394 with a $451.4 million sales, Time Inc., 217 with $1.038 billion, RCA, 31 with $5.32 billion, Gulf and Western, 57 with $3.39 billion, Times Mirror Co., 232 with $964.7 million, Gannett, 426 with $413.2 million, Knight-Ridder, 295 with $677.5 million, and the *Washington Post*, 452 with $375.7 million.

Their principal operations are wide. The Knight-Ridder chain, for example, includes newspapers in approximately 50 cities such as the *Miami Herald*, *Philadelphia Inquirer*, *Anaheim-Fullerton Independent* (California) and *Walla Walla Union Bulletin*. The *Washington Post* not only has its controversial newspaper in the capitol and in Los Angeles, and its magazine *Newsweek*, but also four broadcasting stations. RCA owns NBC plus TV stations in Chicago, Los Angeles, Cleveland, New York City and Washington, D.C.

It also owns electronic firms, Random House publishing company which controls 17.6% of the market, Banquet Foods, Orient Foods, Coronet (carpets), Hertz which is a vehicle renting service, etc. CBS owns five TV stations, records, publishing companies, and some 25 magazines that range from *Mechanix Illustrated* to *Woman's Day*.

There is a case to be made against monopoly of news and information. Kevin Phillips states, "Opinion samplers tell us that Americans are recovering confidence in political institutions, and even in the bureaucracy, but not in media institutions. Among the key elites, business, political and intellectual, the unhappiness is more specific— media are *too powerful*." Justice Hugo Black addressed the linkage between free press and antitrust when he said the First Amendment "rests upon the assumption that the widest possible dissemination of information from diverse and antagonistic sources is essential to the well being of the public."

Kevin Phillips, "Busting The Media Trusts,"
Harpers 255, pp. 23–34.

MEDIATE EFFECTS   The final way we are affected is mediately. I use the term "mediately" to refer to a special case of serial communication in which the interpersonal chain begins with information or opinions someone has acquired by attending to the mass media. Others pass us information they have acquired from the mass media. For example, when young Steve Allen, his mother, and aunt heard the broadcast about Martians invading the United States, they decided to flee. Note that the Allens were influenced directly by the radio announcements that the Martians were attacking. They were also influenced indirectly by the format of the program. That is, the announcements were presented in the form of special bulletins interrupting a dance program. For the Allens, this format confirmed the truth of the "news flashes." In the hotel hallway, they ran into a young woman with a little girl and urged her to run for her life because Chicago was under attack. Here the information had gone two steps: from the radio to the Allens and from the Allens to the woman.

Not all chains of mediated influence are this simple. Sometimes many steps occur. That is, the woman could have told her neighbor; the neighbor could have alerted her husband; and the husband could have warned the children. So you see this type of influence can cover a lot of territory.

Indeed, in any modern society, most of what is known or believed can ultimately be traced back to the mass media. Take academic knowledge for example. Primary research on specific topics of communication, economics, physics, and the like are carried out by a few experts who then write up their conclusions as books or articles. Other specialists, such as your teacher, read these summaries and pass on what seems like appropriate information, as the opportunities arise. Of course, mediators do more than just passively pass on information. Sometimes they change messages unwittingly, as research on serial communication indicates. Sometimes they explain or evaluate the information. And sometimes, as, for example, a teacher does, they synthesize information from several sources before passing on the amalgamation to others.

Outside the classroom we are most likely to receive mediated messages when we are not particularly interested in the information, when the information is of little importance, or when the information is of great importance.[31] When topics hold only small interest to us, we seldom pursue them and we seldom pay attention to them. Consequently, we often learn about them only as a result of the idle conversation of others. When information of little importance is carried by a mass medium, it receives little prominence and is likely to be noticed only accidentally, or only by people who are interested in it. So, again, it is often through the conversation of others that we become aware of this material. On the other hand, information of great importance, such as the assassination of a president or other important public figure is considered by us to be so significant or shocking that we quickly rush off to share it with others.[32] Thus one reason 90 percent of the people in this country knew about the shooting of President Kennedy within two hours is because half of them heard it by word of mouth.[33]

Mediated messages are a combination of mass and interpersonal communication. The interpersonal messages, of course, tend to have a large impact on us because we feel compelled to pay attention to people speaking to us in person, because their message can be tailored for us specifically, because our feedback can be quickly noted and adapted to, and because we tend to converse with people we know and consider trustworthy and informed. As a result, mediated messages are more effective in changing our central beliefs than are either direct or indirect messages.

Considerable research has been done on the topic of how influential the mass media really are. Much of the study is done by people with training in sociology or mass communications; and it often concentrates on how knowledge of technical innovations is distributed and how new ideas or products are adopted by consumers. The kinds of products include, new grains, weed killers, various new health practices, contraceptives, and appliances. Results of the research are typified by what investigators found when doctors in four Illinois cities began prescribing a new drug.

> A team of sociologists interviewed over 200 physicians, almost two-thirds of those in active private practice in these [Illinois] communities, about their use of a recently introduced antibiotic called "gammanym" (a fictitious name). Drugstore prescriptions were also examined in order to determine when the doctors had first used this drug. The sociologists found that the social networks linking the physicians with their colleagues greatly affected the usage of gammanym. Only about 10 percent of the doctors prescribed the antibiotic on receiving the first information about it (often from the manufacturer's salesmen or from direct mail advertisements). More often than not, the physicians waited until the product was legitimated by articles in the professional journals and especially by their colleagues before they took it up.
>
> The new item was a highly ambiguous stimulus that had to be given definite shape by the appropriate reference group. As the doctors discussed this novelty among themselves, they pooled their information and formulated a common conception of its merits and demerits, arriving at a more or less social decision as to whether or not it should be used. Indeed, when the antibiotic was still very new (and thus very ambiguous) the early adopters were likely to have written their first prescription shortly after one of their friends or close professional associates had also prescribed gammanym.[34]

This study and others[35] indicate that the role of the media in introducing new innovations is largely informative. There is considerable delay between the knowledge of a new product and its actual adoption. And the decision to try a new product is more often based on the recommendation of a colleague or friend than on some commercial message.

Another area of research concerns the effects of the camera angle and other technical aspects of the mass media production process. In "Should the Camera Look Down at Me?" we get an idea of the problems and research that is being conducted to help determine the effect the technical production of a message can have on the viewers' perception.

SHOULD THE CAMERA LOOK DOWN AT ME?

Basic Question: Does the video camera angle influence the credibility of the person on screen? It has generally been reasoned that looking down upon a person conveys an impression of weakness whereas looking up to a person contributes to an impression of strength, dominance, and power. But does a high or a low camera angle affect the credibility of the person pictured?

Method: Five television cameras filmed on videotape the same presentation, a five-minute speech on the topic: Should the grading system be revised? Cameras were placed to shoot from extremely high, subtly high, eye-level, subtly low, and extremely low angles. The same presentation was videotaped using two college men and two women. One of the tapes was then played to a class of introductory speech students, who subsequently rated the presentation with regard to such qualities as competence, composure, friendliness, and dynamism on a scale from little to much. In all, there were 20 conditions, five angle treatments across four speeches. The tapes were randomly assigned to be played to different classes.

Results: Higher angles consistently produced higher credibility than low-angle shots on such dimensions as character, competence, composure, sociability, and attractiveness. Dynamism ratings did not vary,

that is, the speaker appeared equally dynamic whether filmed from a low, eye-level, or high camera angle.

Implications: Because these findings contradicted an earlier study, follow-up studies were conducted with variations of camera angle.

The researchers reason that a camera shooting up toward a performer may increase the impression of power he (or she) conveys to an audience. Looking up may make someone appear bigger than life and therefore able to exert influence or dominate. But such people are not easy for an audience to relate to. More effective communication occurs between people who are similar to one another. Persons who impress us as dominant certainly don't seem similar. On the other hand, eye-level shots may contribute to this feeling of similarity. Shots down on media figures may equalize the increased power and status they enjoy.

Perhaps the most significant implication for research into the power of the camera is that it heightens our awareness of how the cameraman's eyes influence the way we see. The cameraman and television producer select and therefore filter out some pictures and enhance our attention to certain messages.

Abstract of Thomas A. McCain, Joseph Childberg, and Jacob Wakshlag, "The Effect of Camera Angle on Source Credibility," *Journal of Broadcasting* 21 (Winter 1977), pp. 35–46.

SUMMARY

"What hath Gutenberg wrought?" might be the lament of some twentieth-century philosopher once he discovers that television, movies, radio, records, newspapers, magazines, and books consume more of our lives than any other activity except sleep. For Gutenberg's printing press was the beginning of the mass media that are so important to our present-day world.

Mass media, themselves, tend to be defined by their methods of sending messages and by the nature of the audience receiving their messages. Their messages are transmitted (1) through some sort of organization, (2) with the use of machinery, (3) in a rapid fashion, and (4) at a relatively low cost per capita. The audience receiving their messages is (1) relatively large, (2) dispersed geographically, (3) mainly unknown to each other, and (4) self-selected.

As individuals we have probably all been persuaded, informed, and entertained by mass media either directly, indirectly, or mediately, that is, through the message itself, through background or incidental factors, and through messages relayed by others. Still, mass media are not as all-powerful as some would have us believe. And the benefits they bring us far outweigh the problems they create.

INITIATIVES

Media Usage. Total up the individual checklists of media usage (at the beginning of the chapter) and determine the class's pattern of usage.

INITIATING ACTION 1

Weaknesses and Strengths. On the blackboard, write the names of the seven mass media discussed in this chapter. Take ten minutes to brainstorm the strengths and weaknesses of each medium. For example, speed, durability, cost, etc. Then go back over the lists and, for each medium, decide which of the strengths and weaknesses are most important or most characteristic.

INITIATING ACTION 2

Gatekeepers. Choose a local mass medium and try to prepare a flow chart similar to the diagram on page 343 of all the potential gatekeepers who decide what messages will/will not be transmitted. Interview each of these gatekeepers to see what criteria he or she uses. What differences and similarities do you find?

INITIATING ACTION 3

Editorial Decisions. Your teacher will divide the class up into groups of five. In each group, four "reporters" will be given three story topics. Each reporter must decide which two topics to forward to the "editor." The "editor," in turn, must choose and rank in order of importance the five stories he wants to feature in his paper. Compare the resulting papers. Discuss the similarities and differences.

INITIATING ACTION 4

The Medium Is the Message. One of the most provocative theories of mass media is presented by Marshall McLuhan. In a four- to six-page paper, summarize his major hypotheses.

INITIATING ACTION 5

Advertising Choices. Have each member of the class interview a different local businessman to find out what kind of mass media advertising he or she uses and why. Compare and discuss the results.

INITIATING ACTION 6

Television Violence. Spend a class period developing a form to classify acts of aggression and violence. Assign channel monitoring responsibilities, have the form printed up, and monitor two entire days of TV programming. Tally your findings and then discuss them.

INITIATING ACTION 7

INITIATING ACTION 8   *Reflections from the Media.* Divide the class into five small groups. Each group is to choose six American movies, TV programs, or novels it is familiar with. Then, assuming this is the only knowledge you have of America, each group should choose a spokesman and spend twenty minutes helping him prepare a four-minute oral report on what the group believes life in America must be like. Present and discuss the reports.

INITIATING ACTION 9   *Influence.* By yourself, list five different ways the mass media can influence people indirectly. Compare your list with lists made by other members of the class.

INITIATING ACTION 10   *Future Media Impact.* Media innovations and political decisions with regard to media can have profound influences on individuals, interaction among individuals, and society. Assume one of the following changes might occur and prepare a two-page paper on its possible effects.

    a.   Widespread cable TV
    b.   Widespread pay TV
    c.   Home video recorders on all TVs
    d.   A video computer terminal in each home
    e.   An "official" government TV network
    f.   A supreme court decision banning government regulation of mass media
    g.   Development of sensory TV

NOTES

1. Frederick C. Whitney, *Mass Media and Mass Communication in Society* (Dubuque, Iowa: Wm. C. Brown, 1975), p. 261; and Leigh Marlowe, *Social Psychology: An Interdisciplinary Approach to Human Behavior* (Boston: Holbrook Press, 1971), pp. 404–405.

2. U.S. Bureau of the Census, *Statistical Abstract of the United States: 1975*, 96th ed. (Washington, D.C., 1975), pp. 519, 723, and 719.

3. D. Thomas Miller, "Television, the Only Truly Mass Medium Remaining Today: Its Role in Our Society," in Robert J. Glessing and William P. White (eds.), *Mass Media: The Invisible Environment* (Chicago: Science Research Associates, 1973), p. 14.

4. "News Minutes in Prime Time Draw Big Ratings," *Broadcasting*, April 25, 1977, pp. 46–47. Figure is calculated by dividing households by Nielsen rating, then multiplying average figure by Nielsen rating and again by the average number of people in a family (2.3). For a description of how a typical evening

broadcast is put together, see Daniel St. Albin Greene, "Making a Television News," in Michael C. Emery and Ted C. Smythe (eds.), *Readings in Mass Communication* (Dubuque, Iowa: Wm. C. Brown, 1972), pp. 336–346.

5. Ray Eldon Hiebert et al., *Mass Media: An Introduction to Modern Communication* (New York: David McKay, 1974), p. 43.

6. Bob Thomas, *King Cohn* (New York: Bantam Books, 1967), p. 125. For other examples of the oddity of gatekeepers, see Ben H. Bagdikian, "Professional Personnel and Organizational Structure in the Mass Media," in W. Phillips Davison and Frederick T. C. Yu (eds.), *Mass Communication Research: Major Issues and Future Directions* (New York: Praeger, 1974), p. 128; and Robert D. Murphy, *Mass Communication and Human Interaction* (Boston: Houghton Mifflin, 1977), pp. 224–225. For an interesting overview of gatekeeping, see Chapter 3, "Decision Making in Mass Communication," in Steven H. Chaffee and Michael J. Petrick, *Using the Mass Media: Communication Problems in American Society* (New York: McGraw-Hill, 1975), pp. 26–42.

7. Lancelot Hogben, *The Wonderful World of Communication* (Garden City, N.Y.: Doubleday, 1969), p. 24.

8. Wilbur Schramm, *Men, Messages, and Media: A Look at Human Communication* (New York: Harper & Row, 1973), p. 168.

9. "About the Author," in William Stevenson, *90 Minutes at Entebbe* (New York: Bantam Books, 1976).

10. Eugene H. Methvin, quoted in William D. Brooks, *Speech Communication* (Dubuque, Iowa: Wm C. Brown, 1971), p. 253.

11. Stuart Chase, *The Most Probable World* (Baltimore: Penguin Books, 1968), p. 19.

12. E. L. Eisenstein, cited in Edwin B. Parker, "Implications of New Information Technology," in Davison and Yu (eds.), op, cit., p. 173.

13. Marlowe, op. cit., p. 387; David G. Clark and William B. Blankenburg, "The Movie Business," in Alan Wells (ed.), *Mass Media and Society*, 2nd ed. (Palo Alto, Calif.: Mayfield, 1975), pp. 109 and 111; and Whitney, op. cit., pp. 145 and 265.

14. Steve Allen, *Mark it and Strike it* (New York: Bartholomew House, 1961), p. 51. For a detailed description of this event, see Hadley Cantril, *The Invasion From Mars* (New York: Harper Torchbooks, 1940). For a contemporary example, see "F.C.C. Cites Station for Martian 'Scare,'" *New York Times*, July 18, 1975, pt. 4, p. 61.

15. Grant H. Hendrick, "How Criminals Learn from TV," *TV Guide*, January 29, 1977, p. 5.

16. Schramm, op. cit., p. 162.

17. Thomas Pepper, "The Underground Press," in Alan Wells (ed.), *Mass Media and Society*, 2nd ed. (Palo Atlo, Calif.: Mayfield, 1975), p. 27; Paul Klein, "The Television Audience and Program Mediocrity," ibid., p. 75; Robert Stein, *Media Power* (Boston: Houghton Mifflin, 1972), p. 27; and Les Brown, "Survey Finds Local TV News Increased in 1973–74, *New York Times*, March 3, 1975, pt. 1, p. 53.

18. Bagdikian, op. cit., pp. 127–128.

19. U.S. Bureau of the Census, op. cit., p. 791.

20. Hiebert et al., pp. 162–163.

21. Schramm, op. cit., p. 285; and Evertt M. Rogers, ''Mass Media and Inter-personal Communication,'' in Ithiel de Sola Pool et al., *Handbook of Communication* (Chicago: Rand McNally, 1973), pp. 291–292.

22. Schramm, op cit., p. 238; and Stein, op. cit., pp. 74–75.

23. ''By Jove, Novel Idea for Healing,'' *Sentinel Star*, Orlando, Florida, June 24, 1977, p. 3A.

24. *The World Book Encyclopedia* (Chicago: Field Enterprises Educational Corporation, 1967), vol. 13, p. 706.

25. Marlowe, op. cit., p. 418; Neil Hickey, ''Does Violence Really Affect TV Viewers? Yes,'' *TV Guide*, June 14, 1975, p. 9; and Lawrence S. Wrightsman, *Social Psychology*, 2nd ed. (Monterey, Calif.: Brooks/Cole, 1977), p. 231.

26. Chaffee and Petrick, op. cit., pp. 181–182; Hickey, op. cit., p. 10; Harry F. Waters, ''What TV Does to Kids,'' *Newsweek*, February 21, 1977, p. 69; and George Gerbner and Larry Gross, ''The Scary World of TV's Heavy Viewer,'' *Psychology Today,* (April 1976), pp. 41–45, 89.

27. Schramm, op. cit., p. 257.

28. Whitney, op. cit., p. 304; and Edwin Emery et al., *Introduction to Mass Communication*, 4th ed. (New York: Dodd, Mead, 1973), p. 239.

29. Schramm, op. cit., p. 259; Bagdikian, op. cit., pp. 127–128; Brooks, op, cit., p. 291; and Murphy, op. cit., p. 20.

30. Neil Hickey, ''Terrorism and Television,'' *TV Guide*, July, 31, 1976, pp. 3–4; and Neil Hickey, ''The Medium in the Middle,'' *TV Guide*, August 7, 1976, p. 10.

31. Schramm, op, cit., p. 122.

32. *Ibid.*, p. 282.

33. *Ibid.*, p. 122.

34. Leonard Berkowitz, *A Survey of Social Psychology* (Hinsdale, Ill.: Dryden Press, 1975), pp. 350–351.

35. Ibid.

SUGGESTED READINGS

Chase, Stuart, *The Most Probable World*. Baltimore: Penguin Books, 1968.

Klein, Paul, ''The Television Audience and Program Mediocrity,'' in Alan Wells (ed.), *Mass Media and Society,* 2nd ed., Palo Alto, CA.: Mayfield, 1975.

McHale, John, *The Future of the Future*. New York: Ballantine Books, 1969.

Miller, D. Thomas, ''Television, The Only Truly Mass Medium Remaining Today: Its Role in Our Society,'' in Robert Glessing and William P. White (eds.), *Mass Media: The Invisible Environment*. Chicago: Science Research Associates, 1973.

Murphy, Robert D., *Mass Communication and Human Interaction*. Boston: Houghton Mifflin, 1976.

Rogers, Evertt M., ''Mass Media and Interpersonal Communication,'' in Ithiel de Sola Pool et al., *Handbook of Communication*. Chicago: Rand McNally, 1973.

Thomas, Bob, *King Cohn*. New York: Bantam Books, 1967.

Whitney, Frederick C., *Mass Media Communication in Society.* Dubuque, Iowa: Wm. C. Brown, 1975.

glossary

Age of the Universe Clock A digital voltmeter clock that registers the year, month, day, hour, and second since the universe is believed to have begun.

Analogy An explanation which compares one thing with another, point by point.

Antiphonal sermon A sermon in which the congregation participates by responsive alternation with the minister.

Artifacts Objects such as tools, clothing, literature, or buildings which reflect the culture of a society.

Attitude A learned and fairly long-lasting predisposition to evaluate a person, event, or situation in a certain way.

Audience audit The process by which we assess a potential audience; this should be the first step in speech planning.

Autistic thinking People believing what they want to believe; truth confused with desire.

Balance theory A refinement of consistency theory designed to mathematically determine where attitude conflict exists. For example, if two people have negative attitudes toward each other ($-$), and they disagree on an issue (one is against ($-$) and the other is for ($+$)), then there is no conflict ($- \times - \times + = +$). If they agree ($+$ and $+$, or $-$ and $-$) then there is conflict ($- \times + \times + = -$). Developed by Fritz Heider.

Behavior An observable action which a person chooses to perform or not perform: it may not always be consistent with the person's true attitudes.

Behavioral goal Consists of: (1) what behavior you want to happen; (2) whom you want to perform it; (3) when it should happen.

Beliefs Ideas or feelings about what we think or assume to be true or false, good or bad, desirable or undesirable.

Body messages Nonverbal communication of emotions by means of gestures, eye movements, and other physical activity, which may either amplify or contradict our verbal messages.

Bubble Each person's territorial boundary, primarily extending about as far as he can reach. Our bigger bubbles, the physical space in which we live and work, convey messages of our status; the larger the territory under one's command, the greater one's status.

Circadian cycles Daily cycles of human strength and vitality.

Classical Conditioning To modify behavior so that an act or response previously associated with one stimulus becomes associated with another.

Coalition formation In groups, the uniting of two or more persons to influence the remainder of the group.

Cognitive Dissonance Theory A type of consistency theory that holds that we seek to produce consonance (harmony) of our beliefs, attitudes and cognitions (things we know and are directly aware of) and avoid dissonance. Developed by Leon Festinger.

Communication   A dynamic human transaction involving ideas and feelings.

Communication apprehension or anxiety   Fear or lack of self-confidence, which causes one to avoid social encounters that involve talking. Such extremely quiet persons prefer to work alone. Also known as speech fright.

Communication-dependent society   A society such as ours in which people are in constant interaction with the other people around them, and are in turn constantly affected by their actions.

Communication elements   The three parts are expressing, receiving, and interpreting messages.

Communication, expressive   These messages may be in the dorms of art, dance, music, poetry, or speech; and they function to provide a form for the emotions of the expressor.

Communication, instrumental   Messages designed to convey information or to influence others towards a particular end. Also called persuasive communication.

Communication, ritual   A ceremony in which those participating reaffirm their commitment to a particular belief or way of life.

Communication, social   The social interaction that helps each person keep in contact with others.

Concept   A mental picture, real or fantasized, of a situation, principle, or relationship.

Congruity theory   An extension of balance theory, it holds that people have countless attitudes, values, and beliefs which are not all consistent with each other. This inconsistency is not troublesome unless these attitudes come into relation with each other because of some experience.

Consistency theory   The strong tendency for people to make their behaviors consistent with their attitudes, values, and beliefs.

Coping   To deal with and attempt to overcome problems and difficulties.

Core statement   The main point or thesis of a speech.

Credibility   The believableness of a source. Competence and trust in the character of the source are the two most important dimensions.

Decibel   A unit for expressing the relative intensity of sounds on a scale from zero (for the least perceptible sound) to about 140 (for the pain level) and above.

Decoding   Assigning meaning to a communication signal or symbol.

Deductive reasoning   Reasoning from known facts or generalizations to a conclusion about a specific situation.

Description   The presentation of "what-it-was-(or is)-like" information.

Design, speech   The creative process of planning a speech, during which the speaker defines the core idea and develops strategy to influence his listeners.

Devil's advocate   A person who champions the less accepted or approved cause for the sake of argument.

Dialogue   An interaction between and among people who prize each other's essential dignity and welfare.

Dogmatism   A viewpoint or system of ideas based on insufficiently examined premises.

Dyad   A two-person communicating transaction

ELF   Easy listening formula, used to measure listenability by counting the number of syllables above one per word in each sentence.

Empathic listener   An active listener; one who tries to understand and share the speaker's feelings, and appreciate the point of view he is expressing.

Encoding   The process of first selecting a message symbol and then putting it into a form that will be recognized by the receiver, prior to transmitting it.

Epidictic rhetoric   See Rhetoric.

Ethics   The discipline dealing with what is good and bad, and with moral duty and obligation. Ethical communication involves the honest and open expression of intentions.

Evidence   Proof, which can be either (1) extrinsic (coming from facts, observable data, statistics, testimony of an expert, etc.) or (2) intrinsic (application of logic and reasoning, or causal relationships) to arrive at some truth.

Explanation   A statement that clarifies a meaning or shows the relationship between certain ideas.

Extemporaneous speaking   In communications, public speaking from notes.

Extrovert   One whose attention and interests are directed largely outside the self; who likes to work with people and in groups.

Feedback   A verbal or nonverbal response to a communication; usually determined by a person's psychological set.

Flesch's Reading Ease Formula   Used to measure readability by counting the number of words per sentence. Developed by Rudolf Flesch.

Flexibility   In group interaction, a tolerance for ambiguity; also patience in dealing with uncertainty and disputable issues.

Focal structure   The use of shapes, lighting, and structure to focus people's attention on what is considered important; such as locating a king's throne on a well-lit, elevated dais.

Forensic rhetoric   See Rhetoric.

Forms of support   The three methods of expressing the information we gather in the research process; namely, explanations, illustrations, and evidence.

Gatekeepers   In mass media, those people who have the power to determine the fate of a potential message.

Graphic communication   A picture, map, graph, or similar two-dimensional representation of a message.

Group   As distinguished from an aggregate or organization, a group involves frequent interaction of individuals who define themselves and are defined by others as members.

Group, consensual   A group whose members gravitate together because of similar needs, talents, or characteristics.

Group, primary   The family one is born into and in which the early years are spent.

Group, reference   The group each person uses as a standard to evaluate his status and guide his own behavior, using such categories of comparison as social standing, prestige, or economic or intellectual ability.

Group-think   The tendency of a long-established group to develop common attitudes and opinions.

GSR, Galvanic Skin Response   A device which measures a person's perspiration, considered a clue to his anxiety.

Illustrations   In speeches, or written communication, detailed examples that serve to clarify meanings.

Incongruity   The quality or state of being unsuitable or incompatible.

Inductive reasoning   Reasoning from the specific, such as observations or experiments, to general laws or theories.

Influence   The power of a person or thing to affect others.

Infradian cycles   Monthly cycles of human strength and vitality.

Initiative   An introductory step, or actions taken independently; enterprise.

Interpersonal Communication   Interaction by written or oral symbols between or among humans, usually in small groups and face-face.

Introvert   One whose attention and interests are predominantly concerned with his own mental life.

Label   An adjectival term applied to a person, such as "outgoing," "introverted," "sneaky," "a good listener," which may affect his social life, his career, and his self-image.

Language   Words organized into patterns accepted within a culture, a symbolic interaction between people.

Learning theory   Also known as reinforcement theory, it states that people tend to repeat behavior that is rewarding, and avoid behavior that is harmful or unrewarding.

Listening   The main prerequisite of feedback: reception (hearing); perception (using all the senses to help refine the message); and interpretation (decoding all the signals by indexing, cataloging, and arranging them in a sequence that will allow us to assign meanings).

Magical speech   Words become magical when people believe in a special effect inherent in the words themselves.

Mass Communication   Messages (1) transmitted through some sort of organization; (2) with the use of machinery; (3) in a rapid fashion; (4) at a relatively low cost per capita.

McCroskey's Scale   A test given to determine the student's level of speech anxiety.

Mediated messages   A combination of mass and interpersonal communication.

Mediately   Refers to a special case of serial communication in which the interpersonal chain begins with information or opinions someone has acquired by attending to the mass media.

Mental inertia   Intellectual apathy; characterized by a lack of curiosity, an acceptance of hasty generalizations, shallow analysis and solutions, and diversion to irrelevant topics.

Message   The central ideas and information symbolized in a communication. In any communication there are numerous verbal and nonverbal messages and what is said is not always the intended message, nor is the intended message always the interpreted message.

Metaphor   A figure of speech that gives a new meaning to one idea and implies comparison by calling a thing by another name, as in "the curtain of night," or "She's an angel."

Micromomentaries   Rapid eye movements lasting one-sixtieth of a second, which occur at the precise moment a person is telling a lie, according to the research of Professor Roger E. Bennett, University of Texas.

Negativism   A mental attitude marked by skepticism about nearly everything affirmed by others.

Noise, extrinsic   Background sounds, movements, and other sensations we are perceiving while someone is speaking to us.

Noise, intrinsic   Our thoughts, going on in our minds while we are listening.

Nonverbal codes   The meanings assigned by man to almost everything in his environment, including his own actions and rituals.

Operant learning   Learning behavior that operates on the environment to produce rewards and reinforcement.

Outline   To organize research material into a planned sequence for the most effective presentation of a speech, report, book, etc.

Outline, sentence   A topic outline in which each point is expanded into a sentence instead of being written in a phrase.

Outline, topic   The ordered list of main points and subordinate topics, written in phrases, which aids the speaker or writer to identify in detail all the information he needs to cover a subject adequately.

Outline, working   A list of topics to be covered which reflects deliberate thought concerning priorities, sequence of events, or reasoned determination as to what should be presented and when.

Persuasion   The gradual process of securing cooperation, of which good timing is an essential part.

Persuasive communication   See Communication, instrumental.

Phonation   The sound produced by vibration of the vocal cords, which is caused by air forced up through the windpipe.

Policy communication   The presentation of regulations or procedures; usually refers to a principle, plan, or course of action.

Political rhetoric   See Rhetoric.

Process communication   The presentation of "how-to-do-it" information.

Psychological set   A person's readiness to receive a communication. Self-esteem and prior experience are major factors in the formation of one's psychological set.

Public speaking   The art of moving an audience to belief and action.

Rapport   A relationship marked by harmony, conformity, accord, or affinity.

Reach-test spiral   The typical form of group interaction, in which a group hears a new idea and then circles back to find an anchor in previously agreed upon common values.

Referent   The thing that a symbol stands for.

Reinforcement   To reward desired behavior and, conversely, to punish undesired behavior.

Relationships   Interactions with others which may be similar, competitive, or may complement each other.

Rhetoric   Formal persuasive communication. Classical scholars described three kinds: *epidictic* (speeches of praise and blame); *forensic* (speeches arguing points of law); *political* (speeches of policy).

Rites of passage   Anthropological term for certain ceremonies by which a community grants its official approval for an individual to pass on to another role. Examples are christenings, bar mitzvahs, and weddings.

Self-image   One's conception of one's self and one's role.

Sentence   A grammatically independent unit of thought, which begins with a capital letter and concludes with appropriate end punctuation such as a period, question mark, or exclamation point.

Signal   (See also Symbol) The basic component of the message process.

Simile   A comparison, often introduced by *as* or *like*, which does not assign the meaning of one idea to another; for example, "as quiet as a mouse," or "teeth like pearls."

Social distance   The degree of closeness in our interactions with others.

Socialization   The process of developing social relationships in our preparation for life, part of which is learning to get along with and work effectively in groups.

Sound, nonsymbolic   General noise.

Specific instance   An illustration that is only referred to, without mentioning a lot of detail; for example, to indicate poor business conditions, one might mention the Great Depression of the '30s.

Symbiotic relationship   Refers to a group which works together in a social contract for the common good: examples are a married couple, or an orchestra.

Symbol   The basic component of the message process; an object, image, or sound that represents something other than itself.

Testimony, expert   The opinion of an authority in a field of knowledge or of an eye witness. The value of such testimony depends on the credibility of the expert.

Thinking critically   This process is composed of: (1) analysis, the examination of a complex, its elements, and their relationships; and (2) synthesis, the skill of finding meaningful relationships and arriving at solutions or general thoughts about specific data.

Thinking, reflective   A technique for solving social problems promoted by John Dewey and consisting of the following five steps: (1) recognizing the problem; (2) describing it; (3) suggesting possible solutions; (4) evaluating them; (5) developing a plan of action.

Transitions   In communication, groups of words used to move the topic from one main point to another.

Triad   A threesome, making possible a six-way message exchange.

Ultradian cycles   Personal attention cycles, lasting roughly 90 minutes.

Value   An ethical principle to which people feel a strong emotional commitment and which they employ in judging others' attitudes, beliefs, and behaviors.

Ventilation   In group problem-solving discussions, the free exchange of suggestions, expression of problems, and consideration of various solutions.

Voice, attributes   These qualities are: volume, quality, pitch, rate, duration (length of a vowel), regularity and rhythm, articulation and pronunciation, stress, and silence.

Words   Written or spoken symbols. A comprehensive English dictionary lists nearly half a million words with over ten million meanings.

index